QUEER

....

Michelangelo Signorile

Each of us here thinks the other is queer

and no one's mistaken since all of us are!

TENNESSEE WILLIAMS

"Carrousel Tune"

Out of the dark confinement! out from behind the screen!

It is useless to protest, I know all and expose it.

WALT WHITMAN

"Song of the Open Road"

A closet, a closet does not connect under the bed.

GERTRUDE STEIN

Tender Buttons

Sex,
....
the Media,
....
and the Closets
....
# of Power
IN AMERICA

The University of Wisconsin Press

The University of Wisconsin Press
1930 Monroe Street
Madison, Wisconsin 53711

www.wisc.edu/wisconsinpress/

3 Henrietta Street
London WC2E 8LU, England

1   3   5   4   2

Printed in the United States of America

Library of Congress Cataloging-in-Publication Data
Signorile, Michelangelo, 1960–
Queer in America : sex, the media, and the closets of power / Michelangelo
Signorile—3rd ed.
p. cm.
Includes index.
ISBN 0-299-19374-8 (alk. paper)
1. Gay liberation movement—United States. 2. Outing (Sexual orientation)—United
States. 3. Coming out (Sexual orientation)—United States. 4. Homosexuality—Moral and
ethical aspects. I. Title.
HQ76.8U5S57   2003
305.9'0664—dc21   2003050114

Portions of chapter 6 were originally published in different form
in the August 27, 1991, issue of *The Advocate*.

Grateful acknowledgment is made to *Harper's* magazine for permission to reprint two paragraphs from "Closets of Power" by Taylor Branch (October 1982).
Copyright © 1982 by *Harper's* magazine, reprinted by permission.

*To my mother and father,
the most loving, understanding,
and supportive parents in America*

Contents

PART III: QUEER IN HOLLYWOOD

EPILOGUE: QUEER IN AMERICA

2003 Preface

Any doubts I had about the relevance today of the critique of the gay "closet" and the "closets of power" presented in *Queer in America*—and how they cause damage not only to closeted individuals but to all gay, lesbian, and bisexual people—were erased when, in early 2003, I became privy to information about a Washington figure, supported and promoted by President George W. Bush.

There were indications that this individual had been hostile to civil rights and in particular to gay rights. Certainly he was and is part of the far-right juggernaut that Bush has promoted, which includes the ascension of antigay religious conservatives into every aspect of the government.

This man is a deeply tormented, married individual who engages in sex with men, only to lecture them afterwards about the evils of homosexuality, guilt-ridden about what he does. His own self-hatred has him working against gays as a group, battling what he sees as the demon inside of himself—his libido—by fighting against gay and lesbian equality in his position in the nation's capital.

I refer to this man in the opening of this new preface because he is indicative of so many stories from ten years ago (and much prior) that are recounted in *Queer in America*, going back to past Republican and Democratic administrations. As the old adage goes, the more things change, the more they stay the same.

Many people had thought that, with the onset of the Clinton administration, by far the most progay presidential administration America has seen (despite some blemishes, which are discussed in this book), it would be the end of the closet as an institution—in Washington and beyond. That of course wasn't true even in Bill Clinton's White House—though many more people in government were open about their homosexuality than ever before—and certainly isn't true in the second Bush's White House. And what happens in Washington is often a mirror of the political culture on the state and local levels as well, showing the odd and complicated place that homosexuality occupies in 2003.

In many ways we've gone two steps backward after moving three steps forward on gay rights and, more accurately, on gay visibility. The control of the government—the White House as well as the Congress—is now in the hands of Republicans again. And the Republican Party has been very slow to change, with powerful, antigay religious conservatives within its ranks and within its leadership. As long as homophobia and antigay hatred are present—within the government and within culture at large—the closet will be present.

Thus, the message of *Queer in America* continues to resonate today though it was crystallized ten years ago, and though much of what it recounts are events of the latter part of the twentieth century leading up to the early 1990s. A new chapter in this edition discusses the 1990s—a pivotal decade—as well as the first few years of the new century, looking at what has changed and what has not.

The first edition of *Queer in America*, published in 1993, emerged in a time of great activity within the lesbian and gay civil rights movement, energized by the then electric AIDS activist movement of the late '80s and early '90s. That movement—and this book—often focused on how the engines of mass culture cover up homosexuality, making it invisible. While the media has changed over the past ten years in dramatic ways and now covers the gay community a great deal, there is still an uneven approach when it comes to reporting on sexual orientation among public figures. The new chapter discusses this and other issues in detail, looking at the media, Hollywood, Washington, and other locales and institutions today.

Even as gay youth groups have grown across the country over the past ten years, and even as the plight of gay, lesbian, and bisexual teens has received national attention, most young gay people still grow up in the closet. Most people are still raised to be heterosexual, and certainly much of mass media, despite gay depictions, still promotes that idea. The difference today might be that once one realizes that he or she is not heterosexual there's more of a support network and an acceptance. But coming out is still a daunting process for many young people, simply because homophobia still exists within our culture.

•••••

Some changes that have occurred over these ten years should be taken into account while reading this book.

During the 1990s, the transgender movement came to the forefront of the gay civil rights movement, demanding visibility and respect. Transgendered people—including but not limited to drag queens, transvestites, and transsexuals—were at the center of the early gay liberation movement, and rightly felt by the 1990s that the gay and lesbian civil rights movement had marginalized them.

Since the mid-'90s transgendered people have not only challenged the gay movement for inclusion—resulting, most superficially, in the acronym "GLBT" being applied to the movement—but began to challenge our ideas about what "sexual orientation" and "gender" really mean. Through the '90s I wrote about transgendered people and the transgendered movement, most notably in two long pieces in *Out* magazine, trying to parse through the important and complicated issues, give voice to the burgeoning ideas, and challenge gays and lesbians to think more broadly about these issues.

Some transgendered people, for example, have said that our political organizing should evolve to focus on discrimination based on gender perception—no matter whether someone is "gay" or "straight," "male" or a "female"—rather than on sexual orientation or gender identity. After all, if a thug brutally attacks a man because he looks feminine and calls him a "fag," what does his sexual orientation (or his biological gender) really matter? Why separate feminists, gays, straights, lesbians, bisexuals, transgendered people, and others when we can all come together under one banner? These arguments have been put forth with clarity and depth most notably by activist Riki Anne Wilchins, founder of GenderPac and author of *Read My Lips: Sexual Subversion and the End of Gender.*

I encourage people to explore these and many other ideas that transgender activists offer. There are many areas about which we should all rethink, and many areas on which we can find common ground. This book, however, focuses primarily on the homosexual closet, not the transgender closet. While some transgendered people identify as "gay" or "lesbian" or "bisexual" and thus will find these issues relevant—and though there are many areas about which gays, lesbians, bisexuals, and transgendered people are faced with similar issues—the particulars of our closets are different.

Another issue that bears discussion is the use of the word *queer* today compared with the usage in most of this book. In the original edition of *Queer in America*, the word "queer" is used interchangeably with *gay* and *lesbian*. The word queer was very popular at the time in which the book was written, coming out of the grass roots movements of the time and used much more liberally than today, encompassing all of the groups, including gay, lesbian, bisexual, and transgendered. It is a word that activists of the time "took back," as we described it, attempting to take the sting out of a pejorative.

As with many words, the usage of the word queer changed over the past decade, becoming, in my opinion, more defined and specific—and no doubt one reason was that many people have never liked it, finding it an insult. It's generally not used any longer as a noun—as when I use it to describe "all queers"—and is more so used as an adjective. Even then, it is most often applied to creative and academic endeavors than to individuals or groups. We speak today of "queer cinema" or "queer theory" but less so of "queer politicians" or "queer bankers." In the new chapter, going with the usage of our time, I use the words *gay, lesbian,* and *bisexual* when describing individuals, groups, and movements. However, I left the usage of the word queer in the original text because I believe the book should be read with the appropriate usage of the time.

Similarly, because *Queer in America* has a narrative structure, I thought it best to let the new edition read as the book was originally written—including facts that might have changed—and update the book by writing a new chapter rather than trying to make extensive changes throughout the text, altering the flow and rhythm of the book. The reader should thus keep in mind that events have changed and that individuals discussed might be in different places or positions today—and certainly are ten years older.

I did, however, make a few changes within the original text: If I knew someone had moved into or left an important position in the gay movement, in politics or elsewhere, I noted it (often in an endnote) and did the same for those who have, sadly, died in these ten years. I did this to the best of my knowledge and am aware that I might have missed some individuals, and I apologize for that in advance.

Definitions have also changed over time, something that should be taken into account as well. We might look upon "the closet" in different ways today, no doubt due to the expansion of ideas as well as technology. The Internet, for example, has allowed for many people who might not be predominantly homosexual—and who might not have ever acted upon any vague homosexual desire they may have felt—to experiment and explore their sexual desires more fully. This is something of note, in particular, with regard to men, many of whom are married—often happily—and who don't have an animosity toward gays, while at the same time don't identify as gay and often don't even identify as bisexual. They are for all practical purposes predominantly heterosexual—not even feeling truly bisexual, if that means an equal affinity for sex with both genders—though they may have experimented with people of their own gender via the Internet, which provides much ease and low risk in terms of seeking out such encounters.

Encouraging people to expand their own ideas about sexual desire should be something for which the gay movement—and any movement for sexual liberation—stands. Such use of the Internet should thus be seen as a good thing, even though many gay activists might also view the Internet— rightly, as well—as an invention that keeps the closet intact, allowing people to operate covertly and discreetly rather than being challenged. I believe that we can and should make distinctions today between those individuals who might be exploring the boundaries of their sexuality and those who are closeted homosexuals, living tormented and unhappy lives and sometimes working against the gay movement, often because they are filled with self-loathing—a self-loathing inspired by a homophobic culture.

In that respect, and from the perspective of the year 2003, *Queer in America* should be read with the knowledge that changes, some of them great, have occurred, but that its basic message about the destructiveness of the closet applies as much today as at any other time in the past.

Michelangelo Signorile
March 2003
New York

On Naming Names

The strategic ambition of *Queer in America* is larger than what the media has come to call "outing," the identification of gay and lesbian public figures trying to remain in the closet. Though I have been considered outing's pioneer, the normalization of the discussion of homosexual public figures—and the abolition of the homosexual closet—has been advocated by many gay writers and activists since the beginning of the gay movement. Certainly, if there are true pioneers of outing, they are among the writers of the generations previous to mine, people like Armistead Maupin, Larry Kramer, and the late Vito Russo. It is only now that there is some interest in this topic among the mainstream American public.

I consider truthful discussion of the lives of homosexual public figures as legitimate and significant in the larger aim to give courage to millions of gay people who stay in the closet out of fear and shame: They are not as alone as a homophobic America would have them believe. Advocating such a position is controversial. It raises moral and legal issues. Is there an absolute right to privacy? May the individual privacy of sexual orientation be infringed upon when the exercise of privacy in this area clearly damages a larger group? How much privacy is a public figure entitled to, and how do we define a public figure?

Above all, is being gay a private matter, or is sexual identity (the fact of being gay or straight) different from sexual behavior (what one does in bed)? Much of this book is about these important and barely debated issues, about the process of identification and the circumstances under which people emerge from the closet.

Some people are named in *Queer in America;* others are not. There are five reasons for these decisions. First, I have readily given anonymity to various individuals I interviewed who have emerged from the closet but need to protect their identities for reasons that have nothing to do with their sexuality. Second, some powerful closeted people gave me lengthy interviews from within the closet, speaking on condition of anonymity; others spoke for deep background, not for any attribution whatsoever. Third, in some cases, sources who have been victimized by powerful closeted individuals—a scandalous reality—spoke to me on condition that not only they but their victimizer remain anonymous at this stage. Fourth, other sources supplied valuable information in return for my not using their names or the names of the closeted people they discussed. Fifth, in a great many cases, the closeted individuals I discuss, such as congressional staffers, are arguably not public figures but private citizens, and they are afforded the same treatment that the media grant heterosexual private citizens. I have, in particular, not used the real names of many private citizens from my past—both straight and gay—who could not be contacted. The following names are pseudonyms; Mr. Reed, Karen, Jim, Dr. Simmons, Dan, Howard, Sally, Keith, Peter, Gerard, Fred, Ed, Bill, Katherine, Jay, Kathy, Hal, Tom, Vinnie, Ted, Ron, John, and Frank.

In many of the above cases regarding public figures, I felt it was more important to tell the stories of the closeted people in power than it was to out them. I felt that the priority of this particular book was to offer necessary experiences and information to the public that couldn't have been obtained had I intended to out certain individuals.

None of this means that any of the unnamed people will or should be protected in other circumstances. They may well be revealed and openly discussed by other publications, by other writers, and by me.

MICHELANGELO SIGNORILE
March 1993
New York

INTRODUCTION

The Closets of Power

There exists in America what appears to be a brilliantly orchestrated, massive conspiracy to keep all homosexuals locked in the closet. This conspiracy forces many of us to live in shame and tremble with fear. Anyone who dares venture out of that closet is threatened with destruction. The vast majority heed the warning.

The conspiracy is a relatively unconscious one, ingrained as it is in our culture. Most heterosexuals, even well-meaning ones, are party to it—as are many homosexuals. It is more subtle than the conscious antigay conspiracy being carried out by a handful of religious zealots and their followers, who seek to punish homosexuals or change them into heterosexuals. The rest of our society, thinking itself "tolerant," conspires to keep queers closeted. Those heterosexuals who participate in the closet conspiracy, conditioned within a homophobic culture, are threatened by homosexuality, fearful of and uncomfortable with people who are open about it.

Most straight liberals who in fact champion gay rights and maintain that all lesbians and gay men should be free to come out aren't aware how vigorously they enforce the closet in America, but they do enforce it, every day:

- By telling a politician over and over again that his homosexuality must be kept hidden, the straight liberal political aide enforces the closet.
- By making film after film after film without any gay characters, the straight liberal Hollywood director enforces the closet.
- By interviewing a powerful public figure whose secret homosexuality is pertinent to a story but omitting it from the story—or by refusing to ask the official about it—the straight liberal newspaper reporter enforces the closet.
- By disguising a homosexual celebrity as heterosexual because the celebrity's publicist wishes him or her to do so, the straight liberal editor enforces the closet.
- By never offering images of homosexuals on billboards or television commercials—while endlessly depicting heterosexuals in states of bliss—the straight liberal advertising executive enforces the closet.

This widespread conspiracy is carried out within three power structures in America, closeted societies that are uniquely inter-related and dependent upon each other. They form the Trinity of the Closet:

- THE MEDIA INDUSTRY, CENTERED IN NEW YORK: This power structure keeps most truths about homosexuals—including news of who is homosexual—from the public. The media force the public to know *everything* there is to know about heterosexuals who are public figures—including information about their personal lives they would rather not see made public. The media create the impression that there are far fewer homosexuals than there really are and that reporting that someone is homosexual—unless they've "admitted" it—is unacceptable and horrible but that reporting that someone is heterosexual—even if they haven't "admitted" it—is always acceptable. This makes the closeted feel even more isolated and more fearful of ever coming out and tells them that homosexuality is grotesque and unreportable while heterosexuality is normal and right.
- THE POLITICAL SYSTEM, CENTERED IN WASHINGTON: By keeping homosexuals in its own ranks closeted, this power structure ensures

that the uncloseted are underrepresented and never offered legislative safeguards but are, rather, legislated against. The net result is to encourage the closeted to stay that way for fear of not being protected.

- THE ENTERTAINMENT INDUSTRY, CENTERED IN HOLLYWOOD: By distorting and demonizing homosexuals depicted in the products of mass culture—or by keeping them completely invisible—this power structure makes sure that negative and often violent reactions to gays persist. The net result is to ensure that coming out of the closet remains a risky, dangerous, and dubious thing to do.

There are, of course, other power structures, such as the Catholic church and the evangelical movement, that also affect the closeted, but those power structures work through the Trinity: Without the compliance of the media, the political system, and the engines of mass culture, the antigay forces could not peddle their homophobia. Each of the Trinity's power structures relies on the other two to keep the conspiracy going, perpetuating a vicious cycle. If the closet were to be dismantled in just one of these power structures, the other two would be forced to follow suit.

In all three power structures, closeted lesbians and gay men themselves are among the most influential people at the very top helping to orchestrate the closet conspiracy; their heterosexual conspirators often know these people are gay but look the other way as long as the matter doesn't become public. The closeted individuals go to great lengths to keep their closet doors tightly shut, hiring lawyers to protect them and squelching any stories about their gay lives, fearful that exposure will ruin them. Often they marry and have children so as to appear straight and protect their secret. Some hire publicists to actively promote them as heterosexuals. If their homosexuality is inquired about, they deny it outright or offer vague, sometimes ridiculous answers. They also enlist the protection of their straight bosses and friends.

By promoting a system that rewards the closeted with money, power, prestige, and fame—and that shuts out and destroys the uncloseted—heterosexuals in power unconsciously make closeted gays act as role models for all other gays. The message coming from the top down is *If you want to make it, kid, just stay locked in the closet.*

Microcosms of the three power structures exist in hundreds of smaller cities and towns. All across America there are state and local governments and modest local media and entertainment industries; for the most part, they are models of their larger counterparts when it comes to enforcing the closet. This ensures that the closet is kept firmly embedded in American culture.

In the past twenty years or so, a relative handful of people, defying the conspiracy, have escaped the closet. Many of them became determined to tear the institution of the closet down entirely.

.....

This book is about the people still trapped in the closet, the people who have escaped it, and the people who work to end its tyranny. It is about the pain and torture that the closet has inflicted on its occupants. It is about the dangerous combination of the closeted and power: how those who occupy the closets of power ultimately allow their closets to oppress not just themselves, but all those gay people who work for them, as well as the millions of queers over whom they wield power.

This is not a book about the AIDS movement, ACT UP, Queer Nation, or the mainstream homosexual advocates in Washington. It is, however, about how those movements and groups have influenced the institution of the closet in recent years. It is a book not about the history of the lesbian and gay civil rights movement but about one pivotal period during which that movement began to take a fresh look at the closet. It is a book not about the new generation of queers or the new queer culture but about the segment of that new generation that is taking on the closet.

Through hundreds of interviews—conducted with people around the country, but mostly in New York, Washington, and Hollywood—I present a picture of the closet and how it relates to and interacts with the power structures. Through the experiences of many gay people, including myself, I offer a personal look inside the closet. In that way, the style and tone of the book vary—sometimes autobiographical, sometimes polemical, sometimes journalistic—depending on what is appropriate to the subject matter at hand.

All individuals who are directly quoted, including those who are quoted anonymously, were fully aware that they were being interviewed for this book or for related articles I have written in the past. However, many observations and analyses were formulated by undercover explorations of closeted gay-male societies. Obviously, it was impossible for me to study closeted lesbian circles in the same way. However, through interviews with many closeted and uncloseted lesbians, I was able to gather enough information to draw conclusions. Because there are far fewer lesbians in positions of power, many closeted women were reluctant to be quoted—even anonymously—for fear of being recognized, and would often provide only background information.

The closet, as presented here, is not easily defined. What does it mean to be "in the closet" or "out of the closet"? Every gay person—and every straight person—has a different answer to those questions. The closet has many levels, depending on how many people one has told about one's sexuality and who those people might be. Does being "out of the closet" mean that you've got to tell everyone you run into that you're queer? No.

Being out of the closet means not caring if your straight friends see you holding hands with the object of your affections.

Being out of the closet means not worrying about people—from your mother to an old school chum—discovering your dark secret.

It means not hiding letters, cards, and magazines, either at home or in the office.

It means not making up fake plans for the weekend.

It means not taking a "friend" of the opposite sex to the company picnic.

It means not playing the role of the lonely, assumed-to-be-straight "bachelor" or "bachelorette."

Being out of the closet means not thinking about it at all.

Many heterosexuals don't understand the closet because they've never been in it. Because heterosexuality is the order of things, many heterosexuals think that they never discuss their sexuality. They say gays who come out are going too far, making an issue of their sexuality when heterosexuals don't.

Those heterosexuals don't realize that they routinely discuss aspects of their own sexuality every day: telling coworkers about a vacation they took with a lover; explaining to their bosses that they're going through a rough divorce; bragging to friends about a new romance. Heterosexual reporters have no problem asking heterosexual public figures about their husbands, wives, girlfriends, boyfriends, or children—and all these questions confirm and make an issue of the subject's sexuality. The ultimate example of making an issue of heterosexuality is the announcements in the newspapers every Sunday that heterosexuals are getting married.

Because they've never experienced the closet, because they have no idea what it's like to be queer, sympathetic straights often see coming out or being outed as the most excruciating, most horrible thing imaginable. They sometimes lament over the process in a most patronizing way. What they don't understand is that the real pain is in being "in"—not "out." The most torturous part for gays is the years and years of being shoved—by straights—into the closet.

For that reason, heterosexuals are at a complete disadvantage in the debate over outing. They can attempt to get some insight from homosexual friends, but that's another problem: Depending on whom they ask they'll get different answers, all of which are bound to confuse them. Certainly the closeted, as captives, suffer such profound psychological trauma that they develop a relationship to their closets similar to that of hostages to their captors: They defend them—lulled into a false sense of security and blind to the trauma they experience—and are threatened by those who are out.

People who have recently come out have a completely different experience of the closet than do people who have been out for five years—and *they* have a different experience than do people who have been out for ten. Queers of different races have differing experiences, as do queers of different ages and occupations. Lesbians have a different experience with the closet than do gay men.

Yet, while they might not agree on exactly how to dismantle it, most gay people agree that the closet is a wretched institution. There is no question that the institution of the closet must be broken down. One logical way to do that is to vigorously assault the Trinity of the Closet and take on those individuals, gay and straight, who are part of the unconscious conspiracy. So far, among the new generation of queer activists, journalists, and business professionals that formula is proving successful.

It has not been easy nor painless, not for the closeted in power nor for the out—nor for straight liberals, for that matter. But in every revolution there is bound to be some discomfort. The alternative is far more grim: the continuance of the conspiracy of the closet as we enter the twenty-first century, and our own complicity in the torment and anguish of millions of lesbian and gay Americans of future generations.

Part I In response to the AIDS crisis, a movement crystallized on the streets of New York in the late eighties. Among other things, that movement took a fresh look at the closet and made an assault on it.

As children, homosexuals are forced into the closet by straight society; the experience retards

. . . .

QUEER

IN NEW YORK

the development of their personalities and of their identities as gay people. Even when they think they've come out of the closet years later, many gays and lesbians are so psychically damaged that they find themselves in still other closets, living in denial.

The media industry (including the empires of television and print journalism, public-relations firms, and advertising agencies), centered in New York, is a power structure charged with rigidly maintaining the closet in America. Often, influential and well-known people in the industry who carry out this mandate are themselves secret homosexuals whose fears force them to take part in perpetuating distortion and invisibility of lesbians and gays—whether or not they are conscious of what they are doing.

They are the among the occupants of New York's closets of power. They set a strict standard for how all gays in the industry are expected to behave. And they dutifully aid in keeping homophobia firmly entrenched in society.

1

....

Lights, Camera,

....

ACT UP

....

Photo op at the flagpole!" screamed the voice over a loudspeaker. Scores of hungry reporters and photographers darted about in front of the massive glass building. An effigy of Ronald Reagan—a stuffed dummy with a rubber Reagan mask on its head—was being strung up the flagpole, hanging by its neck. A flag went up the pole: a pink triangle on a black background above the words that would soon become an international rallying cry: SILENCE = DEATH.

A crackly voice came over Chip Duckett's walkie-talkie: "They're burning an effigy of Reagan here in the back of the building." Duckett ran to the microphone and podium that had been set up in the parking lot across the street.

"Attention, members of the press: Another effigy is going up in flames around the back. Attention, press: Very hot photo op in the back of the building!"

They scurried like little roaches with notebooks and cameras.

Still at the podium, Duckett was approached by a Latino reporter from a Texas newspaper. "I want a Spanish-speaking person with AIDS, preferably a woman," he said. Duckett took the microphone and spoke to the surging crowds of protestors in front of the building: "Any PWA women who speak Spanish out there?"

A woman came forward explaining that she had ARC—"AIDS-related complex," a term then used for people who were HIV-infected and had one or two symptoms, but were not yet classified as having full-blown AIDS.

The reporter thought about it for a moment, then reluctantly nodded. Duckett rushed back to the mike and looked at the woman. "ARC will do." Her eyes lit up and she ran off with the reporter.

It was at that point that I began to understand what we had done and what we were doing. We were the media committee of ACT UP—the AIDS Coalition to Unleash Power. What we had done was organized a well-rehearsed circus. What we were doing was exploiting each other in order to get our message across.

I knew we had succeeded when a media comrade ran up to me and reported, "We did it. We're gonna get an avalanche of press."

That was what we'd planned for months. In July 1988, four months before the demo, I was first informed that we would "seize control of the FDA," as our slogan described the action against the Food and Drug Administration. In ACT UP's opinion, the FDA was responsible for the deaths of thousands of people with AIDS because of the inaction of its bureaucracy.

I had become chair of the committee a month before, in June 1988. I had relieved Bob Rafsky, who was on staff at the high-powered PR firm Howard J. Rubenstein Associates, which was handling Donald Trump. An eloquent speaker and a smooth PR operator, Rafsky would four years later become known as the ACT UP member who hounded Bill Clinton into having an AIDS plank in his platform.* Together with David Corkery, a former *Good Morning America* producer, they had fine-tuned the ACT UP media committee and whipped it into a sophisticated corporate public-relations department—minus only corporate expense accounts, computers, offices, and staff. Like everything else in ACT UP, this was a purely volunteer corps—and a remarkable one at that: The committee was made up of about twelve publicists, journalists, editors, and writers, all gay men and lesbians, all working out of their homes or in their offices late at night. Everyone had contacts, everyone had connections, and everyone did his or her share of the work: smug-

---

*Bob Rafsky died in February 1993.

gling mailing lists out of offices, using copy machines at night, reeling in favors owed by reporters and editors, dutifully developing strategies to bring AIDS activism to the media. The pace was mind-boggling, but our friends were dying. There wasn't a minute to squander. *We* were dying, too.

Corkery talked me into taking over as head of the committee in June 1988. He was the hypester on the committee and had realized that if ACT UP was to get anywhere, it had to be brought into a more "pop" arena. PR was a game for him and one at which few could beat him. When Corkery was riding a story, there was no stopping him. He'd push it along until it wound up on the front page of *The New York Times* or at the top of *The MacNeil/Lehrer NewsHour*. He taught me well.

I was the gossip columnist on the committee—a *People* magazine free-lancer and a former "column planter" who had worked for a PR firm guaranteeing its clients mentions in columns like Liz Smith's. I dealt in sleaze and dirt and I spoke the language of the masses, which was where David Corkery knew ACT UP's message had to go.

Now I was taking the helm of the media committee at a time when we were organizing the AIDS movement's first national action. It was going to be an all-day affair, a ten-hour demonstration. The place was Bethesda, Maryland, just outside Washington, D.C. The target was the FDA. The issues were that promising AIDS drugs weren't being tested; that drug trials excluded women and people of color; that inhumane placebo-testing was the norm; and that after 47,000 deaths from AIDS, no individual in the government or the medical establishment was taking the lead. Bureaucracy, sleazy politics, and ambivalence were killing people. Worse yet, no one seemed to care. So we—the real experts, the people living with AIDS—were going to take over: "Seize control of the FDA."

I had no idea what to do. A mudslinging hack, I could tell you which famous person was sleeping with whom and why, and how to get that information printed in any newspaper, but I certainly didn't know the first thing about how to publicize an AIDS movement. I needed help.

The media committee had its hands full. We hadn't done anything like this before. People in ACT UP chapters from over thirty-five cities were going to participate and come to Bethesda, under the umbrella name of ACT NOW (AIDS Coalition to Network, Organize, and Win), but ACT UP/New York would be doing most of the work when it came to the press.

"Depending on our budget, we can do bookings in twenty-five markets, thirty-five markets, or fifty markets," Chip Duckett told an enraptured media committee, speaking at my request. "Of course, we'll have to train people to do the bookings on the telephone, and we'll have to give the people sound-bite lessons, you know, how to speak on television. We'll have to design a specific press kit—a nice, glossy black one, maybe with a pink triangle or the SILENCE = DEATH logo. We'll have to target the local TV talk shows in each city. Then we'll have to design a separate kit for radio, and one for print. Oh, and columnists will have to get personalized kits. They've got lots of ego, you know."

I'd known Duckett from the party circuit for about a year. I was a columnist and he was a party promoter and at first I thought that he was getting involved with ACT UP to get on my good side. Later, after we became friends, I saw that his commitment was genuine.

"Every kit has to have a really hokey, tearjerking cover letter attached to it," he continued. "Remember: We're talking to producers in middle America. We have to hook them. We have to talk about *families* devastated by AIDS." Duckett was an energetic man who always wore black and always had the right comment on the tip of his tongue when he met someone prominent. "Then we have to have a totally different strategy for the national talk shows—*Oprah, Donahue, Today.* They're way more sophisticated. You better let me handle those people. We may not grab them. But I'm sure we can get some really decent coverage out of this whole thing."

Duckett never buckled under pressure and rarely showed any outward signs of uncertainty. And he had a shrewd strategy for manipulating the media in just about every circumstance. Before leaving PR to become a nightclub party promoter, he had spent several years publicizing cookbooks at Workman Publishing, sending authors on tour around the country doing radio, television, and print interviews. His talents—not to mention his reams and reams of media lists from cities across America—proved invaluable. "The easy thing about publicizing a national political movement," he said often, "is that you don't have to waste time and money sending anyone on tour. You've got people in every market, ready to do the interviews."

With the help of dozens of volunteers from ACT UP's general membership, we put together over five hundred glossy press kits and sent them out to thirty-five radio and TV markets. An entire sub-group of the media committee formed; it was dubbed the Little Publicists—twenty people who'd shown an interest in working the press. They were trained in how to book people on shows and how to get the producers hooked once they received the press kits. By phone, Chip Duckett trained activists from each local ACT UP chapter who would be going on talk shows in specific markets.

Press releases went out every week, updating the details of the action. The strategy was repetition: We saturated the reporters with information so that by the time the demo neared, they'd feel as if it were a familiar event that they were obliged to cover—and one that was going to be a spectacle. Months before its occurrence, the demo was listed in a publication sent out to hundreds of radio talk shows across the country; the publication described it as a "massive civil disobedience" that was going to "shut down the FDA." For weeks ACT UPers sat on telephones, doing interviews with radio stations in towns and cities across the nation. Because ACT UP had no offices at the time, my apartment was media command central. It was a very large two-bedroom in the East Village, with a huge living room. Throughout the campaign, people sat from morning until night at two long folding tables that stretched the entirety of the living room. They stuffed envelopes, took phone calls, and stacked clippings. Press kits and envelopes lined the walls of every room, including the halls. When we ran out, we bought new supplies and made new ones.

We were taking a tremendous financial gamble. For the first time ACT UP had poured thousands of dollars into publicity for a demo. But, at roughly $6,000, it was costing less than 5 percent of what we would have spent to hire a professional PR firm for such an event.

As the day came nearer, my phone rang off the hook, starting immediately at eight A.M. I'd stay on the telephone until about eleven A.M., then I'd race down to my father's croissant shop on

Wall Street. In the months prior to the demo, my career had pretty much fallen apart. I wasn't going to parties to dig up dirt, and, worse yet, I wasn't seeking any free-lance writing assignments. My life was ACT UP. So now I was working part-time for my dad in order to pay the rent. It was rather bizarre: Many afternoons I simultaneously sold croissants and talked on the telephone placing people on network talk shows.

The pre-publicity was coming in. Magazines and daily papers were planning stories announcing the demo and discussing the issues in advance. Everyone wanted to be first. Radio interviews were being booked by the dozens, and at least two local TV talk shows in each of thirty-five cities across the country booked guests. We had blown this thing into a gargantuan event: Everyone on the committee described it to the media as the "largest act of civil disobedience since the storming of the Pentagon."

The FDA was getting nervous. Suddenly, they were calling people on our issues committee, wanting to have "discussions." They were asking whether there was any way the demo could be stopped, if they agreed to negotiate. "Not a chance," they were told. We knew all too well the way these people operated. We were also getting to know how powerful the media could be for us, if they were harnessed properly. A well-orchestrated protest would accomplish ten times more than a meeting.

Just days before the demonstration, we scheduled film critic, activist, and PWA (person with AIDS) Vito Russo (also a member of the media committee) on *CBS This Morning*. That same week Susan Sarandon came to ACT UP/New York to offer her support and be briefed by the media committee. She was planning to go on *Good Morning America* to discuss her latest film and she wanted to give the action a plug.

That was one week before the demo. The energy in the little room at the Lesbian and Gay Community Services Center, an old schoolhouse on New York's West Thirteenth Street where the five hundred or so people who made up ACT UP/New York regularly met, was intoxicating. People had organized into smaller cells, or affinity groups, and each group discussed the different acts of civil disobedience they were to engage in, from lying down and blocking traffic to illegally selling unapproved antiviral drugs right in front of the FDA.

Each had created props, costumes, and signs, all guaranteed to get maximum media attention.

The legal team, as well the support team, briefed the room. Both groups were vital to the protestors. The legal team consisted of a dozen or so lawyers, some in private practice and others with gay legal-advocacy groups, who laboriously explained the complexities of the legal system to demonstrators and informed them of their rights. The legal team would also be there when arrests were made, and would bail the protestors out of jail. Similarly, the support team offered demonstrators help with things such as medications and notification of parents or friends in case of any problems.

After the support and legal teams spoke, it was time for the media team to address the room. "We're *all* spokespeople," I told the fired-up group, "as we always have been, with no leaders, no officials. Therefore, any and all of us may be speaking to the media about the issues at any time during this demo. It's imperative that we all learn how to give good sound bites."

Jim Eigo, the chair of the issues committee, then addressed the room, going over the actual issues surrounding the demonstration. His explanation was complex and scientific. People listened, absorbed, and took notes.

David Barr, a lawyer who was on the issues committee, then spoke to the group. Only days before, then–Vice President Bush had released a plan that was supposedly going to streamline the drug-approval process, but it was really just another ploy by the administration and the FDA to counteract what effects our demonstration might have. Barr described in scientific detail how Bush's plan was bogus and wouldn't do a damn thing. Then Ann Northrop got up to tell the room how to translate all of this information into five- to ten-second sound bites.

A one-time Boston debutante, Northrop had carved out an impressive career in broadcast journalism. Just before leaving the field, she came out as a lesbian and decided that she wanted to teach lesbian and gay teens. In 1987, when she was thirty-nine, she became an AIDS educator at the Hetrick-Martin Institute for Lesbian and Gay Youth. In 1988 she joined ACT UP.

Everyone loved Ann Northrop: She was poised, articulate, and accessible. Her hair was cut in a smart, trademark silver-blond bob,

and she always dressed casually in windbreakers and sneakers, looking very much like a young yuppie mother chaperoning the kids on
a class trip. Having been a producer with *The CBS Morning News,*
Northrop knew more than anyone else on the media committee
about how to work a camera.

"Okay, what you've just heard is important and incredibly detailed," she said. "Now I want you to forget all of it. Because what
you've got to do is reduce this stuff to the easiest, shortest words
possible, otherwise they're just not going to pick it up. So, when those
cameras swoop down on you and ask you for a comment about Bush's
proposal, you're simply going to say: 'It's a lie! It's a sham! And it
won't work!' Is that clear?"

The group immediately began chanting: "It's a lie! It's a sham! And
it won't work!" The old schoolhouse on Thirteenth Street vibrated
with enthusiasm.

· · · · ·

Several members of the media committee, myself among them, flew
down to Washington a couple of days before the action to meet with
several other media coordinators from ACT UP chapters around the
country as well as with Urvashi Vaid, then the media coordinator for
the Washington-based National Gay and Lesbian Task Force. Vaid
had been feverishly working on the demo too, handling the Washington media. She seemed to know everyone at the networks and newspapers, and almost every reporter seemed to know "Urv." A dynamic
lawyer, activist, and former journalist from Boston, she had been in
Washington, selling gay and AIDS issues to the media, for several
years. Now she was part of the ACT UP press machine.

"There has to be a press conference during the demo," she explained. "We've got to get just two or three people to address a few
issues, very simply and clearly, and we'll put them at a podium with
a great backdrop—maybe the building surrounded by protestors or
a provocative, attention-grabbing sign—so that all of the TV people
can get their sound bites at the same time. This is especially good if
they need backup quotes. Then, I've got a surefire plan for all of the
regional press. Every newspaper in this country has a Washington
bureau. Well, every one of them will have a local angle on this story,

since we have people here from cities across America. Trust me, we will get incredible press in all of those papers."

The pre-action meeting the night before the demo, the first time that ACT UP chapters from around the country had ever met together, was held in an old church in D.C. Even here, the media spotlight was on us. The group of nine hundred or so was eyed by cameras, all local TV newspeople who were getting footage for their eleven o'clock broadcasts, so they could hype further what was going to happen the next day. Each one of them had been summoned by Urv.

The meeting was the last bit of organizing done before the demo. Each affinity group planned its separate acts of civil disobedience and separately announced them on the floor, one by one, to the cheers of the crowds. It was perhaps the most empowering few hours of the entire demo. For the first time people from around the country had come together to put their bodies on the line. When they rose and named the place they came from—Texas, Massachusetts, Florida, California, and so on—their various accents and regional differences brought them even closer together. They had one thing in common, and it had them tightly bonded. The highlight of the night was a woman from Houston, a grandmotherly figure with poufed white hair. When it was her turn, sixty-nine-year-old Sylvia Ayers went to the front of the church, raised her hands, and hollered, "I love all you beautiful kids!" The crowd thundered with applause.

A lot of last-minute work was still being conducted that night. The legal team met in one corner, support people in another. Urv organized the press conference and discussed her regional press scheme with several dozen people from ACT UPs around the country, while Chip Duckett and I organized everyone else on the media committee, going over our tasks one more time.

That night I shared a room at the Holiday Inn in Bethesda, two blocks from the FDA, with Ken Woodard, an advertising-agency art director who is responsible for some of ACT UP's most compelling posters as well as many of the print ads that the media committee later began placing.

Chatting before bed, we both froze as one of D.C.'s local eleven P.M. news broadcasts began: ACT UP was the lead story.

It showed the FDA building, roped off and with cops already stationed outside. The voice-over reported: "Montgomery County police are already guarding the Food and Drug Administration in Bethesda, gearing up for what is expected to be *the largest act of civil disobedience since the storming of the Pentagon over twenty years ago.*" Our words were in the newscaster's mouth.

A chill ran down my spine: What had we done?

Ken began to laugh. The Pentagon protest, he pointed out, had involved several *hundred thousand* people. We'd be lucky if we had a total of *one* thousand. But this was going to be a spectacular demo and a wonderful show for the media. ACT UP *always* delivered.

All the other TV stations buzzed about the demo on their late-news broadcasts. The media had bought into this story and now they owned it. Now they had no choice but to serve up to their viewers and readers the major event they'd promised. It didn't really matter what we gave them the next day; they were going to display "the largest act of civil disobedience since the storming of the Pentagon."

We woke up at six A.M. The demo was scheduled for seven. We needed to get to the site early to set up. There was to be a podium, a mike, and speakers, and a table for reporters to check in with a "media coordinator." There were actually ten media coordinators for the demo, all wearing flashy badges and all handing out press kits.

Still groggy, I entered the motel elevator equipped with two walkie-talkies, one to communicate with the media coordinators and one to talk with the legal team, so we could always get a proper count of arrests to give to the press. I also had a portable, battery-operated television set so I could monitor the live coverage. Michael Nesline, a nurse and member of ACT UP/New York, got on the elevator at another floor, looked at me and all my gadgets, and said hello. Then we both burst out laughing.

In the lobby of the Holiday Inn, everyone was bustling about. It looked like a group of fourth-graders getting ready for a class play. People were in costumes, rehearsing scenarios. Like a stage mom, Chip Duckett was giving orders to the media coordinators, who were only too willing to do whatever last-minute things had to be done. I went to the motel gift shop and picked up that morning's *Washington Post*. They'd done an extensive piece on the impending demo. The issues were clearly defined. I showed the paper to Duckett.

"Okay, someone's got to get about seventy copies of *The Washington Post,*" Duckett told the Little Publicists. "I want seventy copies of the paper, opened to the page where this story is. Oh, and someone's got to go and get donuts and a few urns of coffee. Every press person coming to this demo is going to get a press kit, a morning paper, a fresh donut, and a cup of coffee. It's going to be a long day, and we've got to keep them happy."

Within an hour the real drama began. Several hundred people charging at a building, engaging in civil disobedience, and performing guerrilla theater in front of a battery of cameras. It wasn't all show biz, though. We were angry.

Very little could be heard above the chants: "*We're* the experts! Let us in!" But at one point there was a faint sound of breaking glass. Perhaps the crowd had become a bit too enthusiastic: They'd surged at the doors to the building so forcefully that the body of a police officer had smashed clear through a window.

He was okay—there was not a scratch on him as he emerged—but the incident made for television footage that portrayed ACT UP as both powerful and dangerous.

While most of the crowd charged at the front doors, a few people got into the building through a side entrance; they were immediately arrested. Other arrests occurred in waves, as people refused to move away from the doors and others blocked the buses that were taking away the previous arrestees. One affinity group did "die-ins" all around the building, lying down in front of cardboard tombstones with phrases like R.I.P. MURDERED BY THE FDA printed on them. Another group wrapped itself in hundreds of feet of red tape. Using garbage and assorted other debris from around the building, one group built a wall the entire length of the road so that no cars could come into the parking lot. The affinity group that called itself Seeing Red marched about in lab coats splattered with red paint, chanting, "The FDA has blood on its hands and we're *seeing red!*" Later, they broke into an adjacent research building, took over a board room, and set up shop, telling officials they were "taking over." After doing several interviews with reporters, they were arrested by police.

Most FDA employees didn't come to work that day, anticipating the mêlée, but a handful had arrived at five A.M., determined to work. These people were now trapped in the building, which had been sealed off completely as several helicopters hovered overhead. Employees stared out of their windows, some even holding up their fists in solidarity. FDA officials, meanwhile, couldn't even come outside to defend themselves directly to the TV cameras. Instead, they did telephone interviews from inside the building, claiming that business was proceeding as usual, without disruption.

We held the press conference in the parking lot across the street from the building. Vito Russo spoke, then John Thomas, head of the AIDS Resource Center in Dallas, then Ann Northrop. The media were fixated. They'd gotten shots of people being arrested and dragged away. They'd gotten good visuals of bold signs, of some people tied up in red tape and others selling drugs on the street. They'd filmed smoke bombs going off on the roof, banners going up the flagpole, windows breaking, effigies burning. They'd gotten random sound bites from many protestors. But now, at the press conference, they were getting well-rehearsed and riveting statements from three people who knew full well how to work the media.

"The side effect of AIDS is death," Russo told the crowd of reporters. "I would rather take my chances with the side effects of drugs. I know it takes months to test a drug in Europe. I want to know why it takes five to ten years in this country. I'm here today because I don't want my name on a quilt in front of the White House." He was referring to the enormous AIDS memorial quilt, which had been displayed on the Ellipse for the previous two days.*

"I am here today—we are all here today—because we all have AIDS," said John Thomas. "Some of us have AIDS in our bloodstream. And some of us have AIDS in our minds. We look into the mirror and see a sore that won't go away, and we are fearful that we are going to be diagnosed. And we all have AIDS in our hearts. All of us have lost people we love."

"You think they're doing all they can?" Ann Northrop asked, pointing to the building. "They're not. They're sitting on drugs that can save people's lives. Their message is very simple: 'We're trying.' They're not. They're *lying*. That is the message of ACT UP."

After the press conference, Urvashi Vaid's brilliant plan for the regional press went into play. Providing a local angle for papers

*Vito Russo died in November 1990.

across the country was the key to making big news in Peoria. It was the difference between getting the front page and getting buried in the paper, lost in the national section.

Vaid took to the microphone: "All those members of the regional press, from cities across the country, you will now find spokespeople from your individual towns and cities." She then pointed the reporters in the direction of a wall of activists—each of whom held up a sign bearing the name of his or her city: Milwaukee, Kansas City, Chicago, Dallas, Seattle, and so on. The reporters looked stunned for a moment, amazed at such an impressive move by the activists. Then, like dogs thrown a steak bone, they raced toward the spokespeople. With cameras, tape recorders, and notepads in hand, they lined up to speak to people from the cities they represented. It was all very orderly. Everywhere one looked, people stood before cameras or spoke to reporters holding microphones or jotting down notes, while other reporters queued single file behind them.

Chip Duckett was setting people up to do hourly radio drop-ins (live, on-the-spot reports, telephoned to the radio networks). "The beauty of such a long demonstration," he bubbled, "is that we get morning and evening drive time—on both coasts!" And Ann Northrop was chatting up her old chums from the networks, trying to spin the story our way.

Toward the end of the day, white-haired Sylvia Ayers from Houston held her own impromptu press conference at Duckett's urging. He'd realized the night before that the cameras would eat her up. "These people are dying for nothing," she said to a battery of television cameras and microphones while pointing to the crowd, "and the government could save their lives. And I beg the government, as a mother, sixty-nine years old, who has no one but who loves all of these beautiful people, to do something. Release these drugs. Help these young people." She then began to cry. "Let 'em live!" she exclaimed, weeping. "Let 'em live, *please!*"

She then laid her body on the floor, blocking the doors to the FDA. Within twenty minutes Sylvia Ayers was handcuffed and dragged away, all of those same cameras following her onto the police bus.

That night Tom Brokaw, in a voice-over lead-in before the first commercial break, announced on *NBC Nightly News,* "When we come back we'll take a look at how AIDS activists have a lot of gripes with the Food and Drug Administration." The footage showed the crowd at the demo chanting, "It's a lie! It's a sham! And it won't work!"

The demo had snowballed beyond our wildest expectations. It was the lead story on all of the Washington TV news broadcasts that night, and it played up front on broadcasts across the country, both on local TV news shows and on the networks. We also made the front pages of hundreds of newspapers across the country the next morning. Perhaps the most satisfying moments were in watching Wall Street stockbroker–turned–AIDS activist Peter Staley on CNN's *Crossfire* that night wearing his SILENCE = DEATH T-shirt and calmly making mincemeat out of a rabid Patrick Buchanan.

We had put the word out to millions of people. The AIDS movement was no longer speaking only to bureaucrats in Washington. Now we were speaking to the citizens of America, letting them know that AIDS was an urgent problem and that something had to be done.

For the AIDS movement, the demonstration showed us that the mass media were among the most powerful weapons at our disposal. And for the lesbian and gay movements, there would never again be a major demonstration—on any issue from antigay violence to gay rights—without press kits, pre-publicity hype, and publicists. Urvashi Vaid had polished these techniques on 1987's massive Supreme Court civil disobedience following the 1986 *Hardwick* decision, which let stand Georgia's sodomy law, but after the FDA demo, the entire movement of younger activists that was now burgeoning on city streets across the country became media-conscious. People realized that in order to get a message across, time and money had to be put into publicity. Suddenly every street activist was a "press whore," and all of us were speaking in sound bites. In-your-face activism took shape nationally, and being out of the closet and in the media became the ideal for a new generation.

A turning point was reached in a decades-old movement that had previously feared the homophobic media or, at best, courted only the elitist press, such as *The New York Times*. Before, we had tried to change the minds of politicians. Now, in the aftermath of the FDA demo, the potency of the *popular* press—and the possibility of manipulating it through sophisticated means in the same way that Democrats, Republicans, Hollywood, corporations, and the right wing always had—was realized. The desire to effect massive changes in social thought could be fulfilled.

And after this ten-hour demonstration, my life—like the lives of so many of us—was never the same. In spite of the AIDS crisis we were battling, I had a feeling of exhilaration, the kind of feeling I hadn't had since childhood.

A Queer's Own Story

Brooklyn isn't the easiest place to grow up, especially if you're a homo.

My cousin Marilu (short for Maria Lucia) was my best friend when I was five. It was perhaps through her, at that young age, that I realized I was queer. I use "queer" in the most traditional sense of the word, because I discerned that I was very *different* from most other little boys in the neighborhood. Like Marilu, I had felt affection toward boys as far back as I could remember. She and I used to talk about the ones we had crushes on. I sensed at that age that I wasn't supposed to be like Marilu in this regard, but still, it felt natural. And Marilu, bless her heart, didn't mind.

Marilu and I were inseparable playmates as toddlers. We were the same age and lived in the same building on Eleventh Avenue in Park Slope, Brooklyn, on the southwest side of Prospect Park. She and her family were on the second floor, while my family lived on the third floor of the building owned by my father's parents, Maria and Michelangelo Signorile, who lived on the first floor.

I remember always perceiving that Marilu and I were the same. I knew that she was a "girl" and I was a "boy," but I didn't understand the difference and certainly didn't feel it. And yet, even when I was five it seemed that the world was already trying to separate us, condemning our playing together and demanding that we be interested in different things. She was supposed to like dolls. I was supposed to like baseball. But I refused to follow those rules. I had something powerful in common with Marilu and it was something intrinsic. I wanted to play with her—and if that meant playing with dolls, then so be it.

My father didn't like that idea. After the first time I got caught dressing Barbie, I remember, I had to sneak play sessions, playing during the day, when my father wasn't around. My father was much more stern about my playing with dolls than my mother was. But I got caught again and again. Soon he became quite alarmed.

"Only sissies play with dolls," he angrily said, and punished me by not allowing me to ever go down to Marilu's again to play with her dolls.

What's a sissy? I thought to myself. Whatever it was, I concluded, I must be one. I also remember wondering why, if I was this thing called a sissy, everyone couldn't just accept that I was a sissy and let me play with Marilu and Barbie.

At the same age, I was discovering that I was left-handed. I remember being told that left-handedness was uncommon; yet people seemed to accept it. But things weren't always that way. My parents and aunts and uncles told me stories of how, just one generation before mine, nuns in Catholic schools used heavy wooden rulers to smash the left hand of anyone they caught trying to write lefty; sometimes they hit hard enough to make the pupils' hands bleed or fracture their bones. Lefties were forced to write with their right hands because left-handedness had for centuries been associated with the Devil in the eyes of the church. It wasn't until the late fifties (at least in Brooklyn) that Catholic schools had accepted lefties, decades after science had decided that left-handedness was natural and normal.

I remember asking myself, when I was five, why, if they could look at being a lefty as uncommon but acceptable, they couldn't view being a sissy in the same way. I soon realized that when it came to religion, especially Roman Catholicism, logic didn't matter. I also discovered that in the culture in which I was being brought up, preserving *la famiglia* was more important than anything else. And being a lefty was one thing, but being a sissy just didn't fit in with preserving *la famiglia*.

.....

My mother and father both grew up in Brooklyn. They met in the fifties, at a dance for the children of immigrants from Bari, a city in southern Italy on the Adriatic coast.

When my parents married in 1958, my mother was a beautiful eighteen-year-old, olive-skinned brunette. Her parents lived in downtown Brooklyn with her mother's parents, who'd come over from Bari in the early part of the century. My mother was the oldest of four children in her family, while my father was the youngest in a family of six children.

My father was twenty-one when he got married. With blue eyes, dirty-blond hair, and fair skin, my father resembled both his parents, Maria and Michelangelo, who were fair-skinned Italians. My father's parents had come from Bari separately, with their families. My paternal grandmother's family had already arranged for her to marry someone else, but my grandfather spotted her, wooed her, and convinced her family to let him have her. He had some money and bought a house in Park Slope. While my grandmother had baby after baby, my grandfather became an iceman, selling ice on a truck to families in the neighborhood. Over the years they lived in several different houses in the neighborhood, before settling in the building on Eleventh Avenue.

Soon after they married, my parents moved into that three-story building, taking over the top apartment. I was born almost two years later, in December 1960. Marilu, who was nine months older than I, lived on the middle floor with her sister and her parents, my father's brother and his wife. All of my father's other brothers and sisters lived with their wives, husbands, and children within walking distance—in fact, none of them lived more than five blocks away: *la famiglia*.

Like most Italian-American families of the time, we were an extremely tight-knit extended family. Individuality was discouraged; developing close bonds with outsiders was okay as long as those outsiders were brought in as part of the family. People in the family saw each other all during the week—at the market, at school, often at work—and then, every Sunday, we got together in my grand-

Sex,

the Media,

and the Closets

of Power

IN AMERICA

The University of Wisconsin Press

The University of Wisconsin Press
1930 Monroe Street
Madison, Wisconsin 53711

www.wisc.edu/wisconsinpress/

3 Henrietta Street
London WC2E 8LU, England

1   3   5   4   2

Printed in the United States of America

Library of Congress Cataloging-in-Publication Data
Signorile, Michelangelo, 1960–
Queer in America : sex, the media, and the closets of power / Michelangelo
Signorile—3rd ed.
p. cm.
Includes index.
ISBN 0-299-19374-8 (alk. paper)
1. Gay liberation movement—United States. 2. Outing (Sexual orientation)—United
States. 3. Coming out (Sexual orientation)—United States. 4. Homosexuality—Moral and
ethical aspects. I. Title.
HQ76.8U5S57   2003
305.9'0664—dc21   2003050114

Portions of chapter 6 were originally published in different form
in the August 27, 1991, issue of *The Advocate*.

Grateful acknowledgment is made to *Harper's* magazine for permission to reprint two paragraphs from "Closets of Power" by Taylor Branch (October 1982).
Copyright © 1982 by *Harper's* magazine, reprinted by permission.

To my mother and father,
the most loving, understanding,
and supportive parents in America

Each of us here thinks the other is queer
and no one's mistaken since all of us are!

TENNESSEE WILLIAMS

"Carrousel Tune"

Out of the dark confinement! out from behind the screen!
It is useless to protest, I know all and expose it.

WALT WHITMAN

"Song of the Open Road"

A closet, a closet does not connect under the bed.

GERTRUDE STEIN

Tender Buttons

mother's basement for a huge meal. I looked forward to those weekly events because everyone would be there, all my cousins and aunts and uncles. I truly enjoyed the family. After my grandfather died while I was fairly young, my grandmother kept the family together. She was a true matriarch, a woman for whom everyone had undying adoration and respect. There were sometimes thirty people at the table, and on Thanksgiving, Christmas, and Easter there were more.

As far back as I can remember, the Sunday meal was immensely important to the family. It was a place where everyone would laugh and have a good time, a weekly meeting where we would connect. In the outside world, all during the week, we were different from everyone else, but on Sunday we were only among ourselves—*la famiglia*. But *la famiglia*'s basement was also a battleground in a war that was tearing the country apart, leaving deep wounds on these first-, second-, and third-generation Italian-Americans, all of whom were assimilating at different speeds and to different degrees.

All through the middle and late sixties and into the early seventies, the discussions at the Sunday dinner table were sometimes fierce, with much shouting and screaming. The country was in the midst of dramatic change. The black civil rights movement, the sexual revolution, the war in Vietnam, and the feminist movement were coming into the forefront. Some of my cousins, teenagers at the time, espoused the emerging ideologies, and their political stance resulted in heated arguments. One or two of my female cousins got into shouting matches regularly with the older men about the women's movement and about racial issues. Almost always, the men would become enraged, yelling at the top of their lungs and silencing the discussion. The men always won, of course. They had to: That was the rule of *la famiglia*.

One of my cousins at one point began dating a Jewish boy. That caused an uproar like I had never seen before. Difference was not acceptable in my family—not at that time. And I knew that I was even more different. I was truly afraid, though I didn't know what it was I feared: I didn't know what homosexuality was. There was never any talk of it at the table, except for the occasional homo joke or antigay slur. One of my cousins had married a man who was effeminate, and the men in the family poked fun at him. The words "queer" and "fag" and "quiff" (an antigay slur prevalent in the outer boroughs of New York City) were thrown around a lot. But there was never any serious discussion—certainly there were no yelling matches—about homosexuality in those days. It was completely in the closet, especially in the church. Cardinal O'Connor may rail against homosexuals today, but back then there was no antigay rhetoric coming from the Roman Catholic pulpit, at least not at Holy Name, our local parish. There was no need for it: Gays weren't a threat because they weren't visible. As far as the church was concerned, there were no homosexuals. And homosexual acts were sins of the worst kind—the kind you never discussed, not even in confession.

I was religious at a young age, and remember feeling very spiritual. When I was five years old, my mother told me the story of Jesus dying on the cross, and it burned in my mind. It frightened me. Yet it also intrigued me. Even though I was a rambunctious individualist, a spoiled child who got whatever he wanted, I always did what the church said to do: I went to mass every Sunday and I prayed regularly. The church was all-powerful and fascinating.

We moved to Staten Island when I was eight, becoming the first unit of our extended family actually to leave Brooklyn and the neighborhood. Staten Island was where upwardly mobile Italian-Americans from Brooklyn went soon after the Verrazano-Narrows Bridge was built, an exodus that caused some bigots to dub the bridge the "Guinea Gangplank." My father had opened his own luncheonette in downtown Brooklyn when I was five, and business was great. By the time we moved to Staten Island, he'd moved his restaurant to a larger place. Eventually, in the eighties, he moved his business to Manhattan.

At the time, much of Staten Island—though it's always officially been a borough of New York City—was still rural. But in the late sixties the island was rapidly being converted into a suburban mecca, with tract housing going up at lightning speed. We lived in Dongan Hills. I was enrolled in the second grade at St. John Villa Academy, a private Catholic boarding school run by the Sisters of St. John the Baptist. Those of us whose families lived on the island (which was then a majority of the school's students) didn't board there. We were picked up by a school bus every day.

I had excellent grades and was a generally happy kid. With sandy-blond hair, blue eyes, and a button nose that everyone tweaked, I knew I was cute and played it to the hilt. I was a loudmouth too, always trying to be the center of attention and always managing to be popular. But by third or fourth grade things began to change: Suddenly, the boys were calling me a faggot. My happy nature grew more subdued.

It wasn't that I was particularly effeminate, but I hung around mostly with girls, rarely with boys. Just as I had with my cousin Marilu, I'd found that I had something powerful in common with the girls. Kids are extraordinarily perceptive: They know who's queer at a very young age. Little gay boys seem to find refuge with little straight girls: They bond, perhaps because both the girls and the gay boys feel oppressed by the straight boys. For young lesbians, it must be more awful than for the young gay boys: Baby dykes are ostracized not only by the boys, but by the girls as well.

I couldn't understand why I was being called names. It was devastating. "Sissy!" "Faggot!" "Queer!" The boys were cruel. I *wasn't* those things, I kept telling myself. Still, that word "sissy" stuck out in my mind because my father had used it, too. I realized that this sissy thing must be lot worse than I'd thought at first; it must be absolutely unacceptable. I would have to prove that I was just like the other boys. I would have to prove that I was a man, not a sissy, a faggot, or a queer.

In the working-class Brooklyn Italian tradition, my father had taught me that if anyone used an ethnic slur, hurling a remark at me like "wop" or "greaseball," I was supposed to punch that person in the face. He'd taught me how to fight.

I decided to transfer this strategy to being queer—even though I wasn't accepting, or even admitting to myself, the fact that I was such a ghastly thing—and so I began hitting whoever called me names. That got me in a lot of trouble in the early years. Worse yet, I wasn't only hitting the kids who were calling me names. I was going after *other* kids who'd been called faggot too, so that I could prove that I agreed they were freaks and distance myself from them. I became a queer-basher to prove I wasn't queer.

Still, the name-calling continued. My personality development was stunted and deformed. I had been a bubbly, smart kid when I entered school, but now I was defensive and belligerent. Whereas I might have developed into one of those kids who was funny, irrepressible, and well liked, instead I was a "faggot," laughed at and ostracized. All my time and energy were consumed with trying to prove I wasn't this horrible thing, this sissy-faggot-queer.

As we got older, entering the fifth and sixth grades, and people began hitting puberty, the girls also started to call me a fag. They now had to distance themselves from me because they wanted to date boys who made fun of me. I, in turn, to prove my manhood, asked out just about every pretty girl in my grade. All of them turned me down. I was a laughingstock.

The name-calling got worse. Every day was hell, and I began to dread going to school. I did everything I could to avoid being noticed. I stayed quiet and tried not to answer questions. I didn't even laugh at jokes. At home, I had my few friends on the block who'd always been my pals. I spent some time with them but I spent more and more time alone, in my room or walking in the woods. I would fantasize about other places, other worlds. I started writing these ideas down, and was soon writing science fiction stories thirty and forty pages long. Escaping into those worlds kept me going. But I always had to come back to reality.

I felt myself becoming distant from my mother. We'd always been close. She was like my best friend, and I thought I could tell her anything. But I couldn't tell her *this*. If I told her the kids were calling me names, she'd want to know why. Even I was refusing to face the true reason. I couldn't just say, "Well, actually, Mom, maybe there's something to it. You see, I do have these feelings I can't explain, and I don't think that fact should be seen as any different from being left-handed, and I just wish the kids would stop." No, I knew my mother wouldn't be able to accept my telling her any of this at that age, and I was afraid of what action might be taken. Would I be put in a home? Would I be punished? Would I be taken to a priest for some sort of ritual? Both the larger culture we lived in and the subculture I grew up in were homophobic. I was like an outsider in the family, an alien—something the family didn't like. As long as I could stay in disguise, however, I was safe. I had to stay that way to protect myself, since there was no telling what they might do. I was absolutely amazed that life had turned out this way—that there could be something about me that I couldn't tell to a soul, not even my mother; that I could be blamed and shamed for something I had no control over.

It was all very hard to comprehend. I knew that somehow the name-calling was tied to these feelings I'd always had toward boys. On top of it all, I realized that these feelings were sinful—they just *had* to be—and I felt dirty for having them. I alternately asked God for forgiveness and cursed him for making me this way. That, in turn, made me feel even more guilty. I pleaded with God, begging him to change me, to make me normal. *Why,* I asked him over and over again, *did you do this to me?* But I couldn't blame God. After all, he was flawless, I was told. I concluded, time and time again, that this was all my fault and that I was simply a bad Christian. I felt that the only way to redeem myself was to confess it all. But I wouldn't dare tell this to a priest. I was literally afraid for my safety, so I lived with the shame.

By sixth grade, people were pairing off. All the girls who had once been my friends were now dating the boys who'd always called me a faggot. The boys' attacks got worse. Sometimes they would gang up on me and beat me up. Many times I thought about going somewhere else, to a place where people weren't so mean and vicious. I often fantasized about running away. At the end of my fantasy there was almost always a reunion with my family and all the kids at school. I didn't really want to run away; I just wanted to get attention, to show everyone how horrible this was.

One day I raised my hand in class and asked one of my teachers, Mr. Reed (in the higher grades there were lay teachers because of a shortage of nuns), if I could go to the bathroom. It had been a particularly rough day; earlier, a group of kids had spat on me while shrieking "Queer!" I went into the bathroom and began crying and banging the walls. I then tore out of the building and walked around the school grounds for a while, eventually hiding in some bushes. About two hours later, I came back. The entire faculty was in a panic. They had been searching the building and were just about to call my parents. My whole class was concerned, too. Mr. Reed saw that I'd been crying. We went for a walk outside.

"Did something happen at home?" he said.

"No," I replied. "It's the kids at school."

"I think I know what it is."

I began to cry.

"Are they calling you names?" he asked.

"They call me a faggot and a sissy," I answered. "I just can't take it anymore. I don't know what to do. It drives me crazy. Everyone hates me."

He looked me in the eye and said, "Listen to me. I'm going to go inside and talk to the class before you come in. But I'm warning you, that's not going to change things too much. This is going to go on for quite some time. It's horrible. I know. But you have to be strong. Do you understand me?"

I nodded.

"One day," he continued, "everything will be fine. You will be happy. But that may be a long time from now. You've got to endure this. I promise you, if you do, everything will be great. But you've got to be strong, okay? Do you promise?"

I nodded, although I didn't really understand what he meant at the time. Years later, of course, I realized that Mr. Reed, a forty-year-old "bachelor" at the time, was also queer. He was trying to reach out to me but was limited in doing so for fear of losing his job, especially then. If only he could really have spoken frankly with me about this. If only there had been some older person—a teacher or a counselor—with whom I could have openly discussed these feelings. I'd have been spared so much pain and suffering. But, of course, there wasn't such a person.

When I went back into the classroom, Mr. Reed had chastised the class for being hateful and calling me ugly names. Everyone was nice. People came up to me separately and told me they were sorry. Some actually said they'd never realized it bothered me. Others said that if I ever wanted to talk to them about it, they would be there for me.

But within a month, the vicious name-calling resumed.

I was forever a "faggot."

· · · · ·

Not too long after that incident, at the age of twelve, I had my first sexual experience. It was with a thirty-year-old man who worked in a bagel store near my house. I wasn't forcibly abused or otherwise coerced. On the contrary, I sought him out. I had heard about him from a friend in my neighborhood—a friend who was warning me about the man because he'd been propositioned by him. The tale intrigued me. My own hormones were beginning to rage. I was an early developer, with hair on my chest as I turned twelve. I found myself hanging around the bagel shop, hoping to be propositioned. Finally, I was.

While I willfully sought out sex with this man, some people would say he, as an adult, was grossly irresponsible. That may very well be true; certainly I, as an adult, would never have sex with a twelve-year-old and would consider anyone, straight or gay, who did so as behaving irresponsibly. But if it hadn't been him, it would have been someone else—most likely another twelve-year-old. I was curious and wanted to experiment.

Although I enjoyed the encounter, when it was over I ran home, crying. I promised myself—and God—that it would never happen again. The guilt was insurmountable. I was physically ill for days, throwing up, disgusted over being such a bad Catholic and doing such grotesque things. In the ensuing months and years, I developed an extreme weight problem, losing weight by starving myself and then gaining it by binging out of control. My sexual habits would later develop the same pattern: I'd go for long periods—months— without sex, only to gorge out of control at some point. And always I was racked with guilt. Somehow, I knew that all this was tied up with my hating myself.

At that time, I sought out some information on homosexuality. I was desperately hoping to be offered a "cure." Our family encyclopedia told me that this "deviant behavior" was difficult to root out after the individual had engaged in it for a long time, and it blamed mothers for the "problem." It said that homosexuality was caused by environmental factors, and there was a reference to the "homosexual-producing mother"—who, the encyclopedia said, was more prevalent among Italians and other Latins than among other ethnic groups. At first I was devastated, but I soon became suspicious of the information. It wasn't that I knew at that time how false and misogynistic the analysis was; I simply knew that my mother had nothing to do with this. However, I grew extremely depressed. There was no accurate information available to me.

In another attempt to prove my manhood, I joined the Pee Wee football league at thirteen. To keep in shape, I began running on the Franklin D. Roosevelt Boardwalk at nearby South Beach. This was about eight months after my first sexual encounter, after I'd sworn to myself that I would never have another homosexual experience. But in the dark, cool recesses under the boardwalk, I found a whole new world.

There, dozens of Italian boys, my age and a little bit older, regularly met in the afternoons and had sex. Sometimes it was group sex; most times it was one-on-one. The boys were all in the same boat as I was: None of them would ever have called themselves gay. They were all kids who were trying to deal with this madness that had seemingly taken over their bodies. Most would have said they hated it and wished they weren't that way; all would have said this was just a phase, a time that was going to pass. None of us were ever going to be homos when we got older: We were all going to get married, just like everyone else.

Actually, we didn't speak to one another about homosexuality all that much, except when the bashers came. Every now and then straight guys with baseball bats would show up under the boardwalk. Everyone would run, and a lot of times someone would get his head bashed in. The bashing was worse at night, I was told. Some said that people had been murdered under there. This danger was really the only thing that had us talking to one another; otherwise we'd just meet discreetly, have sex, and leave each other.

In the beginning, after each visit to the world under the boardwalk, I'd go home and cry. Each time, I'd not go back for quite a while. But eventually the guilt subsided. I started to accept this thing, whatever it was, as something manageable. It was my secret world and—well, yes, it was fun. But of course I could never tell anyone about it—and I could never let it become my whole life. It could only be a phase.

I felt I had to date girls to prove not only to everyone else, but to myself, that I was a heterosexual. I began seeing a girl at school, a new girl who'd transferred in. The affair helped my image. I was in the eighth grade by then, and the guys stopped calling me names, it seemed, out of respect for my girlfriend. It appeared as if I'd proven my heterosexuality to them.

Karen was a pretty blond girl but she didn't really interest me. More than that, I didn't really enjoy being physical with her. Kissing was okay, but I had no desire to have intercourse with her. After a while, she got bored and dumped me.

I was devastated—not because I'd lost her, but because I'd lost my cover. Some of the guys actually started saying Karen had left me because I was a fag. Thank goodness I was graduating that year. High school would be a whole new world, a clean slate. No one would know anything about me. And I'd make sure that I appeared completely heterosexual. I would not hang around with girls, and I would keep playing football—even though I hated it.

I was enrolled in Monsignor Farrell High School, a private, Catholic, all-boy school. It was the best school on the island and one of the finest in the state; it accepted only those who scored highest on the entrance exams. Farrell was a competitive school that prepared students for the top universities in the country, and it had the best high school football team in New York State.

I spent weeks trying out for the football team. I was a good player, but two conflicting forces were battling inside of me. One part of me wanted with every fiber and bone in my body to get on that team so that I could prove I was a man; the other part—the true me—hated the game and didn't want any part of it. I sabotaged myself, making slip-ups in tryouts, and didn't make the team. But the other side of me—the false me—pushed me to go to football camp anyway, as a second-stringer, so that I could still be part of the team and would of course be playing the next year.

Surprisingly, at football camp, a two-week preseason ordeal out in East Hampton, New York, it seemed that everyone became queer. Well, not everyone, but a lot of boys who were probably straight were experimenting with homosexuality, as usual in any all-male environment, especially when all the males are teenagers. Others probably were queer. I had sex with a few of the guys on the team.

But when we got back from camp, *everyone* was again heterosexual. I had actually developed a crush on one of the players with whom I'd had sex, and I kept pushing to be with him when we were back at school. He, of course, labeled me a queer. Suddenly, once again, I was the class fag, reviled by everyone. I got into a lot of fights.

But football had beefed me up. Now I was beating people up everywhere—in the cafeteria, in the library, in the bathroom. Anyone who called me a fag received a punch in the face. I had learned one thing: how to shut them up. I was a strong kid with a powerful left hook, and I could take on guys twice my size. My temper would rage, and I'd pummel my enemies to the ground and then sit on them, claiming victory. It was humiliating for them because a "fag" had beaten them up in front of everyone. But they'd never say anything nasty to me again because they were afraid I'd go crazy on them. However, no matter how vicious and mean they were to me, no matter how ugly their taunts, I felt terrible after beating them up, after that aggression dissipated. Each time, I'd cry myself to sleep that night, upset that I had hurt someone else.

This went on for almost two years. Then I got into one fight too many and was called into the principal's office. He said if my fighting didn't stop I'd have to leave the school. He wanted to know why I was always in fights, but I refused to tell him. After an hour or so, he called in one of the brothers to counsel me. This was a man who I always suspected was gay. In fact, there had been some rumors about him.

I told him, in private, that I was fighting the other guys because they were calling me a queer.

"You know," he said, "because this is an all-boy school, and because people are so envious of the students who attend, many on the outside say cruel things, I know, in order to intimidate the students here."

That was true. If you attended Farrell, you were a "Farrell fag." It was a running joke all over the island.

"Because of that," the brother continued, "many of the students here internalize that name-calling and take it out on each other. They're so afraid of being called these things themselves that they attack others in the school first."

"Well," I responded, "it's not entirely untrue."

"What's not entirely untrue?"

I was getting up the gumption to actually tell someone about myself, someone who I felt understood the situation.

"I do have these feelings," I continued. "And things have happened."

"What are you saying?" He seemed to become incensed.

I suddenly realized he was not the person to tell.

"Nothing, sir. Forget it."

"Wait right here," he told me.

He went back out and spoke with the principal for quite some time. I then was called into his office. The dean of students, Father Finn, was also there.

"Mike," the principal said, "we don't think you're happy here. We think you would be better off on the outside, at a public school. We're not going to expel you. It's up to you. But I think you should go."

My mother was then called in and was told that I wasn't happy at Farrell, that I'd been in fights and that this type of disciplined environment wasn't right for everyone. They told her that I'd suggested I'd like to leave and that they had agreed.

I was enrolled in the local public high school, New Dorp High. Public school was much rougher, I knew. There were lots of tough kids, the kind who formed gangs and hated queers and enjoyed pouncing on them. I had to survive. I sensed that once high school was over, a lot of the nightmare would stop. Somehow I just had to get through this, as Mr. Reed had told me back in sixth grade. Of course I wasn't yet admitting to myself that I was really homosexual. I was still going to the beach, under the boardwalk, regularly. But that was my secret world, and it didn't mean anything. All of the years of name-calling had taken their toll: I hated myself. *Why,* I began to ask myself over and over, *do I want to live any longer? Why do I want to go through any more of this?* I contemplated suicide. Over and over I'd go through the scenarios: Take all the pills in the medicine cabinet. Jump off the Staten Island Ferry into the harbor. Run into oncoming traffic. Slit my wrists.

I couldn't go through with it. I vowed that I was going to make it—any way I could. I had to make sure that I'd never be labeled a fag again, so I sought out the toughest crowd in the school. I figured if I hung around with them, I'd be considered macho. I beat up a lot of boys over the silliest things, showing my new friends that I could handle myself. Then I got into drugs, to prove to the guys that I could take it. We were doing the hallucinogen mescaline a lot. When I was high, everything was easier to deal with. I found myself doing more drugs as time went on.

Another way to show the guys that I was heterosexual was bashing queers, just like they did. There was a skinny, quiet kid named Vinnie, one of those nerdy guys who rarely said a word to anyone and always took whatever abuse was hurled at him. And there was plenty. Everyone called him a fag and a queer. Lots of the tougher, meaner guys pushed him around a lot, sometimes punching and kicking him. He just took it all, never uttering a sound. Everyone laughed at him all the time, pointing and cackling.

In gym class, Vinnie always sat on the bleachers, participating in sports as little as possible. While he sat against the wall, the other boys hurled basketballs at him, as a sort of target practice. His glasses flew off most of the time, or broke. Still, he just sat through it. I knew Vinnie was living a hellish existence. So was I. Yet my way of dealing with it was to hurl basketballs at him too, to show everyone that I wasn't at all a fag like him. I remember vividly how the guys would egg me on and laugh, having a grand time as I whipped those basketballs at Vinnie. His head, over and over again, smashed against the wall. Still, he never moved. He never did anything. Passivity was his way of getting through the nightmare. And beating him up was mine. Each time, I went home and cried.

At the same time, I began to fall in love with my friend Jim. It was not a physical relationship. Jim was straight for all I knew, but I felt a powerful emotional bond with him. I was so emotionally disturbed, so messed up, that I was looking up to this tough, muscled guy, who really was a loser: His grades were lousy; he treated people terribly, using them for all of their money and anything else they could give him; and he was on drugs every day. I was easily taken in by him, partly because I was attracted to him physically and partly because he was telling me that I was a great guy. He was lying, scamming me. I think I knew that but I didn't care. Anyone who treated me well and told me that I was wonderful could manipulate me.

Jim and I did a lot of drugs, almost every night. I was a senior in high school by then, and we were hanging out with the rest of my gang in a nearby park. The drugs were costing a lot of money, and I was buying them for Jim too. He slept over at my house a lot, in my basement. I always fantasized about having sex with him, but I never dared to try anything. Soon, I began selling drugs in order to make money to fund our habits.

At home, things had hit rock bottom. Since I'd turned twelve, my parents had caught me with cigarettes several times and had punished me—which only made me more rebellious. I still did everything I could to get them mad, it seemed, to prove to them that I was straight—which, to me, meant doing macho things and standing up to your parents. I was very defiant, running out on them, not coming home on time, saying the nastiest things to them. My mother was a nervous wreck. When she finally found my stash of pills, all hell broke loose. She and my father sat me down.

"I need help," I said. "I need someone to talk to about things."

My mother called the pediatrician and got the name of a psychiatrist. Within two weeks I was in therapy.

Dr. Simmons knew that the drugs were not the problem, but rather were a symptom of a larger dilemma. I had no identity. My personality was stunted and damaged.

Therapy went well. I was more positive, thinking more about myself and what I wanted to do with my life. As a result, I pulled myself away from unhealthy influences and I was happier. But strangely, we never discussed my being gay, even though I was starting to feel good about that fact.

During therapy, which went on for almost two years, I graduated and enrolled at Brooklyn College, still unsure of what I wanted to do for a career.

During that time, I dated a woman and had sex with her several times. In terms of sheer enjoyment, the sex didn't compare to sex with men. But there was also something else missing. While I had always looked to girls rather than boys to be my best friends, I didn't bond emotionally with women in the same way that I did with men; there wasn't a sexual edge. But I had never bonded with any of the men I'd had sex with; that feeling was always reserved for the straight friends on whom I had crushes. The men I had sex with were quick encounters, men I met at the beach or on the subway, at the library or in cafés. I never attempted to see these people again or to have a conversation of any depth with them, because I was afraid of getting involved, afraid that it would mean I was a homosexual.

Now, toward the end of therapy, I started to think that I wanted to experience a bond with a man that was both emotional and sexual. For the first time, I felt good about being queer. It was exciting. Looking back, I realize that just dealing with my lack of confidence and repairing my damaged sense of self had equipped me to come to terms with my homosexuality. However, I didn't dare discuss that at length with Dr. Simmons because I knew that he was homophobic—even though I didn't know that word at the time. What had me leery of frankly discussing my homosexuality with him was his response after I'd first tested him on the issue. I told him that I'd had a sexual experience with a man I met outside his office, and he told me that it probably meant nothing.

"That's normal," he said. "Everyone has one or two homosexual experiences. I'm sure it's nothing. If it becomes something more, let me know."

"But what about people who are gay?" I asked. "People who live a gay life? Do they have some sort of problem?"

"Ninety-nine percent of homosexual men just have a fear of women," he said. "It's a fear of something different, since a woman has a different organ. It's easier to deal with the familiar and so they stick with men. All they really need to do is get over their fear."

I knew that wasn't it. My whole life was getting better because of therapy, and I was also feeling better about being gay. I didn't want to go into this with Dr. Simmons because I figured it would keep me in therapy much longer for something that I wasn't feeling so bad about and that I didn't think he had a handle on. I sensed that he was going to try to tamper with an aspect of my life that he shouldn't be tampering with. I wanted to pursue this—this homo thing—and see what happened.

On leaving therapy, I decided to study journalism. I transferred to the S. I. Newhouse School of Public Communications at Syracuse University. I also knew that if I wanted to be happy and live my life, I needed to move away from Staten Island.

At Syracuse, for the first time in my life, I was completely out of the closet in my day-to-day activities. I socialized in a gay environment. All of my friends were gay, and much of my life revolved around exploring my sexuality and exploring the rich gay culture I'd been denied. With distance, I realized how corrupt my church was. It wasn't preaching love and respect—it was ordering its members to hate and to exclude. So much of the madness I had lived through for twenty years was caused by the church's teachings on homosexuality. I discarded Roman Catholicism entirely. However, I would always retain my spirituality.

I was the happiest I'd ever been, as if I'd finally found that fantasy world I'd always dreamed about. But I also realized how lucky I'd been to make it through those rough years: Thirty percent of the teen suicides in America, I came to learn, are among lesbian and gay adolescents who feel that life has nothing to offer them and that they are freaks. I'd only made it, perhaps, because I was strong and because I had parents who loved me and cared about me enough to stick by me and get me help when I sent them a message—even though it would be years yet before I told them about my being queer. I thought about the kids whose parents didn't send them to therapy. I thought about the kids whose parents sent them to therapists who tried to "cure" them. What about the kids whose parents were troubled themselves? What about children from broken homes or children of alcoholics? What about the kids who weren't strong enough, who weren't survivors?

I thought a lot in those years about Vinnie and the others whom I had pummeled. Had they made it? How badly had I hurt them? Still, I wasn't at all political and had no interest in gay politics at that time. I was filled with a lot of unhealthy ideas about homosexuality, and I was at the beginning of a road that would take years to travel.

At that time I told two close straight male friends from home that I was gay. John and Paul were great guys—typical macho Italian guys—who had been my constant companions during my two years at Brooklyn College. I wasn't sure how they'd react, but they accepted it well. I also told my cousin Marilu. Incredibly, she was shocked—but very supportive, and even delighted. "That's great," she said. "At least *someone* in the family is doing something exciting." And I had my first relationship, a one-year-long, intimate affair, while I was at Syracuse. Then I had another that lasted just as long. I graduated and decided to explore this new life. I'd been denied a real adolescence, even a real childhood, in which I could grow and learn.

Growing up is hard, especially if you're a homo. I headed down to Fort Lauderdale to meet some men and get a good tan. I'd been through a horrible ordeal for the first two decades of my life but I had survived.

Now I wanted to make up for a lot of lost time.

3

....

Hype Anxiety

....

I got back to New York and my parents were pissed. They'd spent a lot of money sending me to journalism school and all I had to show for it was a fabulous tan.

I needed a job, but even with a degree, you had to have fast typing skills in order to get so much as an entry-level position. I went to one of those loud, crowded employment agencies on Forty-second Street—the ones that advertise in *The New York Times*. I failed the typing test, but the agency itself offered me a job—a sort of scam they pulled on people who couldn't be placed elsewhere.

I didn't get a salary. The job worked like this: I was supposed to go through the telephone book, call up companies, ask the personnel directors if they needed office help, and try to place the employment agency's clients. Usually the people on the other end hung up, or said no. But if I got a personnel director who needed help, I was supposed to offer the perfect person with the perfect skills for a fee of roughly $10,000. If the personnel director was crazy enough to say yes—and if the person I sent over was actually hired—I would receive a commission.

After several days, I knew it wasn't working out. I decided that I had to sell *myself*. I turned to the listings under "Public Relations

Firms" and began calling them up. Instead of asking the firms to pay $10,000, I offered myself for no fee at all. By the time I got through the letter "F," I had landed a job.

I started immediately, answering telephones and running errands at Faces, Inc.,* a company that produced advertorials, those slickly produced advertising sections that are a cross between editorial content and ads. The agency would get five or six advertisers together, buy five or six pages of *Vogue, Mademoiselle,* or *Glamour,* and fill the pages with a scenario that involved all of the advertisers' different products.

But the company itself was something of a sham. Though we would always talk about our "studio," it didn't exist. The company was made up of three individuals, one of whom lived in the apartment we worked out of. They did everything second-rate, using the worst models, the worst makeup artists, and the worst photographers. One of the principals, Dan, a middle-aged amateur photographer who did many of the shoots himself, had made one of the bedrooms into an office. It consisted of a mattress, a chair, and a table with a light board. Pounds of used and unused film as well as stacks of paper—mostly unpaid bills and junk mail—lined the floor. On a good day, Dan could be found talking on the telephone or sitting in the chair, which wobbled on top of a pile of papers. On a not-so-good day, he could be found *under* a pile of papers, passed out.

Howard, the second partner, still hadn't gotten over his divorce—which had taken place ten years earlier—and was subject to mood swings. When he got depressed, which was often, he'd leave without a moment's notice and take long drives upstate, which sometimes lasted for days. His function in the organization was to sell space to potential advertisers, which put him face-to-face with rejection every day. Each time Howard was rejected by a major company, he'd jump in the car and take another long ride.

The third partner was Sally, the creative force behind the trio. She wrote and edited the copy and came up with the concepts for the ads. Perhaps because she—an experienced former magazine editor—was the smartest one among them, and perhaps because they were sexist swine, Dan and Howard expected a lot from her. They treated her

*This is not the company's real name.

terribly. Sally organized the shoots and secured the models and the make-up artists. She was also the stylist, the decorator, and the lighting assistant. Sally was high-strung to begin with, and all of the pressure made her a nervous wreck. On top of everything else, Sally was romantically involved with Dan, the alcoholic, who abused her both mentally and physically.

Me, I was twenty-two, lucky to get paid—in cash—and excited to be working in Manhattan. I moved out of my house, into an apartment in St. George, on Staten Island, just across the street from the Staten Island Ferry. I spent a lot of time in the city after work and began doing the club scene with a gay friend from college who had moved to New York to be an art student at Parsons School of Design. Michael and I made a lot of friends—art and design students mostly. I became a fashion freak, attired in whatever was at the cutting edge, ornamenting myself with whatever was hip.

It was the early eighties, as garish a time as ever there was. Michael and I spent hours dreaming up flamboyant things to wear and making the garments ourselves—we couldn't sew, so we used iron-on adhesive tape. We made our own kiltlike skirts, which we'd wear with heavy black shoes and white socks, no shirt, and a navy-blue or black blazer. We always wore trinkets with such outfits: fake-jeweled crosses on chains, or crown pins attached to our breast pockets. It was important to create a look for yourself—something to confound people, to excite them and make them think that you were the hippest thing.

At first, I liked the fact that Faces, Inc., wasn't what it seemed. I learned that nothing in this new world I was in had any substance. Everything was just a shimmering, seductive façade. It was my job to make the façade look substantive. It became exciting trying to pull off the charades we maneuvered. But the company couldn't last—it was about to fall apart. I had to get out of there right away, and they had taught me how to play the game. I stayed after work one day, went back to the telephone book, opened again to "Public Relations Firms," and picked up where I'd left off—the letter "F." I had gotten better at the game, having just learned from three of the industry's sleaziest. By seven o'clock I'd gotten to the letter "H" and Mike Hall Associates, where a soft-spoken man answered the telephone.

"Good evening, sir," I said politely. "I hope I'm not disturbing you. My name is Mike Signorile. I'm a recent college graduate, having majored in journalism with a concentration in public relations, looking for an entry-level position, anything that will give me some experience." Then I worked my façade. "I like to work long hours, and I'm impressed that you're still at the office at this hour. Mike Hall Associates sounds like my kind of place."

"Come on over and see me," he said in a monotone.

If Faces was about putting on façades, then Mike Hall Associates was where they were polished. A fifty-year veteran entertainment PR man, Mike Hall was not at all the quintessential pushy Broadway press agent. He was a slight man with a quiet demeanor who pleased almost everyone in the business with his low-key approach. In a world where publicists vigorously push themselves and their clients, Mike Hall always sat in the background, his arms wide open. This strategy made him far more credible than many other publicists, and has brought him much admiration and respect.

"You're going to get some valuable experience here," he told me in our first meeting. "The kind of stuff you won't get anywhere else." I didn't realize until years later how right he was.

Within days it became apparent that this was one of the most specialized of media operations imaginable. We weren't really public-relations people in the full sense of the phrase, nor were we publicists or press agents. We were column planters: We promised our clients mentions in gossip columns—and we delivered. The clients might have a regular publicist who would book talk shows or arrange feature stories and interviews; they came to us strictly to get their projects into gossip columns. And in the world of entertainment, gossip notes aren't taken lightly. They're considered great mentions, the most visible kind of publicity, especially if the columnists are nationally syndicated. Our client list proved the point: We had major film companies like MGM/UA, Columbia Pictures, 20th Century Fox, Universal, Touchstone, and Disney; Broadway producers; book publishing companies; and a string of performers who came to us when they were working on special projects. Across the street from our offices was the famous Russian Tea Room, the celebrity spot where so many deals are made daily.[1] It was an "exchange" client—

we put the Tea Room in the columns, while it provided Mike and sometimes others of us with free meals and good tables—as was the famous Stage Deli.

I worked in a small room with the company's two other staff members. One of them, Mitch, was an openly gay man who was there because he was a Broadway buff more than a media person. Sylvia was a straight British divorcée in her forties who had worked for years for the British singer Tom Jones. Mitch and I sat at desks facing each other, and between us was a six-by-ten-foot wood partition about a foot thick. Dozens of cake trays fit neatly into slots carved in the partition. On each tray was the name of a columnist. Inside the trays were strips of paper, each with a "gossip item" printed on it. Items would go something like this:

> Wags at the Stage Deli say **Elizabeth Taylor** is aching to star in a picture based on the story of her life. They say she wants to do it first before anyone else can so that she can have complete control over it. But she's afraid she won't be able to play herself if she keeps on eating those triple-decker sandwiches. . . .

> **Dustin Hoffman**'s looking to reprise his "Death of a Salesman" act on Broadway. Any backers? . . .

At the end of the day, all of the items would be typed up and sent to the particular columnist, part of an elaborate and tedious system that had been devised over the years by Mike's wife, Fran.

Fran and Mike had an apartment in the same building as the offices, about five floors above. But Fran rarely, if ever, came down into the office during business hours. Instead she'd "buzz" us throughout the day. When she buzzed, we had to drop everything. If it took too long to get to the phone after she buzzed, we had to have an explanation.

Fran did a meticulous job of monitoring things from upstairs. She would come down after hours and on weekends, when no one was there, then play dumb and ask us about things she'd noticed. She loved to catch us in lies.

She and Mike had been in the business since the forties, when there were half a dozen daily papers in New York, each with several columnists. Those were the days of the Broadway press agent, the days of Walter Winchell. Mike and Fran had been among his main sources. They were reliable and hardworking, and they knew how to dig up dirt.

Each day, we'd send a few pages of items, from one sentence to a small paragraph, to each columnist. Sometimes these were "fresh" items, meaning they just had been written or hadn't appeared anywhere else yet. Other items were "recycled," meaning they'd been to another columnist, who had decided not to use them.

Some items were "client" items: announcements about a client's new film, a tidbit about a client in an upcoming Broadway show. Other items were "free" items—juicy pieces of dirt about celebrities who were not our clients. We would put four or five items on a page, spaced a few inches apart. Every other item was a free item. If a columnist decided to use a free item, it was understood that he or she would use a client item. In other words, they would pay us off for hot gossip by plugging our clients' projects. A typical free item would be something like:

New Two You: **Jessica Lange** and **Sylvester Stallone** have become the hottest couple on the French Riviera, spotted day and night, cooing at each other in cafés. . . .

When we typed up pages for any given columnist, we made a carbon copy. The items on the carbon were cut up, so that each was a strip of paper. The columnist's name was scrawled in the margin. When a columnist used an item, his or her name was circled. Then the strip of paper went into a file of "Used Items," where it stayed forever. However, if the columnist didn't use an item, his or her name would be checked off in the margin, indicating that columnist had received the item but rejected it. It would then become a "recycled" item. This process went on until the item was used. Some items would have ten or more names scratched out before they found a home with a columnist somewhere.

Each time an item went out, it was rewritten for the specific columnist it was going to. Since the goal was to place as many client items as possible, we made sure the items were written in the columnist's style, so that he or she would be more inclined to use it. Most of the time, when we did our jobs right, the columnists ran our items word for word.

We feverishly studied the columnists' writing styles and idiosyncrasies, what they liked and what they didn't like. We knew what excited them and what insulted them. We even knew about their personal lives.

Sylvia, Mitch, and I were each assigned to cover several different columnists. I serviced the less important ones at first, but eventually I worked my way up. Mike himself did the powerful syndicated columnist Liz Smith. She was the queen bee and her column was the one that all the clients wanted to be in. She only received the freshest, hottest items. And Mike sometimes spent hours rewriting and reworking her copy.

Mike went all around town, collecting information. He'd go to the Russian Tea Room every day, watching for celebrities, schmoozing with producers, directors, writers, editors, actors, and agents. If Yoko Ono was at the Russian Tea Room having lunch with Brian De Palma, he'd feed Liz an item like:

There was **Yoko Ono** splitting some blinis with filmmaker **Brian De Palma** at the Russian Tea Room yesterday. Were they cutting a deal for the film rights to her book?

At night, Mike took in a Broadway show or went to a screening of an upcoming film. His entire life revolved around that area: Fifty-seventh Street from Fifth Avenue to Broadway, and Broadway down to Times Square. There were cocktail parties and dinner parties, and Mike would have us attend so that we could chat people up and get dirt out of them. Sylvia, full of poise and British charm, could melt almost anyone who came within ear range. An attractive redhead who told hilarious stories, she could be incredibly pushy at times in a very seductive way. She always got what she wanted, and people gave her the information she needed.

That Mitch and I were openly gay was an enormous asset to Mike. There is a network of homosexuals who trade information—or who just plain gossip among themselves. Many of the top publicists were lesbians, and scores of gay men worked throughout the film industry, the fashion industry, and Broadway. Perhaps because information is power, gay people, traditionally powerless, love to revel in gossip and dish. Mitch and I cultivated friends who were gay and likely to give us information.

I found myself constantly scouting for items. While Mitch's social life centered around the Broadway and theater crowd, mine became the nightclub scene. I started digging up what Mike liked to call "subculture items." Anything could be an item: an outfit, a billboard, a scene on the street—the kinds of trends my friend Michael and I followed.

Our sources didn't just come from our social networks; many of them were people we could do "favors" for: Makeup artists, costume people, grips, studio assistants, and junior scriptwriters were our Deep Throats, but almost *anyone* was a potentially valuable source. It was common for individuals in service professions to rush to telephone us after overhearing some delectable dish. Celebrities for the most part are stupid—all too often they say things in front of waiters and maître d's in restaurants, people at cosmetics counters, ushers in theaters, taxicab drivers, caterers, florists, and delivery people. Anyone might hear something valuable and call us. In return, we'd give the Deep Throats screening passes or tickets to Broadway shows. Others were simply born gossips who just loved the thrill of being part of it all and didn't want anything in exchange. It was an almost sexual release for them to open up the paper, turn to Liz Smith, and see a bit of dirt they'd spread. In their otherwise powerless lives, this was a brief moment in which they had power. These were the most reliable sources imaginable; they had no social, financial, or political agenda, and thus had little reason to lie. They also knew that they could always be found if they did lie, as these public jobs afforded us easy access to them.

Few topics were off limits. But one thing that was never discussed in print was homosexuality. This was a cardinal rule, and even the subject of breaking it rarely came up. We'd constantly discuss people's *heterosexuality*, writing about new love interests (whether or not the subjects wanted them reported) and weddings, and speculating on divorces (again, whether or not the subjects wanted them reported), but never mentioning homosexuality. We—meaning those of us at Mike Hall's, as well as the studios, the agents, the managers, and the columnists—disguised homosexual public figures as heterosexuals. Love interests of the opposite sex were assigned to queer stars, many times in cooperation with the manager of the star the celebrity was being matched up with so as to give them both publicity. Sometimes both stars were closeted queers, making it all very convenient. We'd send these items to columnists, who also knew that the celebrities were lesbian or gay. The person who was covering for the gay star was called a beard. When writing about heterosexual liaisons, we had to be meticulous, but when writing about homosexuals, we were *expected* to cover for them. It simply wasn't "right" to tell the truth. We were doing this all so unconsciously and automatically that no one—including me—ever protested any of it, nor did we think it was problematic. It was simply how things were always done—and how they had to be. There was no sense at the time that we might be misleading the public.

Every one of our clients wanted a mention in Liz more than any other column.[2] Liz was considered a massive "break": She reached millions of people who read her religiously. Having spent years cultivating a down-home Texas-gal image, Liz was very well liked and well respected. She appeared six days a week in the New York *Daily News* and was syndicated to hundreds of other newspapers throughout the country.

Aileen Mehle wrote the "Suzy" column, which was then also in the *Daily News*. She and Liz were fierce rivals, always at war and often backhandedly swiping at each other in their columns. Suzy's beat was New York and international society; Liz's was entertainment. But Suzy loved running juicy Hollywood items whenever she could get them, and Liz loved hobnobbing with the upper crust. The two columnists competed against each other for items, and it was sometimes hard for us to service one without the other getting bent out of shape.

It was well known that Liz had been involved with another woman for many years. It wasn't something Liz tried to hide in her social circles, but she never mentioned it in interviews, and certainly never in her own column. Some people baited her. Frank Sinatra, in an antigay tirade, once made a crack about it.

Suzy—Aileen Mehle—was a real character. The glamorous photo of her that graced her daily column dated from many years before. In the photo she had a luxurious head of blond hair styled into a

Dynasty coiffure. She was close to seventy years old, but her writing was crisp—even if what she covered was stale. Her colorful, fantastical writing style was admired by many. Mike was able to imitate it perfectly. Often he realized that a certain client needed a "Suzy" break—though she wasn't widely syndicated, like Liz, Suzy was a prestigious break since she was read by all the "right" people. Mike would spend days crafting a "Suzy" column, getting all of her words and phrases down pat, but his work paid off: Often she'd run his copy as large chunks of her column, word for word.

Suzy lived on the first floor of a well-kept four-story townhouse in the East Sixties, just off Central Park. There was no doorman, just big iron gates and a dark lobby with a huge rotunda. Elaborate frescos were painted on the walls and ceilings, and a huge chandelier hung overhead.

No one was allowed to deliver any copy to Suzy before noon, when the help arrived. She was out at parties all night, we were to believe, and couldn't possibly be up before noon. Once I got there at about ten to twelve to deliver copy. Something seemed to be wrong with the buzzer, so I rang again and again. Finally Suzy came out, in a bathrobe, undone hair, and a temper.

"What time is it?" she thundered.

"I, uh, don't know," I said.

"I'll tell you what time it is. It's ten to twelve. *Ten to twelve!* And what time are you *not* supposed to come here until?"

"Look," I answered, "I'm very sorry, I—"

"If you *ever* do this again," she said, staring me in the eye and grabbing the envelope of items, "I'll make sure you *never* work in this town again."

I bolted out of there like the Cowardly Lion in *The Wizard of Oz* and never went back before noon.

Cindy Adams, a gossip columnist at the *New York Post,* lived with her husband, Joey, a "humor" columnist at the *Post,* in a high-rise on the Park, not far from Suzy. But that was as close as Cindy and Suzy got. Adams was considered a third-rate break. She wasn't syndicated widely, and no stars clamored to be in her column—they considered it tacky. While the other columnists courted the crème de la crème of New York society or the power brokers of Hollywood, Cindy trafficked in such people as Ferdinand and Imelda Marcos, Roy

Cohn, Dewi Sukarno, the Trumps, and the Helmsleys. These were among her best friends. She always had the scoop on their latest ventures, and she was always a mouthpiece for them.

Most clients who wanted to be in the *New York Post* opted for the popular and racy "Page Six" column (then written by Richard Johnson, who now has his own column at the *Daily News*), which we regularly serviced as well.[3]

We also fed items to other columns, like *People*'s "Chatter" page and the Associated Press and United Press International's "People" wires, which were simply gossip wires. Many times we'd exaggerate things for the wires. We'd decide that a new trend had started—one that just happened to have a connection to one of our client's projects. We'd write fashion items, claiming that the costumes in clients' films had inspired street fashion. Many times, our items turned up as expanded stories and would go on to actually create the trend on the street. It began to dawn on me that we were regularly reaching and influencing millions of people with hype. As silly as this all seemed, we were having an impact on mass culture.

While working at Mike Hall's, I began to write a nightclub and party column for *Nightlife*, a tacky Long Island monthly that was soon to kick off a city edition. It was my first column, good practice, I thought, since I eventually wanted to be a free-lance writer. It also got me invited to a lot of parties, the private nightclub parties of the time.

The time was 1984, and the nightclub of the moment was Area, a space in Tribeca that changed its decor every six weeks with extravagant art installations, each of which had a theme: "Sex," "Food," "Suburbia," and "Religion." Area was the ultimate in downtown overstimulation, packed with the fashion and art world's elite as well the usual Hollywood and society types who brought television cameras and media people. Dressing up in the most garish, outlandish attire was de rigueur. Area was soon outdone by the Palladium, a mammoth club that opened in 1985. Its decor incorporated the work of the downtown artists—people like Keith Haring and Jean-Michel Basquiat—whose work was being bought up by uptown yuppies. Owned by Steve Rubell and Ian Schrager, who had run Studio 54, the Palladium and the private Mike Todd Room upstairs were where the celebrities and the extravagant downtown crowd flocked when they weren't at Area.

Straight and gay mixed in what seemed to be perfect harmony. The scene was *fabulous*—that was actually the word everyone used, along with many variations: "Darling, you look *fabulous!*" you'd say to girl-of-the-minute Dianne Brill. "*Fabulousness* becomes you," you'd whisper to deejay Anita Sarko. "Don't wallow in your *fabulosity*," you'd tell drag creation and self-styled "celebutante" James St. James.

It was all about how much press you got: Even if you *were* press you wanted to get press. The amount of press you received was the ultimate indication of how *fabulous* you were. And you just had to tell everyone else how *fabulous* they were too, even though behind their backs you'd insult them. Sometimes you would insult them to their faces in a public confrontation, which could make both of you look even more *fabulous*.

My life was moving faster than it ever had. I had no idea what was going on in politics or in any other aspect of American life. The outside world didn't matter; it was too scary anyway.

By day, I was digging up bits of information and dirt to feed to egomaniacal columnists in return for their help in hyping a client, and by night I was running around with the party elite, meeting movie stars and fashion icons and getting lots of good gossip to use the next day in the office or to write about in my own column in *Nightlife*.

After a while, I left Mike Hall's to concentrate on my column and on free-lance writing. I began reporting on the downtown scene for *People* and for the fashion trade publication *Daily News Record*. I started writing regularly for the British publication *The Face*, and I was getting work at various other newspapers and magazines.

I also began my own segment on a local cable-television entertainment show, *Tomorrow's Television Tonight*, on which my beat was the club scene. I'd report on the parties and serve up some dirt, but I also had a gimmick: I made dolls of the celebrities. I'd create outfits and hairstyles that had the dolls looking uncannily like the stars—then I did dastardly things to them on the air. When Madonna's henchmen had me thrown out of a club during a party for her *Like a Virgin* album, I made a Madonna doll and nailed her to a blood-red crucifix on the air. (She was into cross imagery at the time.) Another time, Boy George came into the Milk Bar with his drag friend Marilyn and had the manager make people get up and give their seats to his entourage. I had an elaborately coiffed and attired Boy George doll thrown into the Slime Pit, a volcanic crater in which a dinosaurlike creature oozed gobs of thick green slime onto the victim.

My life was truly fantastical. Like Suzy, I'd wake up around noon, write until six or seven, and head out to a cocktail party—a gallery opening or fashion party. It might then be up to Broadway for a show or off to Susan Anton's birthday party. Or it was downtown to a party for a film at which Eddie Murphy, Sylvester Stallone, or some other Hollywood type was the guest of honor; then over to another private affair for a British rocker, an artist, or a designer. Several hours and parties later, I might wind up at an after-hours club, eventually crashing home at five or six A.M. During peak seasons—fall and spring, when many affairs are thrown—this might go on every night, except perhaps Saturday, when the downtown A list stayed home. For most of the crowd it was the only night of no drinking and no Ecstasy, the drug of choice since the early eighties.

Village Voice columnist Michael Musto was becoming one of my closest friends. With his trademark head of curly black hair and black sunglasses—prescription glasses he wore even in the darkest of clubs—Musto was sometimes intimidating to strangers. In reality, he was a shy, sensitive man from the Bensonhurst section of Brooklyn who'd grown up in the same strict Italian-Catholic environment I had. He was a genuine, original thinker and one of the few people on the club scene with whom I had any substantive conversations. Like James St. James, Musto enjoyed doing drag and was endlessly photographed.

As taken with the glamour and glitter as he was, Musto had one foot in reality. He took his work very seriously, rarely drinking, never doing drugs, always carrying a pad and pencil, and not staying out too late. He also knew that many of the club people were his friends only because he could give them publicity and because he got so much publicity himself. While no one else on that scene had analyzed why we all were behaving in this frenetic, self-indulgent fashion, Musto had a handle on it all. Musto knew that far in the background, behind all of our theatrics and all of our excesses, was AIDS.

·····

The first time I heard anything related to the disease, I was on a dance floor in a gay club in Syracuse in 1982. One of my friends passed me a bottle of poppers and told me about some new disease that had killed a few gay men. He said that it was caused by poppers. We laughed it off and did another hit.

Throughout the early eighties, while I was at Mike Hall's, AIDS seemed to have no relevance to my life. There wasn't much written about it, and when there was, it was a farfetched story about tainted blood or quarantining. I didn't pay attention. I was young and didn't know anyone who was sick.

Of course, I must have known scores of people with AIDS and people who were HIV-positive in the early 1980s. Lots of men in our business, in fact, mysteriously went away and never came back. No one ever asked about them, but deep down, we all knew. AIDS was something no one would dream of telling you about, especially in the worlds I occupied, where we didn't even talk about being gay. We were so liberated—or so we'd convinced ourselves—that we didn't need to discuss it, certainly not politically. Everyone was free to do whatever they wanted to do, whether they were straight or gay. By talking about it you were making an issue of it—you were drawing attention to it.

The truth, however, was that we didn't discuss being gay because it *wasn't* so acceptable. Discussing it made people queasy. And now that this weird disease was circulating there was even more reason to keep quiet: You didn't want people to think that you *had* it. You didn't want people to think you might give it to them. After all, no one really knew how it was transmitted. Maybe we *all* had it.

AIDS stayed in the background, and we in the industries most full of queers, the industries that could do the most in terms of raising money and awareness, went further into the closet. AIDS was just too close for us to deal with. We needed to distance it, to make it less threatening. That was easy for us: We were the experts at creating façades.

And so, as the eighties wore on and others around me were beginning to deal with AIDS, I was still putting my head in the sand. With
only a little bit of effort, it was easy to block out. At Mike Hall's, I
remember Sylvia warning me to "be careful." I remember discussing
AIDS with Mitch on several occasions. And I remember the entire
scandal surrounding Rock Hudson. But I was deep in denial.

Musto later observed that the panic surrounding AIDS was what
had us all running around in outlandish outfits looking for press
mentions. We were out to prove that we could be fabulous—in spite
of AIDS. "I also think," he says now, reflecting on his own motivations, "that I was dressing up in so many crazy outfits as a way of
expressing my homosexuality, because I felt I couldn't express it
through sex, which I was petrified of. I also think that it was a way
of scaring people away—so that I couldn't have any sex. No one
would want to have sex with someone who looked so weird."

Our reactions to AIDS were revealing much about us—to ourselves and to each other. Though we were supposed to have been so
comfortable and open and liberated with regard to our sexuality, we
were still racked with internalized homophobia. I had come out
several years before, in college, but I had no sense of gay history, and
in the years to come, the only gay culture I learned was club culture.
To the people in the clubs in the early and middle eighties, gay
politicos who identified themselves as "activists" were boring. They
were so *serious,* we would say, and they were wasting their time. We,
on the other hand, were *living* the revolution. Or so we thought.

Musto, five years older than I, was in the age group first affected
by AIDS. Many people he knew personally were becoming ill, and
he was stunned by AIDS. The safer-sex message hadn't yet been
widely disseminated, and since there still was so much misinforma-
tion about the transmission of HIV, Musto—like many gay men—
had stopped having sex altogether. Although I only vaguely
remember discussing sex with Musto at that time, he now says that
we discussed it often and that I was out having a lot of it, like most
of those my age who were oblivious to AIDS. I do remember that
whenever AIDS was even alluded to, the attitude was something like
"Just make sure you don't get it." But even that callow response was
disingenuous: Few of us practiced safer sex. We simply believed we
couldn't get AIDS.

As time marched on, however, the impact of the disease began to shake our false beliefs. Some began to realize our club world was a fragile world—one that could be taken away at any moment. We began to realize that homophobia, coupled with apathy about the concerns of queers, was as powerful within our world as it was on the outside. As AIDS progressed, we saw the straights and gays on the scene separate. Suddenly, queers weren't trendy and chic to run around with. By 1986, Nell's had opened. It was the club of the moment, the new place where celebrities and the media flocked, a return to Victorian decor and a return to a Victorian way of behaving: You sat down and listened to a jazz band or danced downstairs on a floor with no spinning lights. Dressing demurely was suddenly de rigueur—and so was being heterosexual. Drag queens were no longer fabulous: They were over. Soon, friends who'd previously been full-fledged homosexuals were declaring their bisexuality.

By the next year, 1987, AIDS had down cut down scores of former club habitués: performers, designers, artists, writers, actors, publicists, musicians, dancers, photographers, and party promoters—all dying around us. It was impossible to look the other way. The highly publicized death of Madonna's onetime roommate, artist Martin Burgoyne, so well liked by so many, made a lot of us pay attention.

It was also in 1987 that *And the Band Played On*, Randy Shilts's riveting and frightening chronicle of the epidemic's early years, made its impact. The book made headlines for days and forced AIDS into the forefront of our minds. AIDS soon reached down deeper into the community and started to affect the next generation. Close friends of mine began getting sick. Old boyfriends were calling me up to say they'd tested positive.

The entire party circuit began attending memorial services. For some of us, these were simply social events at which to wear *fabulous* outfits—if only in memory of someone's fabulousness. But others of us were becoming more aware, and more alarmed. AIDS had reached a point where the people on our scene were going to go one of two ways.

It was at one of those memorial services that I began to realize which way I had to go. The dreadful feeling that came over me was at the same time a good feeling: I awoke from my dream and noticed that Musto had been awake all along. We began talking more and more about AIDS and about how nothing seemed to be getting done. We were irritated and anguished. And together, we were being jarred.

It was a Thursday night in late 1987: Musto and I were at the Boy Bar, a trendy queer dance club in the East Village. We were approached by two guys with finely sculpted bodies who easily pried us from the group of people with whom we'd been in conversation. One was tall and dark, the other blond and much shorter, but with cheekbones to make up for it.

"You guys should come to ACT UP," one of them said. "You know, maybe you could write about it or something."

4

....

Out of the Closets

....

and into the Streets

....

The blond with the cheekbones was Howard Pope, a local musician and bartender. The tall and dark one was Adam Smith, an art assistant at *GQ*. They began telling us about ACT UP, which I'd only vaguely heard about. The way they spoke about it, the group seemed like a cult. It all sounded too weird for me . . . but they *were* cute.

"Sure, we'll come," Musto said. "When and where does the group meet—and will *you* be there?"

"It's seven-thirty on Monday night at the Center," one of them said. "And, yes, we'll be there."

I'd never been to the Lesbian and Gay Community Services Center—I didn't even know there was such a place. It was a beat-up old school building on West Thirteenth Street where, I came to learn, every lesbian and gay group imaginable was based.

Musto was looking forward to the meeting. It wasn't just the cute guys that had lured us there. By then he and I had had our few dark conversations about the AIDS crisis. In the days prior to that meeting, we spoke more about it, hoping, it seemed, that ACT UP would help us cope a little better. But we'd been told ACT UP protested a lot, and we weren't sure how we felt about that.

The auditorium was filled with several hundred people sitting on folding chairs. Musto and I sat in the middle of the room. He took out his pad and pencil. Two facilitators, a man and a woman, came to the front of the room, ready to guide the meeting. They immediately made us feel very comfortable—the man, David Robinson, was extremely handsome, and wore a dress. The woman, Maria Maggenti, was a beautiful lesbian with long, blond hair. Both students, they were years younger than I and had an impressive command of the crowd and the discussion.

The meeting took off, and I was dumbfounded. It followed *Robert's Rules of Order*, sort of, and was all excruciatingly democratic.

The group discussed a myriad of issues: drug policies, insurance, symptoms, drugs, politics, cures, and the media. Sometimes the talk was very scientific and over my head; the politics alone was unfamiliar. But there were two sensations we all shared: fear and anger. People were letting those emotions out with passion and fervor. Crying and yelling were almost rituals. Musto and I were exhilarated, and Musto was writing feverishly.

Some people from the issues committee got up in front of the room and began rattling off facts and figures. It was all horrifying. But to listen was, at the same time, what can only be described as "empowering": These people had information—and it was information that simply wasn't out there anywhere else. The facts and figures—and the power behind them—gave the information junkie in me an adrenaline rush.

The meeting went on for hours. I'd never experienced anything like this, and hadn't felt as stimulated by anything I'd done before. Several groups took to the front of the room to propose "zaps"—fax zaps, phone zaps—and actions. A zap was a quickly organized protest; sometimes people were needed immediately, to organize a demonstration or a picket line, but often a zap required the flooding of the target's phone lines or fax machines with angry complaints. An action was a larger protest that took several weeks of planning. Everyone voted and clapped and committed themselves to various zaps and actions.

One protest that was announced was an upcoming zap of Josef Cardinal Ratzinger, the German prelate who was head of the Congregation for the Doctrine of the Faith. He had written a paper for the Vatican in which he said that homosexuality was "intrinsically disordered" and a "moral evil." Cardinal Ratzinger had said the church had to fight the homosexual movement and fight against legislation that "condoned" homosexuality.

Now he was coming to New York for a speaking engagement, at the behest of New York's John Cardinal O'Connor, and every big-time Catholic was going to be there. ACT UP, which is an AIDS activist organization and not a gay rights group, wasn't really planning the demo, which wasn't an AIDS-specific protest. But Dignity, a gay Catholic group, had come to ask ACT UP to endorse their protest. ACT UP voted overwhelmingly to support Dignity's actions, and several people said they were going to go to the demonstration.

When the meeting was over, Musto and I both were filled with energy. He raced home to write a column about ACT UP, the first piece written about the group for *The Village Voice*. I decided to go to Dignity's demonstration.

·····

The Ratzinger appearance was at St. Peter's, a church known for its modern architecture, at Citicorp Center. I had never been to a Dignity meeting—I barely knew what Dignity was—and I didn't really know what form the protest was going to take. When I arrived, the place was packed. It was a big amphitheater that looked more like the United Nations General Assembly chamber than a church. This wasn't going to be a Catholic mass; St. Peter's wasn't even a Catholic church. Ratzinger may have been a religious figure but he was also a political leader, especially since he was the church's official antigay crusader, here to fight against gay civil-rights legislation. The church wanted him to speak in a slick, modern, secular-looking space, free of ornate and intimidating religious decor and adornment. It made the gathering accessible and open to people of all faiths and political persuasions.

Ratzinger sat at the altar, along with Cardinal O'Connor and several other prelates. Judge Robert Bork, the conservative Supreme Court nominee who'd just been rejected by the Senate, sat in the front row. Mrs. William F. Buckley, Jr., was there too, as was an incredible array of Upper East Side women, the upper crust of New York's Catholic society. There were prominent Wall Street businessmen and local government officials. And rows and rows of nuns, brothers, and priests, perhaps the heads of orders and parishes. I began to feel very small—I hadn't seen so many priests since Catholic school. The room, a semicircle, gradually sloped downward so that the altar was down in a pit, a reasonable distance from those who were standing in the back, where I was. There were several marble platforms that jutted out from the back into the seating area.

I looked for the protestors, but I couldn't see anyone with a sign or a T-shirt. I wondered for a few moments if anything was really going to happen. I had decided to go there strictly to watch, to check out how these people operated when they conducted these demonstrations. As for myself, I didn't know the first thing about protesting and I still wasn't sure about it. I certainly didn't like the idea of getting arrested.

A brother stood up and motioned the crowd to be quiet. Then Cardinal O'Connor rose, to a round of thunderous applause. He gave Ratzinger a brief introduction, which was followed by another round of thunderous applause. Ratzinger took the podium and began to speak. As soon as he finished his first sentence, a group of about eight people to the left of the crowd leaped to their feet and began chanting "Stop the Inquisition!" They chanted feverishly and loudly, their voices echoing throughout the building. The entire room was fixated on them. Activists suddenly appeared in the back of the church and began giving out fliers explaining the action. Two men on the other side of the room jumped up and, pointing at Ratzinger, began to scream, "Antichrist!" Another man jumped up, in one of the first few rows near the prelate, and yelled, "Nazi!" All over the church, angry people began to shout down the protestors who were near them; chaotic yelling matches broke out.

It was electrifying. Chills ran up and down my spine as I watched the protestors and then looked back at Ratzinger. Soon, anger swelled up inside me: This man was the embodiment of all that had oppressed me, all the horrors I had suffered as a child. It was because of his bigotry that my family, my church—everyone around me—had alienated me, and it was because of his bigotry that I was called "faggot" in school. Because of his bigotry I was treated like garbage. *He* was responsible for the hell I'd endured. He and his kind were the people who forced me to live in shame, in the closet. I became livid.

I looked at Cardinal O'Connor, who had buried his head in his hands, and I recognized the man sitting next to him. It was O'Connor's spokesman and right-hand man, Father Finn, who had been the dean of students back at Monsignor Farrell. A vivid scene flashed in front of my eyes: The horrible day when I was in the principal's office talking to the principal, the guidance counselor, and the dean, the day they threw me out because I was a queer. I looked back at Ratzinger, my eyes burning; a powerful surge went through my body. The shouting had subsided a bit because some of the brothers had gotten in front of the room to calm the crowd. The police had arrived and were carting away protestors.

Suddenly, I jumped up on one of the marble platforms and, looking down, I addressed the entire congregation in the loudest voice I could. My voice rang out as if it were amplified. I pointed at Ratzinger and shouted: "He is no man of God!" The shocked faces of the assembled Catholics turned to the back of the room to look at me as I continued: "He is no man of God—he is the Devil!"

I had no idea where that came from. A horrible moan rippled across the room, and suddenly a pair of handcuffs was clamped on my wrists and I was pulled down.

I was shoved against a wall and frisked along with some other protestors. I was mortified. What had I done? *I can't go to jail,* I thought to myself: *I have a dinner party tonight.*

While we were standing with our faces against the wall and our hands cuffed, one of my fellow protestors introduced himself, as if this were a routine occurrence.

"Hi, I'm Joe," he said. He smiled.

I thought he must be nuts, but I introduced myself in return. I smiled too.

They took us outside, where a huge crowd of supporters and reporters and photographers was waiting as we were taken to the paddy wagon. My only frame of reference was a film premiere: There were flashbulbs popping and we were being cheered as we were rushed to a waiting car. My hands were cuffed behind my back so I couldn't wave to my fans, but I smiled. A cop's shove brought me out of my reverie.

That night, after we were released from jail, I ran to the dinner party I was now very late for. It was at a restaurant on the West Side. Musto was at the table, having saved me a seat. I sat across from Don

Munroe, a videomaker who used to work with Andy Warhol, and Jill Selsman from *Interview* magazine. I was bubbling over with enthusiasm. As I told my story, I could sense that the somewhat uncomfortable crowd, except, of course, for Musto, thought I had lost it.

I had, in a way. I'd lost the desire to sit through boring dinner parties. I'd lost the desire to attend affairs where talking about being queer was considered gauche. And, somehow, I'd gained the desire to scream at the top of my lungs that I was homosexual. For the first time, too, I was excited to see something in the *New York Post* the next day besides the gossip columns: a headline—GAYS RATTLE POPE'S ENVOY—next to a photo of an anguished Cardinal Ratzinger.

I joined the ACT UP media committee. The meetings were held at Vito Russo's apartment. I had been aware of him but had never read his book, *The Celluloid Closet*. Now I bought it and started to read it, as well as books by Larry Kramer and Martin Duberman and other writers on lesbian and gay history, politics, and activism.

At my first meeting, I realized that ACT UP members were masters of manipulation who knew how to get attention through their actions. Everything was planned, from the kinds of actions they chose to do, down to the costumes, props, graphics, and slogans. I realized that with such sensational material to work with, the media committee could get ACT UP's not-so-popular message out to a more widespread audience. David Corkery, the former *Good Morning America* producer who'd helped whip this media committee into shape and put together its mailing lists, sensed that I had some ideas. He urged me to get more involved, but I wasn't sure exactly how deep I wanted to get in all of this. My arrest had been cathartic, and the meetings energized me, but I was afraid of how powerful this experience was, afraid of how it could really change my life. It was all too attractive and I just wasn't sure if I was ready for that kind of change and commitment.

I was also about to go on a business trip to Brazil for a few weeks. Getting away, I decided, would help me sort things out. I told Corkery I'd call him when I got back.

I was still a nightclub columnist, and the nightclub crowd was regularly sent on junkets, all-expense-paid trips to other cities. Nightclubs and other businesses would fly in New York writers, photographers, and assorted *fabulous* people for openings so that their establishments would be associated with the fashionable downtown crowd from New York. The most lavish of these were regular sojourns in Miami's South Beach art deco district. We were flown down, put up in nice hotels, given just about anything we asked for no matter what the price, and thrown grand parties.

This time, the Rio socialite Anna Maria Tornaghi was bringing us to Brazil for Carnival. On the trip with me were Musto, photographer Patrick McMullan, colorful deejay Anita Sarko, *Details* columnist Stephen Saban, and then–*New York Post* gossip columnist Richard Johnson.

We were out every night, soaking up the Carnival madness at ball after ball in the ninety-degree nighttime heat. We received VIP treatment—always chauffeured around, never having to deal with the crowds, the lines, or the craziness in the streets. Each night at around four A.M., we went to a huge stadium where the various samba schools competed. The stadium was once a long boulevard in the heart of the city, but the celebration had gotten so large that the government turned the boulevard into a narrow stadium, with cement bleachers that went up several stories on either side.

We were in the governor's box, an enclosed carpeted room with sofas. Huge windows looked out over the spectacle, and there was an outdoor balcony. There was food and drink from eight P.M. until noon the next day, when the competition ended. It was there, in the governor's box watching samba-school competitions, that I realized that ACT UP had already changed the way I viewed the world— even in Brazil.

The samba schools weren't educational institutions; they were places where people went after work and after school to rehearse their pre-Lenten extravaganzas. The costumes and dance numbers were lavish and gaudy, yet elegant and majestic. The hard-driving samba music pounded constantly; the entire stadium rumbled out of control; colorfully dressed throngs and elaborate floats paraded by. Most fascinating to me, however, were the messages of each samba school and the stories they told. The lyrics of the songs were very political. So were the costumes, the banners, and the scenes played out through dance. Brazil had a history of turmoil and strife and the people had endured great hardships. The nation was rife with poverty and unemployment, and inflation was skyrocketing out of control. The middle class was shrinking fast, leaving only a few rich people and great masses of poor. The government was rocked with scandal after scandal; corruption seemed so widespread that it occurred in the open. The natural beauty and balance of the rain forests were being stripped, threatening the entire planet, and crime in the cities had reached the point where everyone, even wealthy socialite women, carried guns. AIDS was becoming an even greater catastrophe in Brazil than it was in the United States, because Brazil's health-care system had already collapsed. All of the country's turmoil was played out in the samba schools' parades: The lyrics of the songs, the banners, the dances, the costumes, all called for massive protest and revolution. And yet, as soon as Carnival ended each year, the people would go home and join a new school for the next year, begin to practice their dances, make their costumes, and come up with a new message, usually a reworking of the message from the year before. The aristocrats and politicians realized that this was good, for all those in the samba schools helped everybody let off pent-up steam so that things could go back to normal days later.

As I watched the spectacle, it became clear to me that Carnival was a tool for those in power in Brazil—they hyped, exploited, and poured millions into it each year—and a brilliantly chosen tool, at that: The vast majority of Brazilians, unhappy and oppressed, were given this illusion of liberation for a few days. It kept them busy for the rest of the year so that they couldn't think about or plan a *real* revolution. They were too busy making their costumes.

At once I saw how this wasn't very different from what my crowd was doing back home. We weren't the "cutting edge" we thought we were. We weren't "pushing the envelope." We were having our own Carnival every night. Suddenly, ACT UP and its message came to mind. Not only for me—it was time to wake everyone else up too.

When we got back to New York, I buried myself in ACT UP. It the winter of 1988: I worked on several actions, coordinating the media and working the PR. Our tactics were sensational. The message—that nobody was doing anything about AIDS—challenged people in the media. It was a message they didn't like, but it made them think about the issues. Nobody wanted to believe the worst: that political leaders were ignoring a major catastrophe. As long as AIDS was a gay disease (or a black disease or a junkie disease), the media didn't have a personal investment in uncovering the scandals behind the disease. Our only recourse was to create a spectacle, something the media could sell.

With the others on the committee, I worked on the first-anniversary action, "Wall Street II." ACT UP's first protest had been on Wall Street in March 1987. It was then, as the legend goes, that the playwright Larry Kramer—the prophetic father of the AIDS movement—made his impassioned call to action at the Community Center, where he was a last-minute replacement for Nora Ephron, who had canceled a speaking engagement. The people who took up Kramer's call and formed ACT UP targeted the stock market, urging people to sell their shares of Burroughs Wellcome, which owned the patent to AZT, the exorbitantly priced drug that was the only approved treatment for HIV infection.

For the anniversary action, the group was targeting not just Burroughs Wellcome but all of Wall Street, for AIDS profiteering while people were dying. The group had grown substantially, and more people were going to come to this protest. People had planned all sorts of colorful, creative actions.

I decided this was a perfect item for Liz Smith's column: theatrical but also important. I had kept in contact with her office over the years, sending her juicy gossip items when I got my hands on them. She had sent me a note asking what I wanted, what mention I'd like. I wasn't really pushing anything so I held on to the IOU.

Now, as the Wall Street action neared, I wrote up an item about the demonstration. I also typed up some "free" items for her, treating ACT UP as my client. My heart and soul went into that demonstration; it was all I cared about in the days leading up to it. Each day I opened up to Liz's column, and saw one of the "free" items I'd sent her. But Liz never ran the item about the protest and never let me know why. It hadn't occurred to me how controversial ACT UP was or that someone like Liz, who raised money for AIDS, would not want to publicize such a protest.

At that time I met James Revson, a reporter at *New York Newsday*, at a birthday party for the nightclub owner Peter Stringfellow. James was one of *the* New York and East Hampton Revsons; his uncle was Charles Revson, the founder of Revlon. A tall red-haired fellow who always wore a suit, he'd done several notable stories for *Newsday* about AIDS and was smart about analyzing the politics behind the crisis. I went out with him on a couple of dates. I liked that he was sort of political minded; Revson liked that I was one of the party people. I told him that I was increasingly bored with the party life and more excited about other things, like ACT UP. We were crossing paths, from opposite directions. What I didn't know at the time was that both of us were motivated by AIDS: I was becoming more involved because I felt it was important, and he had recently tested HIV-positive and wanted to have all the fun he'd never had.

He dropped his AIDS beat and began writing a society column for *Newsday* called "Social Studies." His was not the typical gossip column. He wrote about AIDS often, covered protests, and even eventually participated in an ACT UP civil disobedience and wrote about his experiences in jail. But Revson was also fast becoming caught up in the gossip world and wanted to make a splash. From the beginning he had asked me for advice. I suggested he'd get a lot of press if he went after Suzy. I told him how fake she was, how publicists wrote much of her column, and how she often didn't go to many of the parties she covered, instead taking information about the events from press releases sent beforehand and writing the column as if she had been there.

Soon, Revson caught Suzy in one of her scams. She'd written about a big party and listed all the people who had attended. Revson, who had been there, hadn't seen a lot of the people listed and hadn't seen Suzy either. She came back from a vacation to find herself in a major gossip scandal: It turned out that not only was she not at the party, she'd written that column *before* it even occurred.

Believe it or not, this became a major story in the New York papers. Every columnist wrote about it and every paper covered it, not as gossip but as news—even the *Times*. The media know how important gossip is in shaping American culture and politics and how influential gossip columns are, if only in selling papers: *The Wall Street Journal* put the story on the front page and headlined it SUZYGATE.

The other columnists, especially Liz Smith, were delighted. Liz wrote endlessly about the scandal, patting Revson on the back and building him up for shooting Suzy down. Little did Liz know that the whole thing was my idea. Little did we all know that, in the not-too-far-off future, there would be other columnists on my list too—and for bigger reasons.

Revson became completely taken with the party scene, loving all the attention he was getting. I was becoming more and more immersed in ACT UP. We had become "just friends" months earlier. Now our relationship grew tense, and we argued a lot. I thought everything he was doing was frivolous; he thought I was being too serious. We drifted apart.

I worked day and night on ACT UP, it seemed. My nightclub life almost completely stopped, and I found I was going out less and less. It seemed pointless to go to these plastic affairs and have dull, irrelevant conversations after spending all day on ACT UP. Soon, I wasn't pursuing any free-lance work. Eventually, I lost my column.

I went to work for my father down on Wall Street, in one of his croissant shops, while running the ACT UP media committee. My life was rewarding, though I was still telling myself this activism was "temporary." I'd never felt so close to people I worked with. My friendships at ACT UP were more substantial than any I'd ever had on the club scene. We were putting our bodies on the line for each other, going to jail for each other. I loved these people—and was loved back—in a way I had never known.

I was feeling powerful about being gay. Feelings from when I was a child came back; I had longed for people to tell me that being gay was great.

My closet was opening. These people were the most out-of-the-closet, in-your-face people in the world. Everything they were doing, all our activism, was based on this fact: *Not only was being out of the closet absolutely essential, but advertising homosexuality through the media and utilizing the media to show the face of AIDS were even more essential.* One of our most popular demo chants was "Out of the closets and into the streets." Everything we were doing was about the strange marriage between the closet and the media. It was a marriage that was only going to become more complicated as time went on. It was a marriage that was about to end in divorce.

And yet, my closet wasn't totally open. I was, of course, out in Manhattan, but I wasn't out on Staten Island. I had convinced myself that I had once told my parents I was gay. It was in the kitchen, I remembered, and I had brought up the subject. But the truth, looking back, was that my father had been asleep on the couch in the living room and my mother had busied herself in the kitchen. We had a short discussion about homosexuality, in which I vaguely implied that I was gay.

Now I was on the radio as an ACT UP spokesperson. My mother might see my name in the newspaper. When I'd told my parents that I was doing work for ACT UP, I explained that it was an AIDS group. They didn't ask any questions. It was time for the truth.

At the same time, I was realizing that I'd spent over thirteen years, from 1973 until 1986, having unsafe sex. Right into '86 and '87 I was still not practicing safer sex. I had been in a couple of short-lived relationships, but basically I was dating a lot and sleeping with several different people during those years. Painfully, I knew it was time to deal with this truth, as well.

I was living in the East Village still with my friend Michael, my roommate from Syracuse. We decided to be tested together, both sure that we were positive. The latest info coming out of ACT UP and other grass-roots organizations—and nowhere else yet—was that you could perhaps arrest the replication of the HIV virus if you started treatment early.

So many people I worked with at ACT UP had AIDS. I was almost resigned to the idea that I was infected. In essence, I was ready to join the club. On a morbid level, I thought it would also validate my ACT UP credentials. Many in the group shared that unhealthy attitude.

Our results came back on different days. First Michael's came in: positive. Michael was unemotional—he didn't cry or reach out for help. He hated people who were "mushy." He didn't react negatively at all to his result. He even laughed it off—though I knew he was burning inside. My heart sank with fright: If Michael was positive, I must be too. We had never had sex with each other, but we had lived through the same years, in the same cities, among the same men. We'd both even had hepatitis B at the same time years before.

Our results were not the same: I tested negative. For a few brief moments I was exhilarated, but then I realized I had to tell Michael. I felt guilty. We hugged and held each other, and for the first and perhaps the only time I can remember, Michael showed a trace of emotion: We both cried.*

Only clichés about "a new lease on life" and having "a weight

*Michael Santulli died in July 1992.

lifted off your shoulders" can describe being a twenty-seven-year-old gay man in New York in 1988 and testing negative. I became more resolute in the work I was doing, more determined. It was my duty to fight even harder. This wasn't just the guilt of the survivor—it was a responsibility. Everyone of privilege, everyone who'd gotten by somehow—either by testing negative or by sitting in a powerful position in this society—was obligated now to do whatever she or he could to end this disease.

The storming of the FDA in October 1988 determined my fate. I was an activist forever, whether I liked it or not.

Soon thereafter, around Christmas, I began dating Gregg Bordo-witz, a handsome, dark-haired videomaker in the education depart-ment at Gay Men's Health Crisis who was part of ACT UP's actions committee. Our relationship thrived on our activist work. Gregg loved the activist in me: the communicator who maximized the message. I loved the activist in him: the documentarian and political organizer with a powerful vision. Our relationship was sexy and exciting—not to mention combative and polemical.

ACT UP was planning its March 1989 action, "Target City Hall," a major demo protesting then-Mayor Ed Koch's negligence and the city's mismanagement of the crisis. Gregg and I were both involved, he as a chief organizer of the action, me running the media commit-tee. The demo drew five thousand people, a record for ACT UP. We never dreamed that many people were actually going to show up. What had been our hype was now starting to come true.

During the months of planning for "Target City Hall," Gregg sometimes got sick, which was certainly not easy for either of us to deal with. His being HIV-positive was taking its toll on me too, but I didn't want to admit that, especially since I felt it wasn't my right to be troubled—he was the one who was sick, after all. How dare *I* have any problems? This feeling, common among care partners deal-ing with many diseases, was not something I was good at handling. Not many people are, at least not without counseling. Gregg and I used activism.

When the city hall action was over, Gregg and I went on a trip together. But without political work, our relationship could not exist; without political work, so many other problems that had always been there, beyond health issues, were suddenly more visible. Within weeks of the trip we broke up. Gregg and I still saw each other at meetings, but it was awkward. I needed a change. Burned out, I left the media committee, passing the chair on to Jay Blotcher, a friend from journalism school who would keep ACT UP in the media.

One day Gabriel Rotello, a former keyboard player and downtown party promoter who was a writer, asked me if I wanted to start a magazine. Rotello had been drawn to ACT UP and had joined its fund-raising committee. He had also done a lot of research and was now getting backers together for a lesbian and gay newsmagazine to be called *OutWeek*. It seemed like a great idea.

ACT UP had exploded across the country and around the world. Chapters had popped up in all the major metropolitan centers and in many rural areas also, and the organization was having a profound effect on the lesbian and gay movement. That roomful of five hundred people at ACT UP in New York had energized an entire community nationwide. With a publication that would serve as a forum for its views and ideologies, ACT UP could have a major impact.

This was also the new challenge I needed. I felt strongly about getting the facts out and having them packaged properly. When it came to AIDS or queer issues, so much of the media at that time was clearly biased. The lives of lesbians and gay men were grossly distorted. The media needed to be taken on, to be criticized in a way that would have people taking notice. I was thinking more about everything I'd learned at Syracuse, about the precepts of journalism. I was now intent on doing good, solid reporting and criticism. I wanted to show that the notion of so-called advocacy journalism was bogus. We would tell the truth about our lives and expose the lies of the institutions surrounding us. As far as I was concerned, that was journalism in the most traditional sense of the word. In my mind, everyone had it backward: It was the rest of the media that was advocating—for the status quo and for homophobia.

Rotello had the financial backing of Kendall Morrison, a young, successful Boston businessman with AIDS who was committed to being the publisher of something that shook people up. Rotello became the editor in chief and I became the features editor. We tapped Andrew Miller, a writer and journalist who had run ACT UP's actions committee, as the news editor, and we began publishing in June 1989. For a while it was just the three of us editors, the art director, and James Conrad, our receptionist–copy editor–therapist, in a little room on dingy lower Lexington Avenue. We quibbled over politics and policies, sometimes focusing on the most minute details. The publication was special to each of us. Sarah Pettit, a Yale graduate who'd worked at St. Martin's Press, was a welcome addition as our arts editor, not only because she was a lesbian but because her point of view was that of someone who had not come through the ranks of ACT UP yet still shared much of our vision.[4] The same was true of Victoria Starr, a WBAI New York radio announcer who later joined the staff. Nina Reyes, who became our staff reporter, brought the perspective of someone from another ACT UP in another city, Boston.

Throughout that time, I found myself avoiding my family, not returning calls and not visiting. Finally, my mother mailed me a letter asking what the problem was and why I was ignoring her. I was filled with so much frustration and anger that I fired off a diatribe and mailed it back.

I wrote that I couldn't deal with visiting because I was sick of hearing all the wonderful, great, suburban things going on in their lives while my life, and the lives of so many people I loved, were in turmoil. I said that I felt I couldn't even discuss these problems with my family. I told her that I was gay and that I had been involved in a relationship with someone who was HIV-positive and that it was very stressful.

I received a letter back. My mother was very upset. I called her, and we got into a yelling match. I treated her unfairly, expecting her to come to terms with my life overnight. This was all very difficult for her to take, and there weren't many people with whom she could talk about it. And yet, I was in such a state of grief and despair that I couldn't be the one to help her.

I got off the phone angry and upset. I'd lost my mother. I'd lost my lover. Because of this fucking crisis, I was losing my friends. I was filled with rage.

Because of my anger I made connections: to my past, to my childhood, to my days at Mike Hall's and the club scene, to the gossip world. I saw how the columnists—and the publicists and the studio people and the others in the business—were keeping us invisible by lying about our lives. I saw that the entertainment-fashion-art-media industry, which shaped mass culture, was violently homophobic in spite of the fact that gays dominated it. I felt a surge like the one I had experienced at St. Peter's when Cardinal Ratzinger spoke. I was to feel it often. It would take over my body. When it did, I sat down at the keyboard to write columns for *OutWeek* and the anger simply came out in the form of capital letters:

DOES ONE HAVE TO TAKE A C.I.A. CODE–BREAKING COURSE IN ORDER TO FIGURE OUT WHAT THE FUCK IS BEING SAID IN THE PAPERS THESE DAYS? IT'S UTTERLY HOMOPHOBIC OF US AND THE MEDIA TO CONSTANTLY BEAT AROUND THE BUSH, SPEAK IN CODES AND TREAT HOMOSEXUALITY AS SOME SCANDALOUS SECRET, THE NAME OF WHICH WE CAN'T INVOKE. . . .

I was going through something and tens of thousands of people would soon be going through it with me, as I targeted those I saw as the perpetrators of a sham:

YOU SLIMY, SELF–LOATHING HYPOCRITICAL MON-STERS. YOU GO TO YOUR PARTIES, YOU WHIRL WITH BIGOTS AND MURDERERS, YOU LIE AND ENGAGE IN COVER–UPS, YOU SELL YOUR SOULS—MEANWHILE, WE'RE DYING!

5

···········

Outing, Part I

···········

It wasn't long before *OutWeek*, like ACT UP, was making headlines. Each Monday morning, the magazine exploded with the
ideologies and demands of a new generation of activists. With its
hard-hitting exposés and in-your-face journalism, *OutWeek* was also
a catalyst for action during a revolutionary period in the lesbian and
gay movement.

Almost from the beginning, *OutWeek* became fodder for the front
page of *The New York Times*. Marion Banzhaf's article offering
women instructions on safe, at-home, do-it-yourself abortions, and
Rotello's exposé about incoming health commissioner Woody
Myers's penchant for quarantining and closing down gay bars both
played on the top of the front page—above the fold, in newspaper
parlance. And that was only within the first few months after we
began publishing. When we reprinted a broadside handed out at the
New York City Gay Pride parade and put its headline—I HATE
STRAIGHTS—on the cover, there followed an uproar that was paral-
leled only by the fuss over the cover that depicted a lesbian pointing
a gun at the reader under the headline TAKING AIM AT BASHERS.

From the controversy regarding the National Endowment for the
Arts in the late eighties to the scandal that rocked Covenant House

and Father Bruce Ritter, *OutWeek* offered new facts and data and spun out biting commentary, the kind of stuff most people had never seen before—not in print, anyway. *OutWeek* was always unpredictable. It infused a generation of activists in New York with their weekly fix of anger, wrapped in a slick, sometimes irreverent, always media-savvy package. Even if you hated it, the magazine was a must-read every Monday morning at city hall, in the media, and even among the most conservative types in the gay movement.

OutWeek tapped into an energy coming off the streets, popularizing the use of the word "queer"—previously used only among some segments in the activist community who were claiming the word as their own to take the sting out of it and at some other gay publications like *Gay Community News* as a new form of self-identification—and the idea of "bashing back." The magazine's letters page was a battleground where conflicting points of views waged war. *OutWeek* encouraged furious polemical debates and put forth the shocking opinion that everyone *must* come out of the closet.

But what came to be called outing—declaring closeted public figures to be gay—was not a preconceived program on the part of the magazine or its editors. It just happened. Contrary to popular perception, outing was a *by-product* of a revolution rather than a conscious invention of that revolution. At *OutWeek* there were sharply divergent views on outing, but everyone agreed that the closet was an ugly institution that had to be broken down.

With all of the discussion about the closet that had gone on in the past few years, and all of the talk about how to break it down and how to make the media stop lying and stop making lesbians and gays invisible, outing was bound to develop. No matter how much some older and more conservative activists wince at the thought of it, outing was a natural, inevitable outcome of the work that everyone in the larger lesbian and gay movement had done for over twenty years. By 1990, outing was the next logical step. In that way, there was no one factor that made me out multimillionaire press magnate Malcolm Forbes in March of that year, except the something inside me that told me it had to be done, that it was the right thing to do.

When we founded *OutWeek,* my colleagues and I had very few ground rules: Basically we were committed to being a cosexual publication—that is, one that was read by, and spoke to, lesbians as well as gay men. We were determined to be a forum where news about the AIDS crisis could be found. We wanted to be an outlet for progressive journalism and to espouse the political viewpoint we'd acquired from our experiences working within ACT UP and other activist groups. Since much of my own work in the organization had involved manipulating the mainstream media, it seemed only natural that media would be the area I'd concentrate on at *OutWeek*.

I decided to write a column that would analyze the popular press, rather than the elitist press. Looking at media columns in gay publications, I thought that too much attention was given *The New York Times* but too little was given *People* magazine, which I thought was far more important than the *Times* in reaching vast numbers of Americans and shaping their opinions about many issues.

My column was called "Gossip Watch," and it was just that: a watchdog of gossip columns, gossip magazines, and gossip reports. It deconstructed and commented on how these forums dealt with queers.

I'd known since my days at Mike Hall's that most gossip columns lied about lesbian and gay celebrities and public figures, helping them appear to be heterosexual even though the columnists knew better. Even worse, many of the gossip columnists were also closeted homosexuals trying to appear straight themselves.

As a journalist who was mandated to report on the media, I felt that I had to tell the truth about what I'd observed. How could I criticize columnists for helping gays disguise themselves as straights without using the subjects' names? And wasn't it pertinent to the story to include the fact that the columnist herself or himself was also a closeted queer and thus had personal motivations for helping other gays to hide?

Here were gay columnists, editors, reporters, and publicists faced with the most devastating crisis ever to affect their community, who rarely reported on the government's negligent response to AIDS. Of course, this helped preserve their closets. They plugged the glitzy benefits, they raised a lot of money, they even sat on the boards of AIDS organizations, but what we needed were political action and loud voices criticizing the government. At the same time, they gave a lot of positive space to homophobic entertainers like Andrew Dice Clay or Sam Kinison. I also observed what I considered Uncle Tom–

like behavior by these people: The queer media people would hob-nob with the very men (and their wives) who are responsible for, or who bolster, the oppression of lesbians and gays in this country. Doesn't that relationship imply collusion and hypocrisy, and aren't collusion and hypocrisy newsworthy? *I* thought they were.

On one page in one newspaper, a closeted gay columnist praised the socialite Pat Buckley, her husband, conservative columnist William F. Buckley, Jr., and their parties, while just a few pages away Bill Buckley complained in his column that there were no newspaper editorials lambasting gays for bringing AIDS upon themselves and the rest of society. And while most of the gay community had come to hold Ronald Reagan personally responsible for his heinous inaction with regard to AIDS and the deaths of thousands, the columnists celebrated the Reagans and jockeyed for invitations to luncheons in their honor.

Going over the top was the only way to get a lot of attention: The ACT UP formula was that you had to go to the furthest extreme in order to get the center to take notice. And going to the furthest extreme was easy when you were filled with rage. Indeed, ACT UP's rhetoric and shrill tactics fueled many of my early columns, providing a useful device for getting my message out as well as creating a powerful persona, one whose trademark was upper-case invective:

> These monster columnists are oppressing us each day in their spaces—and half the time they're gay or lesbian themselves! But that doesn't stop them from deeming us invisible, making homophobic remarks or schmoozing and worshiping the people who are killing us. When William Norwich [of the *Daily News*] tells us that Liz Taylor and Malcolm Forbes are "dating," millions of people get the wrong impression, though Norwich knows better. How about how Liz Smith and Billy Norwich worshiped the ground that Ronnie and Nancy walked on for eight fucking years while my friends died and the Prez did nothing? How about how Liz and Billy now foam at the mouth over George and Barbara, while millions are infected with HIV, don't have access to health care and don't hear a peep out of our leader? Am I supposed to just let Liz write her ass-kissing bullshit, without saying anything? Fuck her! I say to them, and to every other writer, columnist, artist, designer, etc., who's whirling with the oppressors: I realize you're

oppressed just like the rest of us (which is why you're hiding in the first place). But don't react to it by oppressing *us*. It's much easier for you to break the chain of homophobia than it is for me. You are in enormous positions of power. Use that. This is a crisis! SOMETHING HAS TO BE DONE AND IT HAS TO BE DONE FAST. AND YOU ARE IN THE POSITIONS TO DO IT. Be part of the solution instead of part of the problem. If not, then get the fuck out of our way. Because we're coming through and nothing is going to stop us. And if that means we have to pull you down, well, then, have a nice fall.

My words themselves caused a stir. The ladies' fashion bible, *W*, put us on the "In" list, saying that *OutWeek* was a "must-read" because of its blend of "culture, politics and vicious gossip." The *New York Post* went with a page-four headline, MAGAZINE DRAGS GAYS OUT OF THE CLOSET. Amy Pagnozzi, the columnist who wrote the article, compared me to Senator Joseph McCarthy for revealing "certain columnists' " homosexuality. But it was *Time* magazine that decided that all of this should be called "outing."

The initial flurry died down until March 1990, when my *OutWeek* cover story about Malcolm Forbes sent shock waves throughout the entire media. The multimillionaire founder of *Forbes* magazine had just died, and I felt that the historical record had to be corrected quickly, before a slew of biographies came out falsely saying that Elizabeth Taylor had been Forbes's lover. I conducted a lengthy investigation, interviewing a dozen or so men who had been intimately involved with Forbes, and I spoke to many of his then-current and former employees, friends, and acquaintances who knew he was gay and knew that Elizabeth Taylor and he had a platonic relationship. Most significant about the story was how Forbes's closet forced him to sexually harass and abuse male employees.

Liz Smith had been a focal point of the outing controversy because I had attacked her repeatedly for remaining closeted herself and for not reporting on the gay lives of some of the supposedly heterosexual celebrities mentioned in her column.

Liz's position, as she later told *OutWeek*, was, "I don't want to make statements about my mythical sex life. Millions of people don't want to be defined by their sexuality. I'd like to be defined by my work, my life. These people you see soul-kissing in the Gay [Pride] parade, they want to be defined by their sexuality, and they are. But what happens when their libido dies down? What will they be defined by then? I'm a divorced woman. I spent my adult, mature life married for ten years. Let people speculate. I'll lead my life the way I choose to." Regarding the subjects in her column, she said, "I don't write a column about sexuality. I write a column about what I perceive. I'm willing to let people make their own statements. If they're telling a lie, the public will realize that pretty quickly."

Soon after the Forbes outing, my old flame James Revson, who had been patted on the back by Liz Smith for his Suzy exposé, began to attack outing. Revson had to protect himself since he, too, was closeted. It was clear that he and I were now in two different places. Immediately following the Forbes outing, he issued a blistering attack on me in his *New York Newsday* column, describing me as "truly frightening and offensive" and saying that "outing only creates fear and fear creates more repression."

I fired back, revealing his homosexuality, since it was pertinent to my criticism:

> For Revson and all of his namby-pamby, snobby friends who climb in the hierarchy of the social elite, the construct of the closet validates their very existences. Revson is a privileged white man from a family with a lot of money. YOU JUST DON'T TALK ABOUT THINGS LIKE MEN FUCKING EACH OTHER'S ASSES OR WOMEN EATING EACH OTHER'S PUSSIES. It is the closet that keeps your West 34th Street penthouse; the closet that gets you that house on the island; the closet that keeps that bank account full; the closet that keeps you doing your society column and getting you invited to lots of parties; the closet that puts you in good favor with all of the other closeted columnists; the closet that ultimately gets you what you want—a few measly crumbs and fastidious approval from the rich and famous.
>
> Yes, Revson and his friends are far, far away in a different world, so out of touch with reality that they have no concern for the black lesbian in the Bronx who gets raped and beaten to a pulp because she appears "butch." Nor do they know of the Latino drag queen who is terrorized every day of his life in the neighborhood where he grew up.

It doesn't matter to them that their coming out of the closet might help other queers. THEY HAVE TO PROTECT THEIR OWN FRAGILE, LITTLE, PRIVILEGED WORLD.

I ended the column with an exhortation to Revson to "WAKE UP," pleading with him to "FIGHT FOR YOUR LIFE." Little did I know how relevant that message was: Revson had developed AIDS by then.*

At first the rest of the media wouldn't touch my Forbes story, even though he was a dead public figure and there were on-the-record sources. Eventually I wrote an article for *The Village Voice*, lambasting the media for blacking out the Forbes story. I'd pointed out how *Entertainment Tonight* was all set to run with it, but backed out at the last minute, and how the New York *Daily News* killed their Forbes story, saying it was too "sensational" and instead went with the front-page headline MARLA HID IN TRUMP TOWER. (It was a story about the Donald and Ivana Trump divorce—an acceptably heterosexual scandal—by Liz Smith, of course.)

It was only then, weeks and months after the Forbes outing and after I'd castigated the press, that every publication from *The New York Times* and *USA Today* to *Playboy* and *Screw* zeroed in on the topic. In articles, editorials, and commentaries, many of them came down hard on us. According to quite a few, this was "fascism" and an "invasion of privacy." Of course, none of these seasoned journalists mentioned their own day-to-day descriptions of the sex lives of *heterosexuals*—from Gary Hart and Donald Trump to Liz Taylor and Warren Beatty to Jim and Tammy Faye Bakker to, later on, Bill Clinton and George Bush. Somehow, to publicize heterosexual liaisons was right—it was considered "reportage"—while to cover homosexuality was to invade people's privacy.

I smelled homophobia. It seemed to me that the American media didn't report about the lives of famous queers because they saw homosexuality as the most disgusting thing imaginable—worse than extramarital affairs, abortions, boozing, divorces, or out-of-wedlock babies, all of which are fodder for the press. Homosexuality frightened straight editors and reporters because it forced them to realize

---

*James Revson died in July 1991.

just how many of us there are. The so-called journalistic ethics that they adduced against outing, I realized, were dreamed up a long time ago by straight white men to protect the world of straight white men. They were arbitrary at best, bogus at worst. Many of these editors were hypocrites; they themselves had outed in the past when it was to their advantage, when they perceived it to benefit straight society. For years the media had no problem reporting the names of closeted gay private citizens who had been arrested in dubious public-restroom sting operations or wrongly accused of child molestation— even though in most cases the charges were dropped or thrown out when it was revealed that the person was set up or wrongly accused. These were victims of society's homophobia, and their lives were ruined and destroyed—the lives of private individuals, not public figures, and the lives of people wrenched from the closet for all the wrong reasons.

When it was a public figure who was involved in hypocrisy that was detrimental to *gays,* however, those same editors ushered in their "privacy" arguments and spoke of careers being ruined so that they wouldn't have to deal with this uncomfortable issue.

Back in 1982, Taylor Branch, a former editor of *Harper's,* had written an exhaustive piece entitled "Closets of Power," much of it about the powerful closeted gays in Washington who were working against the gay community. He quoted activists at the time, discussing the idea of revealing these people through the media in the future. He termed this potential practice "outage" and offered his astute and prophetic observations:

> By all evidence, the newspapers and other media organs would simply prefer to avoid the issue. Perhaps this has something to do with congenital machismo among journalists and writers. More likely, the avoidance comes from the fact that heterosexuals live in their own closet, hiding from homosexuals while homosexuals hide from them. It hasn't occurred to them to inquire. Or they don't want to inquire because they know it will be a big mess.
>
> Whatever the reason, avoidance is less becoming to journalists than to other professional groups. Its practical effect has been to ignore one of the most explosive social changes of the past decade. If the "war of outage" comes, and readers suddenly look up to find

a homosexual on every street corner and a prominent official coming out of every closet, journalists will more than likely join in a panic they could have helped avoid.

Now the "war of outage" had come. And, as Branch had predicted, journalists were only joining in a panic that they could have helped avoid. Much of the liberal media's patronizing concern regarding outing, I charged at that time, was a manifestation of latent and thinly veiled homophobia among straight editors and reporters. I also charged that closeted gays in powerful positions in the press had a vested interest in maintaining the closet throughout American culture. As it goes in the media, there was a feeding frenzy. Suddenly, I was besieged with interview requests.

. . . . .

Many people say outing is wrong under any circumstances. Others see it as a weapon and a tool, something that should be used only against those queers who are closeted and harming others. For me, outing has a far larger scope. I agree hypocrisy should be exposed: If gay people are party to hurting other gay people, that fact should be made public. But to out *only* for that reason is to make the revelation of homosexuality into a punishment.

"Some people have compared outing to McCarthyism," observed philosopher Richard Mohr, agreeing with my sentiments in his 1992 book, *Gay Ideas: Outing and Other Controversies.* "And vindictive outing *is* like McCarthyism: such outing feeds gays to the wolves, who thereby are made stronger. . . . But the sort of outing I have advocated does not invoke, mobilize or ritualistically confirm anti-gay values; rather it cuts against them, works to undo them. The point of outing, as I have defended it, is not to wreak vengeance, not to punish, and not to deflect attention from one's own debased state. Its point is to avoid degrading oneself." In that sense the outer, Mohr says, is a person living with "dignity," and his or her action is "both a permissible and an expected consequence of living morally."

For me, the problems start with the word "outing" itself. It was *Time,* after all, that came up with the term, using it to condemn something they felt was wrong. And it is certainly a word that evokes violence—like "wilding." I think the action should simply have been called "reporting." We don't have a special word for any other action that deals with revelation of truth, from describing a politician's extramarital affair to writing about a Hollywood star's latest love interest. So why should there be a specific term for this?

Writing an opinion piece in *OutWeek* in May of 1991, Gabriel Rotello attempted to rename the practice "equalizing":

> What we have called "outing" is a primarily journalistic movement to treat homosexuality as equal to heterosexuality in the media. On a larger scale, that's the goal of the entire gay liberation movement: to raise homosexuality to an equivalence with heterosexuality in all spheres of life.
>
> In 1990, many of us in the gay media announced that henceforth we would simply treat homosexuality and heterosexuality as equals. We were not going to wait for the perfect, utopian future to arrive before equalizing the two: We were going to do it now. That's what outing really is: equalizing homosexuality and heterosexuality in the media.

Unfortunately, the word "outing" had so permeated society by then that it was impossible to replace it. The heterosexual power structure, aided by the single-minded right-to-privacy crowd in the gay community, would be loath to change the name. Rotello is absolutely correct: "Outing" takes on its true and proper meaning—and loses its negativity—when one looks at it as equalizing.

Whenever it's pertinent, a public figure's homosexuality should be discussed and inquired about. This should be true *only* for public figures—rich and famous individuals who've made a deal with the public: In return for the millions of dollars they earn and/or the power they wield, their lives are open for dissection by the media. If the media are going to report heterosexual love affairs—whether that is right or not—it is simply homophobic for them to refuse to report on homosexual ones. By not reporting about famous gays, the message the media send is clear: Homosexuality is so utterly grotesque that it should never be discussed. In many cases—such as those in which a gay person is using a government position to work against gays—by *not* reporting the subject's homosexuality the media are censoring perhaps the most significant information in a given story and thus colluding with the subject—and the government—in deception. In no other instance would news organizations hold back information that, though it might be of a personal nature, had a direct bearing on a story regarding the actions an official is carrying out. Many closeted gay actors hire publicists who are charged specifically with making the actor appear heterosexual. Journalists often know this but accept it. Again, in no other area would journalists collude with PR hacks.

A new generation is questioning that double standard. We don't see any reason why we must police all discussion of members of our own community, and why, in a country that considers itself more sexually liberated than it was twenty years ago, we must continue to whisper about people who are gay. This generation wasn't around during the blacklisting era of the 1950s. We've enjoyed the first few benefits of the gay liberation of the sixties and seventies. We don't see why we can't speak freely about being gay. We don't see why we must be restrained from writing about people who we know are our own kind.

Those gay journalists, in the mainstream and in the gay press, who are pushing editors to change their blanket policies and to look at outing on a case-by-case basis are not "radicals" or "activists." They are journalists who are challenging the status quo, asking that a new set of ethics be applied regarding reportage of their community. They are no different from female reporters, African-American reporters, and reporters of other ethnic and racial minorities who have told the established journalistic order that a new set of standards must apply to coverage of their communities because of the power inequities in our system—whether those differences be in how a group chooses to call itself or how rape and other crimes against members of those groups are to be reported.

Indeed, lesbian and gay activists and journalists alike are challenging the very notion of "privacy." Is being gay or lesbian a "private" issue in this country in 1993, when so many millions of younger, more liberated Americans see their homosexuality as no different from such "public" issues as race, gender, and ethnicity? If, as we've been saying all along, being gay is not about sex acts or about what we do in our bedrooms but is a much larger matter regarding identity and culture and community, then how can the mere fact of being gay be private? How can being gay be private when being *straight* isn't? Sex is private. But by outing we do not discuss anyone's sex life. We only say they're gay.

That is something that escapes most heterosexuals because they don't really see homosexuality as a full orientation equal to heterosexuality; they see it rather as a kinky act that either enhances or detracts from heterosexuality, which to them is the only truly fixed sexuality. Though they might not even be conscious of it, even some of the most liberal straights view homosexuality as a "fetish" on a spectrum of fetishes that includes sadomasochism, infantilism, wearing uniforms, using rubber hoses, and lots of other things. They're afraid of outing homosexuality because they think the next step will be outing their sexual fetishes. The heterosexual rhetoric against outing is constantly tinged with phrases like "What you do in your bedroom is your own business." True enough, but outing doesn't report what acts anyone does in the bedroom.

Attacks on the media for invading people's private lives inappropriately include the outing of gays as part of the argument. Both Suzanne Garment, author of *Scandal: The Culture of Mistrust in American Politics*, and Larry Sabato, author of *Feeding Frenzy*, have espoused the view that the media are much too invasive and that politicians are subjected to unwarranted scrutiny of their personal lives. This may or may not be true, but by including the revelation of people as gay—which they do—as one of the areas where this is happening, both Garment and Sabato immediately accept without question the idea that being gay is a "privacy" issue. In a January 1993 *New York Times Magazine* piece headlined "Who Killed Privacy?" essayist Roger Rosenblatt went even further, adopting the right-wing contention that homosexuality is a choice: "The practice of 'outing' homosexuals implies contradictorily that homosexuals have a right to private choice but not to private lives." These writers seem not to comprehend that outing, when it is promoted *by gays*, is an assault on the media themselves. Outing's proponents, for the most part, start from the supposition that gay is *not* "private," and certainly is not a "choice." They do not imply that invasion of other areas of privacy is ever necessary or warranted.

The media claim that we're seeking role models by outing. Then they say that a homosexual dragged kicking and screaming from the closet does not make a proper role model. Most of us agree. But I personally haven't said I was trying to offer up good role models. In fact, in only one circumstance, that of Malcolm Forbes, was there a discussion in *OutWeek* of a "role model." Forbes was dead and couldn't be dragged out "kicking and screaming." Rotello wrote an editorial holding up the dead Forbes in the way that historical figures like Michelangelo Buonarroti and Leonardo da Vinci have been claimed as queer centuries after their deaths and held up as role models.

The role-model argument became a favorite of the media because it was the easiest argument to rip down. Outing may not be a vehicle to create living role models; it does, however, create visibility. There are gay people all over television and in films, yet most gay kids don't know that. Denied seeing the members of their own community, gay teenagers are left feeling alone, like freaks. The fear and isolation sometimes lead to severe depression. Its consequences: Thirty percent of the teen suicides in America are among lesbian and gay kids, even though homosexuals make up only 10 percent of the population (this is according to a U.S. government–sponsored study).

Thousands of gay actors and newscasters and politicians are covered with a mask of heterosexuality. Kids should know who's gay regardless of whether the people are proper role models. Eddie Murphy isn't necessarily the greatest role model, but it's important for black youth that a top box-office star is black. It's important to the black community that Oprah Winfrey, a black woman, is a top TV personality, and it's important that Arsenio Hall is a top talk-show host, even if their allegiance to the community is not a priority. There's always Jesse Jackson for perfect politics.

There's something to be said for *bad* role models. By exposing Malcolm Forbes we were trying to say to gay kids: Don't let this happen to you. Don't let your life be swallowed up by the closet though you're one of the richest, most powerful people in America.

On many levels, outing isn't much different from other revolutions in the media and society over the past forty years. Homosexuality is only the latest taboo. It's the only topic the media can't discuss openly. Three decades ago the situation regarding issues such as drug abuse, alcoholism, cancer, and extramarital affairs wasn't much different. These were things that *no one* would dare put in print, even though they were prevalent among Hollywood stars—and, indeed, throughout society. But slowly the stigmas broke down and society became more relaxed, largely *because* the media began reporting the issues.

In the 1950s, when the legendary film star Ingrid Bergman became one of the first stars to have the fact of her out-of-wedlock pregnancy reported, it was a major scandal. She had to leave the country for many years until her career bounced back and she was a star again. But that one story, combined with 1964's *New York Times* v. *Sullivan* Supreme Court ruling (which held that public officials could not under most circumstances recover damages for news stories about them that weren't to their liking) opened up the floodgates on such issues. Suddenly the media began reporting more accurately and more honestly about famous people, and society reflected it. Things loosened up. Younger people, always ready to experiment and change, realized that the rich and famous weren't much different from themselves. They began living their own lives more openly. And the rest of society simply came to accept it.

Still, that doesn't mean that outing is directed at the average gay citizen. This misconception is probably the number-one reason why so many are against it. Outing, for me, as a journalist, is only about public figures. Journalistic outing compels the reporter to interview and get testimony of those who've been involved intimately with the subject. There are laws protecting private citizens from that: Technically, revealing that a private citizen is *heterosexual* without his or her permission is grounds for a lawsuit. Private citizens who are gay have as much of a right as do private citizens who are straight to keep facts about their love lives and with whom they are intimately involved to themselves. The notion that, though outing has focused on public figures, some people might be influenced by it and go after the average person is preposterous. The truth is that average people have been outed for decades. People have always outed the mailman and the milkman and the spinster who lives down the block. If anything, the goal behind outing is to show just how many gay people there are among the most visible people in our society so that when someone outs the milkman or the spinster, everyone will say, "So what?"

In many ways, outing represents a maturing of the gay community. As Jews and blacks did many years ago, queers are now calling to account members of our community who have power and privilege. The new generation is saying that those individuals who have power also have a civic duty to the community in which they reside at least part of the time and thanks to which they enjoy the benefits of the liberation that has so far been won. And we're saying that the time has come for them to be known. Certainly, at various points in history, Jews helped each other to hide: It was a matter of life and death. But in modern-day America, no self-respecting Jew would put up with another's hiding, even though anti-Semitism still exists. This generation of gay activists is now telling the rest of the lesbian and gay community that the McCarthy days are over, and that conditions for gays are not going to get better now unless we all come out.

To fight outing at this point is senseless and futile, for, as homosexuality becomes more accepted in our society, outing will become more accepted. The two are inextricably tied: As one advances, the other becomes less of an issue. Outing is a natural process that will eventually make itself obsolete.

Again looking at the Jewish community, that process has occurred earlier in this century. If the *Jewish Weekly* today reported that a Jewish film star or politician had changed his name, the media would not seethe with rage, and fear wouldn't sweep across Hollywood and Washington the way that anxiety over outing has in recent years. Yet forty years ago, most people who were Jewish in Hollywood had to change their names to escape anti-Semitism; and much of the media participated in their subterfuge. But times have changed; the Jewish community has reached a point where it abhors such hiding and chastises those who encourage or participate in it.

In the last two years we've already seen a change in that regard in the gay community. Outing focused so much attention on the closet that more public figures have come out on their own. They see it as important. Outing has also made many journalists take a long, hard look at how they've aided in people's deceptions. Suddenly, "asking" became acceptable, and celebrities from Whitney Houston and George Michael to Sandra Bernhard and Dolly Parton were asked. Of course, stars have the option to tell the truth, to lie, or to waffle, but for the first time reporters are bringing it up in interviews. Homosexuality has entered the dialogue of celebrity journalism.

Those who initially came under attack by outers meanwhile have also moved dramatically. Liz Smith, now at *New York Newsday*, and Billy Norwich, now at the *New York Post*, two people I relentlessly criticized week after week in 1989 and 1990, have turned into virtual heroes of the gay cause. Liz Smith had always written about AIDS and had raised money to fight the disease since 1983, but by 1992 she had become more outspoken. That year she championed celebrities k. d. lang and Rupert Everett for coming out, supported Madonna's stretching the boundaries of sexuality, wrote additional thoughtful and vital information and news about the AIDS crisis, defended herself against critics who said she wrote too much about AIDS, attacked critics of Elizabeth Taylor who said she should be spending less time on AIDS, assailed George Bush for what she called his "family values junk," and loudly applauded openly lesbian Diane Mosbacher (daughter of Bush's campaign fund-raising chief Robert Mosbacher) for standing up to the Republican party's gay-bashing. Liz even called gay rights "one of the most important social issues of our time." And in 1993 she was given an award by the Gay and Lesbian Alliance Against Defamation.

Norwich stood up to Barbara Bush at a luncheon in September 1992, challenging her on the Republican party's denigration at its August convention of women, intellectual Jews, and gays, saying that he belonged to two of those groups. When she asked which two, he replied, "All three, ma'am, on a Saturday night." After the laughter subsided, he pressed her further. In his column the next day Norwich recounted his public coming out.

Within the gay community, outing helped reshape the definition of the closet. Previously, the closet was seen by many as a place people had a "right" to—a safe, comfortable place where everyone had to stay. Even five years ago, many in the mainstream considered it an "embarrassment" to be out of the closet, "flaunting" one's sexuality. People who were doing that were said to be "indiscreet" and were even considered "unfashionable." But outing focused attention on the closet and what a horrible, pitiful place the closet is. Outing demands that everyone come out, and defines the closeted— especially those in power—as cowards who are stalling progress at a critical time. With outing, the tables have turned completely: It is now an embarrassment to be *in* the closet.

Outing was inevitable, the product of the first American gay generation brought up with the luxury of gay liberation. Perhaps the greatest proof of that inevitability is that outing is emerging for the second time in gay history. According to Larry Gross's *The Contested Closet: The Politics and Ethics of Outing*, an ideology of outing was established in the gay movement of Germany at the turn of the century. As early as 1902, when the German homosexual-emancipation movement was forming, there was debate about outing within the Scientific Humanitarian Committee, which had been founded in 1897 by Magnus Hirschfeld. The committee eventually weighed in against outing, but a few years later, Adolf Brand, founder of the first known homosexual publication, *Der Eigene*, espoused the opinion that homosexual hypocrites should be exposed. He outed Chaplan Dasbach, leader of the antireform Center party. "Under threat of libel action Brand printed a retraction," reports Gross, "yet many viewed the incident as a success for the homosexual movement." The leftist press soon began outing too, and what followed was a series of libel suits. In one of those, Hirschfeld testified in favor of the outers, with whom he appears to have agreed intellectually. But that action angered the financial backers and members of his organization. The scandals and trials dealt a crushing blow to the movement, and membership in the Scientific Humanitarian Committee dwindled. Brand was convicted for libeling the imperial chancellor, Prince von Bülow, whom he'd outed, and was sent to prison for eighteen months. Defeated and discouraged, Brand decided that it wasn't a good idea to reveal closeted homosexuals in power: "Decent society cannot stand the truth."

Later in the early 1930s, Brand was at it again. "The rise of the Nazis revived the debate about the tactic of outing because of the prominence of Ernst Röhm, the chief of staff of Hitler's SA paramilitary organization and a known homosexual," Gross notes. Röhm was outed by the leftist press, and in *Der Eigene* Brand once again defended outing: "In the moment, however, when someone—as teacher, priest, representative, or statesman—would like to set in the most damaging way the intimate love contacts of others under degrading control—in that moment his own love-life also ceases to be a private matter and forfeits every claim to remain protected henceforward from public scrutiny and suspicious oversight."

Throughout the decades of the American gay movement there

have always been debates about outing, although it didn't have that name. One could probably argue that there have been dozens of outings over the years too, depending on what one defines as outing.

In recent years, outing has taken place in the streets, among the new generation of queer activists. In the late 1980s, members of ACT UP chapters in New York and elsewhere—Larry Kramer most prominent among them—carried signs at demonstrations outing various closeted politicians, and sometimes even went to their homes to castigate them. But long before ACT UP, some prominent gay people were pointing to the media's hypocrisies. Throughout the eighties, the popular gay author Armistead Maupin criticized American journalism for its double standards and named famous closeted individuals when he gave interviews, although no mainstream publications printed the names.

Perhaps the first outing by activists that made it to the media—months before the Forbes outing—was that of Senator Mark Hatfield, who denied he was gay. Wayne Harris and Tom Schoelder of ACT UP/Portland targeted the Oregon senator, whose record on AIDS funding was abysmal, by altering two of his campaign billboards in downtown Portland to read CLOSETED GAY: LIVING A LIE, VOTING TO OPPRESS. *The Seattle Post-Intelligencer* ran a photo of one of the billboards on the front page, and several papers reported the incident, naming Hatfield. His voting record dramatically changed for the better. Soon thereafter, Washington, D.C., activist Michael Petrelis outed dozens of members of Congress, holding a press conference on the steps of the Capitol and reading their names aloud. Scores of Washington's press corps showed up for the event, and even though no one printed Petrelis's claims, he sent rumbles throughout the capital. Both the right wing and the Washington gay establishment were up in arms about the action. The right-wingers obviously don't want the world to know who and how many people in Congress—in particular how many right-wing politicos in Congress—may be gay. The gay politicos, of course, were concerned with the right to privacy. Much of their work in Washington, lobbying and working within the system, has been based on fighting for that right. But the outing action perhaps made them begin to question privacy's importance. Certainly, all attempts to win it have been futile, the crushing blow having come with the Supreme Court's

Bowers v. *Hardwick* sodomy decision in 1986. Now a new and vocal segment of the community was telling them to go as *public* as possible. The new queers were in fact soon joined by some of their mainstream compatriots who espoused the same view. "Emphasizing this right [to privacy] plays right into our enemies' hands," wrote Benjamin Schatz, executive director of the lesbian and gay doctors' group, American Association of Physicians for Human Rights, in *The Advocate* in 1991. "Private is, after all, exactly what they want us to be. I believe we are in the long run fighting less for the right to privacy than for the right not to have to be private."

Petrelis scored better in 1991, when he spent months waging an outing crusade against Wisconsin Republican congressman Steven Gunderson, who hadn't signed on to the gay-rights bill and who voted with homophobes. Petrelis kicked off his campaign when he approached Gunderson in an Alexandria, Virginia, gay bar that the congressman frequented (along with Badlands in D.C.). Petrelis first urged Gunderson to come out and support gay rights. According to *The Washington Times,* Gunderson replied, "I am out. I'm in this bar, aren't I?" and then brushed Petrelis off. The activist grew angry, threw a drink in Gunderson's face, and called the police on himself. He pushed the story in the press until the papers back in Milwaukee finally printed it. In the press account, Gunderson portrayed Petrelis—and Minneapolis activist Tim Campbell, who, at the same time, outed Gunderson at public events back in Wisconsin—as the lunatic fringe. Gunderson said, "Being single, I have been accused of being a womanizer by some, abstinent by others. . . . The key here is, I'm married to my job. I don't really have a personal life, that's it. I'm here at seven o'clock, and here late at night. For better or worse, I've commited my life to public office. The rest is pretty boring. . . . I have been accused of all these things, but I can't prove it." The papers forced him to defend his record on gay rights, and his voting record has since improved.[5]

In the spring of 1991, in an effort to promote lesbian and gay visibility, a group of New York activists calling themselves OutPost plastered posters around town outing dozens of Hollywood celebrities. It caused an uproar, particularly in the leftist press. Writers at *The Village Voice* had previously remained quiet about outing and my column, but the posters, which termed the celebrities ABSOLUTELY

QUEER, made them finally speak out—and loudly. Several column-ists attacked me along with those who'd put up the posters, bringing in the usual arguments regarding the invasion of privacy. Other writers at the *Voice* defended outing. The issue puts the left in a quandary because neither side—neither pro-outing nor anti-outing—fits neatly into leftist orthodoxy. While the anti-outers said that outing invaded the individual's right to privacy, the pro-outers accused the anti-outers of protecting the privileged and helping them make more millions by lying to the rest of society at the expense of millions of lesbians and gays who would benefit from the truth being exposed.

The anti-outing charges came mostly from older gay and lesbian writers, and from closeted ones. However, on the streets during Gay Pride Week, crowds of young gays, many in their teens, gathered around the posters. None were upset or spoke about privacy; most of them were thrilled and excited to find that some of their heroes and heroines were gay.

Queer Nation, which had formed in spring of 1990, was taking on the closet in a major way throughout much of 1990 and 1991. It was soon after Andy Rooney made horrendous antigay remarks on *60 Minutes* that I and three other activists—Alan Klein, Karl Soehnlein, and Tom Blewitt—called a meeting of people who were willing to take on that kind of homophobia in vigorous ways. Soon after the group began, I left it; I was busy with my work at *OutWeek*. Queer Nation went on to become known as a colorful and brash vehicle to create awareness, rather than a direct-action group committed to civil disobedience (although some chapters, such as San Francisco's, utilized civil disobedience as a tactic more than others). Utilizing ACT UP's in-your-face tactics to take on gay-bashers and increase visibility, Queer Nation spawned chapters across the country. Its members invaded bars and restaurants to hold kiss-ins. Dressed in the most fabulous gay regalia, Queer Nation went into suburban shop-ping malls. Queer Nation also dabbled in outing, altering on-street advertisements that depicted celebrities endorsing products. If the celebrity was queer, like k. d. lang, the ad soon said so. (At the time, lang was still closeted.) Queer Nation also pioneered "fax outing"—faxing around the names of closeted public people—and they confronted those same famous people in person, in front of crowds, outing them on placards and urging them to come out.

These events caused controversy and deviated from my journalistic form of outing, which was trying to challenge American journalism to rethink the reporting of famous people's private lives. My point was that journalists shouldn't gratuitously out people—only if their sexuality was pertinent to a story and, of course, only if it could be journalistically substantiated and verified.

In that vein, when multimillionaire record producer David Geffen made excuses to the press in 1989 for his number-one band, Guns N' Roses, some of whose song lyrics were antigay, Geffen's homosexuality was pertinent, and I reported on it. Again, when Geffen took on the distribution of the homophobic comedian Andrew Dice Clay, his sexuality was pertinent to discuss. There was an uproar, but Geffen subsequently dropped Clay and came out as "bisexual" in *Vanity Fair*. To his credit he has since become involved and visible in several gay causes. Eventually, he came out fully as "a gay man."

Jodie Foster made a film, *The Silence of the Lambs*, which many people thought was homophobic. After having written two very complimentary columns about her, I sent her a letter through a mutual business associate, seeking to discuss the film with her, but she did not respond. I decided to discuss in my column the relevance of Jodie Foster's own sexual orientation. Like many lesbians and other gay men, I was angry at her for not speaking out against the screenplay. I never thought I was saying anything horrendous about Foster—just that she was regarded as a lesbian who'd participated in a film that was perceived to have portrayed a negative gay stereotype. But at the same time, OutPost put her on an ABSOLUTELY QUEER poster. The *Star* picked up the story and ran a sensational, ugly piece about Foster, dubbing her a "manhater," something no queer would say. Suddenly the backlash against outing reached critical mass.

Lesbian activists with whom I'd regularly consulted at the time told me that, because Foster was pretty and feminine, and because she was the epitome of a straight, WASP woman, the outing caused a curious backlash among many women, gay and straight. Foster was a role model they looked up to. After the posters, she was seen—by many women as well as by most men—as a defenseless, innocent victim. But some lesbian activists told me that internalized and externalized sexism, homophobia, and even racism motivated many to protect Foster. This seemed to be true: Few people had come to the defense of many other famous women who were outed at the time and who were not as young, pretty, or glamorous. For whatever reasons, Jodie Foster went from being the poster child for the outers to being the unofficial poster child for the anti-outers. From then on, the debate over outing was fierce and personal.

What went unnoticed was that outing had become very complex. It was now being practiced by different people for different reasons: There were journalists trying to expose hypocrisy and to equalize the discussion of homosexuality and that of heterosexuality. There were street activists utilizing guerrilla tactics to politicize homosexuality in a new way. And there were supermarket tabloids looking for a new vehicle to make a quick buck. Ultimately, these phenomena were a gain: Homosexuality left the realm of the unspeakable and moved into the scandal phase it must pass through before being thought of as just another characteristic of human nature.

Outing by gay journalists continued until there was little debate in the gay press and in the mainstream about the efficacy or ethics of outing. In the winter of 1992, then–*Advocate* columnist Donna Minkowitz investigated and outed Anne-Imelda Radice, who had just been appointed acting head of the National Endowment for the Arts at a time when the endowment was being pressured by the right wing to defund homoerotic art and gay artists. Whether or not Radice intended to fund "sexually explicit" work, her lesbianism was pertinent to the story—as was her conservatism. She was taking over an agency that had been at the center of controversy for several years, most notably with respect to the work of queer artists Holly Hughes, Tim Miller, John Fleck, and the late Robert Mapplethorpe. And she was a well-known dyke in Washington, bringing her lover to affairs and going out in public with other gay couples.

During the 1992 presidential campaign, *QW*, a New York–based queer magazine, outed the son of Phyllis Schlafly, the conservative head of the Eagle Forum and an icon of the radical right. John Schlafly worked as a lawyer for his mother, promoting her right-wing views and helping her to become a powerful figure among the "family values" elite. John Schlafly subsequently came out. During the same campaign, Chris Bull, a reporter for *The Advocate*, did a thorough investigation and named Louisiana Republican congressman Jim McCrery, another ardent promoter of "family values," who denied he was gay but who certainly had refused to sign on to a bill to end the ban on homosexuals in the military and had a horrendous voting record on gay and AIDS issues. All of these incidents were covered, to varying degrees, by the mainstream press and in no case was there an uproar over outing.

The outing of Assistant Secretary of Defense Pete Williams in *The Advocate* prior to all of these in September 1991 was the turning point in the discussion of journalistic outing. It carried the kind of political ramifications that warranted more discussion. The pertinence of Williams's homosexuality to the hypocrisy of the military's policy had forced many people to debate the topic rationally.

Not that the media accepted outing after Pete Williams—certainly they wouldn't engage in it themselves, and most newspeople were still reluctant to pick up an outing from the gay press. But as outing became more accepted in the gay community, many straight editors and reporters learned that many of their gay colleagues favored it.

Still, by 1992 the word "outing" started to be arbitrarily attached to a variety of issues. When *USA Today*, acting on a tip, asked tennis star Arthur Ashe if it was true that he had AIDS, and thus forced him to reveal that he did, it was considered that revealing his HIV status was an "outing," though Ashe actually became infected by contaminated blood after surgery. Most of us who favor telling the truth about closeted gay public officials have always adamantly opposed revealing anything about any person's medical condition, gay or straight. Similarly, some journalists said that revealing the names of women who had abortions was outing. The media's equating a private medical condition (like HIV infection) or a private medical procedure (like abortion) with homosexuality—an issue of sexual identity that carries with it a rich culture and a community in which a supposedly closeted individual is known to hundreds, perhaps thousands of people as gay—was naïve at best.

Rather than trying to understand what outing means to the lesbian and gay community, the media were quick to attach the word to all acts of journalistic disclosure they disapproved of. When George

Bush was alleged to have had an extramarital affair, no one considered that he had been "outed" as an adulterer, though, according to the media's now wide-ranging definition, he certainly had. Every newspaper in the country carried that story, and argued that it was proper to do so since the Bush campaign had referred to Bill Clinton's alleged extramarital affair and also for the bogus reason that Bush had been asked about the affair during a press conference.

By 1992, "outing" had in fact become a brilliant catch-all word that members of the media could throw around in a holier-than-thou fashion whenever convenient. "Outing"—the word—provided journalists, who often feel guilty when they pry into people's private lives, with an easy way to arbitrarily decide what was a responsible disclosure (anything to their own benefit and liking) and what was an unseemly disclosure (anything not to their own benefit and liking).

And making outing seem unseemly keeps homosexuality unseemly too.

•••••

In the early days of outing, back in 1990, I was called every name in the book and fended off angry people everywhere I went. At the height of the controversy over Malcolm Forbes—who was outed posthumously—outing was seen by a great many people as the most grotesque and horrible act one could possibly commit against another person. Their reactions revealed their true homophobia.

The pressure and the attacks were like nothing I'd ever experienced. Neither was the support I received from hundreds of lesbians and gay men, from seasoned gay activists to closeted teens, who wrote and told me not to stop what I was doing.

On a personal level, my relationship with my family improved. At the time of the Forbes outing I sat down with my mother and father and spoke to my three younger brothers, trying to explain all of this to them. The initial publicity I received, and the fact that I had just come out to them in an angry way, had been difficult for them. In a way my notoriety "outed" them to their friends and to the rest of the family. It was no longer their choice when and how to tell those close to them about their gay son or their gay brother; the newspapers and TV had done it for them. But they came to accept it; my family—my parents especially—became among my greatest supporters.

Someone else from my past also became a great supporter. One Monday night at an ACT UP meeting, a curly-haired, skinny man approached me. He had a big smile on his face.

"Do you remember me?" he asked.

He looked familiar, but I couldn't place him.

"No," I responded.

"My name's Vinnie," he said. "We went to the same high school."

A chill ran through my body. I saw a vision of myself whipping basketballs at his head. I was speechless.

"I just want to tell you," he continued, "that I'm very proud of you and all of the work you're doing. You're very brave."

"Thank you," I said. "I've thought about you over the years."

"Really? Are you going to go to the class reunion? It's coming up."

I thought to myself, *Why on earth would I want to do such a thing?* Why would *he?* Why would *anyone* want to revisit all that pain?

"I don't think so," I said. "I don't think I could handle that."

"Well, I'm going so that I can tell everyone we went to school with that I'm gay. I'm going to come out to all of them and tell them how great it is."

Again I was speechless, consumed by my guilt.

As he walked away I thought back to what I had done to him, how I had bashed him in order to protect my closet. I thought about all the closeted people in power today, whipping basketballs at all of our heads, but on a massive scale, abusing their power, ignoring homophobia, working for institutions that oppress us, voting against legislation to help us, and just plain keeping us invisible by hiding—all in order to preserve their closets.

"Vinnie," I called out after him. "*You're* the brave one. And I'm proud of *you*."

Part II Washington's closets of power
have always operated under tacit government
orders. In many cases, those people who have
carried out or defended antigay policies or
institutions are themselves closeted lesbians and
gays. Often, the heterosexual power struc-

QUEER
IN WASHINGTON

ture knows this but looks the other way as long as the hypocritical individuals stay quiet.

The Washington closet is kept in place by the New York closet: Without the media's dutiful cover-ups and rationalized refusals to expose the truth, Washington's closets of power could not endure.

For various reasons, a disproportionately large concentration of gays work in the government. They occupy a spectrum of closet types, from the more erratic Revolving Closet utilized by many aides and staffers, to the impenetrable Iron Closet that some high elected officials and appointees are locked in. The occupants of the Iron Closet usually are tormented people, living a hellish nightmare. In the case of lesbians especially, they are sometimes manipulated by straight people around them who guard the secret.

Closeted gay men in power are often driven to sexually harass and abuse closeted male members of their staffs who are themselves vulnerable. Some closeted lesbian and gay officials legislate against gays or carry out antigay policies to fend off persistent rumors that they might themselves be homosexual. In these and other ways, Washington's closets of power adversely affect the lives of millions of lesbian and gay Americans every day.

6

....

Operation

....

Out-the-Pentagon

....

The first phone call came in December 1989.

"You must reveal the disgusting hypocrisy of the Pentagon and President Bush," a man's voice whispered.

"Sure, no problem," I responded. "What's it about?"

"Pete Williams—the PR guy for the Pentagon—is gay and they all know it. They have a policy against gays serving in the armed forces, but their spokesman is gay and it's all right with them. That's scandalous!"

He hung up.

Over the next few months there would be several more calls, as well as some letters, from anonymous informers, friends, acquaintances, and even sympathetic government officials speaking off the record, all giving me tips regarding the same issue.

Then the Gulf War broke out. Pete Williams was on television every night. And suddenly I got a tidal wave of information about the topic once again, as well as a lot of pressure from colleagues urging me to expose the truth.

"But what do I know about the Pentagon?" I asked them.

I had rattled the New York media world and peeked into Hollywood's most private places, but now I was being urged to invade Washington. The thought was downright scary.

Friends and colleagues pushed me hard, stressing the importance of this mission: The U.S. government's policies regarding lesbian and gay men who serve in the armed forces were infamous and atrocious. The Pentagon relentlessly conducted witch hunts year after year; since 1982, these had netted almost 13,000 queers, all of whom were discharged because they were "incompatible" with military service. People were interrogated and tormented after their homosexuality was revealed, while their superiors demanded to know who else in the service might be gay. They were threatened with having their children taken away, their families informed, and their lives ruined. Whether they cooperated or not, the queers were kicked out of the military and branded with a mark on their discharge papers that stigmatized them forever. Some, demoralized by their treatment and shaken by the disclosure of their homosexuality, were driven to suicide. While a handful of lesbians and gay men fought back and went public with their stories, most retreated into obscurity, humiliated and afraid.

In the face of such horrors, the fact that a top Pentagon official was gay and accepted as such by his superiors—not considered a security risk, which at that time had been the Pentagon's main reason for purging gays—represented a double standard. Certainly this was a story.

And so, as the Gulf War came to a close, the U.S. military was about to find itself with a new kind of battle on its hands.

· · · · ·

The last thing that twenty-five-year-old Brian Ramey wanted to do, he says, was join the service. "But like a lot of people who don't really have any direction when they graduate from high school, I was stuck in a rut," he remembers. "I was working in a factory and getting myself deeper in debt. There was no way to go to school, no way to travel. There was no other alternative, no other way for me to get out of Indiana. I had no money. But I wanted to see the world. I wanted to get an education. The military makes it sound real attractive with the ads that tell of educational opportunities and travel possibility."

The soft-spoken young man laughs when he says he knew he was queer "all my life." Shy and quiet, he flashes a sheepish grin every time he tells personal facts about himself.

Brian knew that Crawfordsville, Indiana—1980 population 13,325—was not a place where he would be welcome as a homosexual. For that reason, he always kept his queerness a secret and never acted on his sexual urges. He never told any of his friends and certainly never told any of his three brothers.

He knew that one day he'd get out of Crawfordsville. While working in the factory after he left high school, he took his first trip out of town, to Chicago. "I realized then that I made a big mistake and should have gone to college," he recalls. "I went to the bars and I saw the big-city culture. I was suddenly itching to get out of Indiana." His mother is a homemaker and his father a manufacturing supervisor. "They didn't have money they could squander away on me," he says, explaining why he didn't ask them to help him get a higher education.

In 1989, Brian decided to join the navy. He knew that gays were no more welcome there than in Crawfordsville, but he thought that if he "never acted on natural feelings it wouldn't come up. I didn't think it would be a problem," he says, "because even if you're straight you're not supposed to have sex." He lied on the questionnaire and denied his homosexuality, because he felt it was unfair on the navy's part to keep him out. "I felt I had a right to do this," he says, "as a citizen."

He was a hit in boot camp. "I was a 4.0 sailor," he says, again with that sheepish grin. "They have a ratings system and do evaluations every seven or eight months. I was pretty much 3.8 and up while in the navy. I was promoted while I was still in boot camp, which doesn't happen often." Brian's superiors were impressed mostly by his fortitude and dedication. He didn't have socializing, let alone sex, on his mind, as he spent all of his time working. His promotion got him sent to a base in Pensacola, Florida, where he was enrolled in school to study what he'd always wanted to study: photography. After three months of advanced schooling, he was put aboard the U.S.S. *Eisenhower* to work in the photo lab and shipped out for a six-month deployment that took him to Israel, England, Spain, Italy, and France.

It seemed then, in March 1990, that all of Brian Ramey's dreams were coming true.

• • • • •

I'd spent several months going back and forth to Washington; the bulk of my investigations of Pete Williams and the Pentagon were completed by the time Washington held its annual Lesbian and Gay Pride Parade on June 23, 1991, a day that was special for air force captain Greg Greeley. He was due to be discharged the following day. Greeley had helped organize the concession stands that year and helped lay out the Gay Pride Festival grounds. In his excitement, Greeley decided to be even bolder. Holding a banner that read TOGETHER IN PRIDE, '91, he led the parade, and spoke to newspaper reporters about how proud he was to be marching.

The next day he was called in for questioning by the air force and ordered by his superiors to appear at the Office for Special Investigations in southeast Washington.

"Are you gay? Were you in the Gay Pride Parade?" asked the OSI investigator, Brett Stern, Greeley recounts. "Who else in the air force is gay?"

"He said, 'I don't want to threaten you, but if you don't cooperate, we'll have to expand the investigation and go back to your high school years.' He said they'd have to talk to my friends, relatives, neighbors, and coworkers so as to get answers to the questions. And he told me the investigation would last weeks, maybe months, and that I wouldn't be discharged until it was over."

Greeley declined to answer the questions. Instead, he sought the advice of veteran Washington activist Frank Kameny, who has tirelessly fought the federal government and its antigay policies for forty years. Both men went to *The Washington Post,* which put Greeley's story on the front page.

Michael Petrelis picked up his paper that morning, saw the frontpage story, and knew he had to hold a press conference. A dark, curly-haired tornado of an activist, Petrelis had risen out of ACT UP/New York and had spent several years touching down in different cities, wreaking havoc on local powers that be. Activists around the country tracked Petrelis regularly.

Now the center of his storm was the Pentagon. Petrelis's press release announced that "Pete Williams, an openly closeted gay man, hypocritically remains silent in his job as Pentagon spokesman, while the Department of Defense continues its irrational policy of ejecting thousands of gays and lesbians from the armed services."

With reporters from *The Washington Post*, the Associated Press, Tribune Broadcasting, and the local NBC affiliate present, several of Petrelis's crew of activists spoke out, some about how they'd seen Pete Williams in bars for years, and one about a friend who had had a sexual encounter with Williams.

Then Petrelis unrolled a poster with a familiar face. PETE WILLIAMS, ABSOLUTELY QUEER, it read. PENTAGON SPOKESMAN, TAP DANCER, CONSUMMATE QUEER.

But no one reported the story, even though the press conference capped off several months of talk among Washington's media corps about Pete Williams's personal life and the paradox it presented in light of the Pentagon's antigay policy.

Most reporters assigned to the Pentagon had known for several years about Pete Williams, and by the time Petrelis's press conference took place in late June, every top editor, every TV news producer, and every network president had been informed that the assistant secretary of defense for public affairs was a homosexual. It had become the chatter of Washington dinner parties, the buzz in right-wing political circles, and, according to insiders, the hottest gossip at the Pentagon itself.

By that point too, many of those same people knew that I had been working for several months on a story that was going to out Pete Williams. My name was—I'd been told—well known in the Pentagon's press room. My phone rang endlessly as network correspondents, major-daily reporters, producers, and editors inquired as to what I was doing. They saw a scandal, much like any other involving hypocrisy within the government, and they were eager to uncover it themselves. Many of them tried, but whenever a decision as to whether to publish went to the top of a news organization, the piece was nixed.

The straight, white, male establishment was once again protecting itself.

And the conspiracy of silence continued to grow ever more deafening.

• • • • •

Brian Ramey was loving his new life, sailing around the world, surrounded by men. The Persian Gulf War lay ominously ahead, but at that time, in spring of 1990, war was the furthest thing from a sailor's mind.

One of the stops on the six-month deployment of the U.S.S. *Eisenhower* was Cannes. The streets were alive with excitement. The famous Cannes Film Festival was in high gear. There were mobs everywhere, partying and soaking up the glitter. Glamorous film types and starlets were all around as flashbulbs popped and TV cameras rolled. It was an exhilarating time for the Indiana boy.

"I went ashore and I ran into a friend from the ship who was really drunk," Ramey recalls. "He said he was getting cigarettes for a friend and wanted to know if I wanted to come along."

The two ended up in a gay bar called Le Zanzi-Bar, where there were several other sailors from the ship. It turned out that the person who had asked for the cigarettes had also told the drunk fellow to meet him at the bar. The drunk fellow had no idea it was a gay bar, but Brian knew even before he walked in.

"I knew the kind of bar it was as soon as we got into port, after I looked around onshore," he says. "I have this kind of radar." Brian hadn't had sex with anyone while in the service, nor had he told a soul that he was gay. For sure, he felt, he was the only queer on the ship. Now he thought that it must be just a fluke that his fellow sailors were all in the bar. "I thought they were just drunk and didn't know where they were," he recalls.

There were about ten guys from the ship, one of whom Brian knew well. After observing them for some time as they carried on, playfully touching each other, he realized that they weren't that drunk after all, and that they certainly *did* know where they were. Obviously, they were all queer.

As the night grew on, they all left for a disco called the Three Bells. American sailors abroad are not allowed to wear their uniforms ashore, for fear that they might be attacked, but their trademark buzzed haircuts give them away instantly. They're certainly not supposed to be in or near any gay bars. "There's an advance party that goes off the ship a week before we pull in," Brian says. "They scout out the porn shops and where the whores congregate and where the queer bars are; they'll make these an off-limits section of town. They call it the 'gut'—it's where all the sleazy bars are. Sometimes a sign goes up over a place that says that this place is off limits to sailors."

On that frenzied and wild night in Cannes, however, Brian and the others didn't have a care in the world. "I drank a little, felt more comfortable, and took in all of the excitement of the town," he says. "It was an incredibly liberating time for me."

Brian came out to his new friends that night and they all swapped stories about queer life on the ship. The other guys had been out to each other for five months and had been going to gay bars in different ports of call. Brian ran around with them for the next few days, but he soon realized that being queer in the navy wasn't all fun and games and had its hazardous moments.

"We were at a gay bar near the Ritz Carlton Hotel," he says. "The place was dead. It was three in the afternoon. We were all playing pinball in the corner. There were some French men drinking at the bar. All of a sudden some straight sailors from the ship came in, obviously drunk in the middle of the day. At least one of them knew it was a queer bar and thought it would be funny to drag his friends in there. We all hid behind the video games, realizing that these guys could make trouble for us on the ship. One of [the straight sailors] asked if this was a gay bar. A couple of the French guys at the bar responded by deep-kissing each other. The straight guys got all offended and shocked and they started yelling. It got pretty tense. The bartender then came around the bar and threw them out. It was really uncomfortable for us because not only did we have to humiliate ourselves and hide, but now the bartender was convinced that [the straight guys] were our friends, since we were all sailors, and that we weren't really queer. We had to convince him that we were."

Frightening incidents like these aside, Brian was feeling great; encounters like the one in the bar, in fact, built even more solidarity between them. He also began meeting more queer sailors and for the first time felt good about being gay. Strangely, he was also getting affirmation from the Pentagon itself, which sent the ships videotaped news clips that included news of the queer movement exploding on the streets and in the media.

"I remember it was way before the war," Brian recalls. "We were watching a tape of CBS's *48 Hours*, with Dan Rather." The segment was one on gay-bashing and the response by the lesbian and gay movement, one in which I was profiled along with other gay activists. "It was great—the whole activist movement thing gave me a great feeling. I wished I was there. It was such a great thing for me and the other queers to see while we were out in the middle of nowhere, wrestling with this problem of having to hide. To see all of that happening back in the United States was so refreshing and affirming." The tape was repeated ten times. "I was thrilled the most," Brian says, referring to one segment shot in a gay nightclub, "to see all of the drag queens dancing about. That made me just want to come home."

· · · · ·

Pete Williams had risen to one of the highest and most visible positions in the Pentagon without his queerness ever being discussed. After the war, after he'd been on television every day, his being gay became the talk of Washington. How does it get to the point where everyone in the nation's capital is suddenly whispering about a top official's homosexuality? How does a closeted homosexual get to the top in Republican Washington?

The answer, curiously, is: The same way any heterosexual does—by possessing a picture-perfect background, making all the right connections, and keeping very quiet about those things that top officials do but don't discuss.

Born and raised in Casper, Wyoming, Pete Williams attended the same public high school as his boss, Dick Cheney. Pete's mother, May Louise, still sells real estate in town, and his dad, Dr. Louis Williams, is an orthodontist and World War II veteran who served as an officer with the famed Merrill's Marauders in Burma.

Williams graduated from Stanford University in 1970 and headed back to Casper, where he embarked on a journalism career. For about ten years, he was a news director at KTWO, Wyoming's largest television station. In 1986, he took a job as press secretary with then-Representative Cheney, the Republican congressman from Wyoming, and moved to Washington.

As *People* noted, Williams lived as a "bachelor" in the Adams-

Morgan section of northwest Washington. He spent countless hours working diligently at the Pentagon, and in his spare time he pursued his hobbies: gourmet cooking, tap dancing, and mountain climbing.

The press bio didn't mention J.R.'s, a Washington bar with a reputation for attracting closeted queers with government jobs, other gay professionals, Georgetown students, and openly gay movement types. Amid the ferns and hardwood of J.R.'s can also be found many Republican gays and even some rabidly right-wing homosexuals. But the mood of the place is surprisingly relaxed, and everyone leaves his politics at the door. People smile, chat, network, and flirt while watching *The Golden Girls* on the huge screen.

On numerous expeditions to this Dupont Circle queer den, I'd struck up conversations with many government men; some had links to high officials, and one was a member of then–Vice President Dan Quayle's personal staff. It's that kind of place.

Although many of Washington's gay Republicans congregate at J.R.'s, many others wouldn't be caught dead in such a publicly gay locale. The most infamous of the closeted gay Republicans—a right-winger—was the late Terry Dolan, who ran the National Conservative Political Action Committee from the late seventies into the mid-eighties and who subsequently died of AIDS. He rarely made appearances at such bars. His was instead a world of private parties and secret liaisons, which included many other ultraconservative queers.

"Dolan had led a double life," reported *Wall Street Journal* White House correspondent Ellen Hume in the Washington monthly *Regardie's*. "He was a homosexual who not only tolerated but at times advanced the gay-bashing that still pervades national conservative circles."

Marvin Leibman, the author of *Coming Out Conservative,* was one of the architects of the conservative movement in America in the 1950s and a founder of Young Americans for Freedom.[6] In 1990, he came out in a published letter to his good friend conservative columnist William F. Buckley, Jr., then the editor of *The National Review*. Leibman notes that a closeted gay man in power can operate with relative ease in Washington's Republican political circles. "Most of my straight friends either didn't know I was gay or didn't *want* to know," he says. "I was a big shot in the conservative community in the fifties, sixties, and seventies. For me to be pointed out as a gay man would have been embarrassing—yes, what embarrasses the straight people most is when the gay people come out or are outed. So most of the straight people look the other way, and pretend they don't know about the gays among them."

These Washington gay men usually remain deeply closeted to their straight—and sometimes even to their gay—friends, colleagues, superiors, and families. Many are married and have children. Some, pathetically trying to mask their identities, publicly speak out against lesbians and gays. They work as lobbyists, public-relations executives, fund-raisers, campaign strategists, White House staffers, congressmen, and party aides. Under Reagan and Bush, they fully accepted that, in order to be part of the inner circles of Republican Washington, they had to remain silent about homosexuality—especially their own—and they never made an issue of gay rights. If they wanted to keep their jobs and move up the conservative ladder, they most certainly could never let themselves be seen at a place like J.R.'s, particularly when the media spotlight was upon them.

So, while several individuals say Pete Williams had been a regular at the bar before the war, no one saw him there after it began.

"As soon as he began appearing on TV, I recognized him from the bar," said Robert Warnock, a writer living in Washington. "He's not really in the closet. It's widely known that he's gay. A lot of other people recognized him too, especially after seeing him on CNN and stuff. But I haven't seen him at the bar recently. He just hasn't been around."

"One night I tricked with a guy and, after we had sex, we were sitting up in bed," related waiter and bartender Stephen Smith. "Pete Williams came on the TV and the guy laughed and said, 'Ha! I dated him!'"

Another gay man, requesting anonymity, remembered having had a sexual encounter with Williams: "At first, when I saw him on television, I couldn't figure out where I knew him from. Then I realized I knew him from J.R.'s. And that was weird—you just don't see people from the bar on TV. But then it got even more strange because, after a while, I realized I'd been with him once. Actually, he was a very charming man."

Indeed, not only was Williams well known, he was well liked.

"Pete is really a sweet guy, who people easily take to," said a gay man who'd briefly befriended him. Another gay man who'd met Williams several times describes him as "one of the nicest people around." And Robert Warnock added, "He's a quiet, nice guy. He doesn't seem mean, like a Roy Cohn or anything like that."

So many gay men seemed to know Pete Williams, and know of his homosexuality, that it becomes questionable whether he was ever in the closet. While several men told of friendships and sexual encounters with Williams, one man, requesting anonymity, said they had had a two-month-long intimate relationship. He said that he and Pete Williams had been "boyfriends."

"We were involved sexually, in a relationship," he said. "I'm not going to discuss it further unless Pete really wants me to, and I don't think he does."

At least half a dozen gay politicos in Washington, if not knowing of his gayness first-hand, had been privy to information about Williams.

"I'd always heard the rumors," said the National Gay and Lesbian Task Force's media coordinator, Robert Bray.

"I'd heard the rumors since the Persian Gulf conflict," noted Tim McFeeley, executive director of the Human Rights Campaign Fund, the Washington-based lesbian and gay political action committee and lobbying group.[7] "Before that I didn't even know who he was."

Several mainstream reporters had asked Pete Williams directly whether or not he was gay. "He refused to address the issue," said Mark Thompson, the Pentagon reporter for the Knight Ridder News Service, "and said that he would neither confirm nor deny it." Tribune Broadcasting's Carl Gottlieb had asked the Pentagon about Williams's sexuality. An angry Williams left Gottlieb a message saying that he would not "dignify that question with a response."

Williams would not return any of my numerous telephone calls made over a two-month period to his office at the Pentagon. He rebuffed several efforts to arrange an interview through a personal friend. Commander Stephen Lundquist in the Pentagon's public-affairs office refused to speak to me about Williams's sexuality. When pressed for a reason, he said that "all such allegations [that Williams is gay], in any story, are based on innuendo, and thus will not be responded to."

I asked the Pentagon's Major Doug Hart, another public-affairs officer, if he thought that it would be a contradiction of the military's policy on homosexuals if someone high up in the Pentagon were gay. He replied yes. When I then said that I was speaking about Pete Williams specifically, he seemed to be caught off guard.

"Pete Williams! Oh, I won't even answer that." He laughed nervously. "I won't get into that one at all. Jeez. Come on." As I pressed him, Hart told me that by answering the question, he'd be participating in "character assassination."

There were rumors that Williams was friendly with Gregory King, media director of the Human Rights Campaign Fund. Williams had apparently been a dinner guest at King's home. The right wing would have a field day with that kind of news: a top Pentagon official hanging out with a honcho from a gay political organization. I decided to give King a call.

"I can't confirm that," he said after a pregnant pause, responding to my questions about Williams and his relationship with him.

An hour or so later, King called me back.

"I *can* confirm that I've had Pete Williams at my home. And I'm happy to confirm he is my friend. We worked together, as press secretaries to congressmen."

"What about his homosexuality?"

"I can't confirm that."

Later, in increasingly frenzied phone calls he made to me, King told me first that he'd never discussed homosexuality with Williams. Then he changed his story and said that he had, but that their discussions were about "gays in general and in the military."

"But wait," I said. "You're gay yourself. And you're saying that you're his friend, but you've never discussed his being gay with him?"

"Well, no," he answered. "I have discussed homosexuality with him."

"But not *his* homosexuality, you're saying?"

"Well, no, I haven't discussed *his* homosexuality with him, but we have discussed the *rumors* of his homosexuality."

"There were rumors?"

"Well, yes—there were rumors generated by *The Washington Post*."

"How so?"

"Well, uh, they reported that tap dancing was one of his favorite hobbies."

I tracked down another friend of Williams's: Dan Brenner, who worked for the Federal Communications Commission during the Reagan administration and then became head of the communications-law department at UCLA.

"In the ideal world I'd totally agree with you, but not in this world," he told me. "I won't discuss Pete's sexual life. All that I can tell you is that he's a very special person and a great person and as far as his sexual preference, that's his business. I'm very open about my own life, but I'm not going to discuss Pete's life. I don't believe in outing. I think it's McCarthyist."

Eventually, I obtained Williams's home number. One night, just around midnight, I called him, sure that he'd be home and figuring he'd answer at that hour instead of letting his machine pick up the call. Not surprisingly, he was already asleep, but he arose and took my call. He immediately recognized my name and knew what I was telephoning about, but, even sleepy, Pete Williams was amazingly poised—almost frighteningly so. He was cordial, even able to joke: "Excuse me if I'm a little groggy, but I work for a place where we get up real early." And he was very eager to find out when and where my story would be published.

"I can only tell you the policies of the department," he replied to my queries about his homosexuality. "They don't pay me to speak about my personal opinions and they don't pay me to speak about my personal life. I'm not going talk about myself. It just wouldn't be appropriate."

"Look, Pete," I explained, "I don't mean you any malice by any of this."

"Well, I can't absolve you, Mike," he politely said. "If you're looking for absolution, I'm not the person who can do that."

"I guess my Catholic guilt is seeping out." I laughed. "What I mean is that I'm doing what I think is best for lesbian and gay liberation, for the community. This has been difficult to grapple with. It's one of those things in this job that you have to do, but which you might not necessarily feel so comfortable with. I'm sure you understand that, and I'm sure you have those times in your own job, times when you have to do things that may make you uncomfortable."

"Well, actually," Williams responded, "I'm completely comfortable with everything that I do in my job as a spokesperson for the Department of Defense."

Perhaps it was with that one comment that Pete Williams sealed his fate.

· · · · ·

It was June 1990 and someone had smuggled Brian Ramey a couple of copies of *OutWeek*. His queer life in the service, after first peaking with excitement, had begun to take a turn for the worse as the Pentagon's injustices became a harsh reality.

"We went to Italy. In Naples the gay bars were all closed for the summer, so a lot of stuff was happening in the streets. That was exciting, but I was missing Israel and couldn't wait to go back, which was our next stop before returning to the U.S.—those Israeli guys were *hot!*" he exclaims, laughing.

Brian Ramey never went back to Israel.

"The last day we were in Italy, Saddam Hussein invaded Kuwait," Brian says nonchalantly. "So we went to this war. We were there for about six weeks."

They were out in the middle of the Red Sea most of the time. "By then, I just wanted to go home," he says. "I had been reading all about the queer movement. The war was really tense because I was looking forward to going back to Norfolk [Virginia] and learning about the queer community and all the bars like the Oarhouse, the Garage, and Charades. The largest naval base in the world is there and there are tons and tons of queer bars."

Life on the ship was also getting uncomfortable. "I never had sex on the ship," he states adamantly. "I was very careful about that. I never was really queeny-acting; I was watching my p's and q's. Word of course had gotten around that I was one of the 'family' and so lots of other queer guys would come up and talk to me. But this one freaky guy came on to me, and when I told him I wasn't interested he kept up the harassment. He was too young to go to the bars, so he would meet guys on the ship and have sex with them in these maintenance rooms filled with pipes. But I wasn't interested. I didn't know what to do. I couldn't report him because if I did I would be turning myself in. So this guy was after me for six weeks in the Red Sea and it was really intense because of the war. He was a freak. He was just a total freak!"

When the war was over Brian was sent back to Pensacola for more schooling. He was looking forward to it because the atmosphere was more relaxed than that on the ship. There were several lesbian officers, one of whom he befriended. One of his former classmates in photography training, a woman, had been kicked out of the military a few years before. The reason given, says Brian, was "mental sickness," but the real reason was that she was a dyke. She was now the lover of the lesbian officer and lived off-base with her. Brian was soon having dinner at the officer's house regularly. They were living pretty much as open queers.

"I met a lot of queers while I was down there this time," Brian says. "They were all stationed on the U.S.S. *Lexington,* which is a training carrier for pilots. It's the only carrier in the fleet that had women on it and there were tons of dykes there."

After two months in Pensacola, Brian returned to his ship, which was stationed in Norfolk. But as soon as he arrived, he was summoned to the commander of investigations. "I'm one of their best sailors and they don't even say 'Welcome back' first," he says. "I knew something was going on."

Brian was told that he'd been accused of being a homosexual. His superiors said they'd been told this by an informant, and then tried to get Brian to admit it. "I acted shocked," Brian remembers. "I denied everything. I didn't know what my rights were in the legal area. They used scare tactics, intimidation, interrogation. I was afraid to go out; I thought someone was spying on me. I quit going out completely and stopped associating with the other queers on the boat."

Brian learned from his photo chief, who he says was very supportive and went to bat for him, that the "freak" had ratted on him. The investigators had no actual proof of Brian's homosexuality—they hadn't caught him in a sexual act with another man and hadn't interviewed anyone who'd had sex with him. They only had the word of the other guy, who said that Brian had come on to him and also had threatened him. That was enough to have Brian investigated and closely watched thereafter.

"I didn't tell on him," Brian says of his accuser. "I was stupid, I guess, but that would have been a bigger mess. He was a bitter queen. As far as I know, he's still in the navy."

Not only did Brian stay away from everyone who was gay, but all the queers on board stayed far away from him, knowing about the investigation. Some were also furious with him because the authorities had also targeted them and told them that Brian had fingered them. He hadn't, but this tactic is used often: Hoping to make a person confess, investigators will say that they were told of his or her homosexuality by someone else who is under investigation.

The whole affair took its toll: Brian became a virtual recluse, racked with fear.

· · · · ·

Several high-ranking Pentagon officials are closeted gays; they were so secretive and removed from Dick Cheney that it is conceivable that Cheney knew nothing about their sexual orientation. But it was highly unlikely that Cheney *didn't* know about Pete Williams's personal life. Williams had worked closely with Cheney since 1986, when the latter was a Republican congressman. Williams "was young and in the right place," says a gay congressional aide. "When the scandal rocked the nomination of John Tower for defense secretary [in 1989], Bush decided on Cheney and wanted the entire thing done quickly—cleaned up so that people would forget all the scandal. Bush didn't give Cheney any time to look for a new staff. Basically Cheney took everyone with him who worked for him as congressman. Williams has access and is a top Pentagon official, so he would have to have gone through a security clearance first, where they find out *everything.* And Cheney probably just waved him through because he needed him and he was good."

According to veteran Washington activist Frank Kameny, who was instrumental in breaking institutionalized discrimination against gays in civil-service employment and with regard to security clearances, since the mid-seventies "the policy excluding gays applies only to the uniformed services. Civilians connected with the armed services are, speaking generally, not discriminated against, but the uniformed ones are unyieldingly excluded." Since Williams was a civilian employee, his high-ranking presence at the Pentagon was not *technically* a contradiction of the department's own policy.

"I assume that his superiors are aware of the fact of his homosexuality," Kameny told me in May 1991, months before the outing. "But being gay has not been an obstacle to getting a security clearance since 1975, except in the CIA or FBI. Gay people get clearances and retain clearances. It's probable that Cheney and others even higher up have known, and there's no rational reason why it's okay for Williams to be gay but not for the uniformed servicepeople. It's absolutely idiotic. But I'm sure the military will give you some fine-sounding rhetoric as to why there is a difference."

"Basically, you have a complete federal employee system of civilians," elaborated the Pentagon's Major Doug Hart at the time, gearing up to feed me some of that fine-sounding rhetoric. "It includes not only the Department of Defense, but all federal employees. And they do not have a policy on homosexuality."

But the armed forces had a ban on gays because, as Hart read verbatim from the Department of Defense policy:

> The presence in the military environment of persons who engage in homosexual conduct or who, by their statements, demonstrate a propensity to engage in homosexual conduct, seriously impairs the accomplishments of the military mission. The presence of such members adversely affects the ability of the Military Services to maintain discipline, good order and morale, to foster mutual trust and confidence among service members, to insure the integrity of the system of rank and command; to facilitate assignment and worldwide deployment of service members who frequently must live and work under close conditions affording minimal privacy; to recruit and retain members of the military services; to maintain the public acceptability of military services, and to prevent breaches of security.

What evidence did the military have for these outlandish generalizations, and were officials at least open to discussion about them?

"We don't elaborate on or debate the policy," Hart firmly told me. "We just say that these are the reasons why—and there it is."

"Some of these same arguments once were used to justify the segregation of blacks" in the military, noted syndicated columnist James J. Kilpatrick. Indeed, since there were no empirical data to support the claims, and since the Pentagon steadfastly refused even to discuss them, the department's "fine-sounding rhetoric" amounted to nothing more than bigoted bellowing to justify heinous discrimination.

But, as Kameny noted, these reasons would most likely be adduced by the government to explain why the uniformed services cannot tolerate homosexuality but why it's okay for Pete Williams to be queer. That is, if officials would even admit that they had known about Williams all along.

If, says openly gay congressman Barney Frank, an official as high up as Pete Williams was gay and the administration had *not* known about it, "our FBI wouldn't be all that it's cracked up to be."

But maybe the FBI realized what this particular closeted gay man could bring to the job of covering up for the Pentagon. "He's helping to win the hearts and minds on the home front," *People* reported at the height of the Gulf War. "In that role, the rangy 6-foot-3-inch bespectacled Williams has proven to be one of the Pentagon's most useful weapons."

Other reporters agreed: "I trust him," said NBC's Washington bureau chief, Timothy Russert. "Pete genuinely tries to be helpful," added George Watson, Russert's counterpart at ABC. "He goes out of his way to be accommodating," said Jack Nelson of the *Los Angeles Times*. And *Washington Post* reporter Lois Romano gushed, "He's thirty-eight and looks ten years younger [and] remarkably like he just stepped out of the pages of *GQ*."

Pete Williams's charm had taken him far. Certainly he had much more influence than the label "spokesperson" suggested. He was, after all, an assistant secretary of defense. Said *People:* "[Williams and Cheney] have an extremely close working relationship. Williams has become a key member of the Pentagon's inner circle. Each morning, he sits in on the briefing given to Cheney in the National Military Command Center at the Pentagon."

"He's a policymaker," one congressional staffer flatly stated. "He's not just a mouthpiece. He's closer to the President and the secretary of defense than many other civilians in the Pentagon. He's in on many key decisions. He decides how things are going to play, and certainly he's involved in hushing up things."

Williams certainly knew about the Perserac Report, a study, commissioned by the Pentagon itself in 1989, that concluded that the military's antigay policies were irrational. The Pentagon rejected the report and attempted to squelch it. Not only was Williams, as head of the department's public-affairs office, responsible for whitewashing the Pentagon's abuse of military queers whenever the press launched investigations of that abuse, he was also presumably the central figure responsible for making sure that no report refuting the policy fell into the hands of the media.

Such squelching was in vain. Openly gay congressman Gerry Studds and several other House members obtained copies of the Perserac Report from other sources inside the Pentagon and leaked the study's conclusions to the press in October 1989.[8] It had long been the Pentagon's contention that queers were more susceptible than straights to blackmail—even if they were totally out of the closet—and that they posed security risks when they had access to classified information. But the Pentagon's own report shot down these warped beliefs, concluding that, as security risks, gays are "as good or better than the average heterosexual."

Besides, if the military was really concerned with blackmail, wouldn't it have been more worried about an assistant secretary with access to all kinds of classified information? Wouldn't someone as highly placed as Pete Williams be more susceptible to blackmail than an openly gay drill sergeant, cook, or porter with no access to sensitive information?

Blackmail, it appeared, was not the Pentagon's real fear.

· · · · ·

After he'd spent some time playing straight and keeping to himself, it seemed to Brian that the situation had calmed down. Months had passed and he'd gone out to sea again, stopping at various ports but no longer feeling that he was being followed by investigators. Things had even been smoothed out with the other guys who had been accused; they believed Brian when he said he hadn't ratted on them.

Soon Brian and the others, feeling that they weren't being watched any longer, were hanging around together and going out to bars again. But Brian was still very unhappy.

"I was miserable," he remembers. "I was scared. I was petrified. I felt that no matter how hard I worked, this was going to blemish my record. The paperwork follows you wherever you go. I couldn't really deal with things. I was under a lot of stress and now I was picking up all of these homophobic remarks from straight guys all the time. There was a lot of whispering, a lot of finger-pointing and glaring. It was all over the ship: I was a queer."

Brian's spirits were lifted at the time by the fact that the ship was pulling into St. Thomas in the U.S. Virgin Islands. It was a beautiful, serene place where Brian thought he could chill out and relax a bit. The only gay bar on St. Thomas was in the off-limits section, which covered half the island. He certainly didn't think he'd be going there.

"I had four straight days off, to do whatever I wanted," Brian says. "I was afraid to go to the bar, but the guys talked me into it."

Lombardo's was a small gay disco atop a steep hill in the middle of the island, which is watched by the ship's shore patrol, or SPs, who walk the area in uniform, carrying nightsticks. The SPs make sure that the sailors aren't anyplace they're not supposed to be.

At one A.M. on a Saturday night, Lombardo's was packed and the music was blasting. The club is very small; the bar and cruising area in the front are long and narrow. Way in the back, through a corridor, is a crowded, pulsating dance floor.

At Lombardo's, queer American sailors were always a hot commodity; they were the stars the locals went crazy for. The night when Brian and his friends arrived wasn't any different. As usual, the sailors, dancing vigorously, were pushed toward the middle of the dance floor as the locals gathered around, clapping and hooting loudly. Then the deejay put on the Village People's "In the Navy." A couple of the boys jumped on chairs. People began peeling their shirts off. The entire place, pounding and pulsating, seemed about to come tumbling down.

Then the music stopped.

For a moment everyone looked up, shocked, but a lot of those present knew exactly what the silence meant. The deejay, in an elevated booth, can see outside and can see who is arriving. A whisper breezed through the disco: The shore patrol was coming. The front of the club was packed with locals, all squeezed into the narrow space of the bar area. As the SPs pushed their way in, locals groaned and hissed and the club's owner speedily pushed through the corridor that separates the bar area from the dance floor. He herded the eight sailors together, pushing them forward, telling them, "Come on, come on, you've got to hide." He shoved them through a hidden door underneath a stairway and shut the door immediately. The deejay put a song on and everyone resumed dancing as the SPs arrived on the dance floor.

"It was really frightening," says Brian. "The owner just grabbed us, thank God, and threw us in this storage space and shut the light and bolted the door. I felt like Anne Frank. This happens, we were later told, every time a ship pulls in. It's like they're searching for Jews in Nazi Germany."

The SPs stayed for ten or fifteen minutes, looking all around the nooks and crannies. One of them asked the owner about sailors; the owner responded, "Why would there be any sailors in our bar?"

When the SPs were well out of sight, the sailors were let out of their hiding place and the crowd cheered and whistled.

"I was literally in a closet," Brian says, "and when I came out of that closet, I thought, I'm not going to do this anymore. I came to a decision."

A week later, Brian went to visit a friend stationed in Washington, D.C. It was the summer of 1991. In Washington for three days, Brian visited Lambda Rising, the famous Dupont Circle gay bookstore, looking for a book that would help him deal with being queer in the military, a book that would tell him how to get out and what legal protections he might have.

"I was getting angry," he recalls. "I was pissed off that this was happening to me. The fear subsided and it turned to anger, all because of that incident in Saint Thomas."

The people at Lambda Rising told Brian that there weren't any books on the subject at the time. They told him he should call Frank Kameny, the resolute defender of queers in the military (and the rest of the government) and a true father of the gay rights movement.

"I called Frank and he told me that he'd have to sit down with me and talk longer to get the specifics of the case," he says. "But he did say that I'd have to have a signed affidavit saying that I was queer and have it notarized and then give it to the military."

That, Brian said, was a "barrier" for him. He was afraid of coming out to military authorities and afraid of putting a statement of his gayness down on paper. "I thought maybe they would lock me in the brig for several days," he says. "I was apprehensive about what would happen, even in the future, if I put it down on paper."

For the next several weeks the debate went back and forth in Brian's mind: Should he take Frank Kameny's advice, come out to the navy and risk whatever consequences there would be, or should he continue to live in this hell for the next two years (the time remaining in his enlistment) and deny himself because to do so might be easier in the long run?

. . . . .

It was on a hot night in late May 1991 when the Dartmouth Gay and Lesbian Alumni Association held a panel discussion at the snobbish Yale Club in Manhattan. "Pink Triangles of the Pentagon" drew a crowd of about seventy conservative, suit-and-tie gay men, all scarfing up hors d'oeuvres, trading business cards, and looking for the answer to the question of the day: How can we end the U.S. government's outrageous discrimination against, and abuse of, gay men and lesbians in the armed forces? The panel included one lesbian and three gay men whose lives had been completely altered when they were discharged from the military because of their sexual orientation.

Moderating the panel was the boyishly cute, quick-witted Bill Rubenstein, director of the American Civil Liberties Union's Lesbian and Gay Rights Project. He explained that the policy excluding lesbians and gays from the military could be overturned by a Supreme Court ruling, an act of Congress, or an order from the secretary of defense or the President.

"With the current state of the court, I'm pessimistic that the judiciary will change this," he said. "And the way Congress is right now, I doubt they'll pass a law. So the key is to put a lot of pressure on the Defense Department, the President, and Congress, which can put pressure on the Defense Department. Public opinion and public pressure could change the policy."

Near the end of the question-and-answer period, Michael Goff, who was a columnist for *OutWeek* at the time (and is now editor of *Out* magazine), stood up. "Since public pressure seems to be the only viable way to end this policy," he asked, "wouldn't outing high-ranking Pentagon officials, like Pete Williams, be an appropriate tactic to use to show the administration's hypocrisy in kicking out thousands of young people a year while other gays continue to work at the highest levels?"

The room grumbled. A short debate on outing ensued, with the usual right-to-privacy issues coming up. Goff then explained that he wasn't talking about younger, rank-and-file enlisted people but only about high-level, policymaking officials in the Pentagon, many of whom the administration knew were gay.

At that point, AIDS activist Dan Baker rose and asked the room if there was any reason why Pete Williams should *not* be outed. No one offered any, and the meeting adjourned.

Discussions at that time with many people in the gay community, including some leaders and elected officials, revealed the same sentiments; many gay people felt that exposing the government's double standard was not only right, but would ultimately bring about abolition of the military's antigay policy. Congressman Barney Frank, though declining to comment specifically about Pete Williams's sexuality, told me that "if you have someone who's gay who's been administering an antigay policy successfully in an agency that says we can't have gay people, I think it helps undermine that policy to expose the government's hypocrisy to the public. In the case of air force captain Greg Greeley," Frank continued, "the military said they were concerned that he compromised 'national security.' But if you expose the fact that there are gay people who have access to secrets in the military, then you undercut the policy and prove it wrong. And that works toward changing the policy because it kills the government's argument."

I asked Frank if he thought it was justifiable to uncover the government's duplicity by making public the fact that one of the Pentagon's top officials is gay, even when there was no way of knowing what that person might or might not have been doing on the inside with regard to gay issues?

"It's relevant to report that a person is gay," Frank replied, "if that person is involved in an institution that has antigay policies, especially if the person is involved in policymaking. It may be valid and legitimate that people are working within the system, but I still think, in general, hypocrisy is pretty hard to wash away. It's wrong for gay people to be administering an antigay policy."

Sandra Lowe, an attorney with the Lambda Legal Defense and Education Fund in New York, had spent the past several years chiseling away at the Defense Department policy. Since 1989 she had represented Joe Steffan, a former naval midshipman who was booted out after he told his superiors about his homosexuality. Lowe at first was vehemently opposed to outing. When I first called her to interview her about the Pete Williams story, she was vociferously against my writing anything about the assistant secretary's sexuality.

"For all we know," Lowe had explained, "he could be working from the inside. I am not for outing people unless we know that they have done things that have hurt us or stood for hurting us. I don't think it's necessarily hypocrisy. There have been various people from the inside who've helped to push this thing along."

Several months later, after what she said were numerous conversations with activists and others in the lesbian and gay community and with members of the mainstream press, Sandra Lowe had changed her mind, as had many people.

"I realized how thoroughly a spokesman and a policymaker for the department Pete Williams is," she explained. "There are rare times in history when I think extraordinary steps must be taken. I've talked to many reporters about this now and realize that everyone has always known that Pete Williams is gay. And that fact shows there is a conspiracy of silence. Pete Williams's silence, in the last couple of years, has hurt us. And I think his silence right now is hurting us. If his homosexuality being known becomes a major media issue, it can make a difference in the policy. We all have an obligation, when we see injustice, not to hide behind privilege when our brothers and sisters are being hung out to dry. It almost seems like being a Jew in the SS."

With those words, Lowe was quoted in a story I wrote for *The Advocate*—"The Outing of Assistant Secretary of Defense Pete Williams"—which hit the newsstands in August 1991.

. . . . .

Norfolk, Virginia, while it was a queer sailor's paradise with all of its gay bars and hot men, was not a happy place for Brian Ramey in the last week of July 1991. His mind was exploding: He didn't know what to do. He wouldn't be leaving Norfolk, where his ship was stationed, for quite some time. But he wanted out. Harassment from straight sailors had increased dramatically; his superiors again suspected him of being queer; and he couldn't get that night at Lombardo's disco out of his mind. Brian was miserable. He knew he had to get out, but in his talks with Frank Kameny he'd realized that leaving would take some courage.

"I was in sporadic contact with Frank, but just when I'd decided I should do it [come out to his superiors and be discharged], I kept changing my mind," he remembers. "I'd talk with him and he'd reassure me, and the next day I'd change my mind and think: I would really screw up my future, I wouldn't be able to get a job. I was buying into all the bullshit that the military told me [in past interrogations] would happen: My family would disown me. I would lose my benefits. I'd get a dishonorable discharge."

Then, a week later, during the first week of August, Kameny called with the pivotal news that would move Brian to act.

"You've got to get the new *Advocate!*" Kameny commanded Brian. "Dick Cheney's assistant is on the cover. You've got to get the *Advocate* with Pete Williams on the cover. It's selling out all over Washington!"

The issue had just been delivered to newsstands and bookstores. Brian searched all over Norfolk. He was the first sailor in Norfolk to get a copy, he says. He wasn't the last.

"I was appalled at the hypocrisy, that the man who was on the news every night during the war was a fag," he says of his first reaction upon reading the article. "During this very war where [Williams was] talking about collateral damage, here I am being harassed because of my sexuality and this man is a spokesman for the military!"

Brian was suddenly jolted to move. "It was the catalyst," he says. "I now wanted to do this. I'd been wrestling with this idea, but now the Pete Williams situation just incensed me so that I decided enough was enough and I'd take whatever consequences I had to take."

Within hours, Brian had rented a car and left for Washington, for Kameny's house. He signed documents Kameny had drawn up and, several days later, he had them notarized. "The notary public called me a sinner," he says. "But I didn't care. I took the papers to the captain's office and turned them in to the yeoman. I had faith in what I was doing. I knew it was right."

Soon after Brian received his discharge, he became a role model for many of his fellow sailors. "A lot of the guys on the ship had to come out afterwards," he recounts, "when they saw what I had done." The outing of Pete Williams and all the coverage surrounding that, Brian says, affected many others in the military as it had affected him. "A lot of people who came back to Norfolk later came out, as a statement of anger over the Pete Williams scandal."

While many soldiers who had valiantly fought in the Gulf War came out to their superiors in protest and were summarily discharged from the armed forces, hundreds more, discovered through the Pentagon's investigations, were booted out on their return from the front. The military used them for cannon fodder. *Newsweek* proclaimed in June 1992 that "someday, Desert Storm may be viewed as a major turning point for gays in the military" because "*The Advocate*, a gay magazine, outed a senior civilian DOD official who had access to classified materials during the war." They and the rest of the media missed the most important aspect of the Williams affair: Brian Ramey and many others came out in protest or were purged by the military in witch-hunts, while one privileged, closeted man who had suffered none of the military's brutality continued to be silent.

While the outing may have exposed a hypocritical "Pentagon official" and turned the media's attention to a brutal and equally hypocritical institution, it had also revealed hundreds of true fighters like Brian Ramey, who, when push came to shove, put themselves on the line. They were the true heroes of Operation Out-the-Pentagon.

7
....

Inning the Outing
....

Initially, my story outing Pete Williams was to run in *OutWeek*. But just as it was about to go to print, *OutWeek* folded. Over the next several months, the story had gone looking for a new home—and almost didn't find one.

Several weeks before the planned publication in *OutWeek*, I made an exclusive agreement with *NBC Nightly News* to have them break the story first, once the magazine had hit the newsstands or perhaps the night before. None of the networks or major papers had the guts to do the story themselves—to do their own investigations and be the actual outers—but there was much speculation among reporters, correspondents, and middle-level producers and editors that the major news organizations would pick up the story from the gay press. One particular person at NBC wanted to see this story come to fruition and contacted me early on; this individual had numerous contacts inside the Pentagon. I agreed to give NBC the story first, the night before *OutWeek* was to hit the newsstands, because those Pentagon moles had kept NBC informed of everything I was doing anyway. I planned to hold a press conference on the steps of the Capitol—or perhaps at the Pentagon itself—the day after NBC broke the story.

Somehow, a week before press time, the well-guarded story, already laid out and ready to go, was mysteriously leaked from the *OutWeek* offices to just about everyone in political and media circles in Washington, New York, Los Angeles—even London. It was being photocopied and faxed over and over again. As former naval midshipman Joe Steffan later wrote in his book, *Honor Bound,* the article fast became "the literary equivalent of the Rob Lowe videotape."

None of this really mattered; the story was still being seen only by an elite group of people in the media. The public didn't have a clue. But the insider-only circulation just added to the hype; all the talk made people want to push the story harder. In a matter of days *OutWeek* was to explode with it.

Just as we were to go to press, *OutWeek*, racked with internal business conflicts, shut its doors. The loyal staff, who had just worked a week of eighteen-hour days on a glorious Gay Pride issue, went into shock. As everyone rifled through filing cabinets, battled with the principals for their paychecks, and made frantic phone calls to lawyers and police officers, and to assorted financiers who might be interested in buying the magazine, I tried to get the story into print somewhere else. Some of my colleagues also wanted the story published.

News editor Andrew Miller, features editor Victoria Starr, and I went to the Greenwich Village apartment of Richard Goldstein, executive editor of *The Village Voice*, the morning *OutWeek* folded. Goldstein was upset by the fall of *OutWeek* but excited by the Pete Williams story.

An out and proud gay man who's been with the *Voice* for over twenty years, Goldstein had decided that outing was appropriate in certain situations. Within two days the *Voice* bought the story. Editor in chief Jonathan Larsen was also pleased with it, and other editors, despite reservations about the issues of disclosure, felt that it was an important story to run.

Everything was set. I was happy and relieved that the story had found a home, that we'd be taking on the Pentagon in a big way, and that I could now deal with the sorrow of *OutWeek*'s demise without having to worry about placing the article.

But word of the story had leaked out around the *Voice*. I had never been popular among certain leftist *Voice* writers. A "commune," as then–*New York Post* editor Jerry Nachman later described the *Voice* staffers, met and demanded that the story be killed. The *Voice* has always been a "writers' paper," and staff opinion carries a weight that the editors would be loath to ignore.

Over the previous two years, I'd had some raucous, and sometimes personal, squabbles with several *Voice* writers on topics ranging from outing to homophobia in films. I had criticized C. Carr, a *Voice* writer who is more open about her lesbianism than she is about her first name, for not asking Jodie Foster about her sexuality and the objectionable killer transvestite in *The Silence of the Lambs* when Carr did a cover interview of Foster for *Mirabella*. Apparently Carr became alarmed when she heard that I'd be outing Pete Williams in the *Voice*. She had in the past launched salvos back at me after my attacks on her, condemning me as an "ayatollah" of outing and defending both director Jonathan Demme and *The Silence of the Lambs*, denying that there was anything remotely homophobic about his portrayal of the killer. She also denounced me for assailing what she called a feminist film.

I had also criticized Gary Indiana, another openly gay writer. I had said that he had pandered to Demme in an profile in *Interview*. He fired back in one of the fiercest attacks on me ever, comparing me to a right-wing zealot, calling me a psychopath, and describing me as an "infant crapping in his diapers." Several more attacks, regarding the same issues of outing and homophobia in film, had also come from closeted gay *Voice* writers. From the beginning, many of the older *Voice* writers had no tolerance for outing, on traditional liberal right-to-privacy grounds. Just a year earlier, when I wrote a piece for the *Voice* about how the media had at first ignored the Malcolm Forbes outing, several writers there complained that they simply didn't want to see such an article in the *Voice*. And so the "commune" would not allow the Pete Williams story to be printed, even though it had the support of three of the *Voice*'s most powerful staff members: executive editor Goldstein, editor in chief Larsen, and the popular columnist Michael Musto.

According to some who were at the staff meeting, Indiana spun himself into a frenzy, putting on an angry show that intimidated what few supporters the story may have had. Only four people out of several dozen supported running it.

For queer activists as well as other progressives, the *Voice* meeting was a defining moment that demonstrated just where the paper stood on the new queer movement: A resolution that would have forbidden outing at the paper forever was shot down, but staffers left the meeting with the impression that the *Voice* was opposed to outing in *all* circumstances with *no* exceptions.

Goldstein called me to tell me the news. I couldn't believe that these supposedly progressive people were doing this to me—to queers—to society in general. As one leftist who writes for *The Nation* asked days later, "Who the hell are they protecting? This is the fucking Pentagon!" And so, Andrew Miller and I made an appointment with Jerry Nachman at the *New York Post*.

An imposing man who looked as if he were attached to his desk, Nachman said he was intrigued with the story, although he was angry about attacks I'd made on him, on the *Post*'s obsessively homophobic right-wing editorial-page editor, Eric Breindel, and on maniacal *Post* columnist Ray Kerrison. But Nachman said that he wouldn't let any of that get in the way of his judgment. He would, however, make a few calls before he considered the story. He would have a chat with Katie Couric, who was then covering the Pentagon for NBC News. Then, if the *Post* went with the story, it would run like a column, with my photo. It would, of course, have to be shorter—maybe even published in two parts—and I'd have to write it, Nachman said, in the *New York Post* style.

That frightened me. I began to wonder why I was there. Andrew and I had figured that only a tabloid would run this story. But even the *Post* didn't want to take the risk.

"Can't do it," said Nachman, when I called him days later, feeding me some excuse about how the *Post*'s metro editor was adamantly opposed to invading people's privacy. (Oh, really?) He went on to say that he thought outing was "ageist" because it was about young gays attacking older gays. (I was thirty and Pete Williams was thirty-eight.) It was amusing to hear such politically correct drivel coming from the editor of the *New York Post*. I knew the truth: The *Post* didn't have the guts after the barrage of criticism that *The New York Times* had just suffered over naming the accuser in the William Kennedy Smith rape case. Suddenly, everyone in the media was walking on eggshells, even the editors at the *New York Post*, and even though the

Palm Beach rape case was a completely different scenario than the Pete Williams outing.

There was a double standard at work. Stories that George Bush had a mistress (as the *Post* later alleged in 1992, based solely on the supposed word of a source who was dead) and that democratic presidential candidate Gary Hart was having an extramarital affair (as *The Miami Herald* discovered in 1988) were, editors felt, worth taking a pummeling for. Standing up for the rights of homosexuals was not. No news organization was willing to take on the Pentagon just for the sake of doing something beneficial for queers.

I sent the story to *The Advocate*. Editor in chief Richard Rouilard had previously been opposed to outing, but, like so many other gay people, he had moved on the issue over the previous year.[9] Several respected mainstream journalists, such as the *Los Angeles Times*'s Victor Zonana, had urged him to run the story. By this time, the story itself had grown. It now included the conversation with Pete Williams himself, as well as interviews with several gays in the military, and the fact that Sandra Lowe at Lambda Legal Defense had changed her mind about outing.

The Advocate was excited about the story. Rouilard, a dynamic editor, had recently turned the magazine around and injected a younger, fresher, more queer attitude into it. The change had been influenced by *OutWeek* and its publicity-garnering tactics. Rouilard put *The Advocate* on the media map by getting some big names like Madonna to give provocative interviews. At the same time, he brought a high standard of journalism to the magazine. Now, with the Pete Williams story, the magazine would take on a political edge and force Washington to stand up and take notice. The *Voice*'s dumping the story was a blessing in disguise, both for *The Advocate* and for the story itself. More time had passed, the story had become bigger, and columnists everywhere were tracking it as if it were a storm, trying to figure out where it would hit next. Even *The Village Voice* covered the story of the story, with media critic James Ledbetter discussing the emergency editorial meeting at which the *Voice* had declined to out someone he called an unnamed "Pentagon official." Both Michael Musto and Richard Goldstein wrote columns criticizing their colleagues for their absolutism. Both announced that the piece would be running in *The Advocate*. Other publications, such as *USA Today*, had been tracking the story regularly. In every instance, these reporters made sure not to mention Pete Williams by name. He was always a "Pentagon official" who was going to be "outed." This was oddly beneficial to the story: No one could scoop me because their editors wouldn't allow them to, so they all reported the outing without divulging the essential facts that only *The Advocate* would reveal.

The Advocate put its publicity machine in place and was ready to roll. My only reservation regarded the way the story was packaged. The article itself did not demonize Pete Williams; it even sympathized with him a bit, portraying him as a charming and sweet guy—albeit a cowardly and hypocritical one. While Williams's position at the Pentagon was certainly hypocritical, it was Dick Cheney, the military, and the President himself who were most disingenuous: They enforced an antigay policy knowing that a talented gay man was in an important position in their administration.

But *The Advocate* cover showed a photo of Pete Williams next to the words DID THIS MAN RUIN 2000 LIVES? KNOW ABOUT THE SUICIDES? WASTE TAXPAYERS' MILLIONS ON MILITARY WITCH-HUNTS? Rouilard, who had previously been anti-outing, wrote an essay in which he made this "a singular case" (*The Advocate* would have several such "singular" cases over the next two years), warranting an exception to the anti-outing rule.

Rouilard's change of mind is fairly typical for gay men and lesbians: First they're adamantly opposed to outing; then it's okay, if the person to be outed is involved in blatant and vicious homophobic actions. Finally, most come to the conclusion that a person's sexuality should be discussed whenever it is pertinent to a news story. Often opinion swings 180 degrees, so that in a vindictive stage we stretch circumstances to say that the person being outed has engaged in the most horrendous, ruthless activities imaginable. I did this sometimes myself—often in capital letters—in my *OutWeek* columns. Even lawyer Sandra Lowe did it, at first adamantly opposed to outing, then comparing Williams to "a Jew in the SS." Pete Williams was not *personally* responsible for people's suicides or for ruining the lives of over ten thousand discharged queer servicepeople; he was a spokesperson for an organization that was. It's hard to say if *The Advocate*'s demonizing him actually helped or hurt the story. I confess that it made me uneasy.

In the late July days before the story ran, *The Advocate*'s publicist, Howard Bragman, began faxing it out to the most important news organizations, the ones that had expressed great interest in it. The media had had roughly two months to deal with this situation, but they were still unsure of what to do, so terrifying and perplexing was the issue of outing for them. They also had mixed feelings about taking on the almighty Pentagon, which only several months earlier had carefully rationed the Gulf War news, denying precious information to any outlet that got out of line.

The networks were therefore most susceptible to the Pentagon's censorship and most fearful of getting on the Pentagon's wrong side. Their competition increased their worries: CNN had outdone all of the networks in the coverage of the war; the others couldn't afford to be cut off now. Treading carefully, ABC did a *Good Morning America* segment on the Pentagon's antigay ban. *CBS This Morning* planned to interview Rouilard about outing before the story hit the stands—although they would not use Williams's name. ABC shot—but held—a segment for the evening news on the ban; producers were still unsure whether or not they would out Williams after *The Advocate* hit the stands. *NBC Nightly News* shot and aired a piece on gays in the military—without mentioning the outing—followed by *CBS Evening News*. Everyone, it seemed, was strategizing.

Actually, reporters from all the networks, including CNN, were trying to do stories that would out Williams. Not only did most of the Washington bureau chiefs agree that the stories should be done, but a number of producers throughout news organizations felt the same way. The decision went to the top of the news divisions at CNN, CBS, and NBC, and it was the network presidents themselves who nixed the stories. Not only did they throw cold water on the idea of revealing Pete Williams's homosexuality in their own stories, they also decided that the networks could not even out Williams secondarily, after *The Advocate* hit the stands, unless Williams himself specifically "admitted" to being gay. This decision jolted the middle- and lower-level NBC people, who had thought all along that they would at least be able to cover the outing after it had occurred in the gay press.

At ABC, the scenario was even worse. The evening-news producers couldn't get the story about gays in the military—which they'd already shot—on the air, even though it didn't mention the outing at all. "That decision has left the news division entirely," I was told at the time by a producer at the network. "It's now in the corporate hierarchy. It'll never get out of that quagmire. This story is hopeless." Someone way up at Capital Cities, ABC's parent company, speculated the source, didn't want the Pentagon coming under *any* harsh or embarrassing criticism just then.

The morning television talk and news programs—*Today, Good Morning America*, and *CBS This Morning*—operate fairly independently of the news divisions, and had more leeway on this story. That's why *CBS This Morning* was able to eventually get Rouilard on; he discussed the outing without naming Williams. *Good Morning America* early on interviewed a few servicepeople who'd been discharged; the interviews were aired only after being announced and then mysteriously canceled for several days. There was not a hint about the "Pentagon official" who was queer. CNN also did some soft pieces on gays in the military, never mentioning the outing.

This was all by the end of July; the *Advocate* article didn't hit the stands until the first week of August. The networks were covering themselves so that they wouldn't have to deal with the outing at all: They could counter any criticism of their silence on the outing by saying that they'd given some coverage to the Pentagon's antigay policies. They would keep the Pentagon happy, too, by not contributing to a debilitating scandal. The Pentagon would remember that and reward them appropriately.

The print media, meanwhile, were now bracing for the story. It had been a hot debate in newsrooms for weeks, but it was still something they wanted to avoid at all costs. Homosexuality has always made straight editors nervous, and exposing someone as a homosexual—especially a government official who wasn't involved in some sort of seedy rest-room scandal—made them extremely uneasy. They couldn't figure out what the real story was: Was it the outing? Or was it *The Advocate*'s actions and the gay community's response? Was it still a story if the Pentagon didn't respond? Was it a story only if the rest of the media made it one? Was it a story if Williams didn't react? And what the hell was it if he *did* react? Editors racked their brains. The controversy surrounding the revelation of the name of William Kennedy Smith's accuser was fresh in everyone's mind. Editors were afraid, having witnessed (and participated in) the bludgeoning of *The New York Times* for having named the woman.

While newspaper editors plotted their strategy, back in Washington Congressman Barney Frank decided to step in. On Wednesday, July 31, Dick Cheney was to appear before the House Budget Committee, on which Frank has an influential position. Frank knew the Pete Williams story was going to break any minute; Cheney knew it, too—and Frank knew that Cheney knew. It was the perfect time to put the secretary of defense on the spot. Although arms appropriations was the topic of the day, Frank decided to grill Cheney on the Pentagon policy—not mentioning Williams but inquiring hypothetically if he thought a homosexual in a high position could be a target for blackmail. Cheney was forced to concede that the security-risk argument was, in words all gays will long remember, "an old chestnut." Twice he said that he had "inherited" the antigay policy. The exchange drew media attention, and the press speculated that Cheney was distancing himself from the policy. He was, of course, also trying to position himself for the eventual outing.

Not surprisingly, the only mainstream news organizations that were aggressively and fearlessly pursuing this story were the smaller ones, which had less to lose, since they didn't have access to the Pentagon to begin with. The Knight Ridder News Service and Tribune Broadcasting had been vigorously investigating the story, even before I had. Then, on July 31, 1991, Tribune became the first broadcast outlet to run a piece about the Pete Williams outing and use his name. They showed Michael Petrelis unfurling the ABSOLUTELY QUEER poster from his now month-old Queer Nation press conference, and they reproduced the cover of the upcoming *Advocate,* which was due out later that week. Tribune, operating out of Washington, feeds its pieces to hundreds of small, independent television stations across the country. In New York, the piece ran on WPIX–TV. Other stations across the country, taking a cue from Tribune, produced their own segments. In San Francisco, CBS affiliate KPIX did extraordinary coverage, using Tribune's footage and devoting the first five minutes of its program to the story for two days in a row. The second day highlighted Pete Williams's response to being outed. KPIX produced several different segments about gays in the military, activism, and outing, and even had live on-air interviews with experts on the topics. CNBC, a cable-television corporate sibling of NBC that reaches 44 million homes, also named the name that week. Like a snowball starting down a big hill, the story began to pick up momentum.

On Thursday, August 1, syndicated columnist Jack Anderson wrote a column about both Queer Nation's press conference outing Williams, and the upcoming *Advocate* story, and sent it out to more than seven hundred newspapers. "Williams says he is not paid to talk about his personal life nor offer his personal opinions on issues," Anderson wrote. "He told us he has 'no plans' to resign, but that could change on Cheney's request. If Williams stays and the questions persist, the Pentagon will have a hard time defending its dubious policy against gay soldiers—a policy that is already on unsteady ground."

The next day, Friday, August 2, many of Anderson's subscribers, including *The Washington Post*, killed his column. Anderson was shocked. "I felt that the little guy, the GI, the enlisted man, was being discriminated against," he later commented. "It was outright censorship."

But hundreds of papers, from the Portland *Oregonian* to the *Oakland Tribune*, ran the column. Cheyenne's *Wyoming Tribune-Eagle*, a local paper back in Williams's home state, ran the column that Friday. The next day there was a front-page follow-up story headlined, PETE WILLIAMS: NO PLANS TO QUIT PENTAGON JOB, in which Williams gave perhaps the only interview on the subject to a newspaper at the time. "I don't think this story will have any legs," he told the *Tribune-Eagle* on Saturday, August 3, "because Mr. Anderson's story is not true—I have no intention of resigning." Referring to Petrelis's press conference, he described Queer Nation as a group "that doesn't like the military policy" and said, "They decided to make me a target. It's a free country, but I'm not going to dignify what they do by talking about it." He refused to discuss his sexual orientation.

That same Saturday, the *San Francisco Examiner* ran a lengthy front-page story that, without naming Williams, thoroughly covered the outing and the issues surrounding the Pentagon's antigay ban. *The Detroit News* took a different tack. It named Williams in a substantial news-commentary piece, syndicated to hundreds of papers throughout the Midwest, which was accompanied by a three-quarter-page photo of Williams. In the savviest move by any paper thus far, the *News* assigned the story to an openly gay man, their New York–based television critic, Michael McWilliams, and asked him not only to explain in detail what had happened but also to offer his opinions and give the topic some perspective. This approach is perhaps the model for how papers should handle outing. (It's not surprising that *The Detroit News*, obviously astute about these issues, later became the first straight newspaper in the nation to have an openly gay or lesbian columnist, Deb Price, to write on topics of concern to queers.)

The McWilliams piece, one of several columns for which he later won a journalism award, was almost irreverent in style. It tied together Pete Williams; the Pentagon's antigay policy; the outing debates in the gay community and the mainstream press; the media; and the story surrounding the story. "The Williams saga," McWilliams wrote, "after all, is the first outing that's really about something, particularly to journalists; it's not about which Hollywood actress is sleeping with which pretty girl pop star. It's about how America conducts itself. It's about hypocrisy, hope, change, betrayal—and survival. . . . The biggest debate surrounding outing is over hurting the individual—does anybody deserve this kind of exposure? But I can't believe that Williams will be hurt by this, and I can't believe he believes it; his constituency after all, isn't the Christian Right, it's the 91 percent of Americans who approved of the Gulf war and hung on Williams' every word to prove it."

As for television coverage, predictably, it was one of the Sunday-morning network news-and-talk programs—also less constrained by the news division—that was ultimately able to kick up some dust. While these shows *seem* to ask hard questions, in reality the questions are not *too* hard on high-profile guests. Otherwise the guests wouldn't come back—or, worse, they would go to another network. On Sunday, August 4, Sam Donaldson summoned all his courage on ABC's *This Week with David Brinkley* and confronted Dick Cheney:

DONALDSON: Mr. Secretary, a national newspaper about homosexuals, *The Advocate,* is publishing a story this week saying that a high-level Defense Department official, a member of your staff, is a homosexual. Does that give you a problem, particularly with regard to regulations which separate members of the uniformed services if they are homosexuals?

CHENEY: Well, I'm not sure that I can comment on it, in the sense that I haven't read the article yet, Sam.

DONALDSON: But you can comment on the general principle of whether high-level Defense Department officials who have to defend policy can in fact defend the policy which separates homosexuals in the uniformed services.

CHENEY: ... The policy in the Department applies specifically to the military, not to civilians, and the fact of the matter is that it's a policy I inherited. It's based upon the proposition that gay lifestyle is incompatible with military service.

DONALDSON: Do you think it is?

CHENEY: Well, I think that there are unique aspects of military service that justify a policy that takes into account the unique aspects of military service.

DONALDSON: Well, Mr. Secretary, if the policy can be justified then for service personnel, why shouldn't it apply to Defense Department officials?

CHENEY: Well, Sam, I have operated on the basis over the years, in respect to my personal staff, that I don't ask them about their private lives. As long as they perform their professional responsibilities in a responsible manner, their private lives are their business—I would also argue that it's none of your business, that from that standpoint, as long as they do their job in a professional manner, that's all that matters. Now, the fact is that there are a different set of regulations that apply where the military is concerned that I inherited, that are based upon the proposition that you cannot make the kind of separation in the military between private and professional life that you can with respect to civilians. When you deploy for six months on an aircraft carrier at sea, it's a very different set of concerns and considerations. So that is the policy that's there today, it's the policy that I've inherited, but I don't think it's fundamentally wrong for us to make a distinction between—

DONALDSON: So I take it, Mr. Secretary, that the individual who must defend Department regulations as a spokesman is not going to be asked to resign.

CHENEY: Absolutely not.

Donaldson may as well have named Williams; unlike all of the others, he didn't use the term "Pentagon official" but rather said "spokesman." Anyone who followed the war saw only one "spokesman": Pete Williams.

The entire exchange seemed a bit rehearsed—as if Cheney already knew what was coming. As one network insider said, "Donaldson blew it!" Either the interview was planned to allow Cheney to give lame excuses, or Donaldson was just not comfortable with (or well versed in) the issues: Why, for example, didn't he inquire what Cheney meant by "concerns and considerations"?

Overall, though, the exchange was positive; the policy was once again chipped away at. Cheney distanced himself from it yet again, saying three more times that he had "inherited" it, giving the impression that it was a relic from the past and that he had nothing to do with it. He also stood up for his spokesperson's "privacy" and declared that he would not ask him to resign. The real news story here was that Cheney was explicitly okaying gays in civilian jobs in the Defense Department as long as their sexuality didn't interfere with their work. Because he said that Williams would not be asked to resign, he had killed the security-risk argument forever. But even more important, Cheney said that government doesn't have the right to intrude on the "private lives" of its employees. Suddenly, a Republican official—defending himself and his policies—was using the same rhetoric gay activists had used for twenty years.

The Donaldson interview provided scores more newspapers with an angle on this story. Usually they cover on Mondays what transpires on the Sunday shows. Now they had Cheney reacting to the outing on national television. But because Donaldson didn't name Williams, anyone who did so was going to be taking a risk. Radio news divisions and talk formats took that risk more easily, and on Monday, August 5, the CBS radio network named Williams all day in its reports that Cheney said it was okay for civilians in the department to be gay.

The New York Times was still smarting from having named William

Kennedy Smith's accuser. After a debate and after gay staffers were consulted, the editors decided against naming Williams in the *Times*'s tiny story about the discussion between Donaldson and Cheney. *The Washington Post* ran a longer story, also without the name. The *Los Angeles Times* handled the matter by printing several opinion pieces over the next few days about outing and the injustice of the military policy against gays—again without naming Williams. The paper also ran an editorial condemning the ban. New York *Daily News* columnist Richard Johnson named Williams, and the next day an editorial in the paper called for "an army for all." *The Miami Herald* attacked the Pentagon's policy as "discriminatory, hypocritical and rooted in stereotypes that won't survive scrutiny," and demanded an executive order from President Bush to end the ban. "The outing of a senior Pentagon official may be the lever that changes the military's unwise and unfair ban on gays," stated the *San Francisco Examiner* in an editorial.

Within days, hundreds of papers across the country followed the leads and, in lengthy, sometimes angry editorials, demanded that the military end its ban. Scores of papers suddenly discovered the story of gays-in-the-military for the first time, and ran investigative pieces on the issues as well as profiles of people who'd been booted out of the service because they were queer. Finally the national spotlight illuminated the issue. *The Wall Street Journal* reported that service-people who'd announced their homosexuality (or had been found out) during the Persian Gulf conflict had been allowed to remain and fight, but would be kicked out now that the war was over. This enraged many editors and reporters who couldn't believe that these good soldiers would be dumped. Some papers used that story, and the personal stories of those who'd been thrown out, as a way to cover the outing of Williams and name him.

At the *Detroit Free Press*, which had to match its competitor, *The Detroit News*, Frank Bruni, an openly gay reporter who had been assigned to Saudi Arabia during the Persian Gulf War, named the name on August 12 in a front-page story headlined GAY TROOPS FACE UNFRIENDLY FIRE:[10]

> With Scuds blazing over their desert camp and troops on alert for terrorists, Marine Cpl. Erik Barker's superiors decided to spend their time investigating him for being gay. . . .

In the U.S. military, it doesn't matter how fierce your courage or deep your commitment. If you are homosexual—and Barker is—you're not wanted. That policy came under fresh scrutiny last week when a gay publication asserted that Pentagon spokesman Pete Williams is gay.

The Washington Post, meanwhile, came under fire for censoring Jack Anderson's column. Michael Petrelis wasn't about to let assistant managing editor Karen DeYoung off the hook. Petrelis had been propelling the story, keeping the media informed and vigorously pushing for them to cover it and to name Williams. First Petrelis called DeYoung at her office. She was adamant about not naming Williams. Then he called her at her home. She was even more adamant. By the time I called her, also at home, she was extremely tense. I could hear her baby crying in the background, and a man was talking loudly. I lost my temper and hung up on her.

A *Post* staffer later informed me that, at the precise moment when I called, DeYoung and her husband were having a fight about whether or not the *Post* should name Williams—a fight that had been going on for weeks. At NBC, where he was a producer, DeYoung's husband had supported naming Williams; this was to no avail, and he was trying to persuade his wife that it was the right thing to do. Within weeks, perhaps as a compromise in the DeYoung marital dispute, there was a front-page story in the *Post* about the Pentagon's policy; it mentioned only an outed "Pentagon official." It followed by days an editorial demanding that Cheney act as Harry S Truman had when he ended segregation in the armed forces.

In sheer impact and column inches, the *Washington Post* editorial was outdone weeks later by *The New York Times*'s, a tardy piece that came, perhaps, only after some prodding. When the *Advocate* article first appeared on newsstands, I sent it to *Times* national editor Soma Golden. Shortly after that, I spoke to her on the telephone. The only reference to the issue in the *Times* had been the seventy-five-word squib about Cheney's comments on the Brinkley show. No stories on the problem of gays in the military, although the *Times* had covered the issue in the past. No commentaries about the Pentagon's antigay policy. No opinion pieces about outing. And no editorial condemning the Pentagon.

"Ms. Golden," I said, "what the military is doing to these people is criminal. There is a contradiction evident. There is a story here."

"Tell me some angles on the story," she said.

I began: "Well, there's the issue of how the gay community is examining one of its own members, calling him to account and pointing out how, with this antigay policy, it is hypocritical of Pete Williams to—"

"Tell me another one," she interrupted, making it clear that the *Times* wasn't going to go near the outing issue. Golden had been one of the editors who made the decision to name the Palm Beach accuser, and had been at the epicenter of the criticism.

"Well, there's the story of how the Pentagon seems to be backing away from the policy—as indicated by its reaction to assertions that an 'official' is gay—and may actually be reviewing it internally, since some documents were recently revealed that indicated that," I said.

"Right, well, that may well be a good story," she said. "Yes, that seems like something that we could do. I'll look into it. Thank you."

When no story showed up in the next week, I sent a copy of the *Advocate* article to assistant editorial-page editor Philip Boffey, who used to cover the AIDS beat in Washington. I included a note pointing out that much of the media had extensively covered the Williams outing, or the issue of gays in the military, or both, and that many papers had run editorials condemning the ban, but that the *Times* really hadn't done much at all.

Within two weeks—two weeks *after* everyone else had done it—the *Times* ran an unusually long editorial, complete with a graph showing increasing public support for overturning the ban. Well worth the wait, "Gay Soldiers, Good Soldiers" pointed out the Pentagon's hypocrisy:

> The Defense Department is actually two-faced on the subject of homosexuality. Homosexuals are allowed to serve in civilian jobs, even at the highest and most sensitive levels. . . . That is why Secretary of Defense Dick Cheney has no trouble retaining a trusted aide who was identified as homosexual by a gay magazine.
>
> But the department bans homosexuals from military service and has discharged more than 13,000 people as homosexuals since 1982. What consenting adults do on their own time is their business,

not the military's. The military and its overseers need to reexamine the case; there's no evident justification for discrimination on the basis of sexual orientation.

Though the editorial was immensely valuable, the most powerful news organization in the country had some of the worst coverage of the entire affair. (The only paper with a poorer record was the *San Francisco Chronicle*.) The *Times* put its head in the sand rather than deal with the issue because, according to a staffer, editors didn't want to appear as if they had been manipulated by activists. (Of course, they don't think twice about the fact that politicians manipulate them regularly.)

Newspapers weren't the only print outlets that were all over the map about how to handle—or avoid—the story; the newsmagazines scrambled too, each taking a different approach. *U.S. News & World Report* waited several weeks, only to run a small squib about the policy and the "Pentagon official." *Newsweek*, anticipating early on what was to occur, did a major piece, which ran the very week the Williams story hit. "The Age of 'Outing' " mentioned "a Defense Department official" who was going to be outed "this week." That made moot the question of naming Williams after the outing: The magazine had already covered the issue. *Time* went with "Marching out of the Closet," an excellent article that ran the week after the *Advocate* piece and, unlike the sensationalistic *Newsweek* piece, covered the topic of gays in the military in depth. "Marching" profiled four individuals who had been thrown out of the military, showed how other countries have dealt with the issue, and pointed out "gay warriors" of the past, including Alexander the Great, Richard the Lion-Hearted, and Lawrence of Arabia. "The Pentagon found its rationale [for banning gays] under severe attack last week when *The Advocate* . . . claimed that a prominent Defense Department official was homosexual," *Time* reported. "The flurry of criticism has Pentagon officials squirming to justify a policy whose existence and enforcement seem at so at odds with the realities of American society."

While the metropolitan dailies and the national newsweeklies contorted themselves strangely in dealing with the outing of Pete Williams, *USA Today*, "The Nation's Newspaper," had by far the most peculiar coverage of all. Tracking this storm for weeks, printing little items here and there about where the story was going next, the national daily dutifully ran a longer piece when Cheney backed away from the policy. This article mentioned the "Pentagon official" being outed. But, on August 7, the paper printed another story about an interview that Cheney and Williams had given *USA Today* days before. The two were in the *USA Today* offices to discuss the fate of the U.S. military bases in the Philippines. In the weirdest twist thus far, *USA Today* mentioned the unnamed "Pentagon official" and quoted Williams's defense of the antigay policy—both in the same paragraph—without letting on that Williams *was* the "Pentagon official":

> Cheney also said Tuesday that he has no plans to change a policy barring homosexuals from serving in the military. "It is not under review at present," he said. "I can't say no, absolutely never, that it wouldn't happen. But I don't at this point have any plans to change the policy." He stressed that the ban did not extend to civilian jobs at the Pentagon. At least one newspaper for homosexuals has reported that a senior Pentagon civilian official is homosexual. "The policy is different because military service is different," said Cheney. Earlier, Pentagon spokesman Pete Williams said homosexuality was "not per se solely grounds for denying" a security clearance to a Defense Department civilian.

That was actually what Williams had said the previous day, during a Pentagon news briefing, soon after he was asked if reports of his gayness were true.

The *Advocate* story had been out for several days by this time, and the outing had been covered nationally, yet none of the dozens of reporters who gathered in the Pentagon press room twice weekly for Williams's press briefing had yet popped the "Is it true that you're gay?" question—and it didn't appear as if they would. While most Washington political reporters, bureau chiefs, and middle-level editors and TV news producers wanted the story to be reported, most Pentagon reporters of those same news organizations were adamantly opposed.

These reporters, concerned with protecting their sources inside the Pentagon and their relationships with those sources, don't like to make waves. Making waves would cost them that next scoop about other issues that, to them, are far more important than antigay bigotry. The Persian Gulf conflict, which had occurred only months before, had made them even less likely to go after the Pentagon.

Pentagon reporters had been mesmerized by Williams during the months prior to Operation Desert Storm, when information about the impending conflict was guarded more closely than that concerning any other conflict in U.S. history. They sat before him twice a week for the regular briefings; he fed them small scraps of information carefully selected by the Pentagon. His hold over them became even firmer during the war itself; in news-poor briefings, the Pentagon strictly controlled all information disseminated. Unprecedented press restrictions kept reporters from the front lines. There were never any photos or television footage of actual combat, and few reporters were able to glimpse the reality of the fighting. All reports of what was occurring on the battlefields were given out by the Pentagon itself. A lawsuit launched jointly by many news organizations failed in getting them access, and newspeople were at the mercy of the Pentagon for the duration of the war. This put them in a terrible bind: Beyond their simple thirst to get the truth, reporters had jobs to do—they had to get *something* on the air or in print. Suddenly, those little bits of news and information dangled by the Pentagon became commodities for which the news media had to compete against each other. Anyone who misbehaved wasn't going to get thrown a bone at all.

The Pentagon had trained the reporters like Pavlov's dogs; attacking Williams would be like biting the hand that made them salivate. The reporters admired and respected Williams—and they weren't averse to saying so in interviews. For that reason, Williams was one of the best weapons in the Pentagon's arsenal during Operation Desert Storm. He kept the dogs at bay and kept criticism of the Pentagon's censorship to a minimum. By the time he was outed, his charm had enraptured these reporters utterly; they were almost irrationally defensive about him. An *L.A. Times* Pentagon reporter lashed out at anyone who brought up the subject of the outing. A London *Times* reporter characterized the entire affair as "despicable." One network correspondent said with sorrow, "This is just so awful for Pete." A reporter from *Defense Week* said he had orders not to bring up the subject. Other reporters said that word had come from the very top that under no circumstances were they to broach the issue. It didn't take much for them to comply; the Pentagon press dogs were mad as hell at the crazed activists who had assaulted the privacy of their master.

Of course, not every reporter jumped through the Pentagon's hoops, but even the few not jumping weren't about to risk their Pulitzers for a few thousand queer soldiers. The gays-in-the-military issue was *not* at that time an issue to straight reporters looking to make a big hit, not one they were willing to antagonize the Pentagon over, not one that would get them very far in their own careers. The public didn't care about this subject, they reasoned. Their own editors and producers weren't so interested either. If a reporter was going to take on the Pentagon it was going to be over something that would make a big splash: the 25 percent of American casualties that resulted from "friendly fire" (in other wars the figure was less than 2 percent) or the truth about how the Pentagon used bulldozers to bury thousands of Iraqi soldiers alive. But revealing that hardworking American queers were being driven to suicide because of an unjust policy, while a top Pentagon official was gay and wasn't being put on the spot about the issue—well, that wouldn't win anyone an award. That was only going to get them in trouble.

Disingenuously, many of the Pentagon reporters referred to *The Village Voice*'s refusal to run the Pete Williams outing as proof that outing was wrong. After all, many of them said, if the politically correct *Voice*, a supposed champion of gay rights, wouldn't touch it, outing couldn't be the right thing to do. Of course, most of the time these same reporters laugh at the *Voice* and other leftist journals; they certainly don't take cues from them. In fact, most of what is printed in the *Voice*, even its criticisms of the ethics of the mainstream media, goes unnoticed by the arrogant mainstream press corps. Suddenly though, working themselves into a moralistic fervor, reporters deferred to the *Voice*'s ethics in the most devout way. In the end, as usual, the left and its press, so caught up in pedantry, were being used to .stall the liberation of their own. To get out of this mess, every mainstream press person had only to feign *Village Voice*-style moral indignation.

But on the morning of Tuesday, August 6, the Pentagon press

corps, as up in arms as it may have been about the pressure to out Pete, had to deal yet again with Michael Petrelis. The intrepid activist—uncharacteristically dapper in a white shirt, red tie, and blue blazer—showed up at the entrance to the Pentagon where the reporters enter for the Tuesday- and Thursday-morning briefings, with a box filled with copies of the *Advocate* story. There, half an hour before the briefing, he held a press conference in which once again he outed Pete Williams and this time chastised the press for trying to avoid the story. The gathered journalists, as irritated as they may have been about the outing, were nonetheless hungry reporters, and snapped up copies of the article. They hovered around Petrelis, getting sound bites and interviewing him. None of their stories, of course, ever saw print or made it on the air. After the press conference, Petrelis badgered the reporters to ask Williams about his outing and about the policy. He received an avalanche of hostility. "How can you violate Pete's right to privacy?" reporters kept asking, annoyed and upset. Petrelis simply replied, "As Barney Frank says, there is no right to hypocrisy."

After Petrelis held court for a while, several Pentagon office workers came out and began heckling him. "Leave Pete alone!" one of them angrily screamed. "Pete's a nice guy. What if he loses his job?" Petrelis shouted back, "The thousands of lesbians and gays who've been discharged are also nice people. What about *their* jobs?" By then, most of the press people had gone off to read the *Advocate* article and confer with each other. CNN's Wolf Blitzer, still present, covered the shouting match and interviewed Petrelis extensively. Even Blitzer's story never ran.

Only one reporter watching the press conference was interested in following up on what Petrelis had to say. Rolf Paasch had spoken to Petrelis the day before; they'd known each other from some of Petrelis's previous actions with Queer Nation. Paasch is a German reporter who at the time was working for Berlin's *Die Tageszeitung,* a leftist daily. Petrelis knew, from the reactions he'd gotten from Pentagon reporters in the previous days, that if anyone was going to put the question to Williams, it was going to be an outsider.

"Although I'm usually against outing," Paasch says, "I thought this was one of the few cases where the right of privacy should be waived. I thought it was hypocritical for Williams to be gay and yet defend the policy. But what weighed most in my decision was that Dick Cheney had already said [on *This Week with David Brinkley*] that he would not ask Williams to resign. Thus I believed that by naming him, by asking the question and getting it in the public record, it would not harm his career."

Paasch, who doesn't usually cover the Pentagon, called the Pentagon that morning so that he could get credentials for the day. Foreign correspondents are usually afforded this courtesy because they are only in town for a short time and can't go through the usual waiting period. Strict rules determine American reporters' access to both Pentagon and White House briefings. Background checks are carried out, and there is a waiting period; officials can refuse a reporter credentials, or terminate them, without offering any reason for the decision. This is all part of the government's way of controlling who gets into the briefing room and then keeping those admitted in line. (In one instance during the 1992 presidential campaign, CNN White House correspondent Mary Tillotson asked Bush at a press conference at his Kennebunkport, Maine, vacation home about press reports of the alleged affair between him and his former appointments secretary Jennifer Fitzgerald. White House spokesman Marlin Fitzwater subsequently told a *New York Times* reporter that Tillotson would "never work around the White House again.")

Paasch had asked some of the other reporters, beforehand, if they had intentions of bringing up the *Advocate* story. "They were waffling," he recalls. "Nobody said no, but nobody said, 'Yes, I'm going to ask the question.'"

The press briefing went on for over half an hour; it was mostly about MIAs in Vietnam and people killed by "friendly fire" in the Gulf. Paasch raised his hand. "There are some groups and newspapers that challenge [*sic*] that the Pentagon spokesperson is gay," Paasch began. "Can you confirm or deny that? And have you talked with Secretary Cheney about possible resignation?"

A collective groan reverberated throughout the room. Some reporters even hissed. "I felt as if I had intruded on some cozy little club," says Paasch. "I'd said the wrong thing."

Williams, a master of poise, didn't flinch, and quickly answered: "Well, if you're asking me whether some groups have said that, I can confirm that some groups have said that, yes. But I assume that's not your question. As a government spokesman, I stand here and I talk about government policy. I am not paid to discuss my personal opinions about that policy or talk about my personal life, and I don't intend to. And the other answer I'll give you to your question is one that won't surprise people in this room. Government people don't discuss in public whatever they may say to their bosses."

Suddenly, another reporter in the room became brave, and threw out another question:

REPORTER: Pete? Following up, did the Secretary's comments on the Sunday talk shows reflect a change in official policy toward the granting of security clearances to DOD civilians who are homosexual?

WILLIAMS: No. My impression was he was stating the current policy.

REPORTER: Well, if so, then how— It appears that people in the past have been denied clearances on that basis.

WILLIAMS: My understanding of the policy is that it is not per se solely grounds for denying someone security clearance.

At that moment, an Associated Press reporter, clearly seeing that Williams was uncomfortable, ended the briefing.

"Afterwards, I was standing around and some of the journalists— only a handful, maybe four or five [out of approximately thirty-six reporters]—took down my name," recalls Paasch. "I remember somebody saying, 'Oh, maybe I'll be able to get this in now that someone else asked the question.' A few people made complimentary remarks, saying they were glad that someone brought it up."

Glad as they may have been, few of them were able to "get it in." But the exchange would forever be public record, available on the media database Nexis and in an official Defense Department transcript. Several news outlets were able to use it at the time: KPIX, San Francisco's CBS affiliate, televised it.

Paasch's popping the question also proved invaluable to all the reporters who later wrote stories on gays in the military and on the Pete Williams outing. In the following weeks and months, as monthly magazines published stories about the outing and the issues surrounding it, and as newspapers did follow-ups, they'd quote Pete Williams responding at that press conference, more secure in naming him months later when the spotlight wasn't on the media regarding the hot issue.

In that respect, newspapers like *The Philadelphia Inquirer*, which waited several weeks and then printed a commentary piece that named Williams, and magazines like *Details*, which named Williams months later in a story on gays in the military, not only would have Williams's response to the outing in their pieces, but—because they waited—would avoid the barrage of initial attacks by anti-outing pundits on all those who'd named Williams. In previous weeks, it had been precisely the fear of these frenzied attacks that made so much of the media tremble, and eventually cower, not using Williams's name. Dreading censure by grandstanding columnists (some of whom, of course, were closeted gays) and doing whatever they could to avoid it, the American media were once again effectively crippled. Pertinent questions regarding a major American scandal within a hypocritical American institution were left to be asked by a lone foreign journalist—and only at the urging of members of the very group that had suffered brutal treatment by that institution for decades.

Even so, in the ensuing debate over the ethics of outing, for the first time defenses of outing began to appear in the mainstream press, both in commentaries and in letters to the editor. Almost uniformly, the gay press moved on outing too, not only naming Williams but often championing outing. A change also occurred among some leaders of established gay organizations. Previously opposed to outing, they now stayed quiet or, in some cases, voiced approval.

In the past, the anti-outers had been criticized only by a small group of radical queer activists. But now those same anti-outing arguments started to crumble under scrutiny in the mainstream as well. Public opinion on the left, in the gay community, and among members of the media themselves began to shift dramatically. Outing was now seen to be justified at least in cases of hypocrisy.

This shift had the anti-outers furious—more so than ever before. They were losing ground and their desperation was starting to show. Beginning the week after the Pete Williams outing, what seemed like a concerted effort got under way not only to attack outing, but also to demonize the outers.

8

Outing, Part II

Whatever the differences among gay men and lesbians, there was always a sense that everyone was essentially on the same side," wrote Andrew Sullivan, now the openly gay editor of the influential Washington magazine *The New Republic*, responding to the Pete Williams scenario and referring to outers.[11] "Now I'm not so sure."

Sullivan had come out as gay in the late eighties, when he was a writer for the magazine. When he was named its editor in 1992, at the age of twenty-eight, Sullivan became a media personality. Young, gay, and unabashedly conservative, he offered opinions that not only angered many lesbian and gay activists but disturbed many feminists as well.

Sullivan came to the defense of Dan Quayle in the early nineties but had harsh words for queer activists. A devout Catholic, he had been incensed by ACT UP's actions, especially its civil disobedience inside St. Patrick's Cathedral in New York in December 1989. He had also lambasted *OutWeek*. "That some of this material [in *OutWeek*] is presented as camp merely heightens the ugliness of the message," he wrote in *The New Republic* in 1990. But despite his criticisms, Sullivan acknowledged "cogent arguments" in favor of outing.

Many gays and lesbians were readier to accept outing by the time the Pete Williams outing article appeared a year later in *The Advocate*, but Sullivan seemed to go the other way. Perhaps that was partially because Pete Williams is a friend of his, a fact that Sullivan declined to include in his *New Republic* critique of the outing, published the week after the outing occurred. Entitled "Sleeping with the Enemy," the piece offered the right-to-privacy arguments against outing and, of course, did not name Williams:

> It's not so much that, within the gay world, there are now those who have assumed the rhetoric of the historic enemy. Nor even that, in the heat of battle, some have taken to desecrating others' religious beliefs and practices, embracing the very forms of intolerance that homosexuals, of all people, have historically shrunk from. It is that they have attacked the central protection of gay people themselves.... The gleam in the eyes of the outers, I have come reluctantly to understand, is not the excess of youth or the passion of the radical. It is the gleam of the authoritarian.

Regardless of his conservative and religious views, Andrew Sullivan has brought some important stories about gays to his magazine. In commentaries he has offered some enlightened, thought-provoking arguments.

However, he failed to view outing from a journalistic perspective and was resolved to look at it only from a personal one. This is fairly common among gay journalists, but it was strange coming from Sullivan, who had always advocated that gay journalists must be journalists first and gay second, that they should operate in the supposedly unbiased way that journalists have traditionally been told to operate. Yet outing proponents seek just that objectivity; they ask that editors and reporters look at the issue of homosexuality from a purely journalistic perspective and treat it just as they treat heterosexuality.

Certainly outing does not "take into account the complexities of people's lives," as Sullivan has said. But how much of journalism does take into account the complexities of people's lives? It's impossible, in the space a reporter is given, to do so—no matter what the topic.

Still, the news must be reported, and the reporter must do the best job he or she can do given the constraints.

As for the anguish outing causes, so much else of what journalists report to the public is *equally* painful to the people scrutinized. Journalists are not in the business of providing comfort or making people feel better. They're in the business of telling the truth, whatever it is, whenever it is pertinent to a story. This doesn't mean that journalists can't, on a human level, feel for their subjects, especially if they're friendly with them.

Sullivan reduced outing to something initiated by "fringe activists" against "gay people at odds with [the fringe's] agenda." Outing might have been originated in recent times by queer street activists and subsequently been taken up by journalists who are gay, but by the time of the Pete Williams affair, it had become a larger movement within the media. Contrary to Sullivan's assertions, journalistic outing is not aimed at all gay people who are not following an "agenda," but at *public figures* and only when pertinent to a story that may or may not have anything to do with an "agenda"—liberal or conservative.

Like Sullivan, openly gay *San Francisco Chronicle* national correspondent Randy Shilts, who died of complications from AIDS in February 1994, had waffled on the issue of outing, yet often came down hard on those who espoused an opinion favoring it.

Shilts wrote for *The Advocate* and other gay publications in the late seventies and early eighties and was involved in San Francisco politics in those years. In 1985, he won raves for his first book, *The Mayor of Castro Street*, about the life of slain gay San Francisco supervisor Harvey Milk. Joining the *San Francisco Chronicle* in 1982, Shilts was one of the first people covering the AIDS epidemic in the eighties. In 1987, shortly after Shilts tested positive for HIV, *And the Band Played On*, his powerful and momentous best-seller about the AIDS crisis, was published. It was a landmark book that documented the epidemic and the bungled response to it by the government, the medical establishment, and the gay community itself. With the publication of *And the Band Played On*, Shilts had become an important gay media spokesperson.

There was an overriding reason why the media took to Shilts at the time: The scandal that propelled his book to fame wasn't the most dangerous one—the fact that the government had willfully neglected the AIDS epidemic—but the most palatable one: how the gay community was also to blame for letting the crisis go on. While the bulk of the book documents the scandalous ways in which the government refused to handle the epidemic, the first wave of press about it focused on the thesis that HIV was spread by the recklessness of one man, a flight attendant named Gaetan Dugas, whom Shilts dubbed Patient Zero. The media, seizing upon the story, called him the Typhoid Mary of AIDS. (Shilts's farfetched scenario later came under sharp criticism from health experts and others.) The press also focused on the owners of gay bathhouses, whom Shilts charged with reckless behavior. The third aspect of Shilts's book the press initially picked up on was that some gay leaders, initially seeing AIDS as a public-relations problem, tried to downplay the health crisis and stymied efforts to educate and enlighten the gay community.

That first wave of publicity on the book, in the first week of October 1987, took the form of a backlash against gays. THE MAN WHO GAVE US AIDS, blared the front-page headline of the *New York Post*, referring to Shilts's Patient Zero. The Associated Press ran two stories on the wire, headlined PORTRAIT OF THE MAN WHO MAY HAVE BROUGHT AIDS TO NORTH AMERICA and GAY COMMUNITY WAS SLOW TO REACT ADEQUATELY TO AIDS EPIDEMIC. It was, thus, inevitable that a week later the more sensational press would have a field day. *People* headlined its story PATIENT ZERO, ALSO KNOWN AS GAETAN DUGAS, WHOSE FIERCE SEXUAL DRIVE GAVE IMPETUS TO AN EPIDEMIC THAT CLAIMED HIS LIFE AND THOUSANDS MORE. The right-wing ate up the new "proof" that homosexuals were dangerous. "If Gaetan Dugas had not introduced the virus here," opined *The National Review*, "some other homosexual undoubtedly would have."

It was the media's negligence and homophobia—not Shilts—that impelled them to shamelessly and sensationally focus on these issues and only secondarily cover (if they noticed it at all) the larger message of Shilts's book. But Shilts seemed to play right into the circus that took place in the mainstream media soon after his book was published. Seen less as an activist attacking the powers that be than as a critical commentator on the gay movement itself, Shilts was just the kind of television-talk-show spokesperson the media liked at that time. In interviews, in op-ed pieces, and on talk shows, Shilts attacked the establishment—the media, the government, private industry—for its homophobia and negligence, but as long as he also attacked the gay community for this disease that straights were now afraid of getting, editors and producers would be sure to invite him back. In their bias-tinged perceptions, Shilts was "fair" and provided "balance" rather than behaving like what they called a pure "advocate." The problem, of course, was that, in this virulently antigay society, the messages that resonated most were the ones faulting the gay community for the AIDS pandemic.

Shilts continued to call for the government's closing of gay bathhouses, touching off a firestorm of controversy. Many AIDS-education professionals in fact felt that the baths were a way to reach people and teach them about safer sex and that closing them down was a moralistic action that benefited no one.

Shilts soon came under attack by AIDS activists for that reason as well as for what they saw as his exploiting of the gay community's role in helping the epidemic to mushroom. He stood his ground, however, explaining that he had to do his job: He couldn't hide the fact that the community hadn't wanted to face the epidemic in the early years, he said.

Soon after ACT UP formed, Shilts began attacking the group— once again getting a lot of press attention for bludgeoning gay radicals, and ceasing only when the media came to realize, years later, that ACT UP was a productive organization in the fight against AIDS. Later, Shilts went after Queer Nation as well. He had clearly developed a pattern: He consistently allowed himself to be used by the media to chastise gay activists. And the media played him up, just as they had for years spotlighted prominent women who attacked feminists.

In early 1990, when *OutWeek* outed Malcolm Forbes, I had appeared on *Larry King Live* with Randy Shilts, who agreed that the media cover up for people who are gay. He condemned the media for bearding closeted gays, and he criticized powerful closeted people for hiding, but he made sure to point out that as a "professional" journalist, he could never out a living person. I was marginalized as a "radical," and Shilts positioned himself as the voice of reason.

Weeks before the Pete Williams story ran in *The Advocate*, but after it had been circulated throughout the media, I spoke with Shilts on the telephone. He had been working on a book about gays in the military and was certainly an expert. Our interaction was cordial and friendly, as our past dealings had been, and, though we discussed some of the reservations people had about outing, he was fairly supportive of what I was doing. He also agreed that a lot of the media were going to jump on the story.

However, as the publication of the story neared, I began to hear conflicting reports about what Shilts planned to do as national correspondent of the *San Francisco Chronicle*. He'd told someone that there was no way he was going to advise his paper to take the lead, and that he'd go with the story only if the networks did.

When it became clear that most of the major news organizations were not going to take the risk and name Williams, Shilts not only advised his paper against outing Williams but wrote a piece in which he attacked outers more strongly than ever before. The article appeared in the *San Francisco Chronicle* and the *Los Angeles Times*. Shilts acknowledged that "before this Pentagon outing, no national reporter found the issue important enough to ask the questions that have resulted in some very serious backpedaling on Cheney's policies." But, as he had always done in the past, he bashed the radicals:

> No matter how high-sounding the rhetoric, outing makes some of the most august gay journalists and leaders look like a lot of bitchy queens on the set of *Boys in the Band*, bent not on helping each other but on clawing each other. It's not a pretty sight.
>
> As for the nastiness of outing, whether outing is done to Army privates by Pentagon policy or to prominent officials by the gay press, it's still a dirty business that hurts people.

In asserting that outing is a "dirty business that hurts people," Shilts failed to grasp that outing is simply another part of journalism, which itself is a business whose first priority is not to protect people or their feelings but to tell the truth. His remark that outing makes gay journalists look like "bitchy queens," and his references to *The Boys in the Band* and "clawing," reeked of self-loathing.

Almost a year after the Williams outing, at the landmark first conference of the National Lesbian and Gay Journalists Association in San Francisco, Shilts continued to demonize outers and Queer

Nation, both of which he attacked disingenuously, calling them "lavender fascists" and comparing them to Nazi "brownshirts." He didn't seem to catch the irony: He—a man who had called for the government-imposed curtailing of sexual activity years earlier—was attacking others as fascists. Invited to speak about gays in the military, he spoke mostly about "some gay journalists" at "some gay magazines" (I was at that time writing a regular column for *The Advocate*), whom he lumped together with the outers and the "lavender fascists." All of these people, he said, wore "piercings" and "bandannas" and had "tattoos" and wanted all gays to dress that way too. He warned that they also wanted to control the thoughts of everyone in the gay community as well. Shilts then told the dumbfounded audience that these fascists and proponents of outing—something he now compared to "a third-grader stomping his foot and yelling, 'Do what I want you to or I'll tell on you!'"—must be "banished" from the community.

By then, it had become clear to what lengths people would go in their attempts to exploit the emotionally charged issue of outing.

· · · · ·

Time magazine's William Henry III, an original anti-outer and the man who coined the negative term "outing" back in 1989, again attacked outing after the Pete Williams story appeared.[12] Henry is obsessed with this issue, and that obsession has led him to dabble in distortions.

Accompanying *Time*'s excellent piece that week on gays in the military was Henry's one-page commentary, "To Out or Not to Out," in which, knowing that the vast majority of his readers would never have seen the *Advocate* story, he altered facts and dwelled on irrelevant circumstances. "In a blatant bid for publicity and newsstand sales, [*The Advocate*] faxed dozens of advance copies to mainstream journalists," he smugly reported, as if *Time* had never done anything of the kind with a hot story. Henry gave the impression that the *Advocate* article was shabby and unsubstantiated:

> Most of the people Signorile quoted had only hearsay knowledge. Their main "evidence" was that the official had supposedly been a regular customer in years gone by at a predominantly gay Washington bar. The few sources who claimed firsthand knowledge

about him were generally permitted to remain anonymous. Even some unnamed sources knew nothing themselves but were merely quoting still more obscure acquaintances; in one anecdote an unidentified man said an apparent one-night stand, picked up in a bar, told him of having dated the official.

Hardly any serious newspaper, magazine or network would accept so loosely sourced a story from its own staff. Yet few journalists tried to verify the claims in *The Advocate* before repeating its main point.

On the contrary, *most* of the people quoted in the story who discussed Williams's sexuality knew *firsthand*, not from "hearsay knowledge." The main "evidence" was not, as Henry wrote, that Williams had been a regular in a bar; it was direct quotes from people who had slept with him and been involved with him and from people who were his friends; there was also Williams's own refusal, when I spoke to him on the telephone, to deny that he was gay. Williams wasn't "supposedly" a regular at that bar—he *was a regular*, as several people pointed out. That wasn't "in years gone by"; it was several months earlier, as was stated by one patron cited in the article. The bar wasn't "predominantly gay"; it was gay all the way, and very well known to be—even, one assumes, known to William Henry III. There were no "unnamed sources [who] knew nothing themselves but were merely quoting still more obscure acquaintances"—Henry simply made that up. And the man Henry says had "an apparent one-night stand" with a man who had "dated" Williams was not "unidentified." His name, Stephen Smith, was in the article with his permission. Henry failed to mention my lengthy telephone conversation with Williams. Nor did he report that I'd spoken to friends of Williams's, and that those conversations also implied that Williams was gay.

Many prominent newspapers have run with stories based on sources that met much less stringent criteria than those Henry said were *The Advocate*'s. Woodward and Bernstein's Watergate stories, of course, were based on unnamed sources. Clearly the reason that papers ran with the Williams outing story was because they felt the sourcing was solid—more solid than Henry suggested in *Time*. Besides, Pentagon and Washington reporters had known for a long time that Williams was gay. It was common knowledge in Washington. Other news organizations checked my sourcing themselves. Still others, not for attribution but for their own background purposes, had their own sources, independent of mine.

When the topic is outing, however, logic and facts don't seem to matter. At the respected *Washington Journalism Review,* then-editor Bill Monroe compared the Williams case to the Palm Beach rape trial and applauded the bulk of the press corps for not "savaging the privacy of a public figure" in both cases. Congratulating American journalism, he said that "critics of the press" should "remember the summer of '91 when most of the press respected the privacy of a Florida woman in a sensational rape case and the privacy of a Pentagon official targeted as gay."

Such comparisons are insulting to all gay people—and to rape victims as well. Rape is a horrible crime committed against a person; homosexuality is an identity equal to heterosexuality. A closeted individual is asking a community of lesbians and gays—and straights as well—to be complicit in his or her cowering silence—is even asking them to lie—in order to cover up something that those other lesbians and gays don't think is a bad thing. Being gay is not something that is forced on a victim in an act of violence; it is a part of an identity, something that has always been there and something that, free from moral judgments, feels normal.

Monroe's primary reason for saying that the media acted wisely in not naming Williams falls even flatter: "Signorile himself seemed uneasy about what he was doing," he wrote. Monroe then recounted my conversation with Williams, pointing out how I told Williams that this was "one of those things in this job that you have to do, but which you might not necessarily feel so comfortable with." Monroe strangely omitted the conversation's most pertinent line: Williams's statement that he was "completely comfortable" in his job as spokesperson for the Department of Defense.

The editor of the *Washington Journalism Review* surely could not think that the basis for doing a story should be the reporter's easiness or uneasiness about it. Following that logic, half the stories in print would never be done. It's a rationale against outing that runs along the same lines as Randy Shilts's "dirty business" argument. No editor or reporter worth his or her salt needs to be reminded that journalism is not a feel-good profession or that reporters often have to do research and interviews that may make them "uneasy."

WJR is read by people in the news media and by students and professors in journalism schools across America. Its readers regularly write letters and communicate with the publication, which, like the *Columbia Journalism Review,* is at the center of the regularly occurring debates in American journalism.

Not a single letter agreeing with Monroe appeared in the next issue of *WJR.* Several people wrote in to criticize him; all of them tried to name Williams in their letters, only to find the name replaced with "[name deleted]." Someone identified as M. Burton, from Austin, Texas, canceled his or her subscription to *WJR* in protest:

> Monroe wrote that the issue of privacy was more important in this case than the public's right to know because [name deleted] . . . "had no record of anti-gay activities." But the Department of Defense has a long and vicious record of anti-gay activities. [Name deleted] was quoted in *The Advocate* as being "completely comfortable with everything I do in my job for the Pentagon." If that is so, then his gayness is relevant to report. To compare this person's gayness to the Palm Beach rape case, as Monroe did, is to compare apples and oranges. . . . This blatant censorship only serves to insult the intelligence of your readers. I am not gay, but I am outraged at your magazine's conduct. My renewal money is not enclosed.

Thom Prentice, a lecturer in the journalism department of Southwest Texas State University, was even more harsh:

> *The Washington Journalism Review*—the sword and shield of the First Amendment and the scourge of the censors, news management and flackish spinmeisters—decided it, too, liked to wear the drag of the heavy-handed, self-righteous censor. The perverse, twisted, obscene sense of *noblesse oblige* that motivated *WJR* and its editor to "protect" the so-called privacy of [name deleted] is sick. . . .
>
> Surely we can all understand that Washington reporters are dependent (co-dependent? addicted? slavish?) to their Washington sources—sources such as [name deleted] and his minions.
>
> The censorship of this issue and *WJR*'s sick, self-righteous justi-

fication of censorship make me want to vomit. Everyone at *WJR* involved in this Nixonian/Zieglerian decision to cover up the [name deleted] hypocrisy in high public office story should apologize or resign. If you don't want to cover the news, then get out. Sell shoes.

Indeed, the letters pages of many papers, if they are an indication of the public's feelings on issues, were reflecting a change. There was little moral outrage about the Pete Williams outing; there was no barrage of letters attacking the publications that had named him or attacking the so-called radicals who had outed him. On the contrary, there were many letters, à la those in *WJR*, attacking the newspapers themselves for *not* naming Williams. While *Time* printed only one letter on the subject (from *The Advocate*, correcting Henry's inaccuracies), the *San Francisco Chronicle* and the *L.A. Times* both printed several letters criticizing Shilts's anti-outing piece as well as the papers themselves for not naming Williams. Both papers had, alongside Shilts's original piece, printed a pro-outing article by Marshal Alan Phillips, who writes often on public-policy issues. Readers wrote in supporting Phillips. His argument compared homosexuality to other facts that reporters regularly reveal:

> If a public figure is Jewish or Jehovah's Witness or Hindu, divorced or married or single, Asian or Icelandic or Kenyan, those personal and private facts, if verified, may be duly reported. No need for an on-the-record admission. Only in the case of gays does this silly rule of invisibility apply.
> It is based on the hackneyed straight assumption that, somehow, being a gay person is innately bad. Never mind that such a person may be well-bred, well-educated and doing a terrific job, have a stable romantic relationship, even attend church every Sunday. If he or she is gay, the media pulls a pious veil of privacy around that fact. Why? Because doing otherwise would confirm the terrifying (to straight folks) truth that gays are normal, happy, well-adjusted, hard-working, capable and everywhere. If you're not gay, you know someone who is.

"We know everything about heterosexuals, every affair, every gynecological fact," agreed *The Detroit News*'s Michael McWilliams in a *WJR* story that accompanied Monroe's musings. "But you won't see anything in print about homosexuality and that suggests that it's the worst thing in the world." John Corporon, news director at New York's WPIX, the first broadcast outlet to name Williams, told *WJR* in defense of his station's actions that "the Pentagon has a harsh policy toward gays, and here's a gay man in a high-ranking position—you put those facts together and you've got a story."

"To run a huge story and then not use the name is chickenshit," said openly gay reporter Hank Plante of KPIX–TV in San Francisco. Eric Newton, managing editor of the *Oakland Tribune*, which named Williams, felt his paper's action was right because Williams "must have known the consequences before taking a job in the public eye." When the press had a field day after Pee-wee Herman was arrested for indecent exposure in a Florida movie theater, Newton said the paper received fifty or sixty angry letters attacking them for violating the entertainer's privacy rights. They received no letters regarding Pete Williams's outing. "This doesn't seem to have stirred up the average person," concluded Newton.

Like *WJR*, other media outlets tried to grapple with how the story was being reported, only to fall flat on their faces. The week of the outing, *New York Newsday*, in a story weirdly headlined COLUMNIST STOKES GAY-NAMING DEBATE, all about Jack Anderson's column being killed by many papers, used the opportunity to have its own editor spit out an excuse for not naming Williams. "Someone's personal life is personal unless there are compelling reasons to make it otherwise," said editor Anthony Marro—as if the interrogation, abuse, expulsion, and, in some cases, suicide of queers in the armed forces were not "compelling." He then added, in what had to be the most bankrupt reason given during the entire affair, that "I don't feel any need to say that an official at the State Department is heterosexual, so why should I say that someone is gay?" Somehow, it never occurred to Marro that every time his paper printed photos of Norman Schwarzkopf with his wife and family, he was revealing that Stormin' Norman was a heterosexual.

In February 1992, six months after the outing, *New York Newsday* named Williams. The "compelling" reason? None apparently: He and his outing were just mentioned in passing in *Newsday*'s gossip column as part of an item regarding another gay issue.

The *San Francisco Examiner* also took the moral high ground, only to realize, eventually, that it was a slippery slope. "Outing is a political statement, and we don't put political statements on the news pages," then–managing editor Phil Bronstein told *WJR*, causing many to wonder how the paper goes about covering protests and demonstrations of any kind. Do they tell the readers about a demonstration but not tell them what it is about? Do they cover up placards in the photographs?

Ten months later, in June 1992, in a story about *The Advocate*, the *Examiner*'s Sunday magazine not only named Williams but reproduced in color, in what certainly could be perceived as a "political statement," the *Advocate* cover with Pete Williams's face on it.

And *The Village Voice*, a week after the outing and several weeks after the staff meeting that so affected how outing was reported nationally, also named Williams. One of the *Voice*'s media critics, Jim Ledbetter, had tracked the story from its beginning. Weeks after the meeting, after the media had begun naming Williams, Ledbetter named him too, and explained that the story had "created a boiling pot of ink even before hitting the newsstands. At this point," he wrote, "withholding Williams's name is a futile exercise."

Hundreds of lesbian-and-gay papers and magazines across the country, while previously divided on the issue of outing, also named Williams. Few engaged in polemical debates about outing; rather, they focused on the policy and on Cheney's backpedaling. *The Washington Blade*, a moderate Washington, D.C., weekly whose publisher, Don Michaels, adamantly opposed outing, seemed to focus more on the fact that *The Advocate* had actually done the outing. Thus, the *Blade*'s headline: ADVOCATE OUTS DEFENSE SPOKESMAN WILLIAMS.

HAS OUTING AS A POLITICAL TACTIC BECOME ACCEPTABLE? asked the headline in *Sappho's Isle*, a New York lesbian newspaper. The answer, by the end of the article, was clearly yes. Similar stories and commentaries appeared in many other lesbian and gay publications.

Many gay papers even went on from the Williams outing to integrate outing into their journalism in a business-as-usual fashion, although they tried not to focus attention on it and even denied that they were outing. The editors of *QW* (formerly *NYQ*) magazine, a New York weekly that filled the void after *OutWeek* folded (and that itself folded a year later), stated emphatically in interviews that the publication was "opposed to outing—except in cases of exposing hypocrisy." But that was misleading. Most or all journalistic outing fits that description, and *QW* outed more people in its news stories than *OutWeek* ever did. More accurately, *QW*'s editors should have said they favored outing—except gratuitous outing.

Although even then they would have been stretching it. *QW*'s gossip columns outed lots of people, either directly or by innuendo. Rarely were the people involved great hypocrites, and rarely was their sexuality really pertinent to the story; they simply were mentioned for the sake of gossip.

Many gay publications do this all the time. Yet their editors would never say that they are in favor of outing. The word had been defined by the media as something so ugly and disgusting that most gay people want to disassociate themselves from it immediately even though many of them actually believe in responsible outers' basic premises. Similarly, social scientists have found that, after the media demonized "feminists," most women would deny they were feminists even though when surveyed about issues of women's liberation and equality they certainly gave answers that would define them as feminists.

In the case of *QW* as well as that of the glossy bimonthly *Out,* founded in June 1992, there were pragmatic reasons for the editors to publicly distance themselves from outing while privately supporting it: When these magazines were starting up, in the wake of *OutWeek*'s demise, the first thing the media wanted to know was whether they were going to out people. The word "outing" was so frightening to potential advertisers—which the gay press, because of homophobia, has enough trouble wooing—that to espouse a pro-outing position would have been a death sentence. *QW* even went so far as to have *The New York Times* run a retraction the day after they printed a business story that stated that the magazine, "like *OutWeek*," favored outing.

The same dynamics have always worked on leaders of established gay organizations such as the Washington-based National Gay and Lesbian Task Force and the Human Rights Campaign Fund, who get their clout and their funding from wealthy, more conservative corners of the gay community. As gay journalist Michael Bronski, a movement analyst who has observed gay politics for several decades, put it:

> Acutely aware of their tactical dependency on those in power and their economic dependency on broad-based, heterogeneous donor populations, [leaders of established gay organizations] are forced to always take the most prudent, least-extreme position on any given debate. No matter what they might really think or feel about outing—and their personal thoughts are as varied as their politics—their public opinions reflect the more conservative end of the discussion.

But in the wake of the Pete Williams outing, some leaders changed. Tom Stoddard, then–executive director of the Lambda Legal Defense and Education Fund, and previously one of the staunchest attackers of outing, gave backhanded support to the Pete Williams outing, telling *Details* magazine in December 1991, "This is the *only* example in which outing has advanced the interests of gay people."[13] Bill Rubenstein of the American Civil Liberties Union's Lesbian and Gay Rights Project noted that the Pete Williams outing did "more to chip away at the [military's antigay] policy than anything else and, in retrospect, I fully support it."

The outing and its aftermath did indeed make a big dent in the military's policy against gays. The publicity generated put the policy on the front burner in 1992, thrusting the issue into the presidential campaign; the issue became so visible that every Democratic presidential candidate had to say publicly that he would end the ban. Bill Clinton, speaking to a gay fund-raiser in Los Angeles, promised to do so, referring to the hypocrisy of the "Pentagon official" who was gay. And even independent Ross Perot, who at first favored the ban, gave in after the uproar from gays and promised to overturn it if elected.

The outing also brought the first serious discussion—and acceptance—of outing among writers on the political left (beyond *The Village Voice*), whose attention span for gay issues has never been long, despite their supposed sympathies. *The Nation*'s Alexander Cockburn, in his "Beat the Devil" column, named Williams and quoted the gay documentary maker John Scagliotti (*Before Stonewall*) who, in an interview with Cockburn, discussed the closet and outing:

> There's a difference between a passive closet, in which you simply survive and hope for the best, and an active closet, which involves putting on a heterosexual mask and promoting yourself as such, which is an ethical contradiction to your actual life. You've made the choice. You're living an actual lie, bringing girls to the company ball and so on.
>
> Take Barry Diller, who is in a position of enormous power at Fox. Why doesn't he push for a gay and lesbian TV show, which I could produce, which would be a gay version of *In Living Color?* Now, no one wants to out little people, gay teachers and so on— unless gay teachers are publicly anti-gay—but I would out people who are gay and yet are promoting heterosexuality.

Cockburn attacked the mainstream press for resolutely "inning" Williams by "attending but not reporting press conferences held by gay outers," and writing and then killing stories about the outing. Cockburn concluded:

> There is something bizarre about the hyenas virtuously strapping on their muzzles, but not so surprising when you think about it, since the mainstream press thrives on exposés contrived on its terms and not the terms set by people like Signorile. . . . Outing, which itself is shifting from a kind of anarchic dada to something more responsible, has clearly changed consciousness. Williams's boss, Cheney, has been compelled to distance himself from traditional Pentagon policy toward gay people, something he certainly would not have done, or been pushed toward by the press, before Signorile began the journalistic exercise of outing Williams.

While the left was beginning to champion outing, the right wasn't feeling so good about it—but that certainly wasn't because they cared about the privacy rights of queers. *The National Review,* of course, didn't name Williams: "When his magazine, *OutWeek,* folded, homosexual activist Michelangelo Signorile went over to *The Advocate* to 'out' a Pentagon official. High-minded reasons were given for exposing the man's putative preferences, of course: he's a hypocrite, the military oppresses gays, etc. What the vice squad can no longer do, gay activists are doing instead."

This was absolutely correct: Outing was no longer a tool of the right wing. It had been virtually stolen from them. Forty years ago, *The National Review* would probably have done the outing, and *The Nation* would have called it McCarthyism. Now the situation was reversed. The right was forced to face the fact that revealing who is homosexual would now advance the lesbian and gay movement, especially if the subjects didn't lose their jobs and especially if their bosses were then forced to back down on government policies. While a few continue to lesbian-bait feminists and powerful women, for the most part, right-wing zealots can no longer out people without wondering whether they're helping the gay cause.

Within the gay movement itself, those on the left of the spectrum (such as many of the gay *Voice* writers), who held an orthodox, traditional leftist view of the right to privacy, had rejected outing. And those on the right of the spectrum, the more conservative gays who wanted to keep their closet as they became public figures, or wanted to protect their friends who were doing so, had a vested interest in abhorring outing.

Contrary to what many people thought, both the far right *and* the far left of the gay political spectrum had rejected outing. In the aftermath of the Pete Williams outing, it was actually a growing number of middle-of-the-road gay journalists and opinion makers— along with some leftists and progressives and a sprinkling of conservatives—who came to support outing. Some believe it's okay to name someone whenever his or her sexuality is pertinent to a given story; others believe that outing is only warranted in cases where the individual is personally carrying out grossly homophobic policies.

In the year and a half following the outing of Pete Williams, those journalists and opinion makers who came to support outing publicly began to push for change in the reporting of closeted gay public figures. What started in the streets with militant queers has moved into the newsrooms of America—propelled, ironically, by the exposé of one closeted man who worked for the Pentagon. Indeed, the Pete Williams case brought out more public support of outing than there had ever been before.

Pete Williams, meanwhile, became a hero of sorts himself. Proving wrong all those who claimed that outing ruined careers and destroyed lives, Williams, after his Pentagon post was terminated with Bush's defeat and after mulling over several offers, in March 1993 took the position of Washington-based general assignment correspondent with NBC News—ironically the very news organization that first showed interest in outing him two years prior. He is, according to friends, content and happy.

9

....

All the Presidents'

....

Queers

....

Sex is power.

That's why sex is so important in Washington. While San Francisco, New York, and Los Angeles are sexually liberating cities, Washington is full of pent-up, repressed sexual tension that makes it ten times more libidinous than they. Everyone is on guard, everyone knows that sex can be used against them, so libidos ride under cover. Washington sexuality is all about furtive glances from people in business suits on the streets of Capitol Hill and Foggy Bottom and in the halls of Congress, anxious and apprehensive looks that reveal more than they acknowledge. Everyone is painfully aware of one general rule: Any clandestine circumstance from your past can eventually come back to haunt you at any moment.

In early September 1991, Anita Hill, an African-American law professor at the University of Oklahoma Law Center, was wrestling with just such events from her own past. She had lived in Washington in the early eighties working at the Equal Employment Opportunity Commission under its then-chairman, Clarence Thomas. Now Thomas, also an African-American, was a Supreme Court nominee. His nomination had been controversial from the start because of his conservative positions. Following up on some leads, the Senate investigating committee charged with looking into Thomas's background sought Hill out. Hesitantly, she decided to speak up.

Thomas had sexually harassed her while she worked under him at the EEOC, she contended at a closed-door meeting of the Senate Judiciary Committee, then holding hearings on Thomas's nomination. Her testimony, she was promised, would be strictly confidential.

But a month later, just two days before the final vote of the entire Senate on Thomas's nomination was to take place, someone leaked Hill's affidavit (previously belittled or ignored by the committee) to the press. Quickly ferreted out by two reporters—National Public Radio's Nina Totenberg and *New York Newsday*'s Timothy Phelps— who were after a hot story, Anita Hill had to go public. Once thrust into celebritydom, Hill was dissected like a frog in a biology class by several Republican senators well trained in the use of the political scalpel. Skillfully, they ripped her guts out. In their eyes, Hill was part of a last-minute political conspiracy to stop Thomas just as his controversial nomination was about to be confirmed, ensuring that the right wing would dominate the Court for decades to come. The White House and the Republicans were furious, but the Democrats on the committee were running scared. At first they tried to rush through the proceedings and not take Hill's charges seriously. But after an uproar among female members of the House, as well as hundreds of thousands of angry telephone calls from constituents across the country, the committee decided to postpone the vote and hold public hearings on the allegations. The hearings were broadcast live on television.

Though her testimony was logical and credible, Republican senators on the committee went all out to portray Anita Hill invariably as a "fantasizer," a "schizophrenic," and an "erotomaniac." She was denounced for colluding with "slick lawyers" and accused of committing "flat-out perjury," even of basing her charges against Thomas on a reading of *The Exorcist,* the onetime best-seller about satanic possession. Every aspect of Hill's personality was distorted and subjected to the scrutiny of the television-watching nation.

Later, among pundits, the word "outing" never came into the discussion, even though according to the loose definition that the media had by then come to use, this certainly was an outing. On condition of anonymity, Hill had revealed private facts of a sexual nature to a select group of individuals. These were facts that, if reported in the media, could (and did) alter her life dramatically. And they were painful circumstances whose publication could damage her psyche. But the media had to do their job. After all, they would say, this was a matter of grave importance.

Anita Hill certainly had done nothing wrong. Unlike Pete Williams, she was not a public figure. Nor was she in a hypocritical position, as Pete Williams was. She simply had experiences that were relevant to the question of Clarence Thomas's character and his fitness to be a Supreme Court justice. But no matter how personal those experiences were, Hill had no choice: The media expected her to deliver. They decided it was time for Hill to stand up for what was right, time for her to be shoved into the spotlight. The media decided that what was personal for her was now a public matter.

It is that very double standard that betrays the media's heterosexism and self-interest. Reporters were reluctant to cover the outing of Pete Williams because it wasn't *their* humanity that was at stake. It didn't matter that the lives of thousands of soldiers had been ruined, that people had been tortured and humiliated, that gay and lesbian members of the service had been driven to suicide. Pete Williams's "privacy" was important, but Anita Hill's was not.

If Hill had been a man charging Thomas with sexual harassment, the media would have had to give credence to charges that implied Thomas was homosexual, and thus would have engaged in outing. Especially in a case where the subject is someone they don't like, the media care only about who benefits from the outing. When the outing serves their agenda (and when they're certain that they won't get beaten up for it), then it's okay. In fact, conservative members of the media attempted to "out" Anita Hill herself, implying that she was a dyke. Hill was first lesbian-baited by Republican senator Alan Simpson of Wyoming during the proceedings, when he referred to her "proclivities" in describing the nature of information he said he'd received about her. "I really am getting stuff over the transom about Professor Hill," he told reporters. "I've got letters hanging out of my pocket. I've got faxes. I've got statements from her former law professors, statements from people that know her, statements from Tulsa, Oklahoma, saying, 'Watch out for this woman.' "

Later, on NBC's *Meet the Press*, Simpson described one of these letters as "the most derogatory letter I have seen to date." When correspondent Andrea Mitchell asked, "Isn't this McCarthyism of the worst order?" Simpson replied, "Well, not in my mind." Yet even with all of this coded discussion it was unclear to many people what Simpson was actually talking about until the next day—two days before the rescheduled vote—when *New York Times* columnist William Safire, a staunch Thomas supporter, summarized Simpson's baiting of Hill in a column in which he charged that Hill "lied, and lied again, and lied a third time." Cleverly, Safire made it appear as if he were chastising Simpson for what he did, but it was clear that Safire was trying to clarify Simpson's coded allegation and float the information further: He portrayed Thomas as a victim of what the right continually asserts is a cabal of man-hating lesbians running the women's movement. "[Simpson] hinted darkly of Ms. Hill's 'proclivities,' " wrote Safire. "That is a code word for homosexuality; if Mr. Simpson has evidence that the accuser's sexual preference is related to her reluctance to bring a charge of sexual harassment, let him make his case or shut up." Without realizing it, Safire—who had previously condemned outing in his *New York Times Magazine* column—had offered a defense of journalistic outing: A person's homosexuality should be discussed whenever it is pertinent to the story.

Hill's being brought forward as a victim of sexual harassment proved in the end to be a galvanizing force for the women's movement, just as the outing of Congressman Gerry Studds had galvanized the gay-and-lesbian rights movement. (Studds had been the target of a sting operation that found him to have had sex with a male congressional page.) Beyond the women's movement, however, Hill became an icon to millions of victims of sexual harassment who were personally affected by her in profound ways.

One of them was Keith, an aide to a powerful legislator. On the day of the final vote, Keith met with the Legislator. He'd already sent the Legislator a letter, pleading with him not to support Thomas. Keith believed Anita Hill because he identified with her in a way that most people couldn't. As he watched her on television and listened to her rationale and her apparent confusion as to why she kept putting up with the harassment, he painfully saw himself.

·····

Sex is power—the kind of power that can hold a person's life in another's iron grip for years, the kind of power that preys upon the naïve and unsuspecting.

Keith is a handsome, big, all-American sort of guy with gleaming eyes, a Pepsodent smile, and an innocent demeanor that suggests he would be hard-pressed to tell a lie. Bashful and quiet, he tends to the traditional. Now thirty-two years old, he's only been with a few men, all of whom he's had long-term relationships with. He thinks often of settling down with a lover for the long haul, and his family is very important to him. He grew up the son of devout Roman Catholics.

Keith remembers seeing and reading about the Legislator from his earliest childhood, at the time when the Legislator was in low-level state government positions. As a boy, Keith heard his father and his uncle discuss politics on Sunday afternoons at home. The discussions fascinated him, as he soon developed a keen interest in politics. "I was always interested at a young age in making an impact and changing things for the better," he says. He particularly liked the Legislator, who was then a local politician popular with Keith's family. Keith's mother and father had voted for him in the past, and Keith, like many others, found him charismatic; Keith looked up to this man as a model statesman and followed his career vigorously.

In his early teens, Keith campaigned for the Legislator for the first time. The Legislator was then making a run for a statewide seat. He won, and remained in that position for several years before being elected to federal office. Throughout his teen years, Keith had volunteered his time and energy to the Legislator's campaigns. Working in politics at such a young age, thrilled by the excitement it generated, Keith decided that perhaps he'd like to go into politics himself when he became older.

"When I was in school, I was tired of having my decisions made by people no brighter—or no more caring—than myself," he recalls, "so I thought I'd run for office one day so that I could do a better job." But, perhaps not so facetiously, he notes that he was interested in politics for another reason. "I wanted to be on TV or in the paper someday," he says, laughing. "I suppose a psychoanalyst would now say that I was running from my sexuality—to be a public person and lose my private side so that I could feel better about myself."

Keith was very much in denial about his homosexuality throughout his teens and into his early twenties. "I had some obvious feelings, but I never faced them," he recalls. "For years I dated women, but my feeling was that it wasn't right for me." Nonetheless, he continued to date women, refusing to confront his sexuality.

One summer in high school, when he was campaigning for the Legislator-to-be (then in a state seat, making his first run for federal office), Keith received an urgent message from one of the campaign workers: There was going to be an emergency press conference—damage control to head off a rumor that had appeared in the press that the candidate was a closeted homosexual.

"I guess I was curious about it, but I thought it was a dirty campaign trick," Keith says. "My mentality towards gays was not positive at the time. I thought [the charge] was crazy."

The future Legislator, a married man with children, denied the rumor. No evidence or witnesses surfaced. Because of certain policies he'd pushed, the candidate was unpopular at that time with a number of people in the state government. So the media attributed the charges to nasty rumors created and circulated by disgruntled state workers. The unsubstantiated claims were deemed false. The candidate went on to win the election; perhaps he was even helped by the scandal, because people sympathized with him, viewing him as the victim of the most vicious kind of smear campaign. But the incident was indelibly etched in the candidate's mind—as well as in the minds of everyone who worked for him.

During college, Keith had one isolated sexual encounter with a man—his first. But, he says, he quickly blocked it out, ashamed of the experience. He continued to resist his homosexuality.

After graduating from college, Keith landed a job with the Legislator, working in his home state. After the Legislator's reelection, Keith moved to Washington to work for him at his request.

Keith believes that the Legislator's brush with homosexual scandal affected the way he voted on gay issues. On several occasions the Legislator supported bills with antigay and AIDS-phobic amendments tacked on by Senator Jesse Helms and others, even though Keith and other aides discussed the injustice of such amendments with him. "He didn't want to open himself up to potential opponents who would remember the scandal and interpret his [support] as 'Well, he's gay and he's trying to protect his friends.' But I was more upset when he [voiced support for Supreme Court justice nominee] Robert Bork, who has no respect for privacy rights." Yet Keith, who still hadn't come to terms with his own sexual orientation, continued for the most part to revere his boss.

The two grew closer. "My long-standing relationship with the campaign and him allowed him to feel a deeper sense of trust in me," Keith observes. "I certainly trusted him. He never felt I would be threatened by him. I worked hard for him and there was a mutual respect and a relationship that went beyond the professional." Keith had by this time come to admire the Legislator more than ever. "I had a great deal of respect for him professionally as well as personally."

But the relationship still wasn't as personal as the Legislator would have liked it to be. And he decided to do something about that.

"His wife was out of town on one of many projects," Keith recalls. "When you're working for a member, contact can be sporadic. Some aides can be [in the office] an aggregate of thirty minutes a day. At the time, that was not the case with me. When I got called in, it was a big deal. He called me in and asked me to come over to his place that night. He said he was baching it and we can have a nightcap.

"I thought, what a great chance to visit. I figured we could have an intellectual discussion. I saw it was a social thing, but also the opportunity to talk about important things going on policy-wise.

"I showed up at nine-thirty and he greeted me. I noticed more of a physical greeting—not a hug per se but an arm around the shoulder, more friendly than before. In the living room, he offered me a drink. He poured screwdrivers—extremely strong drinks. We drank and talked candidly, gossiped about office people. Within an hour, his eyes started to wander and he started to look at my crotch. I was starting to feel uncomfortable about that. He got up to make us another drink and then sat next to me on the couch. He turned off a lamp, then put his arm on my leg, on my knee, as he continued eye contact. I felt very uncomfortable about it, but I was shocked. Going through my head was that the rumors were true.

"The situation progressed speedily, as he put his hands on my crotch, trying to arouse me, telling me to relax. I was very nervous. Alcohol was having an effect on me, obviously, but I was alert as to what was happening. He tried to get my hand over to his crotch to get him off. I found a way to slip out from under his arm. I got up and said, 'It's getting late and I better not drink any more and I should get going.' He intercepted me by putting his arm around me and saying, 'You don't need to hurry off; we're friends—nothing we share has to go out of here.' I was still heading for the door, hoping he wouldn't notice how uncomfortable I was, so he'd just let me go. He turned me away from my path to the door and walked me toward the bedroom, which was completely dark. He steered me into the bedroom, where he took off his pants, started fumbling with mine, took mine down, and then lay me down and tried to jack me off, tried to get me to do the same to him.

"All I remember was wanting to be out of there. I knew I had to get out of there. Luckily, he had a very low threshold in the orgasm department and with very little stimulation was able to have an orgasm. He didn't play with me any longer. He went to the bathroom to clean up. That's when I made my move to get dressed and position myself by the door. He came out of the bathroom, acting more drunk than I knew he was—he really can hold his liquor. He said, 'Gosh, we can really get in trouble when we drink too much.' I couldn't look him in the eye. I told him I had to go and that I'd see him tomorrow."

Keith departed, confused and upset. He was in a state of shock. He says that everything happened so fast that he couldn't figure out what was right and what was wrong. He felt he couldn't say no to his boss, a man who was in a position of authority over his life, a man for whom he had enormous admiration and by whose power he was mesmerized. Keith was not yet fully in touch with his own homosexuality. On one level, the incident, as it was occurring, had appealed to him, because he knew deep down that he was gay; homosexual sex seemed enticing. At the same time, he was not physically attracted to the Legislator, and he sensed that the situation was unethical and even immoral because he worked for the man. Keith feels that as a person who was still confused about his sexuality, he was preyed upon and manipulated.

"[The Legislator] knew I was lonely and needed companionship," he recalls. "He knew I didn't like D.C. very much and that I was very much into my work, working long hours. He knew I didn't socialize or date. Considering how intuitive he is, in hindsight, he could have sensed, 'Here's a young guy who's not getting out and may have questions about his own sexual identity.' He may have known about me before I did."

But at the time, Keith didn't think any of this through. Terrified and upset, he tried to do what he'd done before: simply block the event out of his mind.

The next day in the office, the Legislator pulled him aside at the end of a meeting, after others in attendance had left the room. "He made a similar comment like the one the night before," says Keith, "about how we had too much to drink and that we should be careful about that. He said that this was something to be kept between us. Then he apologized, saying he didn't want me to feel uncomfortable. He again blamed it on the alcohol and left it at that.

"I felt pretty dirty. I wasn't in any way attracted to him and it certainly wasn't pleasurable. And I now knew this big secret, something that could destroy the man if I ever told anyone. It was something other people had suspected but now I'm the one who knew firsthand. It was very frightening, very intimidating, very burdensome. I was pretty depressed, very confused."

Perhaps Keith was trying to rationalize and even deny the situation: He says he felt a bit of relief because the Legislator suggested to him that the sex had been an isolated incident. "He characterized it in terms of the drinking," Keith says, "leading me to believe that he didn't do this to other people. It was just something that got away from him." Thus, in spite of the past rumors, Keith convinced himself that perhaps nothing like this would happen again. It was all he could hope for. "He knew how uncomfortable I was, and how I was trying to break the restraint he had over me," he says.

But the sex would not be an isolated incident. For the next two years, Keith says, the Legislator sexually harassed and sexually abused him on roughly twelve separate occasions. The circumstances were usually the same: The Legislator's wife would be out of town and he would tell Keith to come over for a drink. On two occasions, they had sex back in their home state, once at the Legislator's home and the other time in a hotel room. "There was also one time in the Capitol," Keith recalls, "where he and [many legislators] have hideaway offices." In most cases, the encounters included drinking, and amounted to fondling, mutual masturbation, and sometimes oral sex, with the Legislator being in the "active" role. Keith says the two never had anal sex.

How could anyone let something like this go on for so long? If Keith didn't like it, why didn't he just put an end to it? Why didn't he become firm with the Legislator, report him, or quit his job? And why didn't the Legislator—knowing each time that Keith was uncomfortable and didn't like what was happening—stop?

Those questions are not easily answered. As with men's sexual harassment of women, issues of sexual harassment and sexual abuse between men are complex; so are the motivations of both the abuser and the abused. The circumstances that keep gay men in abusive situations in Washington have more to do with society's overall oppression of gays and the competitive nature of the nation's capital than they do with the simple desire of one man to either put an end to or encourage the advances of another.

As it does for so many lesbians and gays who move to Washington, the big-city life, coupled with being far away from home, forced Keith to address his homosexuality soon after he'd arrived. "It was a little bit exciting to come here, challenging at first," he says. "I was definitely having mixed feelings about my sexual orientation. In the beginning, I was lonely. I wasn't out [and] didn't talk to anyone about it."

But shortly after the second incident with the Legislator, Keith became involved with another man his own age and soon was taking his first steps out of the closet, albeit with fear and trepidation. "I remember my first gay bar in Rehoboth, [Delaware,]" he says. "I went to a beach house with friends of [my new lover,] Peter. They convinced me to go for a drink at the Blue Moon and I didn't know it was a gay bar at first. When I was told so, I wasn't interested in going. I was afraid someone would see me. But I went. That was a hundred and twenty miles from D.C. and I went in the bar and saw [another legislative aide,] who worked around the corner from me in the same building for a conservative Republican. I knew then that I could not be out working on the Hill." Keith felt that he had to be more deeply closeted than other staffers because his boss had once been suspected of being gay, and thus, if Keith were known to be gay, it would put the spotlight back on the Legislator.

"Everyone [on the Hill] is representing someone else," says Joe Martin, an openly gay man who was an aide to Congressman Barney Frank. "You don't want a spotlight brought to your behavior. You're potentially living in a fishbowl. When you're working for an elected official you can't do anything that would harm that person's stance for being elected."

"I was really torn in my allegiance to my boss," says Keith. "That was a factor in my decision [never to be out]."

But Keith was definitely beginning to feel good about his own homosexuality. He soon fell in love with Peter. As first gay relationships so often do, Keith's made him more defiant of the heterosexual establishment and more proud of being gay.

There was one problem: Peter also worked for the Legislator.

"Soon after he was hired we went out for a drink socially," Keith says. Eventually, they were having a full-blown office romance. Peter's job didn't require much interaction with the Legislator. He was never sexually harassed by him, and had never suspected the truth of the situation. After Peter and Keith had been together for four months, Keith told Peter about the Legislator. "He was upset. His advice, of course, was 'Don't go there!' " Keith explains, referring to his trips to the Legislator's home.

Why did he keep going?

"I was fearful [of refusing] for a number of reasons, the first of which being my job," he says. "Not that he would fire me. He wouldn't be so stupid as to do that. But I couldn't sit him down and say, 'No, don't do that to me!' I just didn't have the ability to say that back then at any of those times. If I had been out for four or five years, I'd have been able to do it, but I was just dealing with all of this myself.

"If I had a confrontation [with him], he would close me out of the loop. He wouldn't answer my memos or follow my recommendations on new initiatives and bills. We were working on a very important [bill] at the time. These people are constantly busy, traveling back to the state or making speeches to special-interest groups or submitting to media interviews. The legislation for a hundred different issues is divided between five to eight legislative assistants. So five to eight policy people are competing for his interest in introducing a particular bill on a particular issue. And that competes with the press people and the scheduling people. You're always struggling to get his attention. There's intense competition for a [legislator's] time."

Keith says that he very much liked his job overall; he felt that the matters he was working on were important social issues and that his work helped many people. He felt obligated to see his goals through, and to do so he needed to have constant access to the Legislator. He also thought that he had no choice in the matter in that firmly refusing the Legislator would have put Keith in disfavor, while leaving the Legislator's employ would certainly have risked angering him, perhaps enough to make him give Keith a bad job recommendation, a sure death sentence on the Hill.

"It's a great motivator in this town to have influence," Keith observes. "If you don't have influence with your boss, then you're a nobody. You might as well be answering the phones out front. If I wanted a job in D.C. as a lobbyist so I could improve my worth in D.C. or if I wanted to return to [my home state] to work, [having had this access] would then allow me to meet local leaders who would be important in my next career move.

"I also knew enough about the way [the Legislator] treated his enemies to know that I didn't want to be one of them. I knew that for all the congenial appearance he put out, he was a pretty cutthroat politician and he could find ways to harm people. People who were complainers, asking for more resources and assistants, were treated differently, put on a different list. I knew that if I threatened him— well, I wasn't ready to risk what that would mean to me. If I left his staff without a good recommendation, what would that mean? I'd be back to where I was before college. I was lucky as hell to get a good job in the first place."

Complicating matters was Keith's unending admiration for the Legislator as a statesman. "It was a terrible struggle," he says, "to see this guy making speeches on the floor and to have immense respect for his intellect, his ability, his leadership—and then to know that he ruined that in private by approaching me in ways that I didn't want to be approached and touching me in ways I didn't want to be touched."

Many times in the office, following an encounter the night before, the Legislator would half apologize and tell Keith that he seemed uncomfortable; Keith would politely say that they shouldn't do it again. But then it would happen three months or so later. They never spoke about homosexuality or "being gay" during or after the encounters. "I always had the feeling that if I told him out front that I was gay, it would be an admission of something awful," Keith says. "As honest as we've ever had an after-morning talk was him saying, 'Gee, we got drunk last night—it sure felt good to me. Did it to you?' to which I would either not respond or say that we shouldn't do it again. But the word 'homosexual' never came up."

Shortly after his first year with the Legislator, Keith learned that another male employee, back in his home state, had received the same kind of abuse. "He's gay and we came out to each other," Keith remembers. "It was all very platonic. We built a strong bond. And he told me that the same thing was happening to him."

Almost all of the men who work for the Legislator are handsome and appealing, and Keith feels that the Legislator hires them on that basis, perhaps for the possibility of having sex with them. "Are they gay for sure? No," says Keith. "Young, attractive, potentially gay, recruitable [as sex partners]? Yes."

Keith, coming under more pressure from his lover and realizing that, for the sake of his own mental health, he couldn't stay in this situation much longer, began to think about getting away, no matter what the cost. Adding to the pressure was the gossip around the office about Keith and Peter's romance. When the two eventually decided to move in together it became common knowledge among the staff.

"[The Legislator] was told by someone that Peter was gay," Keith says. "Then he was told that we were moving in together. He talked to me about it. He didn't think it was a good idea. Of course, he was worrying about *his* image. He let me know that if I needed to talk about a better salary to keep my own apartment then we could talk about that.

"A lot of this had to do with what was going on politically at the time: Early 1988 was the time frame of the consideration of the civil-rights bill [which the Legislator favored], the overturning of which [Republican senator Jesse] Helms said was important because, among other reasons, voting in favor of it would expand rights to gays and AIDS patients. After the consideration of the civil-rights bill, our office received a fax, a two-page flier that was entitled 'The Committee to Recall [the Legislator].'* One of the reasons listed was that he supported the civil-rights bill and he had liberal, 'homosexually sympathetic advisors' on his staff who pushed him to support this expansion of civil rights, which was interpreted to include gays and people with AIDS.

"For all these reasons, [the Legislator] was concerned that his chief legislative advisor would be the roommate of someone outwardly gay, and thus would be known as gay. This is an illustration of the paranoia around being gay on the Hill or having someone that is gay working for you."

Keith was outraged by the Legislator's suggestion that he not move in with Peter, but the last straw was another incident that occurred shortly after that one. A straight male employee on the staff was accused of sexual harassment by a woman in the office. The matter was all kept very hush-hush. Keith was appalled at how the Legislator ignored the situation, not addressing it properly and not reprimanding the male employee. Soon after, Keith was finally empowered to do what he had to do: He handed in his resignation.

"I wrote that I was leaving to do other things—that I was going back to school and would be looking for another job—but that if he ever said anything that was an attack on me or any characteristic about me, I would certainly set the record straight," Keith recounts. "I felt free but I felt bad for him because his life would still be miserable. I might not be as comfortable as I once was, but at least by then I had supportive friends who knew me for who and what I was. For him, on the other hand, I was one of the few people who knew who and what he was, but now he didn't have me anymore. When he lost me from his staff, he lost control over me. What I gained when I left his staff was my freedom. I had lived my life for years basically being manipulated by someone who was able to take something from me that should not have been taken."

After receiving Keith's letter of resignation, the Legislator took him for a drive and had a talk with him, during which he apologized profusely for all that he'd done. "I don't know how deep the emotion really was," Keith says. "He got choked up and said, 'I hope that what

*Other legislators received similar threats that they too would be recalled.

we have done has not made an impact on you in any way that you don't want.' Translation: 'I hope I haven't made you into a homosexual.' "

It took Keith a year to find another job. Though the Legislator did not produce the scathing evaluation that Keith had feared, Keith's particular skills weren't very marketable in Congress, he says, because he'd worked mostly on social issues. The job he eventually took was in another field altogether. It's not a job that he particularly likes or finds challenging, and it doesn't pay very well. He no longer harbors aspirations of running for office or otherwise going into politics. But he is much more at peace with himself, and in retrospect he's not only able to see more clearly what actually happened, but he has also stood up to the Legislator.

"The first time I listened to Anita Hill's testimony, and how people responded, I realized it was so sterotypical of what people would ask you," he says. "People who think rape is a sex crime as opposed to a crime of power, they're the same people who think that sexual harassment is a flirtation instead of the use of power. With me, [the Legislator's] use of power fed off of my sexual confusion. After Anita Hill's testimony, I sent [the Legislator] a letter, saying [that Congress] looked stupid. Thomas was mediocre at best and the Senate wasn't prepared to take the issue [of sexual harassment] seriously. I told [the Legislator] in the letter that his conduct toward me had been sexual harassment, that I knew that at the time but I didn't know how to deal with it, that my career was seriously impacted by having to leave his staff prematurely, and that I had considered legal action."

Within hours after Keith hand-delivered the letter to the Legislator's personal secretary, the Legislator called him. They met for lunch on the day of the Thomas vote. But all of Keith's explanations and veiled threats did not persuade the Legislator to call for Thomas's defeat. For the usual political reasons that had nothing to do with his conscience, the Legislator was supporting Thomas and was trying to explain his actions to Keith.

"I suppose he knew I wouldn't press him on it," says Keith. He realized that the Legislator knew that Keith would never go public about what had happened between them. "All things being equal, he figures I've got as much to lose as he does."

Keith has a point. On several occasions he has considered going public. But his greatest concern, he says, is that his own life would change forever also. He realizes that if Anita Hill was handled the way she was by both the media and Thomas's supporters who denounced her as a liar, Keith, as a gay man, would probably be treated more severely. He doesn't think he could ever deal with it. Keith still has great respect for the Legislator as a politician and is conflicted about bringing him down. In spite of what was done to him, he says he'd feel terrible about ruining the Legislator's career.

Two other men, both of whom worked for the Legislator in his home state, say they were also sexually harassed by him; both, for the same reasons Keith offers, are reluctant to come forward.* Fred worked for the Legislator only briefly, while he was a student. He had been out of the closet for several years by then and says he "knew from the very beginning" that the Legislator was a closeted queer "just by watching him." Fred says that several times the Legislator invited him to come to his home after work, when his wife was away, but Fred declined. Once, while they were working late in the office, the Legislator offered Fred a drink, which he accepted. Over the next hour or so the two had several drinks and chatted about political events. Then, in the same manner Keith described, the Legislator made advances to Fred, touching Fred's leg and moving his hand up to Fred's crotch. Fred, however, stood up abruptly and said he wasn't interested. "I hadn't really spoken about my being gay in his presence, so he may have thought I was closeted and confused," he says, "and that I'd just get flustered and go along with it. But I know a bad situation when I see it. I said, 'I'm sorry, but I don't think this would be a good idea, and I'm leaving now.' He tried to stop me but I left. He attempted an apology the next day, but from then on, he was very cold to me. I was leaving there soon anyway, and it was just as well."

Gerard, like Keith, was in denial about his homosexuality and hadn't ever had sex with a man. He also looked up to the Legislator and was excited about working for him. When the Legislator invited Gerard to his house, he accepted, exhilarated about being in the company of a man he admired. They had drinks, and events developed much as they had with Keith. The two had sex, after which

---

*Neither is the one who told Keith that he too was sexually harassed, in whom Keith confided.

Gerard left. The next morning the Legislator apologized, as usual, but Gerard says he never accepted any invitations to the Legislator's home again and quit his job fairly soon after. He told his friend Ed about the event at the time, which was during the mid-eighties. "He was shaken," says Ed. "We were friends for years but we were both closeted. I came out to [Gerard] and he told me that he thought he too was gay and then he told me what had happened and how horrible it had made him feel. I didn't know what to do. I was new to all of this myself, but I said, 'Look, he's a disturbed man and it's because of the system and what it does to gay people. Let's hope we don't turn out that way.' " Like Keith, Gerard says he'd feel uncomfortable with bringing down the Legislator by coming forward.

If Gerard and Keith seem altruistic in their concern for the Legislator's life, it is because they see the Legislator as a tragic victim of society's homophobia—just as they once were. The Legislator was groomed for office when he was very young, before the 1950s, by a political family in a conservative part of the country; he was manipulated into living the life he now leads. Life as an openly gay man was never an option for him, nor was homosexuality something that he could ever face up to in his closed world, even as times changed. Tortured and ashamed, he suffers a ghastly existence in which he is compelled to deceive all those around him—his wife, his children, his parents, his friends—and forced to abuse his power as a lawmaker.

Keith and Gerard are wrong, however, to value the Legislator's life above their own and those of others. As much as the Legislator is a victim, he is one who has in turn victimized many more people. The tragedy of the Legislator's closet is not only in the damage done to him and his family, but also in that done to countless naïve, sometimes confused men who work for him. And this is not to mention the damage done to millions of lesbians and gays whose civil rights he votes against in order to create and preserve his closet.

Perhaps even more frightening, this is a situation in which the person in the closet tried to control his life—but eventually lost control of the closet itself. For that reason, a closeted gay male's sexual harassment of another gay male is probably not motivated by the same circumstances that motivate straight men's sexual harassment of women. While certainly many men in power harass their female employees for the sake of obtaining sex, often—perhaps, for instance, in the Thomas case—it may not matter to the man whether he ever has sex with the woman. Rather, it's his complete control of the situation—it's the power he exerts by means of intimidation and harassment—that gets him off. And unfortunately it's power that many heterosexual men must constantly reassure themselves they still have as women empower themselves in society.

But in the case of a tormented, closeted homosexual man like the Legislator, the sexual harassment and abuse are fueled *specifically* by the passion to have sex and only to a lesser degree by the desire to exert power over someone. While the situation certainly involves the abuse of power, the motivation is homosexual activity. Like Malcolm Forbes, these men set up their entire work lives in a way that enables them to have sex with men who surround them in their daily functions. This is the only way, in most such cases, that they can have intimacy with other men. As public figures who are married to women and have images to keep up, they cannot be seen in gay bars or at gay parties. Even male escort services are risky. Sexual harassment and abuse of gay employees becomes the easiest and most practical way possible for them to fulfill their sexual desires.

· · · · ·

People who claim that all closets are equal and that there isn't a compelling reason why any should ever be violated obviously don't care to comprehend the complexities surrounding closets of power, like that of the Legislator. His desire to keep his homosexuality a secret does not affect only *his* life. Beyond the obvious fact that it influences the lives of millions of his own kind whom he votes against, his closetedness also causes him to sexually and psychologically abuse people who work for him. The damage done to these young men is incalculable. Certainly there can be lifelong trauma. While some, like Keith, may eventually find a way out and come to terms with the situation by discussing it, scores are still locked into horrible realities, experiencing abuses of power and doing what they think is right but what is actually tearing their lives apart.

Those who hold that outing is wrong in every circumstance say that even in cases of harassment or abuse it is unwarranted to reveal a person's homosexuality. This rigidity sets up a double standard:

The media would think nothing of exposing a man who abused his *female* staffers. And they don't consider that "outing."

In March 1992, when eight women anonymously claimed that they'd been sexually molested by their former boss, Senator Brock Adams of Washington State, over a period totaling twenty years, the entire American media placed complete trust in one paper, *The Seattle Times,* and the allegations of eight unnamed women. None of these women had ever filed charges with the police. No other newspaper had met with the women or asked to see the affidavits. But all reported the charges. They could have chosen not to run the story, as many had chosen not to run the Pete Williams story because, as they claimed, some facts were documented using anonymous sources. In defending their actions, some papers stated that Adams had been previously accused of sexual abuse, although the earlier case had been thrown out because of what investigators had called inconclusive evidence.

Other newspapers defended themselves by pointing to the fact that Adams responded to the charges in a news conference—as did Pete Williams when he was asked about his sexuality at a Pentagon briefing. Pete Williams had refused to give a firm answer, but Adams vehemently denied the charges, saying they were completely false. Still, the media rightfully saw no reason to squelch the Adams story.

According to the story in *The Seattle Times,* Adams was given to plying vulnerable young women with drugged drinks as well as to making unwanted advances. One woman said he had raped her nearly twenty years before. Adams denied all the charges, but with pressure mounting in the days following the media barrage, he was forced to announce that he would not run for reelection. His career was ended, not because of a trial outcome or the official filing of charges, but because of one newspaper report citing unnamed accusers.

In the days that followed, outraged citizens wrote scorching letters to papers across the country accusing the media of playing judge and jury in this case. "American politics has reached a low point with the sudden announcement by Senator Brock Adams of Washington that he would not seek re-election in the aftermath of anonymous accusations concerning sexual improprieties and rape," wrote Professor

Mark Petracca of the University of California, Irvine, to *The New York Times*. "Neither our political nor our legal system is supposed to work like this."

But the media themselves, in editorials and commentaries, almost universally defended the *Seattle Times* story and the subsequent stories that appeared in hundreds of newspapers and all over radio and television news programs. "The bottom line is that we thought the basic choice we had was to withhold an important story we believed to be true or to tell the story without named sources," said Michael R. Fancher, executive editor of *The Seattle Times*. The paper's own ombudswoman, Colleen Patrick, admitted that out of over two hundred calls the paper received in the first two days after the story ran, 60 percent had opposed publishing the story with anonymous sources. But still, she concluded that the paper had done the right thing.

"Is there any excuse for printing anonymous accusations?" asked Maggie Boys in a column in the *Minneapolis Star-Tribune*. "The only justification I can think of for breaking such a story without the names of the accusers would be to prevent more women from being harassed. . . . Between the legal system and the press, it should be possible for women to get some justice in this country. But nobody said it would be easy or comfortable." Boys's logic seems reasonable, in light of the fact that *The Seattle Times* assured readers and the rest of the media of the accuracy and validity of the story and said that it had thoroughly gone over the information, which had been supplied over a period of years.

Imagine now what the reaction would have been if a newspaper or magazine printed a story in which eight anonymous *gay male* staffers revealed that their married boss was secretly gay and had been sexually harassing them. Would the same editors feel that, for the sake of preventing more gay male employees from being harassed, they were justified in printing the story? They probably wouldn't reveal such allegations unless formal charges were made to the police or federal investigators. More than likely, most of the media would think the whole affair was pretty disgusting; many would see it as a gross invasion of privacy and a horrible attack on a good man by a cabal of homosexuals. Many might question the notion that the men were abused at all—especially if they were unwilling to come forward. All would be leery of the story. If a news organization did use it, the anonymous sourcing would become a violently contentious issue. If the story broke in a mainstream newspaper, the rest of the media would be likelier to pick it up. But most news outlets still probably wouldn't. If the publication that originally broke the story was from the gay press, the story would not be touched by the mainstream media. Wherever it broke, gay anti-outers, and editorial-page editors across the country, would condemn the writers and the publications for shoddy journalism and invasion of privacy without proper sourcing.

When abuse is heterosexual, however, it seems to be understood that privacy is forfeited and that hunches and gut feelings are more important to go on than ironclad journalistic principles. Tim McGuire, the *Minneapolis Star-Tribune's* executive editor, said that it was "impossible" for him "to be completely sure of the propriety of the Adams story," but that "it certainly looks like a piece that needed to be printed."

At *The Washington Post,* columnist Judy Mann wrote: "Like a lot of other people I know, I started out feeling very uncomfortable. . . . But after two days of talking to experts [on sexual harassment], I've changed my mind." Art Nauman, *Sacramento Bee* ombudsman, said, "I support what the *Times* did. . . . [The fact that Adams] is a public official with his power in the Senate bears on the question of his character and his ability to serve the public properly." And the *Boston Globe* ombudsman, Gordon McKibben, accepted even less justification to run the story: "Our Washington bureau people say those stories about Adams have been around for years. They say everybody knows they are true."

Gay activists who have outed closeted, hypocritical gays with similar evidence "everybody knows" have been looked upon with contempt even when reporters show up time after time for the activists' press conferences. If "everybody knows" about a particular closeted gay public figure, you can bet that *The Washington Post* or the *Los Angeles Times* knows, but the editors never run the stories. Somehow the fact that "everybody knows" is just not good enough in the case of a closeted homosexual, though it is in the case of a man sexually harassing women. "Everybody knows" usually means that dozens, if not hundreds, of people have discussed the individual's homosexuality with him or her, have friends who know for sure, or have socialized with the individual time after time in a gay context; "everybody knows" means that dozens or hundreds have seen the individual over and over again at lesbian and gay bars and parties, at public events with an openly homosexual date, being affectionate and playful with a same-sex date in public. In some cases, people have even seen the closeted individual engaging in sex at a gay sex club.

"What is a newspaper to do with such damaging information as that on Brock Adams?" asked an agonized *New York Times*. "Verify, verify, verify. Then publish what it believes to be the truth, however painful. *The Seattle Times* appears to have followed this high standard."

The New York Times refused to print Malcolm Forbes's name in its story about the outing phenomenon two years before. It refused to discuss the sexual abuse he perpetrated, and editors made no attempt to "verify, verify, verify." Certainly, if there was ever someone about whom "everybody knew," it was Forbes: Among the editors, executives, and publishers of *The New York Times*, many were intimate with Forbes and with members of his family.

The Forbes story was a story about sexual harassment and sexual abuse not unlike the Adams case or the Clarence Thomas case. Forbes had harassed and coerced employees to have sex with him. The men felt intimidated. They believed they had to engage in sex with him in order to keep their jobs. Two conspicuous differences made the Forbes story even more ethically reportable than the Adams case: The Forbes story had *named* sources, people who could have been interviewed and checked out; and the subject was *dead*.

In light of the Adams case, it's astonishing that the Forbes exposé caused such an uproar among members of the media at all. The outrage and anger caused by the revelations of male-on-male sexual harassment perpetrated by Malcolm Forbes were motivated solely by homophobia. *OutWeek* had dared to claim for the gay community an American icon who had supposedly dated the most glamorous movie star in the world. We had dared to describe him as someone whose closet forced him to sexually harass his employees. Just as in the case of Pete Williams, those who reported that Forbes was gay were seen by media critics to be participating in the vilest of invasions. They'd never vocalize it, but deep down the critics believed it was terrible to say that someone was gay, even if that person was dead. Papers like *The New York Times,* which reported about outing but referred to Forbes only as "a famous businessman who recently died," were seen as being responsible and "tasteful." The media will continue to view revelations of homosexuality as tasteless and ugly until they are pushed hard enough to do otherwise.

Where sexual harassment is an issue, the media's resistance to outing undercuts the justice system, allowing abusive, destructive actions in the workplace to go on unreported. While male-on-female sexual harassment is rightfully exposed, male-on-male sexual harassment will continue to be made invisible by a homophobic press, except when the abused files official criminal or civil charges. As we've witnessed in recent years, however, two extremely powerful cases of sexual harassment did not involve criminal charges, and one of those cases was based solely on anonymous sources. It is hard for a person who is being harassed to speak up at all, let alone file charges. Scores of cases escape public scrutiny. If the media waited until actual criminal charges were publicly filed before reporting allegations, the issue of sexual harassment would not have gained the visibility and significance it now has. No one would have known anything about Anita Hill, and Senator Adams would still allegedly be abusing women in his office. Ultimately, as Maggie Boys pointed out, sometimes the media must be the institution that offers justice for those whom society steps on.

Journalists and others who say they are opposed to outing in general might say that when sexual harassment is involved, it would be right to publish a story exposing the truth. However, they should not be fooled into thinking that these are exceptions to the rule: Closeted gay public figures who are sexually abusing others do not represent only a small number of isolated cases. It is more likely that they represent the vast majority of deeply closeted, powerful men in our society, simply because sexual abuse of employees and others in their lives offers the easiest—and often the only—means of sexual interaction with other men.

· · · · ·

What would happen if Keith's former boss, the Legislator, were outed? On the one hand, he might do what Brock Adams did: deny the entire scenario and decide not to run for reelection. Or Keith's boss could resign outright. In that case, someone who was abusing many young gay men and voting against the lesbian and gay community though he himself is gay would be brought down and prevented from abusing his power any longer. He would forever become an example of the horrors of the closet, of the massive damage that one man's powerful closet perpetrates and how it can adversely affect the lives of many.

There is a third possibility: He could rise to the occasion, admit his wrongdoing, attribute it to society's homophobia and to being forced to live a lie, and stay in office as an openly gay man. He might realize that exposure, though traumatic at first, has freed him. He might get divorced and come to terms with his sexuality. If he did, he might become not only a happy and more productive individual but also an enormous asset to the gay community. This is what happened to Congressman Gerry Studds after he was outed in 1982.

Massachusetts Democratic congressman Studds was brought out of his closet in a sting operation initiated by a tip from a congressional page, who claimed that House members used illegal drugs, which they bought from pages. The investigation found no evidence of drug sales or use but did find that in 1973, almost ten years earlier, Studds had been sexually involved with a male page and had made advances to others. It was also found that Representative Daniel Crane, an Illinois Republican, had had an affair with a female page.

The sworn testimony of several male pages (who, some speculate, were coerced into cooperating) revealed that Studds had had a relationship with a male page for roughly one year. The former page, who testified, was sixteen when he and Studds began engaging in sex. They had even gone to Europe together. There is some question whether these actions constituted sexual harassment or abuse, or whether the boy had been making his own decisions. In his testimony, the boy did not characterize the affair as abusive; in fact, he went out of his way to disassociate Studds's actions from such behaviors. However, some child psychologists would argue that sixteen-year-olds are unable to distinguish between sexual harassment and consensual sex and are not mature enough to make decisions about sex, even though they may feel that they are. The report of the House Committee on Standards of Official Conduct read:

Q. When the congressman first invited you to have dinner and as you got to know the congressman, how did you feel in that environment, that a congressman was talking with you?

A. I was flattered and excited.

Q. Did you feel intimidated?

A. No, I did not. I would like to state at this time—it would probably have been better if I had stated this in my opening statement—but the congressman or the Honorable Gerry Studds was an intelligent, witty, gentle man with I think a high level of insecurity. He did nothing to me which I would consider destructive or painful. In another time, in another society, the action would be acceptable, perhaps even laudable. Unfortunately this is not the case. I have no ax to grind with him. I have nothing negative to say about the man. In fact, I thought that he provided me with one of the more wonderful experiences of my life, if we exclude the instances of sexual experience which I was somewhat uncomfortable with. But I did not think it was that big a deal.

Q. You said you felt uncomfortable with it, did you continue with him because he was a congressman, because he was someone you were impressed with?

A. No. Well, I kept company with him because he was an intelligent man, a fun person to be with. If I could have had my druthers, I would have had the friendship that I had with the man without the sex. And I mentioned that to him.

Q. Did Mr. Studds ever offer any preferential treatment or offer you any inducement to have a relationship with him?

A. No, he did not.

Q. Did he ever threaten you or coerce you if you did not have a relationship with him?

A. He did not. Essentially all I needed to do to stop the relationship was walk out the door, or not go in the door, as the case may be.

Studds told the committee that he did not believe that a "relationship which was mutual and voluntary, without coercion, without any preferential treatment express or implied, without harassment of any kind, which was private and which occurred 10 years ago constitutes 'improper sexual conduct.'"

Whether or not Studds's actions were "improper," the circumstances surrounding them were the result of his closeted life. Like Congressman Barney Frank while he was closeted, like the Legislator who employed Keith, like all the scores of closeted powerful men, Studds was not able to lead an open life or go out to gay bars, gay parties, or other gay social gatherings. He was forced to negotiate sexually intimate relationships within the workplace.

"I feel better than I ever felt in my life," Studds told *The Advocate* soon after being outed. "I suspect that's something that would be easy for your audience of gay people to understand. But I've found that in giving that response to the media in general, to folks who have not had this experience themselves, that it requires a great deal of explanation as to how in the midst of what for a lot of reasons appears to be a disastrous situation, one can candidly say, 'I've never felt better in my life.'" In 1990, Studds told the *Los Angeles Times* that his outing was the best thing that had ever happened to him and said he saw a case for outing public figures.

One of Studds's strongest supporters during the scandal was Republican congressman Stewart McKinney of Connecticut, a relatively conservative member who surprised some with his support. "Ladies and gentlemen of America," McKinney said on *The MacNeil/Lehrer NewsHour*, "one slightly psychotic teenager went to the FBI and the press of the United States and said there was something evil in Congress—drug selling. Wrong. And that there was something evil between '81 and '82—illicit sex. Wrong. . . . I would suggest to you that no Rotary Club, Lions Club, corporate entity, board of directors or anyone else would have spent a million dollars and more investigating this type of process and in fact masochistically beating themselves over the shoulder." Years later, McKinney's support would be understood. In 1988 he died of AIDS. A married man with several children, he too had had a secret gay life—and a lover, who later became involved with McKinney's wife in a bitter public tug-of-war over his estate.

Studds was censured and then put the scandal behind him. He went on to use his position in Congress as a platform, taking on the Reagan and Bush administrations' policies on AIDS education and fighting immigration laws that exclude HIV-positive people. Studds has become a loud voice against antigay bigotry throughout our society. He has been instrumental in the fight against the military's ban on homosexuals.

The Studds outing marked a turning point. He was the first closeted official who came out—proudly declaring his homosexuality to the American people—after he was outed (in a scandal perpetrated by the government) whose career was not only unaltered but actually enhanced. In 1978, Representative Fred Richmond of Brooklyn, New York, had been charged with paying a sixteen-year-old boy for sex and using his own Washington home to solicit sex from a male undercover cop. But, after sending out a confessional letter to constituents admitting wrongdoing, he later pleaded innocent to the charges and never discussed his sexuality in the media. (The charges were dropped after Richmond completed a D.C. first-offender program.)

Right-wing Republican congressman Jon Hinson was arrested in 1981 for having oral sex with a Library of Congress clerk in a House office building. Although he pleaded innocent, the scandal forced him to resign. It hadn't been his first brush with the law: A year earlier, it was revealed that Hinson had been arrested for "committing an obscene act" at the Iwo Jima Memorial, then a popular gay pick-up spot. (He pleaded guilty and paid a fine.) Like the Legislator whom Keith worked for, Hinson allowed his closet to control him. He admitted to Deb Price at *The Detroit News* in 1992 that by having sex in public he was doing "incredibly risky, stupid things," torn between his desire to be out and his perceived necessity to stay in the closet. "I knew the minute I was arrested that my career was over," he said. "I look back now and see that I was a gay man trying to lie to myself."

Right-wing Republican congressman Robert Bauman, who had been vocally antigay, was also outed in 1980 when he was charged with soliciting sex from a teenage boy in a Washington gay bar, a scenario that many said at the time was a set-up by the Carter administration. Only four weeks later, the charges were dropped, but he lost his bid for reelection.

But Studds stayed on as a vocal, openly gay man, was reelected several times, and became a valuable asset to his community. Little wonder that a new generation of lesbians and gay men, perhaps perceiving this sea change in the way that revelations of homosexuality played out in the public arena, would come to consider outing as a way of advancing their rights. And no wonder that the right wing, which had historically delighted in outing, would now condemn the new, young generation of queers for this gross "invasion of privacy."

Sex *is* power, and often the tables can be turned completely.

• • • • •

Lesbians, like all women, have known for centuries that sex is men's ultimate means of control over them. But when lesbians themselves are in power, sex is still a tool used against them by straights.

There are so few women—and even fewer lesbians—in powerful positions that it is difficult to deduce a clear and predictable pattern among lesbian closets of power in the nation's capital. However, certain similarities prevail among lesbians in high elective office, as well as in other powerful positions throughout the government.

High-ranking lesbians do not seem to engage in sexual harassment. Perhaps that is because lesbians in such positions aren't forced to resort to extreme measures in order to have emotional and sexual intimacy with other women. They're actually not as closeted as their gay male counterparts. Closeted lesbian entertainers and pop stars, as well as lesbian government figures, have tended to remain unmarried and let their homosexuality be known to their immediate staffs and even their families. Some quietly have lovers with whom they live. The rules are different for men and women in Washington, as they are throughout society: Men in power must be the breadwinners of the family, they must have wives to bring to events, and they must have children and live by traditional "family values"—even though they're given permission to fool around on the side, as long as they keep it "discreet."

Women in power, on the other hand, are subverting the system just by being in power, and thus there are no rules. While having a husband might deflect rumors that a woman is queer, women in Washington don't have to be married. Women in Washington aren't taken seriously enough to begin with—or haven't been until now, that is. "It goes hand in hand with lesbians being invisible," says openly lesbian Vivian Shapiro, a board member of the Human Rights

Campaign Fund, who has socialized with prominent Washington lesbians. "It's easier for them to stay in the closet and still maintain a relationship."

One closeted lesbian member of Congress is convinced that her entire career would be jeopardized if she ever stated publicly that she is queer. She believes this in spite of the fact that her constituents are, for the most part, working-class Democrats, many of whom have speculated for years that she's a lesbian, as have many people in government and the media in Washington. The force behind this member's closet is a straight woman who masterminded her early campaigns and who is to this day her closest political advisor. When the member decided she wanted to lead a more open life, the straight female advisor, using feminism in the most deceitful way, told her she was being selfish and consistently pressed the notion that, if the member came out, she'd destroy her own career and make people think that every prominent woman in politics was a dyke.

The homophobia—and lesbophobia—of this straight female advisor and several straight men who also work for and advise the member and run her campaigns are so pervasive and obvious that it was apparent, at least at one point, even to some other heterosexuals who worked for the member. At the time, the straight female advisor seemed to have an unbreakable hold over the member, observers say.

The female advisor urged the member to vote against gays in order to prove that she wasn't queer. Thus the member, like the Legislator who employed Keith, voted time after time in favor of antigay legislation and legislation that discriminated against people with AIDS. After initially supporting a gay-rights bill, the member retreated in fear.

Other lesbians, further out of the closet and working in women's groups in Washington, went directly to the member to speak with her. By then, the straight female advisor had left the member's employ, though she was still close to her. Also, by that time, outing had developed in the gay community, and this member knew that she certainly was "on the list." Those who worked in her office at the time say that she was terrified of outing and that even the straight advisor realized it was time for the member to change her voting pattern.

Today, the member's votes on gay issues are nearly perfect, and she is once again behind the gay-rights bill. But she still will not be seen in public with openly gay individuals. She still will not attend any gay political functions. Nor will she take any money from the Human Rights Campaign Fund's political action committee. Even though the member's voting has gotten better, she is still the victim of people who control her life. She changed only out of fear that her career was in danger. Living in fear, the member still leads a closeted life; she is still constantly anxious and worried about exposure.

·····

Closeted lesbians are probably much better than closeted gay men are at maneuvering through the maze of moralism in Washington. As women, they're forced from childhood to maneuver through a man's world. If they want power, they're forced to "pass," forced to downplay the fact that they are women.

For these reasons, someone like Anne-Imelda Radice, named acting head of the National Endowment for the Arts in early 1992, can weather quite a storm. George Bush forced John Frohnmayer out as head of the Endowment when presidential contender Patrick Buchanan attacked it for funding art that had gay and lesbian themes, most notably the Marlon Riggs film *Tongues Untied,* about the lives of black gay men. The NEA's funding of the Riggs film was the straw that broke the camel's back in a controversy the right wing had been instigating for several years regarding the funding of gay artists' projects about gay life.

A right-wing, conservative NEA staffer, Radice was made acting head at that time. There was speculation that she had originally been brought into the job with the eventual rise in mind. Soon after he was replaced, Frohnmayer said on *Nightline* that Radice had always reported directly to then–Vice President Dan Quayle, an icon of the right. Upon her arrival in the top spot, Radice told the media that she would veto applications with "difficult subject matter" and works where "the sexual nature is the first thing you see or the overwhelming thing you experience." Jesse Helms, a leader of the movement to defund gay art, immediately called her "a lady with good sense and guts to match," exclaiming, "My hat's off to her!" Quayle's aide William Kristol said that there was now "no need to be involved because the NEA was in good hands."

What no news organizations wrote at first, however, was that Radice was a lesbian. Unlike the deeply closeted gay men who live and work in Washington, Radice had never "bearded" herself by marrying someone of the opposite sex. She had never hidden her sexuality in any way.

Rochelle Thorpe, who interned with Radice at the National Museum of Women in the Arts in 1985, told reporter Donna Minkowitz that, among the staff, "everyone knew Radice was a dyke." Other women told of going to rather public gay parties with her and of going out to dinner with her and her lover, with whom Radice lives openly in the Dupont Circle area of town. One man who worked closely under her at NMWA told Minkowitz that she was very open at the office and had actually helped him come out of the closet himself. He met three of her lovers during that time, and went out in public with her to many gay and lesbian bars.

Minkowitz, a rigorous reporter for *The Village Voice*, launched her own investigation and reported on Radice in *The Advocate*. Soon after, some of the mainstream press, including the *Los Angeles Times*, acknowledged Radice's lesbianism. Some compared her to Clarence Thomas, pointing out that both were conservative members of oppressed groups who were brought in to push the agenda of an administration hostile toward gays and blacks.

Many other papers refused to write about the issue, buying the NEA's response to inquiries: "The NEA does not discuss personal matters about any staff members." This made newspeople feel that they should keep their hands off the issue. The incident proved how easily one could "in" oneself to the media at a moment's notice.

Perhaps someone like Radice can hide behind the image of lesbians as sexless. "Because of the public image of gay men as wildly sexual and sexually transgressive and the image of lesbians as asexual and sexually boring," says Minkowitz, "it was easier to put a lesbian in charge of the NEA. She feeds into this image of lesbians as unerotic." Minkowitz is convinced that Radice's lesbianism was known to people in the White House. "They definitely knew," she says, "and thought it would be perfect. I think they made that appointment very deliberately. Radice was so obsessed with her career and rising through those circles. They'd find out right away, certainly through the routine background checks."

Minkowitz observes that closeted lesbians in the Washington power structure are so invisible that "sometimes [lesbians] get away with stuff that gay men can't because lesbians are more likely to be ignored than gay men." She says that lesbians have an "easier time playing up a variety of closet angles—from being fully out to being fully closeted, whenever convenient." But Minkowitz is quick to add that "freedom in passing is really not freedom at all."

· · · · ·

Sex is power and power is sex. And many times both are tucked just beneath a surface of smooth, pristine veneer.

Washington—the official part of Washington—is an immaculately clean place. Sparkling and white, it appears virginal in the most traditional sense: untouched. The city is also highly systematic and uniform. The Metro is always on time. People line up willingly in single file on escalators. There aren't any lines at the bank. And no one is ever late for an appointment.

This neurotic efficiency and cleanliness betray the truth: Washington is a town racked with guilt, a city desperately trying to cover for itself, its Mussolini-like architecture intimating at a lurking evil beneath its rotundas—an evil bred by power.

Like most groups who've traditionally been shut out, lesbians and gays are attracted to power. The city is—perhaps disproportionately—overflowing with queers. Throughout the years, they have occupied the White House. They have sat in high positions at the Pentagon. They have headed the district's top PR firms and lobbying groups. And, if it is true what they say—that congressional staffers, rather than the members themselves, run Congress—then Congress is and always has been run by homosexuals.

This is nothing new, as gay men, and to a lesser extent lesbians, have had a strong presence in Washington for decades. In recent years, evidence has surfaced suggesting that Franklin Pierce and James Buchanan may have been closeted homosexuals. Abraham Lincoln may have had a homosexual relationship with his close friend Joshua Speed. Gore Vidal even suggests that George Washington harbored an unrequited passion for pretty boy Alexander Hamilton. Eleanor Roosevelt was either a lesbian or a woman with many lesbian friends. Nancy Reagan had many gay male friends and acquaintances, two of whom spent a night together in the Lincoln bedroom; her godmother, the early-twentieth-century actress Alla Nazimova, was a well-known lesbian who was best friends with Nancy's mother. Over the years, there have been several sons and daughters of presidents who were gay. Aides to presidents and other prominent politicians have been queer too, and sometimes have been brought out in public scandals. In 1993, it was revealed that the viciously antigay FBI director from the thirties through the sixties, J. Edgar Hoover, was a closeted queer who did drag once in a while. Needless to say, throughout history gays have occupied, and now occupy, prominent positions everywhere in the government hierarchy.

The powers that be have always known this, and journalists and social commentators, albeit with antigay vigor and a penchant for paranoid exaggeration, have even reported it to the public. As far back as 1951, gonzo gossips Jack Lait and Lee Mortimer wrote a ghastly and popular book entitled *Washington Confidential*. In one chapter, "A Garden of Pansies," Lait and Mortimer, a rabidly homophobic gossip columnist for the *New York Mirror*, provided canon fodder for the McCarthy era:

> If you're wondering where your wandering semi-boy is tonight, he's probably in Washington.
>
> The good people shook their heads in disbelief over the revelation that more than 90 twisted twerps in trousers had been swished out of the State Department. Fly commentators seized on it for gags about fags, whimsy with overtones of Kinsey and the odor of lavender. We pursued the subject and we found that there are at least 6000 homosexuals on the government payroll, most of them known, and these comprise only a fraction of the total of their kind in the city.
>
> The only way to get authoritative data on fairies is from other fairies. They recognize each other by a fifth [sic] sense immediately, and they are intensely gregarious. One cannot snoop at every desk and count people who appear queer. Some are deceptive to the uninitiated. But they all know one another and they have a grapevine of intercommunication as swift and sure as that in a girls' boarding school.... There is no geographic section where degenerates generally live. That is part of the general picture, everything,

everywhere, in Washington. Many rich fairies and lesbians live in expensive remodeled Georgetown homes, the nearest thing to a left-bank neighborhood. This is also a left-wing center.

At the time of *Washington Confidential*'s publication, the country was ripe for paranoia. Communism—and its threat to capitalism— had taken hold in many countries around the world. Republicans in the United States, bitterly trying to unseat Democratic President Harry Truman, described communism as the vilest of scourges and grossly exaggerated the threat it posed to America. They portrayed Truman as weak and ineffectual in the face of this supposed menace. Republican Senator Joseph McCarthy, seeing opportunity knocking, began crusading against and rooting out supposed Communists in powerful positions from Washington to Hollywood. Finger-pointing and list-keeping were his methods, and many people's careers were ruined simply because of political beliefs they might—or, in many cases, might not—have had. The anti-Communist strikes were soon accompanied by purges of homosexuals, as the Republicans expanded their campaign to encompass all of what they perceived to be threats to national security.

In his book *Sexual Politics, Sexual Communities: The Making of a Homosexual Minority in the United States,* historian John D'Emilio documented the events:

[In 1950] McCarthy . . . charged that an unnamed person in the State Department had forced the reinstatement of a homosexual despite the threat to the nation's safety. Styles Bridges, a conservative senator from New Hampshire, assailed the laxity of the federal branch in ferreting out spies and homosexuals. After the head of the District of Columbia vice squad told a Senate committee that thousands of "sexual deviates" worked for the government, the Republican floor leader, Kenneth Wherry, demanded a full-scale Senate inquiry. In May Governor Thomas Dewey of New York, who had been the [Republican] party's presidential candidate in 1948, accused the administration of tolerating the employment of sexual offenders. Seven thousand Republican party workers received a newsletter from their national chairman, Guy Gabrielson, alerting them to the new "homosexual angle" in Washington. "Sexual perverts . . . have infiltrated our government in recent years," he warned, and they were "perhaps as dangerous as the actual Communists." Gabrielson implied that party loyalists had a special responsibility to arouse the country's ire over the issue, since "decency" constrained the media from "adequately presenting the facts" to the American people. Finally, in June 1950 the full Senate bowed to pressure and authorized an investigation into the alleged employment of homosexuals and "other moral perverts" in the government.

The Wherry Committee's report was the first of several that led to the expulsions of thousands of lesbians and gays from government jobs during the fifties.

Frank Kameny remembers the era vividly. In the early fifties, he was a graduate student of astronomy at Georgetown University. "There were congressional committees on both sides of the Capitol which were viciously homophobic," he recalls. "That was the story of the fifties. The number of firings throughout the decade was enormous. People were fired throughout the House and the Senate as well as people in the civil service—federal civil servants in the executive branch."

In 1957, Kameny himself became a victim of the purge. He'd been working for several months as an astronomer with the Army Map Service, which was part of the Department of Defense. "They found out I was gay and I was fired on the spot," he says. "They just called me in and told me that they had information on me."

Kameny grew angry. "My feeling was that it takes an awful lot of chutzpah and gall to do this to someone," he says. Determined to fight injustice, he became a gay activist. In 1961 Kameny founded the Mattachine Society of Washington, the city's first gay organization. At first, he says, "the gay movement, which had only begun to loosely form in the fifties, was very passive, very apologetic, very unassertive—they weren't doing anything. But we were now the cutting edge of the movement nationally. In any possible direction you could imagine, we were doing it." Kameny devoted much of his life to fighting the federal government's antigay policies. By 1975, he had won for gays the right to jobs in the civil service and to security clearances for civilians, except in the CIA and FBI. Today, still working hard as an activist in Washington at the age of seventy-six, he has lived to see the raging public debate over dismantling the Defense Department's ban on gays in the military.

"You have to be very careful," he says with caution, "not to fall into a trap of a kind of subtle stereotyping in some way. You'll get a variety of answers [about how many gays there are in the government] from different people. My feeling has always been that the proportion of gays in government positions has been substantially the same number as in other populations."

Other observers sharply disagree.

Joseph Izzo, a psychotherapist who works with gay men and HIV-positive people, is currently head of mental-health services at the Whitman Walker Clinic, Washington's largest AIDS service organization. Izzo has lived in and just outside of the nation's capital since 1965. In his view, lesbians and gays are attracted to Washington and its government jobs in greater numbers than to most other places. "There's no question about it—it's because of the nature of the city," he says. "A lot of gay people move here for the same reason that blacks did after the Civil War: There are many job opportunities and it's a way to access power."

The "transplants," as Izzo calls them, are generally high-achiever types. Landing a job with the federal government provides a way to gain security and even influence.

"This will sound terrible," says Bill, a closeted gay staffer who works for a particularly powerful congressman, "but when you are in a place where you can be a part of decision-making at the highest levels on a regular basis, well, I get a certain charge of excitement. It's watching the exercise of the power, it's interesting and exciting and, occasionally, in the public interest." Bill, like Keith, says he's "always been involved in politics, even as a teenager, working on campaigns."

Bob Adams, one of a small handful of openly gay staffers, is an aide to Gerry Studds. Like other gay staffers, he speaks of his job reverentially. "I went home and turned on the TV and watched the State of the Union address," he says of George Bush's speech in January 1992, "just like everyone else in the United States. But the next day I went to work and I was able to immediately talk to people who were very involved in the legislation that Bush was talking about. I started working on some of the legislation. Most Americans went to work the next day and made cheese in the Kraft plant but I got to start working on that legislation and following it and reading about it and learning about it. It's very exciting. I feel very blessed that I have this job."

Katherine, a closeted lesbian staffer, says that working on the Hill has brought her into much closer contact with other lesbians than she had in college. She feels there are disproportionately high numbers of lesbians and gay men working in Congress. Like several other closeted gay men and lesbians who work on the Hill, Bill and Katherine both feel that the ratio of gay people in the lower echelons of government is probably 10 percent, as in the rest of the population. But on Capitol Hill, they say, among the staffs of the more powerful senators and congressmen on the more powerful committees, there is a much larger number of gay men and lesbians.

There are several reasons why this is true. The more demanding positions require long hours, sometimes ten to fourteen hours a day. The jobs require an enormous amount of dedication and commitment. A person who is married and has children is going to find it difficult to hold down a key position with a powerful member of Congress. Asking around casually, one finds that, on average, of the ten or so top aides to the most powerful members of Congress, six or more are unmarried and over twenty-eight years old. Often the jobs also require much travel. Bill says that, among staffers in such positions, many are gay or lesbian, simply because gays are more likely than straights to remain unattached and in most cases do not have traditional families and children to tend to.

The prevalence of lesbians and gays in the top positions in Congress is also a result of economics. The work force on Capitol Hill is fairly young. Most low-level congressional staffers are in their twenties, having landed a job right out of college. Many move on after only one to three years, having gained valuable experience and a respectable entry on their résumés. If they want to make big money, they have to take that experience and go elsewhere, usually to the private sector. The starting salary on the Hill is anywhere from $12,000 to $20,000 per year. Most young staffers live in group housing and barely get by. After a few years most move on to graduate school or law school, enter a family business, or land a position on the outside. Those who stay must be prepared to work for relatively low wages, in jobs that become more and more demanding as their holder rises in importance and influence over the years. Moving up in a member's office might bring one's salary up to $30,000 after five years, and then, after many years, to a cap of $115,000 (reached in only a few cases). Most of the ambitious young people just out of school are looking to make much bigger money, much quicker. The vast majority, heterosexuals, are always aware of having to pursue careers that will afford them enough money to raise families and put kids through college.

"Conventional wisdom would say that gay people, being single, would work more hours and stay here [in Congress] and not feel compelled to get off the Hill and make more money," says Bob Adams. "Whereas a straight person, after working here for several years, would get a job with a law firm or lobbying firm, make more money, keep more regular hours, and commute home to the suburbs to be with the kids, gay people, still wanting to stay in the mix of everything, wouldn't mind staying here, living here, working longer hours, and getting paid less, because this is where things happen. They're willing to trade off the lack of free time and money in order to maintain their exciting lives."

"The jobs are by definition highly mobile," says Tim Donohoe, a gay man who has worked for various House members for twenty years.[14] He now works for the House of Representatives itself and became open about being gay only in recent years. "It's a way to get out of Podunk," he says. "I can only think of three or four openly gay staff members, but as far as the closet goes, it's very big here. I'd say the amount of gays here certainly far exceeds the Kinsey ten percent. The people who seem to stay on longer in the jobs tend to be gay and seem to move up quickly. A lot of the administrative jobs and the policy jobs are filled by gays. There is a cadre of gay people on the bigger committees, especially Energy and Commerce and Public Works. I know people at the top levels."

Washington is also a very comfortable city for queers. Traditionally liberal, the District has one of the most comprehensive antidiscrimination laws in the country. The local lesbian and gay activist community has been effective over the years in quietly pushing for gay rights. The municipal government is tolerant. The black community, which represents the vast majority of the city, has gained in power and influence over the years and, though there are sometimes huge rifts between some black leaders and some gay leaders in Washington, the local power structure has been very broad-minded with regard to gay civil rights.

Paradoxically, until September of 1993, when it was finally overturned without a challenge, an antisodomy law was on the books in D.C., because Congress still retains much control over the city. Laws as old as the Republic itself leave the nation's capital with little autonomy. Congress, led by its antigay members, has, during the Reagan administration in the mid-1980s, overturned a previous repeal of the D.C. sodomy statute and had passed an amendment prohibiting allocation of funds for an ordinance the city council had passed granting domestic-partnership benefits for D.C. city employees.

Some religious sectors of the black community have fought gays as well. Wilhelmina Rolark, until 1993 a member of the city council, was a staunch foe of the gay community, blocking many initiatives. In general, however, activists in Washington have made much more progress in fostering tolerance for gays than has been achieved in many other cities. Washington was a trailblazer in gaining local antidiscrimination ordinances for gays, years ahead of cities thought to be more progressive, like New York and San Francisco. In 1975, Frank Kameny, appointed to the D.C. Human Rights Commission, was among the first openly gay municipal public figures in the United States. In the late seventies and early eighties, Washington had more openly gay public officials than any other city in the country.

The dichotomy between the liberal municipal government and conservative members of Congress highlights the existence of the two Washingtons: the federal one, which is perceived to be overtly homophobic, and the municipality, which is gay-friendly. The city is constantly in a tug-of-war between Jesse Helms's ilk and a black liberal establishment.

"It's a place where many gay people can comfortably be *socially* out of the closet, away from their original homes and families," Joseph Izzo says, referring to the mostly white "transplants" who work in Congress and in the executive branch. This particular observation reveals, perhaps, the greatest contradiction about the gay people who fill many of the staff jobs on the Hill. The transplanted gays (as opposed to those who've grown up in Washington, most of whom are African-American) move to Washington to work in government and enjoy a lively and openly gay social life, Izzo notes. Because they've left their homes, they don't have to worry about being found out by their families and are stepping out in a tolerant, liberal environment. But they are constantly aware that they're living in the two Washingtons. The business lives of many are extremely closeted because of the nature of their work and the institutionalized homophobia in the government. Their lives become centered around what has come to be called the Revolving Closet; they stay inside from nine to seven, spin merrily out after hours, and then slip securely back in just in time for work the next day.

The Revolving Closet manifests itself in a variety of ways. Washington has as many gay bars and social-service organizations as any other city its size, perhaps even more. It has several neighborhoods known to be predominantly gay, such as Adams-Morgan and Dupont Circle, where many restaurants are filled with gay men and lesbians. And yet, for a community of this size, in a city of this size, a surprisingly low number of people will show up for public demonstrations of any kind. Except when activists come in from around the country for a national action, the local chapters of ACT UP and Queer Nation, as well as other protest groups, have rarely gotten crowds comparable to those in other cities. Washington's Gay Pride Parade is small, doesn't last long, and doesn't run through the heart of town.

"The parade here is nothing compared to the one in Boston," says Joe Martin, an openly gay man who worked for several years as a chief aide to Congressman Barney Frank of Massachusetts and is highly respected among Washington's gay politicos. Having been with Frank through the period after the congressman gave an interview to *The Boston Globe* in 1984 declaring his homosexuality, Martin was a positive influence on Frank for much of the latter's career.

Martin came out of the closet at a very young age. Growing up in Boston, he realized before the sixth grade that he was different. "I identified myself as being attracted to men," he recalls, "and it became evident to me that the majority of people were heterosexual." While in the seventh grade, he saw his first soft-core gay porn film. "It was in 1963 and it was men hugging, not much else," he says. "But it was significant because it made me realize that adult men were attracted to adult men and that it was okay." Over the next couple of years, Martin became more comfortable with his homosexuality.

"I came to realize that the last thing I wanted to be was a closeted gay man," he recalls. He decided at fifteen that he was going to tell everyone in his life, including his family and all his friends. He did, and he's been outspokenly out of the closet ever since. Like many people who came out very early in life, Martin, who still resides in Washington, is quick to spot closeted individuals and not especially tolerant of closeted environments.

"I wasn't working [in Washington] very long when I sensed that it was extremely closeted," he says. "I'd look at someone who I'd sense was gay. Normally, just like black people who pass each other and give each other a nod, there's that sense of fraternity among gays when they spot each other. But on the Hill, that didn't happen much at all. You'd make eye contact with someone in a hallway and figure they were gay, but they'd look the other way. Sometimes they were people I knew from [my] neighborhood [Dupont Circle] who I knew were gay, who were even friendly with me in the neighborhood, smiling and saying hello. But then I'd go to nod at them on Capitol Hill and they'd turn away. That kind of thing happens all the time, and you can just see them freezing up."

Martin feels that because he is one of less than half a dozen openly gay staffers (out of hundreds of staffers) on the Hill, people tend to be afraid of him. He also thinks that his working for Barney Frank, who is openly gay and a supporter of outing, has had an effect. "I have a friend who is gay and is a senior Republican staffer," he explains. "He has told me of several times when in social situations—gay social situations—when he told people that I work for Barney Frank—these are gay Republicans—they tell him that they're not interested in meeting me or being in the same place as me. They're afraid that I'm going to out them. He's introduced me to people who only tell me their first names and won't tell me where they work."

But since he is closeted himself, Bill, a senior aide to a powerful member, has a different experience. He doesn't see queers on the Hill as so deeply closeted, simply because many of those who are closeted in a general sense—and are closeted to Joe Martin—are *not* closeted to Bill or any other closeted staffers. They utilize the Revolving Closet and are out to others in the same predicament. They are among the people one will meet at J.R.'s—or, more recently, the video bar and restaurant called Trumpets—after work during the week and at the huge dance club Tracks on a Saturday night. They're very friendly in the bar and discuss work openly among themselves and even with strangers, but the vast majority are not out at the office. They would never associate their names with something that might identify them as gay, and would never speak as gay people, on the record, to reporters.

Bill says that he constantly runs into people at work whom he knows from social settings and that this isn't uncomfortable precisely because they share a secret. Martin, on the other hand, has revealed his secret, and thus is perceived as dangerous. People don't feel they're on an equal footing with him: He has something on them, but they don't have anything on *him*.

"Unless you go home and sit in your room and don't go out to any gay bar or event, or don't walk down the street for that matter," says Bill, "then you run into people [from work] repeatedly, and you recognize them because you've seen them in the cafeteria, the hall, the gym. I recall being told that a person was an aide to a right-wing fascist senator and that person was lying out on the beach at Rehoboth [a beach on the Delaware coast with a popular gay section] with everybody else who is gay. To not be found out or known to many as gay in this town, you'd really have to be *totally* in the closet. I can't see how you could function in this town, in the bar, gym, or on the street, and be that closeted."

"These people fit in that middle area—the semi-closeted," says Tim Donohoe. "They're part of a large social clique. Everybody involved in government who is gay for the most part knows each other—and knows *about* each other. They meet at J.R.'s or on an occasional night out at the dance bars. They go to the gay-friendly restaurants and the cocktail bars. A lot of them are in couples, and socialize with other couples. They tend to occupy the political spectrum, from Democrat to Republican. It's always been that way."

Thus, unlike those gay members of Congress who are locked in the Iron Closet, the vast majority of gay aides and staffers have a slightly more open society, thanks to the Revolving Closet. In the past few years, they've even begun to organize in the most elementary of ways. In 1992, some gay men (no lesbians) who worked on the Hill formed a group. The members were mostly young staffers: One of their meeting announcements in the gay press crudely asked that only people under twenty-four years of age attend. The group is strictly social; rarely does discussion arise around political organizing or such. And, still afraid of exposure, the group keeps itself shrouded in secrecy. Even if the staffers are quite out to the gay public, keeping their anonymity on the Hill is of the utmost importance. The same is true for those who work in the Pentagon and the White House, and in the higher positions of other government agencies.

The fear, of course, is due to the intense homophobia throughout Washington's government circles and especially on the Hill, where many closeted gay staffers work for unsympathetic and even overtly antigay members. But even most of those whose bosses are more supportive of gay people tend to stay locked in the closet at work.

"You identify so much with the member and his beliefs," says Tim Donohoe. "It's just the nature of the job. You don't usually have a high profile on any issue. You bury your personality in the member. I think the loyalty goes so far that you start to have their opinions. I worked for a Texas congressman and I soon found myself sympathetic to oil and gas constituents even though I considered myself a staunch environmentalist."

"I think one of the things that happens," says Joe Martin, "is that people believe that whatever it is you are has to be submerged for the sake of your boss, because of what he represents to so many people. People feel that they can never be in the spotlight, or attract any attention that might reflect on their boss." Thus, the vast majority of closeted gay staffers keep their true identities hidden from their bosses and everyone else at work; it's a situation that only adds to the internalized homophobia they experience.

In many of these cases, just like the closeted senators and congresspeople who vote antigay in order to deflect gossip about their sexual orientation, the staffers refuse to advocate for gay rights. In some cases they even argue vociferously *against* gay rights and the rights of people with AIDS. But even those closeted staffers who try their best to work in the interests of lesbians and gay men find that their closets compromise them. Bill admits that being closeted often causes him problems. He sometimes challenges his boss when his boss is planning an antigay vote, but at other times, not wanting to seem too strident and thus arouse suspicion, he stays silent. He realizes that if he were out, his boss would find it more difficult to vote antigay, but he has no intention of coming out to his boss, he says, because it would be "uncomfortable."

Yet being in the closet is probably much more uncomfortable for Bill. On at least one occasion he found himself having to submit a proxy vote for his boss through another member (his boss was away on business) on a bill in conference—a vote that was antigay—while gay lobbyists, acquaintances of Bill's, stood nearby, anticipating the vote and giving him stern looks. His boss had told him that if the bill didn't need his vote to pass, he could direct the other member to abstain his boss's proxy. This, Bill was eventually able to do. But he admits he felt "terrible."

Many closeted staffers on the Hill are gay Republicans who basically believe in many of the fiscally conservative tenets of the party but don't necessarily agree with the direction the party has taken on social issues in recent years. Some gay conservatives in Washington—like members of the Log Cabin Federation, the gay Republican group—say they are working for change within the Republican party. But even the Log Cabin Republicans these days stand up against blatant antigay bigotry, as they did when they condemned George Bush after the rhetoric that spewed forth from the Republican National Convention in August of 1992.

However, many of these conservative gays who are staffers on the Hill claim to work for change privately, even as they aid their members in constructing antigay legislation. "Change occurs incrementally here," says Jay, an aide to a notoriously antigay senator. "You can't just demand things. It doesn't happen that way. If you do, you'll just be shut out of the loop. Where does that get you?" Jay espouses the opinion that he is "just doing a job" and that he has to separate that job from his personal feelings. Amazingly, he is out to his boss, who he claims is not personally antigay. "But he must act on behalf of what his constituents believe and want and he must do what they elected him to do," he says. "They are very conservative on sexual matters and certainly do not believe in gay rights." Jay speaks for many other closeted gay staffers when he says that staying in the closet, for purposes of advancing one's career, is not only expected but justifiable. He also is not sure about the gay movement's precepts. "I have trouble with the whole notion of 'gay rights' myself, to be honest," he says. "I do believe in less government."

In this atmosphere, it is easy to see why the bulk of Washington's "transplants" who work for the government would never show up for a public event that would draw television cameras, such as a demonstration, a parade, or a march.

Compounding their desire to remain low-key is the belief among staffers that their work is creating great change. They are adamant, if not smug, when they discuss what they perceive to be their own significance. Almost all of the three dozen interviewed, closeted or not, value their work immensely, feel it is of major importance, and seriously believe in the system. They feel that the work they are doing, no matter how bureaucratic, no matter how sluggish or inefficient, is "activism"—a word several of the more liberal ones use. The thought of being involved in more activism after work, especially direct action, is not appealing to them. They feel they've done their share during the day. Some feel threatened by street activists' in-your-face tactics, seeing them as a direct contradiction to the kind of work they themselves do.

"Washington is a town where you can't turn a street corner without running into someone who is here doing some advocacy work," says Bob Adams. "Either they're working for someone on the Hill or for the Environmental Defense Fund, the Sierra Club, or maybe they're working for the Heritage Foundation or whatever. It sort of struck me as strange at first, that maybe there isn't a lot of gay and lesbian activism in D.C. But when you're working nine to five, being an advocate, trying to change the world, you might want to get off work and just go and watch *The Golden Girls.*"

The notion that everyone in Washington is doing God's work filters from the top down. By constantly reinforcing the belief that the work is of primary importance and that everyone in Washington right down to the lowliest of aides is changing the world, the government keeps its employees under control. Few would dare do anything outside of the system that would upset the perceived balance. For gays that means not rocking the boat in even the slightest—and that, of course, means not being out of the closet. It thus becomes important to those in power in Washington that the closet continue its tyranny, since it prevents lesbians and gays who work in the government from organizing.

If they did, with their sheer numbers and their presence in high positions, there's no telling what they might be able to do. In fact, things may already be changing. In February 1993, in an unprecedented action, some staffers (closeted, mostly) formed a group called the Nathan Hale Brigade. Angered by the Senate's initial resistance to Bill Clinton's desire to end the ban on gays in the military, this group decided that outing was now appropriate. "The rights of gays and lesbians may be determined by a handful of hypocritical representatives and senators whose private 'closeted' behavior belies their public positions," the group's leader, Phillip Detterman, a former navy intelligence technician, told *The Washington Blade*. The Brigade, he said, would activate a network of gay "insiders" on the Hill to gather and publicize information on closet cases.

·····

In hundreds of interviews with current and former White House and congressional staffers, political consultants, family members of politicians, journalists, campaign strategists, State Department employees, lobbyists, fund-raisers, legal professionals, Pentagon insiders, gay activists, male strippers, bar owners, male escorts, masseurs, and members of Congress themselves, a clear picture of Washington's Iron Closets of power—as well as the Revolving Closets of those close to power—begins to emerge. While assigning an accurate percentage figure would be difficult and unscientific, it is safe to say that in some government bodies the number of those dwelling in closets curiously exceeds the Kinsey ten percent. These individuals have diverse backgrounds, ages, occupations, and lifestyles. They cover the political spectrum from right-wing to liberal—although, curiously, a majority are on the conservative end. While all of their stories are sad, some inspire more sympathy—and anger—than others.

In one state, until recently both U.S. senators were closeted homosexuals; both were terrible on gay issues, with one being particularly terrible. Both had been married at least once. Neither was as deeply in the closet as the Legislator for whom Keith worked: Both dated men fixed up with them by friends, and both utilized escort services.

A staffer for the one who was worse on gay issues told two of his colleagues that the senator had sexually harassed him.

In 1992, two female officials started having an intimate affair that began as a friendship. For one, it was her first same-sex romance, and she told many friends about it—perhaps more than she should have. In the past, when she had a different job, this official had tried to block a gay-rights initiative in her home state. She still does not support gay rights.

Within the past ten years, as he promulgated perhaps the most antigay agenda in the Senate, Jesse Helms had two people on his staff who were gay and closeted. Each supported several of Helms's most antigay efforts. One was less closeted than the other, and regularly frequented the now-shut-down Chesapeake House, a gay strip club. At one point, according to two sources close to the office, Helms received an anonymous tip that someone on his staff was a homosexual. In response, Helms held what was supposed to be a top-secret meeting of only key staffers and asked them if they knew anything about the matter. Those present reportedly said that the tip wasn't true. While neither man is now working for Helms, their parting from him had nothing to do with their sexuality: Helms, it is assumed, still doesn't know they are gay.

One prominent elected official has lived a closeted life for many years while serving in several different public positions, always while in a deep, committed relationship with his senior aide. Gay men who have known him for years say that these two traveled in the same circles with them years ago, attending gay parties. One prominent real estate broker remembers watching them have sex one night, as does a new-retired government worker.

When the official began his public life many years ago, the two stopped going to gay events. The official married a woman, and his lover became his chief aide. His wife is completely aware of the circumstances and accepts them. They have had several children, who have kept her busy, and her life has always been separate from her husband's. When the official travels, his wife rarely accompanies him. But he and his aide, the lover, are inseparable. This official has not only voted antigay but has supported the most horrendous homophobes in America.

In what sounds like a variation on David Leavitt's *The Lost Lan-*

guage of Cranes, a married, closeted government official (who is anti-gay) has a closeted gay son who has worked in politics in the past. They were not out to each other during that time, but each of them, through mutual contacts, has always known about the other. Both racked with guilt, they never confronted each other. At one point the son worked on the campaign of a heterosexual candidate who was being gay-baited by his opponent, the incumbent. The gay-baiting opponent is a vocally antigay conservative—and also a self-loathing closeted gay man. The gay son declined to expose the gay-baiting opponent's homosexuality, say former friends, because he was afraid of his own closet—and perhaps his father's—being revealed.

A closeted member of the House agreed to an anonymous interview to discuss what it's like to be a closeted gay elected official. Recently having come to terms with his homosexuality, he has a good voting record on gay issues, and has been privately supportive of people doing work within the gay community. Part of his reason for speaking, however, was clearly a fear of being outed if he did *not* speak. (I did not threaten him in any way.)

"I've always worried about it from the time I entered politics," he says. "I was terrified of it. I certainly knew I was gay when I entered politics, I went to [gay] parties and such and worried about it. Being a congressman and being gay makes being gay much harder."

As was expected of him, this member married a woman but he doesn't feel that—consciously, at least—it was strictly for the purpose of having a "beard." "I don't think that I really did it for that reason," he says. "She was someone that I'd been really close to for a very long time. We had a close friendship. It was not really romantic. She wanted to get married and it was certainly a good move for her, marrying a congressman, and there were many parts of the marriage that were very good. That is no longer the case. It became a frustrating situation for her. She did have romantic interests with others—and so did I."

This congressman has reached the point where he'd like to be out. Psychically, he has left behind his years of complete denial and self-loathing and reached self-acceptance. "This interview never would have taken place earlier," he says, noting the change in himself. "I would rather be honest with people. It's not comfortable. I'd rather be accepted for what I am. I do tend to be a personally conservative person. I've always been private, but I certainly think it would be better to be open about it." Yet he worries about his job, because he has never won by a substantial margin, and feels that if even a few voters were homophobic it could make a difference.

"It's been something I worry about—however, less and less," he says. "I'm older now. My staff must know. I've had male friends come and go in this office. I have a group of gay men I go on vacation with and everyone around here knows that. I have a person I've been involved with who I've worked with. He comes to my house and neighbors see him. My parents know and they've told me to calm down [about being so public], but I don't care. I feel good."

The congressman is in a state of flux, holding mutually contradictory opinions. "I'm actually kind of sympathetic with outing," he says. "I understand it. Gay people who are prominent have an obligation to disclose it. I understand it, but I don't agree with it—if people want to keep that private they should be able to. I understand people who out people, but I wouldn't do it. I even understand this—you know, talking about it. In a way, it's really not a secret for me. I can't imagine that there's anyone in the press, or in politics, who doesn't know."

As for George Bush's White House and his failed 1992 reelection campaign, more than one key figure who put forth the "family values" theme prevalent in the campaign—including its veiled antigay rhetoric—was a closeted homosexual, as were several men who occupied top positions in the Republican National Committee during the campaign. Sources close to several of these men say that they were uncomfortable with both the "family values" cant and the antigay tone of the Republican Convention, but as closeted gay men they couldn't oppose them. Still, there was some conflict. One closeted gay man who worked at the convention and in Bush's D.C. campaign office says there were rifts and fights throughout the 1992 campaign. A closeted lesbian who worked on Dan Quayle's staff says she became disgusted and submitted an anonymous memo to some members of the staff and to the Vice President. Tyler Franz, a Bush campaign worker who said he was fired for complaining about antigay rhetoric in the campaign, went public with his story, garnering much publicity during the election. And Diane Mosbacher, the daughter of Bush's fund-raising chairman, Robert Mosbacher, gave an interview to *The Washington Post* in which she criticized her father and Bush for sitting by silently while the religious right attacked gays at the convention. The Log Cabin Federation publicly denounced the party and the religious right, and before the convention the federation declared that it would not endorse George Bush for president.

These events were far different from those that occurred among gay Republicans during the Reagan years. At that time, say many observers, there were many more closeted gays in the administration and the Republican National Committee, and they tended to be much more conservative, self-loathing, and silent. Some, like right-wing fund-raiser Terry Dolan and the notorious Roy Cohn, were carrying out antigay agendas and did a lot of damage to the gay and lesbian movement in the midst of the AIDS crisis. One right-wing lobbyist, Craig Spence, was outed when it was revealed that he was connected to a gay prostitution ring in Washington and had brought men in for nighttime tours of the White House. Another, Carl "Spitz" Channell, was outed when he was implicated in the Iran-*contra* arms deals in 1990. Kurt Klinkscales, who had worked for conservative congressman James Mann of South Carolina in the early seventies, became one of the most successful fund-raisers of the early eighties. He worked throughout the decade for the National Alliance of Senior Citizens, a right-wing alternative to the American Association of Retired Persons.

In the mid-eighties, in what some say was actually an extraordinary move, Channell, Dolan, Spence, Klinkscales, and other closeted conservative and Republican gays met in Texas to form a relatively low-key group that would solicit funds to be put toward gay rights. Many of the right-wing gays were direct-mail professionals with access to lists of wealthy Republican and right-wing donors. The plan, which never got off the ground, was that they would all put their lists together and send out a form letter asking people to support the gay cause. According to one man who was present, several of the men asked to get back any hate-mail responses so that they could solicit the homophobes for right-wing and antigay causes. Regularly, these men aided the very members of Congress and the White House staff who allowed the AIDS crisis to spin out of control and who advocated stripping people with AIDS of their civil rights.

Dolan, Cohn, and Klinkscales had died of AIDS-related causes by the end of the eighties. Channell died in a mysterious hit-and-run car accident on Capitol Hill—although several people now say that that was a cover-up and that he died of AIDS-related causes. Spence committed suicide in the midst of the scandal concerning him.

"They were all very sick people," says conservative gay Marvin Leibman, distinguishing them from the gay Republicans with whom he works today. "Those guys were totally homophobic. As self-haters and homophobes, they found their home with the right-wingers." The majority of gay Republicans now, says Leibman, are moderates who are "pro-choice" and value "individual rights."

"Those kinds of people wouldn't even come near me," says Rich Tafel, head of the Log Cabin Federation.[15] "I'm just too out of the closet for them. They made a lot of money for the party back then, but they were expected to be completely closeted."

As closeted as they were, they were perhaps less discreet—and more lavish—in their social and sex lives than today's more out conservative gays. Their subculture was a mirror of the larger culture at the time. During the eighties there were excessive, extravagant gay parties all over Washington, thrown by closeted members of Washington's permanent government—the lobbyists, lawyers, public-relations professionals, editors, fund-raisers, and direct-mail and marketing strategists. One of these men, a well-known D.C. power broker, threw huge bashes at his home at which he'd answer the door completely naked. "Those parties were wild," comments one Hill staffer who says they began to taper off by the mid-eighties as AIDS became more of a reality. "Everyone was naked. It was mostly a lot of pretty young guys. Our host would walk around with a hand massager, rubbing people."

Denys Larsen was a flight attendant based in D.C. in the late seventies and early eighties; he was much sought after for his swarthy good looks. "The whole purpose . . . was to come and have sex," he says of parties thrown by several well-known men in town. "And there were prominent figures at many of these. The parties went on all day and all night—all weekend. You got a nice invitation in the mail. Some were out on estates in Virginia. People were naked. There was horseback riding and limousines pulling up. If you got into this group and handled yourself, you'd always be invited back.

They weren't just drunken orgies. You had riding, tennis, swimming, sunning, eating. You packed an overnight bag."

In her 1992 book, *The Power House: Robert Keith Gray and the Selling of Access and Influence in Washington*, Susan B. Trento describes Robert Keith Gray as a closeted gay man who played a key role in the Reagan eighties. Gray worked in the White House under President Dwight Eisenhower, in an administrative job. In 1961 he joined the public-relations firm of Hill & Knowlton. With Gray as an instrumental figure, Hill & Knowlton became one of the biggest commercial public-relations firms in the world, revolutionizing public relations and lobbying in Washington. In 1981 Gray founded his own firm, Gray and Company. In 1986 he sold it and went back to Hill & Knowlton until late 1992, when he left Washington and moved to Florida.

Over the years, Gray represented such clients as the Church of Scientology, the People's Republic of China (after Tiananmen Square), Haiti (under Duvalier), the Reverend Sun Myung Moon, and the Catholic Bishops Conference (for its anti-abortion campaign). He was a darling of right-wing circles and a close, longtime friend of the Reagans.

When Ronald Reagan was elected president, Gray had access to the Oval Office. He was a cochair and the main orchestrator of Reagan's extravagant 1980 inaugural ball, as grand an affair as Washington has ever seen and one that set the tone for the decade. Throughout the eighties, Gray wielded enormous influence, crossing over the worlds of politics, media, and high society.

Also throughout that time, according to Trento's book, Gray kept his homosexuality from all his business associates, and certainly from the Reagans, not realizing that many knew but looked the other way. But his closet always haunted him. In 1982 he was investigated briefly by authorities and racked with the fear of disclosure. The investigation came to naught and no evidence of wrongdoing was found. To protect his closet, he remained silent as huge numbers of gay men died of AIDS over the years, knowing full well that his friend and associate President Reagan was doing nothing about the epidemic.

Trento's book shows how Gray's closet operated and how it ultimately overpowered him as it does other closeted power brokers in Washington. In 1981, Gray had a dinner party for twenty in his home in Rehoboth. In attendance were other closeted gay men, among them some other executives who owned Washington public-relations agencies. During dinner, Gray disappeared with a young man he'd brought out to the house, one of his staffers, and, according to the Trento book, they had sex. Trento recounts the ensuing events:

> A few weeks later the young staffer's supervisor complained that his job performance at Gray and Company was unacceptable. . . . The supervisor was given permission to fire the young staffer, but that did not end the matter. The young staffer filed a complaint against Gray with the D.C. government. The complaint was detailed and graphic. If it were made public, it would be explosive. "The complaint described second by second the sexual act that he committed with Gray," remembered a Gray and Company executive. . . .
>
> Gray and Company retained an outside law firm to handle the complaint. The law firm was successful in getting the file sealed. The young staffer settled for $3,000. Over the years Gray ended up spending over a million dollars in legal fees and settlements, partly in an effort to try to keep his private life a secret.

As the AIDS crisis wore on, Gray lost many friends—including one ex-lover—to the disease. There is no indication, however, that he ever used his power and influence to speak to the President. By the mid-eighties, his longtime companion, Bill Austin, an interior decorator, had developed AIDS. Gray still remained silent.

In 1989, at the Vatican's request, Gray, who was working on the Catholic bishops' anti-abortion campaign, gave a speech at the Vatican's International Conference on AIDS in Rome. He was asked by the church to do so not because he was gay—church officials certainly didn't know that—but because he was a well-known public-relations speaker working in their best interests. His speech pointed out the failings of American policies toward AIDS, as Trento points out, "as if he had not worked hard to put in place the very officials who had designed and were implementing these policies." He also attacked American corporations for not doing their share in spreading the message, yet he had never urged his own clients, some of the largest companies in the world, to do so, nor did he use his own agency's huge resources and ability to disseminate information.

During the entirety of the eighties, Gray was a very public figure, always reported on in the newspapers. It seemed that *The Washington Post* got every angle on him that they could—except one. It was common knowledge that Gray was a homosexual; many journalists knew people who'd been to his gay parties as well, and they knew all of the pertinent facts about his life. And yet the biggest story—and perhaps the most urgent and important—about Gray was covered up by *Washington Post* editors: This powerful man, who was working for the antigay Catholic church and who was best friends with the homophobic President of the United States, a leader whose bungled response to the AIDS epidemic seemed almost willful, was a closeted gay man whose own lover lay at home dying of AIDS. Certainly, *The Washington Post* has created scandals out of less.

Gray is one of a fairly large group of big-time Washington PR executives, lobbyists, editors of resource directories, publishers of newsletters, fund-raisers, and direct-mail honchos who are closeted and who are very powerful in Washington today. As part of the permanent government, they mold themselves to whatever administration, Democratic or Republican, takes over the White House. Their own politics and personal beliefs are suppressed, and they take on the politics and policies of those in power at the moment.

These closeted gay men have a long history in the city and have had many public and private squabbles among themselves over the decades. Sometimes they have stooped to the dirtiest of tricks, smearing each other—even gay-baiting each other—often through anonymous mailings or one-shot anonymous publications.

Their sexuality keeps them together despite their differences. They mix with many other wealthy gay men who go way back in Washington, some of whom are fund-raisers for both parties and some of whom do charitable work for the gay community, such as organizing benefits. Still, even as they attend these events and show their support—sometimes opening their homes for such events and hosting them—many involve themselves in antigay projects, seeing a clear distinction between their work and their social lives. One closeted gay PR honcho, who sometimes works on behalf of the gay community, also represents a foreign government that tortures—and sometimes puts to death—known homosexuals.

. . . . .

Many would say that closeted gay staffers working for right-wing members of Congress should be outed. But they are not public figures. And closeted members of the House who vote favorably for gays would seem to be people whose closets should be protected. But they *are* public figures, and it would appear that their homosexuality should be discussed if it's pertinent to a story.

In 1992, when *QW* outed Phyllis Schlafly's son John because he worked for his mother and supported her views and because she has been an icon of the religious right and a crusader for so-called family values, many felt that the publication made the right call, even though John Schlafly wasn't a public figure. Others, usually in favor of outing, thought this instance violated their basic guidelines because he was a private person.

Obviously, there are hazy lines in the debate. What is absolutely clear, however, is that people espousing a "no exceptions" anti-outing rule are increasingly seen as being on the fringes. A case-by-case approach seems to be best; most people do see some cases in which outing is appropriate.

Some gay groups, like the American Civil Liberties Union's Lesbian and Gay Rights Project, have never condemned outing. Yet the major gay organizations in Washington, which must play by the rules of the town in order to achieve their goals, initially offered a "no-exceptions" position. For several years, beginning in 1989, the leaders of both the National Gay and Lesbian Task Force and the Human Rights Campaign Fund condemned outing in all cases, relying on the predictable right-to-privacy arguments. Their condemnations had on several occasions affected the media's willingness to cover a particular outing: Each time someone was outed these groups took the position that the outers were wrong. Reporters and editors, in turn, believed that NGLTF and HRCF spoke for the community. In reality, of course, they speak for their boards of directors. Some of the members of their boards have a vested interest in maintaining the closet, protecting the closeted with whom they do business, knowing that much of their organizations' money and political support comes from people who are closeted and conservative. After interviewing one or two of these people for an article, reporters concluded that "most" gays are vehemently opposed to outing in all circumstances.

However, many of the gay executive directors, lobbyists, and communications directors in Washington privately have supported outing. In the case of Anne-Imelda Radice there was tacit approval by the staffs of both HRCF and NGLTF. In letters to *The Advocate*, HRCF officials went out of their way to distance the group from the outing, although some HRCF board members had helped Donna Minkowitz on the story.

The national groups' refusal to publicly assault the Washington closet made them parties to its maintenance. Each time they loudly opposed an outing they told the Washington establishment that it's okay to be in the closet. Both NGLTF and HRCF became comfortable refuges for powerful closeted government officials. But even these groups—always slow to change—eventually moved on the issue. By early 1993, both groups were softening their positions on outing, stepping out of the way of journalists doing their jobs and stating that, although they would not engage in outing themselves, they would no longer condemn others for it. The national groups had bowed to a growing sentiment in the gay community: Let the closeted public figures fend for themselves, and the closets of power in Washington will in time break down.

Meanwhile, the closets of power continue to destroy their occupants, all those lesbians and gay men within reach, plus millions of us across America. The vast majority of homosexuals in Congress and in the permanent government are still as closeted as ever. People shouldn't be fooled into thinking that things will change in Washington, or even within the executive branch, when a Democratic presidency comes to pass. All the presidents have their closeted queers. One of the saddest and most harmful individuals described in this chapter is in fact a close confidant and advisor to President Clinton. He is in the same position he was in before the election, but he is more powerful now.

And he's still up to his old tricks.

Part III Throughout Hollywood's history, the closet has tormented lesbians and gay men. Much of the burden has fallen upon actors, who have been expected to stay locked in the closet under penalty of career death. The powerful executives who enforce the closet throughout the industry are, all too often, closeted gays, wor-

QUEER

IN HOLLYWOOD

ried that any "indiscretion" might affect their ability to earn millions of dollars. These closeted actors and executives are the most proficient architects and peddlers of Hollywood's antigay images.

Like the New York closet, the Hollywood closet is essential to maintaining the Washington closet: The film and television industries are propaganda machines that marginalize and demonize homosexuals in American mainstream culture, keeping the electorate ignorant and fearful of gays, giving lawmakers more reason to vote antigay, and creating an environment in which the closeted are too afraid to come out.

Similarly, the Hollywood closet is kept intact by the New York closet: the media's tacit agreement to make all closeted lesbian and gay stars—and power brokers—appear heterosexual is essential to the Hollywood closet's endurance.

Because Hollywood is a private industry worried about its product and its public image, it is potentially more responsive to activists' attacks than is Washington. In the early nineties, gay activists learned that taking on Hollywood in the most sensational ways—and staging a massive assault on Hollywood's closets of power—would provide them with a way to break into the New York–Washington–Hollywood axis of interdependent closets.

10

The Crucifixion

of Zelda Gilroy

I
t was 1947 in America and Sheila James Kuehl—then known simply as Sheila James—age eight, was a radio star.

Kuehl starred with such other unknowns as Gale Gordon and Jim Backus on *The Penny Williamson Show*, one of the last of the family radio shows to air live from Studio B in the old NBC studios in Hollywood. Next door, in Studio A, a young singer named Doris Day was a regular on *The Bob Hope Show*. On the other side, in Studio C, the popular drama *The Cisco Kid* was performed. For a little girl from a working-class family in central Los Angeles, those were exciting times.

"I loved Doris Day the best," Kuehl remembers, laughing. "I was very happy. Everyone was playing, and I was, too. It was a wonderful way to learn. They all taught me a lot about comedy and about professionalism. It was like being initiated into a new club."

Kuehl didn't have the typical stage parents who forever push their children into the spotlight, hoping to live out the stardom they themselves have never achieved. It was Kuehl's dance-school teacher who'd urged her parents to take her on auditions for radio. "This kid is funny," he had said, talking up her comedic talents. While she was still on the radio program, Kuehl's agent urged her parents to take her on auditions for television shows.

Sheila Kuehl was cute and smart. The camera, as they say, liked her. She was soon signed to *The Trouble with Father*, to be shot in front of a live audience in Hollywood, which was trying to woo the burgeoning television industry away from New York. For five years Kuehl played the part of Jackie Erwin, the tomboy daughter of Stu and June Erwin, a prototypical fifties TV-sitcom couple.

It was during those years, just prior to her teens, that Kuehl first became vaguely aware of her sexuality. "I remember playing those adventure games with the other kids, making as if we were knights and ladies," she says. "I always imagined my part as the hero, and the hero always kissed the girl. It felt really weird."

In those days, lesbianism, even the thought of it, was completely outside Sheila's purview. For quite a while, matters never got beyond those childhood games.

When Kuehl turned fifteen and *The Trouble with Father* ended, she worked as an actress for the next couple of years while going to school. She dated boys but never had sex. "It was fine," she recalls. "I mean, I always liked guys. A lot of women in the fifties received antisexual messages. It was your responsibility not to get pregnant. You were expected to resist—which made it easier. I don't know whether my not getting involved with guys sexually had to do with the messages about what you were supposed to do or just that I didn't want to. I guess it was more about doing what you were supposed to do, and I had a lot to lose, so I didn't do it."

Having skipped two grades, Kuehl was attending the University of California, Los Angeles, by the age of sixteen. She eventually moved into a sorority house and spent her summers as a counselor at a children's camp. It was during those years, in the late fifties, when she was away from her parents and experiencing independence, that her homosexuality bubbled to the surface.

"I met a woman and fell in love," she says flatly. "We met at camp. She was a counselor too. It was just this funny attraction that neither of us would acknowledge. Then, one night she and I were sitting together at her place. She was rubbing my back and we just, like, went to bed. It was wonderful. But then we stayed up all night wondering if we were really sick."

They concluded that they were "sick" but that there was nothing they could do about it. "There was no movement then," she says, explaining their conclusion. "There was nothing to read. I knew no lesbians. We just figured this was a rare thing and that we were two women who'd fallen in love and that we had to keep it a secret because nobody would approve. We didn't dare tell a soul."

Kuehl's lover, Kathy, went to school in San Diego. After that summer at camp, the two spent an entire year writing letters to each other every day, longing to be together. "We were madly in love," she recalls. "The letters were very passionate, with us both saying things like 'I can't live without you.'"

By that time, in the fall of 1960, Kuehl had appeared on four episodes of the wildly popular show *The Many Loves of Dobie Gillis*. The first episode she appeared on, in the fall of 1959, was the fourth of the series. Dobie was the creation of author Max Shulman, who wrote the teleplays. The original plan had been to give Dobie (played by Dwayne Hickman) a different love interest or foil in each episode. One of those many girls was Zelda Gilroy, played by Kuehl. Kuehl's was supposed to be a single guest appearance, but Zelda was brought back repeatedly.

"Max loved Zelda," Kuehl says, "because she was the girl who would chase Dobie and the one girl he didn't want. She was smart and she was clever and she was determined and she could do everything except get Dobie. It was victory for Dobie when he escaped."

After four guest appearances, in the summer of 1960 Zelda Gilroy was made into a regular character. Kuehl signed a contract to do twenty-one shows in the next season.

That summer, one of the best she'd ever had, she was also able to see Kathy after a whole year of being apart. She had done well at school that year and was popular; she was an officer in both the student government and her sorority. She'd signed a contract to be a regular on a popular TV show and was on her way to becoming a star. And, above all else, she was having a passionate, secret romance.

But by September things began to topple.

"Somehow, some of the [love] letters had been left behind in the house over the summer," Kuehl says. "Actually, I think that they fell out of the back of a drawer. The cleaning people found them and turned them in to the alumnae council of the sorority. As soon as I walked into the house after summer vacation they called me into a meeting."

The council waved the letters in Kuehl's face and demanded an explanation. The discussion was all coded: The word "lesbian" never came up, but everyone knew what this was all about. Kuehl tried denying the entire affair, but that didn't work; the letters were explicit. "I then just clammed up and took my sorority pin off and put it on the table and left," she says. "I cried all the way home."

Kuehl was officially expelled from the sorority. She was assured that no one would be told why, but she knew the news had gotten out and that the rumor was spreading. "All of them were my best friends," she says of the other women in the sorority. "Afterward, some of them still spoke to me, but others didn't. They avoided me. It was very isolating."

She didn't dare tell her parents what had happened. Moving back in with them, Kuehl gave them the excuse that she'd missed them and wanted to come home to live. But she told them that she was still a member of the sorority. "They knew how much it had meant to me," she recalls, "and they knew I wouldn't just leave it, so I had to tell them I was still involved. Whenever there was a meeting that they knew about, I'd go and sit in a coffee shop and then I'd go home and make up stuff about what the meeting was about."

Kuehl was upset and distraught, realizing she was leading a more and more secretive life and seeing how devastating it could be when people found her out. At around the same time as the sorority incident, Kathy moved to L.A., and the two saw each other every day, which put a strain on the relationship. Kuehl was thinking about her future and her career. "By then the whole idea of being queer was so overwhelming and scary," Kuehl says. "Not the sexuality, but the loss of everything. To be that way for good meant no family, no children, no career, no normalcy, no parents. It seemed at that point that I should really get out of it. I told [Kathy] I didn't want to see her any longer."

Kuehl had casually dated a particular man on and off over the two years during which she was involved with Kathy. Now she began seeing him more seriously. "He came to the sorority dances and I went to the beer busts," she remembers. "We made out but it wasn't sexual. We never fucked. But we almost got engaged."

In fall of 1961, a full year after the sorority incident, Kuehl's contract was renewed. A lot of time had passed and it seemed to her that her fears of being found out—beyond the sorority—might have been exaggerated. Kuehl was about to turn twenty-one and was about to be engaged to a man. But she couldn't get Kathy out of her mind.

"I couldn't live without her," Kuehl says. More successful, and more confident, she felt that perhaps it was safe now for her to be with Kathy. "I broke up with my boyfriend and we started seeing each other again," she says.

Kuehl had by then become a national celebrity, the new kind—a television star—interviewed in all of the fan magazines and in *TV Guide*. Viewers, especially women, liked Zelda Gilroy: She was smart, strong, and independent at a time when women weren't encouraged to be any of those things. They also liked the real-life Sheila James Kuehl too, for the same reason: She was a working actress who was in college, an independent, single woman who was focusing on her education and her future, which was not the norm for most of the actresses in Hollywood at the time.

In the middle of the 1961–62 season, every television actress's wildest dream came true for Sheila Kuehl. "Max [Shulman] came to me and told me with great delight that he and [20th Century] Fox wanted to make a pilot film starring me," she says. "It would be a spin-off of the series—*The Zelda Gilroy Show*. My own show! I was so excited."

Everything was looking up. "I was about to turn twenty-one, about to graduate. I had just made this pilot for my own show. It was all totally fabulous. And I really, really loved this woman. We were very committed. My parents had known her as my best friend all along. They liked her a lot. I decided that was it with men. This was going to be my marriage, as bizarre as it seemed: We only had our parents' marriage as role models. I put the whole school incident behind me. I had all of these people who were friends from camp. I had also been in student government. I felt more relieved that the news hadn't gotten out, but I guess I still was just a bit afraid. It of course was something that [Kathy] and I could never talk about with any of our friends and family. But the whole thing, and the secrecy—it made our relationship more intense because we only had each other to talk with about this stuff."

Making the pilot was exhilarating for Kuehl. "I was a star, and I was treated like a star," she says. "I was consulted with scripts. I was helping doing the casting. I felt important and grown-up. Every night after the shoot I would sit down and have champagne with the producers, the director, and the writer, and go over things."

Working closely together, they'd produced a decent TV pilot. During the fall and early winter of 1961, it was being shown throughout the industry; everyone was talking it up. "The news just before Christmas came back that CBS was high on the pilot," Kuehl remembers. "Fox, the studio that had put money into it, was real high on it too. It was all great." Kuehl eagerly awaited the good news.

But the good news never came. No one—not the producers, not the director, not the writer—would tell Kuehl anything.

"No one was talking," she recalls. "There was a hush. The next thing I heard, weeks later, was that nobody was going to pick up the pilot." Soon after that, Rod Amateu, who had directed *Dobie Gillis,* asked Kuehl to take a walk with him.

"He said to me, 'Well, um, nobody's told you this so I felt I should say something,' " she remembers painfully. " 'Apparently, over at CBS, they thought that you were just a little too butch.' I looked at him kind of funny, like I wasn't sure what he meant. But I of course knew. I suddenly had this feeling like somebody had dropped ice cubes down my back. He said, 'Well, there are these rumors.' That was it. I cut in. I didn't ask him about the rumors and didn't want to know what they were. I knew. I just started babbling, saying I was sorry it didn't work out for all of us and how disappointed I was and how he'd done such a great job."

When she'd signed her contract for the new pilot, Kuehl had had to turn down the renewal of her contract with *Dobie Gillis.* Now that *The Zelda Gilroy Show* was not to be, she thought she might go back to *Dobie Gillis.* But there was no offer of a contract. The show's producers asked her to do a few guest appearances in what seemed like a way for them to ease out the character. Zelda Gilroy had appeared on twenty-one of thirty-nine shows in the 1961–62 season, but she appeared on only four shows in the next.

Zelda Gilroy was crucified, burned at the stake, all for being "just a little too butch." And for all intents and purposes, Sheila James Kuehl's bright and promising career was over; she at first landed some bit parts, but soon even those dried up. Hers was one of hundreds—perhaps thousands—of lives tormented and destroyed in a world that had been hostile to queers since its inception.

11

From McCarthy

to Medved

Several weeks after Bill Clinton was elected in 1992, Patrick Buchanan appeared on *The McLaughlin Group*. Smarting from the beating he'd withstood from both Democrats and Republicans for having injected hate into the Republican National Convention (and perhaps having helped cost George Bush the election) that year, he was nonetheless single-minded in his mission. Fiercely debating the other guests on the show, Buchanan strongly opined that Clinton's plans to open the armed services to homosexuals would "force the cultural war to take place primarily within the ranks of the military." He was of course talking about the cultural war he had declared on homosexuals in his speech at the convention. But this statement seemed naïve, especially for Buchanan: Surely he knows that the primary battlefield in his cultural war always has been—and always will be—Hollywood. And surely he knows that Hollywood is a far more important and powerful place for him to enforce his agenda.

In his landmark 1981 book, *The Celluloid Closet*, gay activist, film critic, and film historian Vito Russo offered an exhaustive look at Hollywood's homophobia from the beginning of films. In many ways, *The Celluloid Closet*—for both the gay community and the Hollywood power structure—was vastly ahead of its time. It took nearly a decade—a decade in which Russo and many others were lost to AIDS—for a much broader segment of the gay and lesbian community to look at films as Russo did: sociopolitically. Ten years after it was first published, *The Celluloid Closet* became a handbook for a new generation of queer activists who had little respect for the closet. Russo helped them see Hollywood and the film industry as a power structure that directly assisted in their oppression—and in which closeted gays participated fully.

Russo showed how lesbians and gay men, throughout the early decades of filmmaking, were either rendered completely invisible or portrayed in vague and coded ways, most of which were negative. He described how the visibility ushered in by the 1969 Stonewall gay riots in New York created a backlash that brought an onslaught of films with more overt negative portrayals of lesbians and gay men: *Staircase,* a 1969 film that starred Rex Harrison and Richard Burton as two swishy fags; 1969's *The Gay Deceivers,* which offended even homophobic critics, who cited it as antigay for its portrayal of two straight guys who, to avoid the draft, played queer in the most degradingly stereotypical ways; *The Kremlin Letter,* a film made by John Huston in 1970 that starred George Sanders as a drag queen in cahoots with a black lesbian spy who was charged with seducing a Russian diplomat's daughter; *The Anderson Tapes* of 1971, which included a dastardly gay thief; *They Only Kill Their Masters,* a 1972 film that starred June Allyson as a killer dyke; 1972's *Blacula,* a blaxploitation film in which an effeminate, depraved gay man is a victim; *Cleopatra Jones,* a 1973 blaxploitation film featuring Shelley Winters as a lesbian gang leader who eventually commits suicide; 1973's *Theatre of Blood,* in which, as Russo described it, "Robert Morley plays a homosexual theater critic who dies when he is forced to eat his two poodles, who have been baked in a pie in the same fashion that a Roman empress's two sons were served to her in Shakespeare's *Titus Andronicus*"; 1974's *Freebie and the Bean,* which showcased Christopher Morley as a killer transvestite; 1975's *The Eiger Sanction,* in which Jack Cassidy played a killer queer who has a pink poodle named Faggot; *Car Wash,* a 1976 film that included a troublesome transvestite; *The Choirboys,* a 1977 film that also featured fags with pink poodles; *Windows,* a 1980 film that starred Elizabeth Ashley as a murderous lesbian; and 1980's *American Gigolo,* whose gay characters were a pimp, a murderer, and a wife-beater.

Other post-Stonewall films in which lesbians and gay men met violent deaths include *Diamonds Are Forever* (1971), *Play It As It Lays* (1972), *The Day of the Jackal* (1973), *The Laughing Policeman* (1974), *Busting* (1974), *Drum* (1976), *Swashbuckler* (1976), *The Betsy* (1978), and . . . *And Justice for All* (1979).

Then in 1980 came *Cruising*, which starred Al Pacino as a police officer who goes undercover in the underworld of New York's gay sex clubs to ferret out a sadistic queer murderer. The film sparked protests while it was filming in and around Greenwich Village in 1979. Further protests occurred when the film opened. The movie offered a one-dimensional view of gays as sexually obsessive, violent, disturbed individuals. It also made homosexuality and the desire to murder seem inextricably tied and presented this supposed pathology as contagious: Al Pacino, the police officer who is investigating the murders by going undercover as a leatherette queer, eventually becomes a sex-crazed queer killer too—simply by being exposed to the environment.

One of the fliers that activists handed out at the time read, with seeming exaggeration, "People will die because of this film." In November 1980, several months after *Cruising* opened, a son of a minister pulled up in front of the Ramrod bar on West Street, the site of the filming. There, he opened fire with a submachine gun, killing two gay men.

As the eighties wore on, lesbians were the victims of increased defamation in films and mass culture. This was directly due to the backlash against the women's movement; independent, assertive women were presented as villainous, man-hating dykes. Negative portrayals of gay men also escalated dramatically amid the AIDS crisis.

By the time Russo published the 1987 revised edition of *The Celluloid Closet*, he knew that he himself was infected with HIV. Not only was he far more alarmed, and more militant in his stance on Hollywood's homophobia, than he'd ever been before, but he had also developed an even keener analysis of a critical, frightening time in American history. In the introduction to the revised edition of his book, he seems to have foreseen the Republican National Convention of 1992:

A vocal minority of right-wing religious fanatics in America, similar in style and viewpoint to the Nazi youth groups found in Germany just before Hitler took power, have been permitted to set the terms of the political debate regarding the existence of gays in society and have used the AIDS health crisis to exploit anti-gay prejudices that already existed. Dangerous political extremists like Lyndon LaRouche, Jerry Falwell and New York's Archbishop John J. O'Connor have fostered the fiction that homosexuality is simply chosen behavior, an act, not an orientation. Such behavior is then termed sinful or illegal, creating a partisan moral issue where none should exist. . . .

Open violence against gay people in America has reached epidemic proportions, fueled by films that encourage young people to believe that such behavior is acceptable. . . .

The same producers, directors and screenwriters who socialize with gay people and give money to support research for AIDS allow the films they create to foster a climate of fear and panic. . . . The situation we have today [is one] in which producers might be privately opposed to institutionalized homophobia and fag bashing but are afraid to hurt their profits by offending the sensibilities of the Christian lobby and conservative elements in the mass audience with films that challenge their prejudices. It's easier to underestimate the general public and bow to religious pressure than to take a stand.

Russo hit upon an extraordinary fact that, in the late eighties and early nineties, became more and more apparent to queers: On gay issues, supposedly liberal Hollywood indirectly takes its orders from the religious right and from conservatives in Washington, as well as from moderate politicians who pander to the right. In this respect, Hollywood functions, and has always functioned, as an effective propaganda machine for antigay operators.

· · · · ·

The strength of the relationship between Washington and Hollywood can't be underestimated—not just because Ronald Reagan, an actor and a homophobe, sat in the White House for eight years, but also because of the historic relationship between the two power structures. An industry built predominantly by immigrant Jews at a time of rabid and overt anti-Semitism in America and the rest of the world, Hollywood has always been a place where the "other" is actually in power, while at the same time it is a victim of society's prejudices and thus easily manipulated by the larger power structure of Washington.

The Washington–Hollywood connection is not one-way. Early on, Hollywood's moguls found that they could influence politics just as much as politics could influence culture. This first became evident in 1934 when the socialist author Upton Sinclair, running for governor of California, announced that he was in favor of assessing higher taxes on the film industry. MGM mogul Louis B. Mayer, along with press magnate William Randolph Hearst, launched a successful propaganda campaign against Sinclair, making newsreels that warned of the danger the public would face if Sinclair were elected. Mayer and Hearst distorted Sinclair's positions as well as his image, making him out to be a disorganized bum whose socialist ideas would bring catastrophe upon California. Sinclair, previously enormously popular, lost the election.

Hollywood has talent, big money, and high visibility, three things that Washington likes and needs. But Washington's effect on Hollywood has always been far more powerful and far more damaging than Hollywood's effect on Washington.

Most people in Hollywood today can't possibly produce work that is overtly political or that questions the status quo. Their day-to-day jobs, and the kind of work they produce as well as the risks it can take, are regulated by influences that are ultimately traceable to Washington, to conservative politicians, and ultimately to the Christian right. In his *The Power and the Glitter: The Hollywood–Washington Connection*, Ronald Brownstein pointed out how the early film moguls' fearful response to being the "other" reinforced Washington's power over them:

> When religious groups accused Hollywood of poisoning the nation's morals in the early 1920s, the studios compliantly brought in Postmaster General Will H. Hays as president of the Motion Picture Producers and Distributors of America and ceded him enormous power, first as political fixer and eventually as censor.

That was typical of the moguls' response to outside pressure: as immigrant Jews, [Louis B.] Mayer and the other studio fathers always remained uncertain and defensive when pressed by forces from Gentile society.

No matter how much money he earned, or how many politicians' pictures he displayed on his walls, no matter even that he celebrated his birthday on the nation's, Mayer never lost his immigrant's fear of being labeled un-American. His anxiety was common in the Hollywood executive suites occupied by men who remembered much meaner lives. . . .

By 1934, the reactionary Production Code of ethics was in force. It banned the portrayal of premarital sex and encouraged marriage in all films well into the fifties. While, in Hollywood's early years, leftists and Communists flourished in the movie community, and liberals and Democrats maintained ideological and political power in the industry for decades (before World War II) with the support of some moguls and stars, the product—the films—remained far from critical of America's system of government or of the religious right and certainly did not offer a divergent view—or even sympathetic treatment—of women, blacks, or other minorities. The bottom line—money—was, as it is now, the driving force in Hollywood. "Like liberals and conservatives," noted Brownstein, "Communists wrote good movies and bad movies—but few with even a glancing impact on national life."

After World War II the right wing finally gained a foothold—and sent frightened moguls into a tizzy with the word "un-American," at a time when communism, rising up around the world, had suddenly become a dirty word in the United States.

Senator Joseph McCarthy's purges of Communists in Hollywood were presented as ridding the industry of "subversives" who might be trying to bring down the government by working with the Soviet Union. But much of McCarthy's real agenda was making sure that liberals did not inject their views into America via the movie screen. During World War II, while many straight (and closeted gay) men went to war, a larger percentage of women—and men who had admitted to being homosexual, thus avoiding the draft—took the open jobs in the industry, especially as screenwriters. Some films with strong female leads emerged; some even had coded, positive lesbian references. During World War II, strong working women were briefly glorified on screen, among them tough, blue-collar types. Rosie the Riveter characters like Ann Sothern's aircraft worker in *Swing Shift Maisie* turned up. Women were also portrayed as heroines, politicians, business executives, agents, managers, editors, and campaign strategists.

Part of McCarthy's agenda, and the right's, was to make sure these influences—including the people behind them—were taken out of Hollywood. Since these people tended to be liberal and leftist, it wasn't hard to find some Communist connection in their backgrounds. In its persecutions, the right believed it was upholding "family values" and making sure that those values—and no others—were embraced on the screen. The irony of it all was that McCarthy's own right-hand man, Roy Cohn, an archetypal self-loathing, closeted homosexual who presents the classic example of the dangers of the closets of power, was targeting other gays as a way to redeem himself.

The blacklist—actually a series of lists—was successfully enforced, because Hollywood's moguls were terrified once again. "Public and private lists of subversives rained on studios faster than unsolicited screenplays," wrote Brownstein, "and the shaken executives dutifully bent over like penitents to take their whacks from each new adversary."

The ice age brought on by the Cold War has yet to thaw. While Hollywood continues to back liberals and exercises its fund-raising might in the political arena as well as for liberal causes from the environment to AIDS research, its product is still as self-censored as ever before. Always afraid that attacks or negative publicity might affect its ability to make money, the industry continues to succumb to Washington's conservatives. It perceives the accurate portrayal of lesbian and gay characters to be risky. Any money that can be made in the gay market has always been outweighed, in Hollywood's eyes, by the amount of money the industry believes it will lose due to conservative attacks as well as by what Hollywood perceives to be the public's visceral recoil from images of homosexuality.

Ronald Reagan's cultural agenda of the eighties was largely responsible for pushing Hollywood ever deeper into the closet. Reagan spoke out against sexual explicitness in the movies, backed critics who railed against rock 'n' roll, and empowered people like Senator Jesse Helms early on in their battles with the National Endowment for the Arts. Modern-day Hollywood, where the new moguls are not only Jewish but in many instances also closeted gays, has responded with the same fear as its predecessor. This has been most evident in television. Prior to Reagan, television was beginning to experiment with new themes, including homosexuality, on a much grander scale than film. In part because of pressure from activists, portrayals of gay men and lesbians on television were prevalent in the seventies. A spate of homosexual characters and episodes about gay people, many positive, others simply benign, soon appeared on *All in the Family, Maude, Barney Miller, M*A*S*H, Baretta, Kojak, The Mary Tyler Moore Show, Phyllis, Medical Center, Mary Hartman, Mary Hartman, The Bob Newhart Show,* and *Family* throughout the decade.

But beginning in 1981, the mood in Hollywood was once again one of caution. As Brownstein noted, "Reagan's landslide election . . . alternately horrified, stunned and amazed Hollywood liberals." Their minds once again burned with visions of the blacklist. Executives became fearful. In 1981, after an uphill battle because of its "feminist" elements, producer Barney Rosenzweig managed to get his TV movie *Cagney and Lacey* broadcast on CBS. It was a smash, receiving a highly impressive 42 share, and the network decided to make it into a series. In her 1992 book, *Backlash: The Undeclared War Against American Women,* Susan Faludi (shyly avoiding the word "lesbian") recounted the lesbophobia that played itself out in the ensuing drama:

> Rosenzweig cast Meg Foster to play the single woman. After two episodes, CBS executives canceled the show, claiming bad ratings. Rosenzweig convinced them to give the show another try but they complained that the women were "too tough" and Foster, especially, wasn't sufficiently genteel and would have to go. "Meg Foster came across in the role as being masculine," CBS vice president Arnold Beck explained later. . . . Rosenzweig replaced her with the blond Sharon Gless.

Throughout the decade, studio executives and standards-division staff, afraid of any reference to homosexuality or other controversial topics, steered clear of issues that would stir up the religious right. Much of their reaction had to do with the fact that Reagan and Bush empowered the Christian right-wing pressure groups who monitor Hollywood. Pandering to these groups, both leaders used what they saw as Hollywood's "permissive" images in their presidential campaigns. Whether or not such calculated attacks always resulted in political gain, they had the residual effect of manipulating the public's fears and injecting poison into the dialogue of American politics and culture, much the way McCarthy had.

During the presidential election campaign of 1992, Vice President Dan Quayle, whom Bush always used as the "family values" arm of the administration, attacked what he called Hollywood's "cultural elite," and specifically the television show *Murphy Brown*, for the series' portrayal of a single woman, played by actress Candice Bergen, who becomes pregnant and decides to have the baby.

"It doesn't help matters when prime time TV has Murphy Brown . . . mocking the importance of fathers by bearing a child and calling it 'just another lifestyle choice,' " Quayle said, regarding what he saw as one cause of the 1992 Los Angeles riots. Quayle's term "lifestyle choice" was in this instance also a code for "homosexuality." The right has consistently perpetuated two myths about lesbians and gays: One, queers have "lifestyles" rather than "lives"—the implications of "lifestyle" include self-indulgence—and two, homosexuality is a "choice," one that Quayle later called a "wrong choice."

In a speech to the Southern Baptist Convention several days after his first attack on Hollywood, Quayle said that "the changes that have occurred in our culture in recent decades" have "created a cultural divide in our country." Painting a picture not unlike the one McCarthy drew in the 1950s, Quayle claimed that the "divide" is so great that "it sometimes seems we have two cultures, the 'cultural elite' and the rest of us. . . . To appeal to our country's enduring basic values is to invite the scorn and laughter of the elite culture." In the same speech, Quayle attacked gay parenting, and sex education and condom distribution in schools. Saying that the "cultural elite" was responsible for "handing out condoms" in schools, the Vice President implied that homosexuals make up at least a part of this dreaded "cultural elite." Indeed, the man behind Quayle, vice-presidential chief of staff Bill Kristol, told *New York Newsday* at the height of the presidential race that much of Quayle's focus in his family values–cultural elite campaign was on homosexuality, which was, according to Kristol, "morally less desirable than heterosexuality."

Although the family-values cant, which became a major theme at the 1992 Republican National Convention, was later softened and eventually dropped, it initially did well in some polls. It was true that people didn't want their elected officials mandating how they were supposed to construct their families or dictating what values were to be important to them, but they were concerned about a conflict between their own families' values and the values they perceived to be part of the larger culture. Much of the media was quick to exploit that conflict.

"Casual cruelty, knowing sex. Nothing could be better designed to rob youth of its most ephemeral gift: innocence," wrote neoconservative Charles Krauthammer in *The Washington Post*, agreeing with Quayle and railing against the film and television industries as well as the Democrats. "[The] lack of decency deserves attack. If Democrats would stop portraying this as a Dan Quayle (ha, ha, ha) issue and help forge a national consensus against this stuff, the culture makers might begin to listen."

Newsweek headlined its story THE ELITE, AND HOW TO AVOID IT, with a subhead that read: "Quayle May Be on to Something: The People Who Make TV Shows Really Are Different." Among the graphics to illustrate the article was a scene of mincing gay men from *The Boys in the Band*. The manipulative story, like many that appeared that same week, was a classic example of how the media subtly whip up and exploit readers' and viewers' latent homophobia. "Quayle wasn't directing his remarks just at the shows," *Newsweek* said. "He was talking about individuals, the Hollywood–New York crowd of writers, artists, producers and stars (except, of course, Arnold Schwarzenegger), and their fellow travelers in places like Boston and San Francisco. Is there a world view that this 'cultural elite' shares?" The story went on to quote a survey done by an organization called the Center for Media and Public Affairs: "The center found that on issues of sexual morality, abortion and religion, the people at the top in television and movie making were far more liberal than the rest of the country," *Newsweek* reported. According to the center's figures, reproduced in a box, 76 percent of Americans believe homosexual acts are wrong while only 20 percent of those in Hollywood do. What *Newsweek* failed to report is that the Center for Media and Public Affairs is a right-wing, corporate-backed organization. It was, in fact, a 1991 study by the center's directors that Quayle's aides consulted when they drafted his "cultural values" speech.

At about the same time that Quayle made his remarks, Patrick Buchanan, in a speech at Falwell's Liberty Baptist College in Lynchburg, Virginia, went after "the adversary culture, with its implacable hostility to Judeo-Christian teaching," that had subverted values "from the public classroom to the TV screen, from the movie theater to the museum." By late June, George Bush jumped into the fray directly, railing about "the content of some of the filth and some of the portrayals that go into the families, into the living rooms through the television."

Like all corporate structures, Hollywood dislikes this kind of controversy, which embroils it in debates with powerful politicians. The industry still shakes with fear when anyone censures it, and is increasingly afraid of pressure groups. *The New York Times* reported at the time of Quayle's attack on *Murphy Brown* that "a senior executive at [CBS] who spoke on condition of anonymity said that at the shareholders meeting last week [the week before Quayle's attack] the issue of the unwed pregnancy on 'Murphy Brown' was criticized by a representative of the conservative media watchdog group Accuracy in Media." The fact that the shareholders would even give time to someone from such a group shows how fearful the networks are, as well as how much power right-wing pressure groups have grasped: CBS executives would not have concerned themselves if someone from the Gay and Lesbian Alliance Against Defamation had shown up at a shareholders' meetings to complain about an upcoming anti-gay portrayal. It's doubtful that such a person would even have been allowed entrance.

A lot of people at the networks get paid a lot of money to make sure such imbroglios as the *Murphy Brown* affair don't occur. At the television networks, the standards division acts as an in-house censor, deciding what is proper and what is not, what will cause an unwanted controversy and what will be acceptably provocative. Producers of shows bring their scripts to standards executives even before production begins. Sometimes, if producers know that a story idea will be especially problematic, they'll tell standards executives about it even before the script is written, so as not to waste time and money producing something the subject of which the network will find unacceptable.

The standards executives go over the script and let the producers know what is potentially objectionable and what should be changed. They also view the finished show to make sure that their original "suggestions" were adhered to.

While it may have seemed that CBS and the *Murphy Brown* producers (and their standards executives) were striking out on their own progressive path by having the single Murphy Brown have a baby in the first place, the truth of the scenario was that the character Murphy Brown, a pro-choice advocate on the show, could not have elected to have an abortion, even though that was presumably her right. "If we had done that," the show's creator, Diane English, told *The New York Times* before the Quayle attack, "it would have been lights out." The writer of the *Times* piece, Jeff Silverman, an editor of *L.A. Style*, observed that, "given today's political climate, where just the mention of issues like abortion, race and sexual preference can fuel tempers, Ms. English may be right. In truth, Murphy had no choice. . . . [The] networks . . . have begun to exercise a new caution about the hot-button issues which divide the country."

By 1992—while the world of independent film was touting "the new queer cinema"—Hollywood releases had also veered toward the safe and comfortable place that television had found. In the summer of 1992, films such as *Unlawful Entry, Lethal Weapon 3, Sister Act, Patriot Games, Encino Man, Class Act, Housesitter,* and *My Cousin Vinny* all espoused conservative themes and highlighted traditional family values. The only major film that overtly dealt with homosexuality was *Basic Instinct*, about lesbians and bisexual women who are man-killers. "Even some of summer's most mindless commercial releases have managed, deliberately or otherwise, to indicate a strong political undercurrent," observed *New York Times* critic Janet Maslin in July of that year. "[It's] not every season that so thoroughly enforces the relatively conservative ideas of mainstream Americana, family values and law and order, L.A.P.D. style, that are now on screen." While Dan Quayle was harping on "family values," the "cultural elite"— rather than making the images that he perceived as adversely affecting America—was churning out precisely what he wanted, having been conditioned for twelve years to do so by both fear and economic and political rewards.

If it is true, as Silverman says, that Hollywood is now more queasy about the "hot-button" issues than ever before, then in 1990s America queers are the hottest button of all, in the political as well as the cultural sphere. Evangelical leaders, who represent a constituency that is 60 million strong and were major players in Reagan's and Bush's election campaigns, told Bush in the spring of 1992 that the issue of homosexuality—and keeping queers out of the mainstream—was more important to them than abortion. The Christian right in America, contrary to what many believe in light of recent evangelist sex scandals, amassed enormous power in the eighties rather than declining. The groups on the Christian right have built their own media empires, infiltrated corporate power structures, and worked their way into state Republican parties.

The Reverend James Dobson's Colorado-based Focus on Family organization has a budget of $120 million. His radio show airs three times daily, five days a week, on 1,450 stations in the U.S. and in thirty-five other countries. D. James Kennedy and his Coral Ridge Ministries broadcast a weekly television show to 309 stations in two thousand cities and on five cable networks. Kennedy also has a radio show that is aired daily on 271 stations. Pat Robertson's *700 Club* TV show is broadcast daily to 29 million homes and has a budget of $135 million. Operating largely as a tax-exempt organization, by fall of 1992 his Christian Coalition had amassed more than $13 million. Robertson told *The Washington Post* that his goals were to elect "pro-family Christians" to Congress and attain "working control" of the Republican party by 1996. The Christian Coalition had outdone Jerry Falwell's defunct Moral Majority. It had tapped state and local affiliates to achieve majorities on Republican committees in more than a half-dozen states. It sent three hundred delegates to the 1992 Republican National Convention in Houston. "I don't want to belittle Jerry Falwell or the Moral Majority," the Coalition's executive director, Ralph Reed, told *The Washington Post* in 1992, "but the Christian Coalition as a model represents a more mature, more developed and more politically sophisticated vehicle for Christian political activism."

Hollywood and the "cultural elite" are on the Coalition's hit list, and the organization has given large sums of money to right-wing watchdog groups that focus specifically on the industry. "The strategy of the Christian right has been to proceed regardless of what was happening on the national level with the presidency," says Sarah Diamond, author of *Spiritual Warfare*, an investigation of groups on the Christian right. Diamond has studied these organizations for over ten years. "They've learned from Robertson being ridiculed and losing [his presidential election bid] in 1988. So they've focused on the state and local levels and on corporations. With regard to Hollywood, it's not only the Christian right, but a lot of secular right-wing groups who are also targeting the industry." Those groups include Donald Wildmon's American Family Association and David Horowitz's Committee on Media Integrity, both of which have gained much attention taking on Public Broadcasting and network television.

When the Christian-right groups aren't targeting Hollywood itself, they're pressuring politicians to do the attacking for them. The religious right's relationships with politicians are based on both the dollars that the right can generate and the votes it can turn out for elections. Robertson's Christian Coalition made political contributions in excess of $31,000 in 1991, including $25,000 to a local Virginia Republican party committee during the state's legislative races. Christian Coalition activists distributed thousands of "pro-family voter guides" in Virginia that year. Local Democrats say the coalition's efforts were responsible for the Republicans' picking up eight new seats. For the 1992 elections, the coalition instituted "in-pew" voter registration and distributed 40 million voter guides that embraced "family values" to influence key races. The largest single contribution to the Coalition in 1990 was in the amount of $64,000 from the National Republican Senatorial Committee, which obviously is aware of the coalition's ability to turn out votes. But money isn't the religious right's only payoff for getting millions of "pro-family" voters to the ballot box.

Both the executive branch and Congress are pressured to launch strikes against Hollywood by powerful conservative watchdog groups and religious zealots. Their critiques on Hollywood are easily outlined for politicians in periodicals distributed to officeholders throughout the country. *Between the Lines* is one of several right-wing publications keeping a reactionary eye on Hollywood. The magazine monitors the words and actions of people in the industry and consistently attacks what it calls Hollywood's liberal bias. It castigates films and television shows that criticize conservative Republicans in Congress, as well as shows that make any statement whatsoever in favor of nonconservative views. Readers are presented with lists of names: names of Hollywood celebrities, directors, producers, and others who speak out in favor of liberal causes or who participate in remotely positive projects about lesbian and gay rights, feminism, abortion, the environment, gun control, and many other issues. *TV, etc.*, another right-wing magazine, focuses solely on television, which it sees as morally vacant and dangerous to children, and regularly attacks shows that deal realistically with any controversial issue. Needless to say, homosexuality is an issue of major concern to these publications. Whenever Hollywood films or television shows present gays in a way that is not negative or that is seen to affirm homosexuality, the publications fire salvos against Hollywood companies and individuals in power—attacks that make the industry's powers that be shudder.

The Reverend Donald Wildmon heads both the American Family Association and the less well known Christian Leaders for Responsible Television, both based in Tupelo, Mississippi. The AFA received its first burst of national publicity in 1989 when it attacked the National Endowment for the Arts for funding exhibitions of the "sexually explicit" work of the late gay photographer Robert Mapplethorpe. The controversy dragged on for several years, and was a boon to the AFA, galvanizing right-wing forces. Today, the organization has six hundred chapters, a $5.2 million budget, and a radio show that broadcasts on two hundred stations. Wildmon's groups, as well as several other right-wing watchdogs, monitor and regularly lambaste television and film for their "permissiveness." Often "permissiveness" means any realistic or positive depiction of lesbians and gay men.

These groups gained strength under the twelve Reagan/Bush years, and their leaders had much influence during both presidencies. The California-based Reverend Louis Sheldon, who heads the Traditional Values Coalition, and who regularly attacks the gay movement and Hollywood, was an advisor to Bush's 1992 presidential campaign and was responsible for prodding the President and especially the Vice President to speak out about "family values" and how the "cultural elite" in Hollywood is a threat.

In these men's view, homosexuals—the new Communists—are taking over.

Because they can reach millions of people via their media empires, right-wing groups, and specifically the Christian right, have power unmatched by any so-called pressure group on the left—certainly unmatched by any group within the lesbian and gay community. Corporate advertisers as well as Hollywood executives are aware and afraid of these groups' ability to reach and sway millions—millions who do whatever "their" evangelist tells them to do. For the same reason, politicians—especially Republicans who court the religious-right vote—equally fear these groups and are easily prodded to join them in castigating Hollywood.

Hollywood is beholden not only to Washington and the right but, increasingly, to Tokyo as well. Beginning in 1989, two Japanese conglomerates, the Sony Corporation and Matsushita Electrical Industrial Company, went on a spending spree in Hollywood. Sony, forming Sony Pictures Entertainment, bought both Columbia Pictures Entertainment and Tri-Star Pictures. Matsushita acquired MCA, Inc., which owns Universal Pictures. While the Japanese companies indicated that they had no intention of interfering with Hollywood's creative decisions, *The New York Times* documented at least one occasion on which Japanese executives stepped in on a film project and made dramatic changes to the script because they weren't happy with the way it portrayed Japan.

Traditional Japanese culture, while homophobic, is perhaps no more antigay than traditional American culture, but without an organized gay movement with years of groundwork laid in battling the government for change, there is much less tolerance in Japan of out-of-the-closet lesbians and gays and of images that depict and affirm homosexuality.

"Many Hollywood executives do worry about their Japanese investors and owners," says one gay casting agent. "They're worried not even so much just about the images on screen but, in the cases where the executives themselves are gay, about their own homosexuality being known. They're much more afraid of being out to the Japanese than to the Americans, since gay life has become more and more accepted [in the U.S.]. The Japanese businessmen are extremely conservative, and definitely are not comfortable making deals with homosexuals."

For the most part, however, right-wingers in this country are and will continue to be the key operators behind the antigay Hollywood propaganda machine, because their interest is not so much in making money off Hollywood's product (the sole interest of Tokyo) but in controlling what America sees on screen. If positive, gay-themed films suddenly became big box office, all those investing in Hollywood, including the Japanese, would be seriously tempted to put themselves behind such projects immediately. Right-wing forces, on the other hand, would be thrown into a tizzy of immense proportions. With a Democrat in the White House, conditions shouldn't be expected to change dramatically. The power of Washington's conservatives, the right-wing pressure groups and the Christian right over Hollywood is so firmly entrenched and independent of the presidency, that their influence will continue unabated.

Hollywood, remembering the blacklisting era, remained cautious regarding gay issues even during the liberal presidencies of Kennedy and Carter. Right-wing and religious groups may not have the President to sound the alarm on their behalf when a Democrat is in office, but they still have a hold over powerful members of Congress and they have deeply infiltrated state and local government. They can also still threaten Hollywood and corporate advertisers directly. The fear that their product may be jeopardized and their money machine slowed or stopped will always have Hollywood in the grips of such groups. As Brownstein put it, the underlying goal of past moguls was simple: "To be left alone, to run the studios without interference from anyone—government, unions, the Legion of Decency." Today's power brokers are no different. Hollywood keeps the pressure off itself by playing into the right's agenda.

In 1990, Donald Wildmon and his American Family Association took on the television show *thirtysomething* because of one scene that showed two gay men in bed; ABC aired the episode but pulled it from the rerun line-up. The network caved in to the AFA's threats to launch a boycott of advertisers, some of whom pulled out of the show. Not only did many analysts believe that an AFA boycott would have been unsuccessful, but others thought that the network pulled the episode because it simply didn't want the controversy and didn't want to risk being branded as "permissive." For the same reason, sources at NBC say, a lesbian character on the network's drama *L.A. Law*, whose presence sent right-wing groups into a frenzy, was changed into a presumably less threatening bisexual after an on-screen sapphic kiss garnered much media attention. The character, previously hailed by the gay community and much of the main-stream media as an example of television's progress in dealing with gays, was "inned" and eventually became, for all practical purposes, a heterosexual. The same scenario occurred with the character of Steven Carrington on the popular eighties prime-time ABC soap opera *Dynasty*. He was originally a homosexual, but the show's creators, Richard and Esther Shapiro, married him off at one point, which they said they did under pressure from the network. Such plot devices are perhaps more damaging to lesbians and gays than total invisibility: They perpetuate—and beam into millions of homes—the myth that gays can "change" into heterosexuals. This fuels the Christian right's warped contention that gays can be "cured" of our "behavioral problem" and dissuaded from a "wrong lifestyle choice."

· · · · ·

Quayle's attacks galvanized the Hollywood community, which rallied vigorously behind Bill Clinton. People feared four more years of Bush/Quayle anti–"cultural elite" rhetoric. "I've never seen a time where people have responded so viscerally and taken the attacks so much to heart," Gary David Goldberg, creator of the show *Brooklyn Bridge*, said at the time. Marge Tabankin, executive director of the Hollywood Women's Political Committee, said that the *Murphy Brown* controversy had "created a chill and fear reminiscent of the fifties. Let's face it: We feel we're used as whipping boys."

In an interview in *Time* magazine, *Murphy Brown* creator Diane English went even further: "I feel like I'm entering a new era of McCarthyism, where one day somebody is going to come up to me and say, 'Are you now or have you ever been involved in the television business?'"

Wildmon's boycott—which he'd announced months earlier, at the height of the campaign—of the opening episode of *Murphy Brown's* new season didn't work: The first show in fact was one of the series' highest rated ever and made a record amount of money in advertising for the network, thanks largely to all the publicity the controversy had generated. But even such big profits don't outweigh Hollywood's age-old fear of being embroiled in controversy and labeled "un-American." Soon after the *Murphy Brown* scenario played out, attacks on the industry escalated, as a newly energized movement to bring "family values" to Hollywood got under way. *Time* magazine declared that "on subjects ranging from religion to the military, TV reflects the values of a pampered, predominantly liberal Hollywood elite." Like *Newsweek*, *Time* quoted the figures of the Center for Media and Public Affairs to show how out of step Hollywood supposedly was with the rest of America, also without pointing out that the group is a right-wing organization. Without challenge or qualification, the magazine quoted the group's leader, Robert Lechter, as saying that because Hollywood is "left of center" it produces many projects about "gay rights"—this, though there had never been *one* major motion picture about "gay rights," and though no more than a handful of television shows had dealt even slightly with the issue.

By late September 1992, syndicated columnist Joan Beck called for even more "watchdog groups" and more "boycotts" in a column headlined IT'S TIME TO CLEAN UP THE TOXIC WASTE THAT POLLUTES THE MEDIA. Other conservative syndicated columnists, such as Mona Charen and Suzanne Fields, railed against the industry, quoting the conservative PBS film critic Michael Medved, author of *Hollywood vs. America: Popular Culture and the War on Traditional Values*, which was published in October 1992. In one interview in the right-wing *Washington Times*, Medved remarked that those who said that this new crusade was a "prelude to McCarthyism" were "paranoid." On talk show after talk show, he completely sided with Quayle.

What was cynical about much of the discussion among conservative columnists and critics, however, was their conflation of many different, complex issues—on many of which they disagreed with each other—under the rubric of "family values." Many of Medved's complaints centered on what he saw as a lack of shows depicting religious people in a positive light; an overabundance of violence, including sexual violence against women; cannibalism; and what he termed an "anti-marriage" bias. It should be noted that Republican "family values" types like Arnold Schwarzenegger are responsible for a great deal of movie violence. To lump these social ills with the issue of accurately portrayed lesbians and gay characters on television and in films—and to say that portraying gays on television and in films promotes these ills—is insulting and homophobic. It's hard to believe that any educated film critic could possibly disagree with Vito Russo's assessment of Hollywood's horrendous treatment of homosexuals. For Medved and others to side with Quayle and the Christian right, without qualifying their criticisms, is not only disingenuous; it's dangerous.

In his book, Medved mentions Hollywood's mistreatment of homosexuals gratuitously, and even softly criticizes those who scapegoat "Hollywood's powerful gay community" for what he sees as the decline of "traditional values" in films. But he hasn't broached the subject in the media, and he has never spoken up when antigay pundits and politicians have used his book as fodder for their reactionary agendas.

The *Murphy Brown* controversy, as insignificant as it may have seemed, will go down as a marker, a first salvo in a war that will become bloodier. The impact on the ignorant of books like Medved's, coming so soon after Quayle's attacks and coupled with the rantings of conservative columnists and the new power and visibility of the Christian right, will only escalate the war against Hollywood and further the push for censorship and distortion of the lives of queers—as well as others whose "lifestyle" is not "traditional."

Patrick Buchanan wasn't kidding when he declared his cultural war at the 1992 Republican Convention. Although the right-wingers lost the election that year, they are determined to win their war.

12

Smashing the

Celluloid Closet

When Jordan Budde arrived in L.A., he expected to find a tolerant, liberal environment. He'd grown up in Tyler, Texas, the son of Methodists who all but disowned him when they found out that he was gay. Budde was then twenty-eight. Without his knowing, his father, an oil-company lawyer, had read his journal before he, his father, and the rest of the family left on a trip.

"My whole family had gone to Maui for the holidays," the lanky thirty-four-year-old recalls. "During the entire trip, they were acting weird." At the time, Budde was working as a writer. He'd left Tyler for New York only a year before, having been offered work on a film.

A week after the family returned from Maui, Budde received a letter from his parents. "We're devastated that you're a homosexual," they wrote. "When we found out, we felt that if our plane had crashed on the way back from Hawaii, our whole family would have been better off than this."

At the time, Budde's lover was sick with AIDS; shortly thereafter, he died. Budde headed for L.A. to start fresh and look for work. There he found that, when it came to queers, attitudes in Tinseltown weren't all that different than they were in Tyler.

His work had always incorporated gay themes. A play he'd written,

Fraternity, had powerful gay characters, and it seemed most of the people he'd shown it to in Hollywood liked it and liked his writing. He was hired by Rupert Murdoch's Fox Television to work on a new show, *Beverly Hills 90210*. That was 1990, and Fox was the enfant terrible of television. With Barry Diller at the creative helm, the company's dramas and comedies were breaking the boundaries of television, in terms of both political content and sexual matters—that is, except for *homo*sexual matters.

"In two years, *90210* only had one episode that ever dealt with homosexuality in the slightest," Budde says of the hit show, which became world-renowned for supposedly discussing some of the "real" issues facing teens—especially issues concerning sexuality— and also spawned two teen idols, Jason Priestley and Luke Perry. "We had this character who'd never been on the show before, who was 'confused' about his sexuality. It was what we call the C story of the show, meaning it wasn't the main plot, or even the B story, but was tangential. His attitude was like, 'I don't know if I want to stick with a woman,' and one of the girls says, 'That's okay' and she acts like, 'Well, you think I'm cute anyway,' and that's the end of it. To have a show that's supposed to have dealt with every issue that's pertinent in the nineties and not ever even get near homosexuality is incredible. They've had condom issues and they've had AIDS issues, but only dealing with heterosexuality."

Budde was one of five staff writers. He was considered very talented and was well liked by everyone on the staff and by his bosses. He was also very vocal about his sexuality.

"I tried over and over and over, every kind of different way to get it in," he says, discussing gay themes he wanted to have in *Beverly Hills 90210*. "Finally, I was assigned a script where a cousin was coming to town and she ends up being gay, and it was all about seeing how the main family deals with that. Halfway through the script, we got a call from Fox saying, 'We can't do that. We're not ready to do that. Maybe next year.' It's always 'Maybe next year when the ratings are better' or 'Maybe next year when we have our feet on the ground.' But it never happened. Nobody would take full responsibility. The staff knew I was gay. I'd come out to everybody. They knew how important this issue was. They were trying to be sympathetic. They were falling over backwards in a way, trying to be sweet and understanding and oh-so-liberal. But I feel if they had taken a stand, it could have gotten done. They just kept saying it came from the top, from Fox, but nobody stood up."

Budde also felt that he was looked upon as an "advocate" who was trying to use the show as a political tool. "I was always told that this was my 'agenda'—that I'd always had that 'agenda' ever since I'd been on the show," he said, noting that the word was used by an executive at Fox. "I found that incredibly insulting, especially since women on our staff always had strong feminist beliefs and were very vocal. They'd say, 'No, the girls can't say that.' 'No, that's insulting to women.' 'No, the girls can't just shop.' 'They can't just go to the mall.' Those were all valid and good points. Everybody listened and took those concerns seriously. But when I would discuss homosexuality, I didn't get the same support. I was always told it was coming from very high up that gay things would offend people, it would be too controversial."

The resistance to the gay issue, Budde feels, had less to do with audience acceptance than it had to do with homophobia and a fear of right-wing pressure groups. The show's audience was young kids in high school who are dealing with the issue of homosexuality every day in their own lives. The audience also included a lot of queer teens yearning for validation.

"They got thousands of letters from gay kids," Budde recalls, regarding the response to the show with the tangential gay character. "They all wrote thanking the network profusely for handling it well—this itty-bitty role. They were saying, 'Thanks so much for having that character.' So many kids would have worshiped that show and watched it constantly if they had a gay character or gay episodes. The resistance is not about a fear of losing the audience."

Budde left the show in the beginning of 1992, wanting to get back to writing plays. He was promised by his former employers that when they were ready to do "the gay episode," they'd call him. As of late 1992, they hadn't. And he doesn't expect them to. "I was very naïve going into that TV show," he says, looking back. "It was such an emotional roller coaster, a power struggle. The networks are so scared with a new show because they put a lot of money into it and they don't really know what they want. They're so eager to have a hit and to please everyone. So twenty different people are trying to do it their way. It's very emotionally draining and crazy."

Budde also realizes that so many of the people remaining silent are gay themselves, locked in the closet and afraid of pushing anything queer. "There are a lot of gay people working in TV but most of them aren't really out about it, and I just kept thinking, 'What do they have to worry about?' I mean, they're not actors. The more vocal I was about being gay, the more people came up to me, quietly, and said, 'Wow, it's great that you can be so open.' They'd kind of reveal to me that they were gay. Most of the people who I know who aren't out—writers, producers, and executives—are just not comfortable with themselves. The saddest thing is that they are in positions to do the most—the power positions. They could really help if they came out."

But, Budde says, because no one will speak up—and until people do speak up—there is a double standard for the portrayal of homosexuality and heterosexuality: "The message coming through loud and clear, over and over and over, is that being homosexual is wrong. That there's something bad and dirty and that you can't talk about it."

· · · · ·

For many reasons, the Hollywood power structure, like the Washington power structure, contains a disproportionately large number of gays. There are many closeted studio heads, executives, producers, writers, agents, and actors at all levels of the business, most of whom are more acutely aware than straight people are of any material that is remotely gay. And as Budde remarks, they're usually the first ones to strike from a project whatever appears too queer and thus not what they are taught is marketable. As Vito Russo observed, "Hollywood is where a gay director makes anti-homosexual films so that he can work with the big boys. Hollywood is where gay screenwriters churn out offensive teenage sex comedies and do it well because there isn't anything they don't know about pretending to be straight."

In the last several years some people in the business, like Budde, have been able to step out of the closet. Those few who are now out—writers mostly, and some agents and producers—agree that closeted gays in positions of power have been among the most detrimental to the advancement of gay people. Richard Kramer is a screenwriter, director, and producer who worked on the critically acclaimed *thirtysomething*. Openly gay and vocal, he was responsible for the show's gay-themed episodes. He's highly critical about how Hollywood treats not just homosexuality but the complexities of everyone's life. "The whole system," he says, "has to be exploded and started from scratch. The myths that it puts out for the world to see are antiquated. They celebrate a system of images and values that nobody can mirror." Because Kramer worked for a show that was a hit, he has been able to be more creative than others. He wrote the scripts for the twenty-two-hour miniseries based on gay author Armistead Maupin's *Tales of the City* books; the series, which was aired in the U.S. on PBS stations, was produced not by American television but by England's Channel Four. But Kramer, whom some call exceptionally talented, understands that there are barriers for other gay people in the business trying to do gay-themed projects. Among those barriers are closeted homosexuals in positions of power. "The kind of scum that Hollywood attracts in powerful positions transcends sexuality," he says with malicious humor. "The agents, producers, and executives—they're all cut from the same cloth, whether they're gay or straight. In a perfect world these people would be executed because of what they have allowed to be propagated about gay people."

As Kramer dramatically implies, closeted homosexuals in the business accommodate themselves to the prevailing homophobia. In the same way, Jews in Hollywood accommodated themselves to anti-Semitism in the twenties and thirties. Jews changed their names, denied their heritage, and refused to make films that in any way attacked fascism, Nazism, and anti-Semitism until well after America was at war with Germany, when Hitler suddenly became Washington's enemy too. In his *City of Nets: Portrait of Hollywood in the 1940s*, Otto Friedrich described a conversation between Jewish actor John Garfield and a Jewish Warner Brothers executive. Garfield had already changed his name from Garfinkle. Now Warner Brothers thought that his first name, Julius, sounded too Jewish:

"But I *am* Jewish," said the future John Garfield.

"Of course you are," said the Warner executive. "So are *we* . . . most of us. But a lot of people who buy tickets think they don't like Jews . . . and Julius is a Jew's name."

Doug Sadownick, a gay journalist, observed in *L.A. Weekly*, "Like the Jews who came to Hollywood in the twenties and thirties, gays have found the industry an extraordinary contradiction: an opportunity to exercise enormous influence over American culture and to reap extravagant financial rewards while, at the same time, being forced to deny their cultural identities."

Hollywood, like Washington, attracts members of disempowered groups. They can receive social status and financial gain in exchange for hard work and ambition, as long as they remain quiet about their "private life." In addition, Hollywood and greater Los Angeles have always had a reputation for "liberalism," which has attracted gays and others, even if they're not necessarily interested in show business. Los Angeles is a haven for outcasts and individualists, a relatively comfortable place for lesbians and gays by comparison to much of the West and the Southwest. The liberal Jewish establishment that built Hollywood has traditionally been tolerant of many different kinds of people. Historically, Hollywood itself has been decadent in terms of sexuality and sexual behavior; national scandals over stars' sexual dalliances have been common gossip for years. In Hollywood, no one really cares whom you sleep with—unless it affects the box office, which means unless the public finds out. This is the contradiction of Hollywood, a town of so-called liberals selling a product to a country they perceive to be conservative. In that way, when it comes down to the bottom line, the most ardent Hollywood liberal can behave like the most orthodox right-winger. Money is *always* conservative.

"You would not believe how things are monitored," says Maxine Lapiduss, a lesbian screenwriter who worked on the top-rated television show *Roseanne* for two seasons. "The stuff that they decide can or can't go on television—it's mind-boggling. You go crazy negotiating for the weirdest things. If something even looks sexual, forget it. We had two cupcakes—you know, those pink Hostess Sno Balls— that we were using on an episode of *Roseanne*. We had them on a plate. We couldn't use them because the network thought they looked too much like a woman's breasts. It's so silly, so arbitrary, so inconsequential. Scripts go back and forth. The fact that anything good is on television is astounding when you see the machinations of the networks, the buyers, the egos. It's an accident when something of quality gets on."

After several years in New York as a stand-up comic, an actress, and a writer in the early and mid-eighties, Lapiduss went to Hollywood in 1986. She was soon writing for several television shows, including *Dear John* and *The Tracey Ullman Show*. In 1990, she joined *Roseanne* for two seasons, and in 1992 she began working on the sitcom *Home Improvement*. She came out to her colleagues on *Roseanne*, including the show's star, Roseanne Arnold, and Arnold's producer-husband, Tom Arnold, because she felt it would be easier to lobby for a gay character on the show if she spoke from the experience herself. "I wanted to write that script about the Martin Mull character," she says of the character who revealed he was gay in 1992. "I was really fortunate at *Roseanne* because Roseanne, for all of her craziness, wanted that stuff out there and she was powerful enough to make it happen. I was lucky to be there and be the conduit. But it only happened because of Roseanne. She can do whatever she wants to do. She has the number-one show in television."

The other reason Lapiduss came out was that she couldn't stand the homophobic remarks that were constantly made in writers' meetings, and yet she knew that Arnold and the rest of the cast and crew were gay-positive enough that coming out would not only be okay but would stop the antigay remarks. "I couldn't take the gay-bashing jokes," she explains, "so I talked to the executive producer. I said, 'Rob, do you know that I'm gay?' He was surprised. I said, 'I'm having a tough time with all of the gay-bashing.' He was shocked—and apologetic. I then told all of the writers. They all had to deal with it. And there was a marked change. It was really positive."

But Lapiduss realizes that hers was an unusual environment in Hollywood. "For gay people, it's extremely tough," she notes. "The industry is very heterosexual-oriented and, with regard to gays, closeted; it's a harsh world." Her lesbianism, she says, has "definitely been a factor" in her being fired from previous screenwriting jobs. "In one instance I think they just *thought* I was a lesbian. When a bunch of writers are in a room for long periods of time, people figure things out. There was definitely a hostility there. In another instance I was open and it was a problem." Lapiduss sometimes writes in partnership with her sister, Polly, and another woman. She notes that her battle in straight male–dominated Hollywood is perhaps harder than that of either gay men or straight women: "Women are just coming into the business. It's very hard to do it on your own. If you look at the successful women in the business right now, their husbands are their partners." She points to Diane English, whose husband, Joel Shukovsky, is the producer of *Murphy Brown*, and to *Designing Women*'s Linda Bloodworth-Thomason, whose partner is her husband, Harry Thomason. Even Roseanne Arnold works with her husband. "I think for gay women it's tough," she says. "You really need to be rooted in this business, because it's so hard. It's great to be in a relationship and I've always found that it's great working alongside the person I'm involved with in a relationship, but it's hard for two women to be producing partners and actually get work."

Lapiduss talks of "doing what has to be done" so that she can attain the "power" to do the projects she'd like to do in the future. In 1992 she was attempting to make one of lesbian novelist Sarah Schulman's books into a film. "I'm trying to do what Richard Kramer has done," she says, describing how she'd like to carve a place in the industry for herself to work on projects she feels passionate about. "I want women and gays to be better represented on television and I plan to do that," she says, adding flatly, "I'm an activist."

For now though, Lapiduss finds it frustratingly difficult to get quality work on the air. She echoes the thoughts of many in Hollywood who consider themselves "activists": They are very vocal about women's issues, civil rights, and topics of concern to queers, but they feel that they must first conform to Hollywood's dictates before being offered the opportunity to achieve their larger goals. Some of them, like Lapiduss, may go on to do socially responsible work that they feel good about, but others will keep rationalizing and playing by the system's rules, rising higher and higher and never using their power in a redeeming way.

In that sense, it's not so odd that Hollywood has given birth to some of the most visible and vocal liberal voices in America—people like Ed Asner, Norman Lear, Barbra Streisand, Whoopi Goldberg, Marlo Thomas, and Jane Fonda—while its product, including many of the projects that those liberals have worked on, does not mirror their convictions and often contradicts them. Vito Russo noted that the same Hollywood people who socialize with gay people and give money for AIDS "allow the films they create to foster a climate of fear and panic." And Ronald Brownstein came to a similar conclusion:

> Accustomed to relying more on emotion than analysis, artists tend to take purist positions on political and social matters. The film community's leftist activists constantly find politicians, who deal in the world of the possible, insufficiently liberal. Partly that is because Hollywood figures, like most activists, have the luxury of criticizing without the responsibility of actually making decisions. But the political extremism of the film industry activists also reflects the unique pressures of working in a creative medium that is above all a business. Compelled to compromise constantly in the making of films, Hollywood figures tend to veer toward the other extreme and become purists in politics, as a sort of psychic compensation; people in the industry have always looked to politics as an arena that allows them to demonstrate that they really have deep convictions about something, even if their artistic choices don't display them.

Producer Howard Rosenman embodies the politically liberal–professionally conservative contradiction. Copresident of Sandollar Productions, Rosenman produced both the Academy Award–winning documentary *Common Threads: Stories from the Quilt*, the moving film about the Names Project's AIDS memorial quilt that profiled several people with AIDS, and the Steve Martin comedy *Father of the Bride*, which was slammed by the Gay and Lesbian Alliance Against Defamation in 1991 as homophobic because of Martin Short's stereotyped portrayal of a gay man.

Rosenman is a fast-talking, robust Hollywood type who always wears dark sunglasses. Highly expressive, he's blunt about his feelings on most things and certainly doesn't cover up his anger at gay activists who target closeted people in the industry and who target the industry itself for homophobia. Responding to attacks on the stereotypical gay character in *Father of the Bride*, Rosenman counters, "Hey, why wasn't I lauded for being a coproducer of *Common Threads*?" (Both he and it *were* lauded throughout the gay press and in much of the mainstream press when the HBO film aired in 1991.)

"Look," Rosenman explains, "there is no homophobia in the industry. That's it. There's no such thing. It's a liberal industry. Actually, in the industry, people are much more liberal and much more tolerant than anywhere else." Then he does a complete backflip and states flatly, "This is a very conservative industry. It's sort of like Wall Street. Not just about 'gay,' but about everything. So people are less likely to have flamboyant people of any kind around." He makes the classic justification for the closet. "You have to establish yourself first. If you set a good impression, you can let people know you're gay. If you're a proven commodity and they know you can make money, then they don't care who you fuck."

Even as he mires himself in contradictions, Rosenman hits upon something that is as true in Hollywood as it is in Washington: It's okay to be queer—as long as you're not queer during business hours. The city of Los Angeles is a comfortable, open place for gays: a sexually liberated, sprawling metropolis where all sorts of people fit in. But Hollywood the industry is as conservative as Washington the industry. While Washington staffers—whether at the White House or in Congress—must not bring any controversy to their elected bosses (and most elected bosses define being publicly homosexual as controversial), in Hollywood the closet has been rigidly enforced to protect the talent—the actors. Actors are Hollywood's bread and butter, and it is believed that their coming out as queer could ruin their careers (and therefore their handlers' livelihoods). People who are out have the effect on the closeted of making them consider coming out themselves. Therefore the best way to maintain a closeted environment among stars is to encourage that same environment throughout the industry. An out person is a threat to the closet.

"There are a lot of gays," says Maxine Lapiduss, "but it's underground, especially among gay women. Mostly, they're in the closet at all levels." In that atmosphere, "discretion" becomes the operative mode. Being out is considered gauche. One is considered to be "flaunting" one's sexuality. The characterization of closetedness as "discretion" plays well to heterosexual Hollywood liberals, who see being "discreet" as preserving "privacy," something liberals have fought to protect for many years.

Among gay men, who are ultimately in much more powerful positions than women, the underground is, as it is in Washington, a playground of abuse. But in Washington, where sex and sexuality can be used against politicians come election time, closeted members of Congress, as well as gay White House and Pentagon officials, are rarely out to each other. In Hollywood, however, many of the powerful gay men are known to each other, part of a secret network. Escort services flourish, but not as much as in Washington, since another form of prostitution occurs in Hollywood, which has always tied sex—straight and gay—with business.

Stars and starlets trying to make it up the Hollywood power chain have always slept with power brokers in order to move up; there has always been an ample supply of young men ready and willing to have sex with those at the top in gay Hollywood. These liaisons are usually arranged by what are casually called networkers. Anyone—a chauffeur, or a friend of a person in power—can be a networker. Sometimes both the networker and the man offering his sexual services get paid. Sometimes the networker works in the sleazier aspects of the business: One producer of porn films rents out top porn stars to the best-known of Hollywood's closeted gay elite. Because the rich are much richer in Hollywood than they are in Washington, money is a much more compromising factor: One power broker offers more money to men who are willing to practice unsafe sex—and many take him up on the offer.

But often, neither the networker nor the sex toy receives cash. If the networker is someone in the mainstream entertainment industry who is trying to ingratiate himself with a power broker—producer, casting agent, director, or someone aspiring to be any of those—he brings attractive, available young men to him as an offering, as a gift. The men, who also want to move up the ladder, are only too willing.

" 'Networker' is another word for 'pimp,' " says a former networker, now a publicist. "It's someone who calculates, schemes, seeks introductions, stays in the good graces of someone he's kissing the ass of. Most of the big shots who are gay have networkers who find them young, handsome men. The networker is a calculator, a manipulator, a schemer. He may not want something now, but it's understood that down the road he'll ask for something. That something will either further his career or help him make some big money."

With "discreet" sex as a commodity that is part of the day-to-day dealings of Hollywood, the closet becomes institutionalized as part of business. It facilitates a hierarchical order that keeps people in their place and gives them an incentive to move up. The history of Hollywood is filled with stars who started out at the bottom of the chain, essentially as prostitutes, became networkers, and went on to become stars or power brokers. Others began as networkers and hoped to move up to power-broker status, but remained networkers, continuing to ingratiate the powerful. Still others, actors mostly, will always be prostitutes, willing to put out for whatever they can get in return. There has never been a shortage of them, male or female: They will always flock to Hollywood.

Another thing attracts lesbians and gay men to a place like Hollywood. Gays have traditionally worked in the arts, and Hollywood has always been the place to try to sell one's talents. Acting is an art form that many lesbians and gay men have excelled at, perhaps because it allows them to be someone else, to escape the horrors of being queer in this society. All homosexuals are probably great actors simply because since childhood they've been forced to pretend they were something they weren't. Many of them start out as actors but eventually wind up behind the scenes when their acting pursuits don't work out.

Jews have also had a tradition in the arts, one that has spanned centuries; they too are prevalent in greater numbers throughout the Hollywood hierarchy. But while anti-Semitism has decreased, homophobia is still so pervasive that even the most powerful queers in Hollywood feel they must hide in a self-perpetuated fear.

Gays in powerful positions in Hollywood, living in an America that is rabidly homophobic, experience the same apprehension that terrorized early Hollywood's Jewish moguls, who lived in a world where anti-Semitism was rampant. Certainly, despite all their wealth and glamour, today's closeted gay power brokers, living amid the Christian right's increasingly vocal gay-bashing, perceive that at any time conditions for queers could become terrible. Some of these people are from a generation that considered homosexuality unspeakable. Many remember the McCarthy era. Their minds burn with fears that were realized in the not-too-distant past.

In 1992, *Spy* magazine included Barry Diller, David Geffen, and producer Sandy Gallin (Howard Rosenman's partner at Sandollar) as being members of "Hollywood's powerful gay tong." From 1990 through 1992 the three bore the brunt of activists' criticism for their association with antigay entertainers like Andrew Dice Clay precisely because they appear more out of the closet than most; they socialize openly within the gay community. They involve themselves with AIDS charities and gay-rights benefits, give large amounts of money to the community, and have responded positively to activists' criticisms.

But there are many other closeted gay power brokers in Hollywood, many of them older, less visible in the gay community, who consistently participate in antigay projects. These older, closeted gays never involve themselves at all in charity events for the gay community. They typify the great majority of closeted people in power in Hollywood.

A closeted television producer made several television series throughout the seventies and eighties that presented antigay stereotypes. Friends implored him to stop, but he excused himself by arguing that such programming was what people wanted and that it was his job to give the public what it asked for.

According to several sources, one well-known film-company executive has been arrested at least twice for having sex in public rest rooms. Deeply closeted and married, he doesn't socialize at all with other gays. The tea rooms provide an easy way for him to have homosexual sex without involving himself in the gay community. Both times the executive was arrested, he was able to get the charges dropped, avoid publicity, and make sure there was no police record. Several gay men told me they've been picked up by him in toilets. One says he met the executive at a male porn theater.

One impossibly handsome leading man is grossly homophobic. He has a well-known closeted gay publicist and a gay agent who have no problem keeping him on as a client. Other closeted queers never challenge the closeted publicist or agent. Like the gay staffers of Washington's Revolving Closet, the closeted Hollywood queers are all out to each other, but they're not out to straight people or people outside of the business. It's understood among them that such homophobia is not only to be tolerated but also to be defended. In Hollywood the closet comes with the territory.

There are countless Hollywood stories of closeted individuals rationalizing their behavior simply by reiterating, "It's business."

These people consistently tell themselves that, given the constraints of the system, they have no choice but to behave in this manner. They are immensely threatened by anyone who is out of the closet, even when these people are their friends. Richard Kramer talks about a former friend, once the head of a studio. "He had gay friends, some of whom were out," Kramer says, "but he was not out to people at work. His reaction to me in private may have been 'Oh, you're so, so interesting.' But in public, he was threatened by me, offended by me, angered by me."

These occupants of Hollywood's closets of power are at once intrigued with and threatened by those who are out. They'd like to be out themselves but are convinced that they can't be until they leave the business—even if they are at the highest levels. "Everybody who comes here," says Kramer, "wants to be the most powerful person in the world—the most glamorous, richest, most powerful person in the world. Coming out jeopardizes that because it defines you. You get power in this town by not being pinned down. A master player would never say what he was, one way or another."

What Kramer says is true despite the fact that everyone in Hollywood knows who's queer and who's not. The golden rule is discretion: As long as you don't say it yourself, no one else will dare say it. It's not until a person's sexuality goes public, in some sort of scandal, that people say in print what they knew all along. This was certainly true in the case of actor Rock Hudson, when shortly before his death, it was revealed that he was gay and had AIDS. By then Hudson's career was over; there was no sense that his life was being harmed by the revelation because it was clear that he was about to die. But Rock Hudson was not a Hollywood power broker.

· · · · ·

Back in the sixties, Merv Griffin was among the most popular of television talk-show hosts, the Arsenio Hall of his day. Thirty years later, he'd built Merv Griffin Enterprises into an empire that encompassed some of the top game shows on television, including *Wheel of Fortune*, after he'd become an Atlantic City casino magnate. Then in April 1991, at the height of his career, Griffin was hit with a palimony suit. Brent Plott, a then-thirty-seven-year-old Florida man, was suing Griffin for $200 million for breach of contract. Plott claimed that Griffin had promised to take care of him for the rest of his life.

"This is a shameless attempt to extort money from me," Griffin replied at the time through his attorney, denying that the relationship between him and Plott was sexual. "This former bodyguard and horse trainer was paid $250 a week, lived in one of two apartments underneath my former house as part of his security function, and left my payroll six or seven years ago. His charges are ridiculous and untrue."

"We lived together, shared the same bed, the same house," Plott told *NBC Nightly News,* which broke the story. "He told me he loved me." Plott claimed that he was entitled to the money he was seeking not only because he had been Griffin's business consultant—claiming he had selected Vanna White for Griffin's *Wheel of Fortune,* for instance—but because as Plott's lover, Griffin had promised him that he would provide "solace and emotional support." (Plott had left in 1985, after living in his apartment for four years, and moved to Florida.)

The story ran on the Associated Press wire and landed in hundreds of newspapers from *The New York Times*'s genteel "Chronicle" column to the splashy front page of the *New York Post. People* magazine ran an article on the lawsuit. They reported Griffin's denial but they also quoted several acquaintances and neighbors in Carmel, California, who said he is thought to be gay. "It's just not a big deal," *People* quoted Carmel art dealer Adam Kramer. The magazine also reported: "A former waiter at the nearby Swank Lodge at Pebble Beach remembers serving the bathrobe-clad celebrity early-morning breakfasts on several occasions—each time in the company of a different, handsome young man. But open as the supposed secret may have been, it was, people understood, a 'secret.' . . . Rumors of romance with Eva Gabor helped preserve the 'secret,' some say, and bolstered Griffin's public image."

At a party for then-President Bush at the home of producer Jerry Weintraub, Griffin called the suit "a lot of garbage." Meanwhile, Eva's sister Zsa Zsa went on talk shows and said that Eva had planned to sue Merv for palimony. She said that she thought Griffin was going "to marry Eva in two months." Eva herself said, "I've been with him for nine years, and I can tell you, this is ridiculous."

Plott's lawsuit alleged that he and Griffin met in Monte Carlo in

1976, the year Griffin had divorced his wife, Julann, to whom he'd been married for almost twenty years and with whom he had a son, Anthony, in 1959. According to Plott and his Florida-based lawyer, Plott had been stationed in Germany for most of his three-year hitch in the U.S. Army; while on leave during that time he says he took a trip to Monte Carlo. And according to the lawsuit, Griffin pleaded with Plott to come and live with him. But Plott moved in with Griffin only years later, after what he called considerable begging from Griffin.

In November 1991, Los Angeles Superior Court judge Diane Wayne dismissed Plott's case with prejudice, meaning that it cannot be refiled. The court also granted monetary sanctions in the amount of $2,000 against Plott. Griffin, who has always had a weight problem, shed some pounds and appeared happy about the outcome of the case. His spokesman said, "This was a totally baseless suit from a guy trying to make a quick buck."

In December 1991, another lawsuit was hurled at him, this one from former *Dance Fever* host Deney Terrio, who claimed that in 1978 he'd been sexually harassed by Griffin. Terrio was now seeking $11.3 million from his former boss.

Terrio claimed in his suit that "commencing in 1978, and continuing through the parties' business relationship, the Defendant, Merv Griffin, made on-going explicit homosexual advances towards" him. Terrio also claimed that "Griffin persisted in said advances often speaking of the financial gains that [Terrio] would enjoy."

Griffin's lawyer labeled Terrio's allegations totally false. The lawsuit was thrown out by the federal court in Los Angeles in June 1992.

In New York, gay men began to wear T-shirts with the slogan I DIDN'T SLEEP WITH MERV.

Griffin has always steered clear of the gay community. He has never put his name to a gay benefit. Nor has he ever backed an entertainment project that even remotely benefitted queers. He has always, in fact, remained silent about gay issues.

· · · · ·

"I was gay and never hid the fact," says Hal, who worked for an entertainment company as a page—an usher who tends to studio audiences. "I was also a very pretty young boy. In Hollywood, I don't think it was hard to recognize that I was gay."

Hal, a quintessential California blond, today works for a major media organization as an investigative reporter. But back then, he was yet another aspiring actor in Hollywood. His story is typical of that of many young gay men (and some lesbians) in Hollywood, who describe same-sex harassment and discrimination based on sexual orientation. Ironically, those in power who harass or discriminate are often gay themselves—albeit closeted. Hal says he was noticed by the mogul who ran the entertainment company after only several weeks of working as a page. "I was twenty-three years old but I looked like nineteen or twenty," he says. "I had just gotten back from Japan, modeling for a year there. I impressed [the Mogul] when I translated a contract for a guest who was Japanese. It came to [the Mogul's] attention. He was thankful. About a week or two later some of the pages were asked if we wanted to work on a Saturday to set up the stage for a special event. I came in jeans and a T-shirt. I'd been working out and [the Mogul] came and put his hand on my chest and said, 'Oh, you're getting pecs.' I took his hand and pushed it away. He was insulted, it seemed. Then I walked away from him. After that, he wasn't as friendly as he had been before."

Hal was an eager beaver, a hard worker when a lot of the other pages were spending most of their time dating and going out to discos. His immediate supervisors liked him. He stayed a page for only two months and then was promoted to the mailroom.

"In the mailroom you see everything coming and going," Hal remembers. "You send mail out and deliver mail in and you always have access to anywhere in the building. I delivered mail to [the Mogul]. I also had to bring him his lunch.

"You were told not to talk to him until he spoke to you if you went in his office or passed him in the hall. He was just very erratic in his mood and behavior. If you saw him smile, then it was okay. Otherwise, you couldn't just approach him to talk. He might blow up at you."

Hal says that discretion was certainly the order of the day at the Mogul's company. "A lot of the men, the executives, were gay," he says, "but they didn't ever discuss it. Two of the executives were even lovers, I recall. They'd all look at you when you came up there, like they wanted to try you out, but they never talked about it."

As in his previous job as a page, Hal was a hard worker in the mailroom. He came to the attention of the talent coordinator, who wanted an assistant unafraid of long hours. "He liked my personality and he asked me if I wanted to be assistant talent coordinator with him," Hal recalls. "I was excited. In six months I'd gone from page to mailroom to the executive floor. As soon as I got up there, I was the best worker they ever had up there—extremely organized."

But within two weeks, Hal was demoted. He was sent back to the mailroom, with no explanation given. He says a reliable source on the executive floor told him the truth, adding that, to save his own job, he'd never say it publicly.

"He told me that [the Mogul] told him that I was too gay and it made him uncomfortable to be around me," Hal says. "He thought that I dressed too gay and looked too gay. I always spoke openly. If I had something to say I said it. I had a sense of humor, which I used. I guess it made him uncomfortable.

"I was furious. I didn't understand why I couldn't have this job. I went to personnel. Someone there who always liked me told me the same thing, that she'd never say it publicly but that [the Mogul] just thought I was too gay. She said, 'You'll never win if you go to the labor board either. He did say that you made him uncomfortable.' She told me that he'd said that when people come up and visit, for meetings and whatever, they might get offended. I was so angry that I quit and I went to work at a Holiday Inn."

Hal thinks that part of the reason he wasn't treated better was that he wasn't friendly to [the Mogul] when the older man touched his chest and admired his muscles. "You could definitely say that got us started out on the wrong foot," Hal says. "Who knows where I'd be if I'd kind of smiled or winked?"

· · · · ·

Sexual-orientation harassment—harassment based on perceived sexual orientation—and sexual harassment of lesbians and gay men are rampant in Hollywood. A great deal of the abuse is executed by closeted gays. "You have no idea—the gay community at large has no idea—what's going on in the industry," says Shawn Plechette, executive director of Alternatives, a network of gay and lesbian professionals in L.A. "It's absolutely scary out there."

Plechette describes Alternatives as a "psychological corporation" that treats primarily lesbians, gays, and people with AIDS who have suffered discrimination, harassment, or abuse at work, although the organization also deals with gay-bashing, civil litigation, and medical malpractice. It's a network of clinical psychologists, family therapists, medical doctors, chiropractors, and attorneys who write medical, psychological, and legal documentation for individuals who are bringing suit against their employers regarding discrimination and abuse. Alternatives opened its doors in January 1992, with no publicity. "Almost immediately, we were inundated," says Plechette. "We get five to ten sexual-orientation harassment, sexual harassment, discrimination, and abuse cases per day. I wish I could say the cases are unbelievable, but they're not. They're frightening, is what they are. And the largest number of complaints we get come from the entertainment industry." A former medical manager who developed treatment centers for alcoholics, Plechette cofounded Alternatives after deciding that he wanted specifically to help lesbians and gay men, who he'd come to realize were being abused in the workplace at dramatically high levels and turning to alcohol and drugs as a way out.

Sexual harassment and abuse of women by straight men is practically a tradition in Hollywood, one that has been publicized and even glamorized in the image of the Hollywood "casting couch." Women's organizations in Los Angeles have dealt with the issue for several years, but none have dealt specifically with lesbians. Many in the business believe that lesbians are targeted even more than are straight women, by straight male bosses who are turned on by dykes or who like the challenge of trying to convert them. These are not only sexual-harassment cases but sexual-orientation-harassment cases as well. "I don't come out to men in this business anymore," says a closeted lesbian casting agent. "With women, or even out gay men, it's fine, although sometimes I'm afraid they'll tell the straight guys and that'll be the end of it. I worked for a producer who degraded me, making remarks and touching me, telling me he could 'eat pussy' better than any woman could. It was horrible but I stayed in that job for eight months before I found another job." Just as in Washington, such harassment is rooted in male insecurity and the desire to exert power over women. Male-on-male sexual harassment in Hollywood, perhaps even more than in Washington, stems from the need of closeted individuals in power to find sexual activity.

But Plechette says that in Hollywood, sexual-orientation harassment of queers *by* queers is also the direct result of the closet. "In Hollywood, gays and lesbians are both the victims and the perpetrators of personalized, internalized homophobia and socialized homophobia," he says. "Oftentimes they're placed in situations where they have to perpetuate heterosexism, where they have to very directly perpetrate a myth and deny their own gay identity or that of other gay individuals by lying, or by marrying people to put on appearances, or by not having openly gay people around them.

"This is heterosexism that trickles down from the top of our society and then into management in this industry, and it makes gays and lesbians here very personally, internally homophobic. It is *they* who perpetuate the heterosexist myth. What they're saying when they claim they can't change it is 'It's the entertainment industry that controls the entertainment industry and it's the entertainment industry that perpetuates the myth.' They have the power. They could change it if they want. They can make it even and equal and they could be very responsive."

Always afraid of being found out, the closeted in power in Hollywood hire batteries of lawyers to protect them and spend inordinate amounts of time trying to squelch the truth and to stop journalists from exposing them. The unrelenting stress created by the enforced closet plays out in ugly ways not only for the closeted gays in power but also for their queer subordinates, who become their victims as shame and self-hatred become prevalent in the closet cases' personalities even as they continue to rise on the professional ladder. Plechette says that most of Alternatives' clients experience one or more of the following: "heavy drinking; heavy drug use; promiscuity and unsafe sex (going out to the bars clandestinely every night to meet people, usually while drunk); involvement in 'hyper-religions,' such as Change Ministries or the Church of Scientology, to keep them from acting on their homosexuality; moving back in with their parents as a way of going back into the closet; having relationships with destructive individuals; depression; eating disorders; and a fear of being alone."

The individuals who come to Alternatives are only the tip of the iceberg. "I think they're only coming forward as a last measure—when they've lost their jobs, or their reputations, or their entire careers," observes Plechette. "Once they've lost everything, there's nothing left, so they come forward. There are many, many more inside in the industry who suffer just the same but just keep going."

· · · · ·

Jacques Rosas is a dark-haired, thirty-three-year-old gay man with high cheekbones and olive skin. Currently, he works in the L.A. field office of the environmental group Greenpeace. But ten years ago, Rosas was an actor and a model who was putting himself through school at the University of California, Irvine. He did mostly television commercials and print ads, he says. "I was out of the closet at school and at home," he recalls. "I came out when I was eighteen. I had two really liberal parents and I told them at the time. It was fine. I had a six-year relationship that began at that time and lasted throughout college."

When Rosas graduated, he realized that acting was not the route he wanted to take. He became a talent agent, landing a job in 1984 with an agency in Hollywood called Coast to Coast Talent. "My role, of course, was to sell artists, to sell their talents," he says. "I was great right away. Within two weeks I had it down pat. I started out with models and commercial and theatrical actors and then, after several years, writers and directors."

But what Rosas found unsettling was the fact that he had to go back into the closet, even though he'd been living openly for the past several years. "At the talent agency, about seventy-five percent of the office was gay—and about fifty percent were *quietly* out to each other. But *no one* was out outside of the office. It just came down to dollars and cents. You had to put up a front. Whenever I went to a function, I always brought one of the female actresses or models with me. There was one woman who worked very high up at [a major studio] who also needed an escort for events. I was her professional date and she was mine. People would assume we were a couple and we never corrected them. I was willing to do that because in the eighties the studio was throwing around some big bucks and I wanted to get in on some good deals and I did."

Rosas says that, for him in particular, the pressure to retreat to the closet was even greater because of the nature of his clients at the time. "I was handling children and had a lot of success right away. I was one of the hottest children's agents in town almost immediately. I remember a reporter from the *L.A. Times* asked me at the time, when she was working a story on children in the business, if I was gay. I lied to her and said no. Being a children's agent, I mean, if it came out, it would have cost me my success. The majority of the children come from Orange County, the deepest, darkest suburbia—Christian fundamentalist territory."

As many closeted gay casting agents report, Rosas says that he was also expected to advise his actor clients who were gay that they had to remain closeted in order to make it. "It was simply understood," he explains. "No one questioned it."

Rosas was becoming more and more successful, but the secretiveness and the constant lying and covering up were making him feel awful about himself. "When I look back now," he says, "going back into the closet almost killed me. I mean, I'd been out. I had told my parents. I had a lover. And now I was going back into the closet for, like, twelve hours a day—we worked long hours—and the stress was taking its toll."

He'd never previously been interested in drugs, but Rosas now found that cocaine made him feel better about himself, and drinking helped him to relax. "I didn't think anything of it at first," he recalls. "All of a sudden, though, I was drinking heavily and doing a lot of drugs." His cocaine habit was up to $125 per day. In order to facilitate it, he says, he needed to make more money and thus got involved in some "dirty deals." He began taking jobs as a casting director while at the same time still working as a casting agent. Thus, he'd cast all of his own clients. "It was a conflict of interest," Rosas says, "but you make money hand over fist. I would be collecting casting fees of five hundred to a thousand dollars per day, plus I was taking a commission from casting my own clients, plus I had my salary."

Things were soon "out of control," he says. "I was living in Beverly Hills, and it was all about the image," he remembers. "I'd be driving my 1965 Ford Fairlane convertible, driving up over Coldwater Canyon, the music blasting, smoking a joint, and snorting coke—doing bullets in the car—while I was on the phone making deals. At night I would drink heavily, then I'd go out to get laid—but never to the bars in West Hollywood, where I might be seen. I'd go to more discreet places. On top of it all, I had to keep a low profile."

Despite all this, Rosas stayed in the business for several more years, moving on and taking different jobs, until he realized in 1989 that he was destroying himself. He insists that "it was all because of the closet." He left the business, sought counseling, and took his job at Greenpeace, where he is very open about his homosexuality. Almost immediately, he says, he was able to stop his self-destructive habits.

Rosas acknowledges that things have changed a little bit in the industry. "What's happened in the past two or three years is amazing," he observes. "More people are out and it's becoming more clear to the world that people at the top are gay . . . being at every major Hollywood event, having tables filled with boys—that's very public and it forces people to accept it more." But, noting that he has many closeted friends who are still in the industry and who tell him horror stories, he thinks Hollywood has a very long way to go. "Of those who have now come out, it's only those who already got there, already moved up. It's okay for them to come out now because they have more power. But the only way they got there was by staying in the closet," Rosas points out. "There are exceptions to the rule. There are certainly some people who are in the right place at the right time or have such exceptional talent or ability that their sexuality is just not going to stop them because, what it comes down to, Hollywood needs their queer creativity—it couldn't work without it and it knows it. But for the average gay person, I still think it's enormously difficult. And I think a lot of the people at the top are still closeted and are creating this climate."

He has it right when he says that many closeted power brokers, especially those of the older generation, are still keeping the homophobic machine going. It's highly unlikely that Merv Griffin, for instance, will ever publicly discuss his sexuality even though it would probably do him a world of good and would have an effect on the way his own gay employees, as well as gay people throughout the industry, are treated.

· · · · ·

Like the Jewish moguls of yesteryear, the closeted power brokers harbor a fear of being labeled un-American and dirty, a fear that something will be taken away. But just as the Jewish community in America, in fighting anti-Semitism, eventually began to demand accountability of its powerful members, so too now a highly vocal and increasingly powerful queer movement is pushing from the other side at Hollywood's closeted power brokers, demanding not only that they come out and allow others within the business to be out (especially those who work for them) but also that they be accountable for their products.

Many people in Hollywood—the closeted among them—feel that the activists' demands are unrealistic. To the first demand, they say people can't come out until homosexuality is completely accepted, or their careers—and business—will suffer. This, they say, is especially true for actors. "There are gays and lesbians on TV that the public isn't the least bit aware of—major stars," noted Mary Buck, an openly lesbian casting agent, who, as a copartner in the agency of Buck and Edelman, has cast over thirty-five TV movies. "If I were a gay or lesbian actor, I wouldn't tell anybody. That's a complete contradiction from how I feel about the behind-the-scenes people. It's a different world for actors and actresses—they get nailed."

Maxine Lapiduss agrees: "I've sat in on casting sessions, where people describe roles, and it does have a derogatory sense. It's like, 'She's too butch,' 'He's too light in the shoes,' 'He's too queeny.' For women, sex is everything in the movies. Every breakdown is about sex for women—all of the roles are 'sexy.' Men can be smart, brilliant. Women are objects. There are actresses I know who are gay who weren't cast after it was found out. They just can't be out." The enforced closet in Hollywood puts actors in the most painful, psychologically tormenting position of all: The combination of the desire for fame and fortune with the fear of being found out can be dangerous. As Shawn Plechette sees at Alternatives, this fear can drive many actors to drastic behavior.

In 1990, the *National Enquirer* ran the blaring headline I WAS JOHN TRAVOLTA'S GAY LOVER. Paul Barressi, a swarthy ex–porn star and former personal trainer in Hollywood, had sold his story to the

Enquirer. Travolta, through his publicist, denied that he had any sexual relationship with Barressi and denied he was gay. The story was certainly a great catch for the *Enquirer,* as Travolta was a hot leading man who had starred in the hit TV series *Welcome Back, Kotter* and went on to make such films as *Saturday Night Fever, Urban Cowboy,* and *Grease.* But Barressi says he hadn't started out with the intent of selling his story.

"I had this idea, because I was the personal trainer of stars like Mary Hart and Joyce DeWitt," recalls the forty-four-year-old Barressi, "that maybe the *Enquirer* would be interested in tidbits on the stars. So they sent a writer over to talk to me. He shook his head and said people don't want to read about that stuff. They want to read about sex. Then he said, 'We know [you know]Travolta.' " Barressi says he declined to discuss the topic with the reporter. A full year went by, in which, he says, the *Enquirer* kept offering him more money if he'd talk. "They offered me ten grand," he says. "Then thirty. Then sixty. I kept saying no. Deep down, I didn't want to do it. But I thought, if I asked them for the moon, which was an impossibility, that would be my way out of it. So I asked them for the moon and they gave me the moon—a hundred grand."

While he was a porn star, a trainer, and a wannabe actor, Barressi claims he had sex with many well-known men in Hollywood throughout the eighties—mostly in exchange for money and arranged through networkers.

In the *Enquirer* story, Barressi said that he and Travolta met in a health club in Los Angeles and made a date. The *Enquirer* quoted Barressi as saying, "During the next two years, we met regularly at a variety of places and were intimate dozens of times." The article quoted Travolta's spokesperson, Paul Block, denying Barressi's story. The article said that the alleged affair took place while Travolta "carried on romances with [Debra] Winger, Olivia Newton-John, and *Taxi* star Marilu Henner."

The mainstream press reported the *Enquirer*'s outing and also reported Travolta's denial.

Since 1975, Travolta has been a member of the late L. Ron Hubbard's Church of Scientology, the religion that is the subject of much controversy and some litigation. One major pending lawsuit is its $416 million defamation suit against *Time* magazine for a highly critical cover story about Scientology on May 6, 1991, in which *Time* asserted that Scientology is a "global scam," with seven hundred centers in sixty-five countries, virtually unmonitored by the government or the media, sucking in billions of dollars. In its suit, Scientology contended that the *Time* article, entitled "The Cult of Greed and Power," contained a series of false statements and was "maliciously constructed from its inception to attempt to destroy the Scientology religion and plaintiff Church while defendants turned a profit in the process." The suit complained in particular about *Time*'s allegations it had intimidated members and critics "in a Mafia-like manner"; Scientology called this label false and said *Time* was using "the hatchet job technique of vicious name-calling." "The history of the article is a history of actual malice," Scientology alleged, charging that *Time* proceeded with "knowing falsity or reckless disregard for the truth."

Time's article had reported, "In recent years, hundreds of longtime Scientology adherents—many charging that they were mentally or physically abused—have quit the church and criticized it at their own risk. Some have sued the church and won; others have settled for amounts in excess of $500,000. In various cases judges have labeled the church 'schizophrenic and paranoid' and 'corrupt, sinister and dangerous.'"

Time had also quoted Cynthia Kisser, executive director of the Chicago-based Cult Awareness Network, whose twenty-three chapters monitor more than two hundred "mind control" cults, as follows: "Scientology is quite likely the most ruthless, the most classically terroristic, the most litigious and the most lucrative cult the country has ever seen. No cult extracts more money from its members." Vicki Aznaran, who was one of Scientology's six key leaders until she left the church in 1987 was quoted with a similar assessment, but Scientology flatly denied Ms. Kisser's assertion, saying: "Plaintiff is not engaged in any acts of terror, classical or otherwise, and its conduct is not ruthless. Plaintiff's policies prohibit the commission of secular crimes and its moral and ethical codes call for peaceful and non-criminal conduct and relationships with others."

Scientology charged that *Time*'s investigation was "merely an effort to string together distortions, innuendo, and falsehoods to produce a derogatory portrait of . . . the Church."

Curiously, many Hollywood actors and others in the industry are Scientologists. (In fact, the church is based in Hollywood: Its headquarters is on Hollywood Boulevard.) Stars get special treatment in the Church of Scientology, perhaps because they have so much money, and are offered counseling and career guidance at "Celebrity Centers."

Doug Lindeman works for a Hollywood production company that represents filmmakers. For the past five years, he's been out of the closet and in a relationship with one man. But for almost fifteen years before that, he was closeted, and during that time he got involved with Scientology.

In 1969, Lindeman, then a student at the University of Ohio, had what he called a "wild crush" on his friend Tom. But back then, being queer was certainly not a concept or a "lifestyle" that he wanted to embrace. "I was the classical homophobic homosexual," he says.

Tom was interested in Scientology, as he had a friend in California who was a member of the church, and Lindeman says this heightened his interest in the cult. He was also troubled. "I was obviously trying to deal with my sexuality," he says, "and I was nineteen and my mother had just died.

"I went to New York for my preinduction physical [before being drafted during the Vietnam War]," Lindeman recalls. "Someone on the street approached me, someone from Scientology. I went to the headquarters and I got into a discussion with a woman. She provided some very simple answers. I took a couple of their courses, and it really made a change in my life and gave me focus. In defense of Scientology, it is very powerful and it works. It put me more in control of my own life. I got very into it."

Though the gay movement was then emerging, Lindeman says it simply wasn't a reality for him because of Scientology. "The further I got into Scientology, the further I got away from anything *gay*," he remembers. "Scientology runs a very tight ship. They demand a lot. The more you are able to deal with your life, the more you are expected to help others. You're expected to work for the organization, and pour your money into it. The courses and the counseling have a high price. Basically you're a zealot. If you have a lot of money, if you're rich, you're expected to give large sums to the church."

Being involved in the church got Lindeman a "ministerial deferment" so that he wouldn't have to go to Vietnam. He and his friend Tom, with whom he lived at school and who'd also gotten deeply into the church, soon began having sex. In Scientology, that was a major transgression.

"Homosexuality is abhorrent behavior, according to the church," says Lindeman. "L. Ron Hubbard was a vicious homophobe. In his book *Dianetics,* he talks about it as a mental illness. It's a [fundamental principle] that Scientology is based upon and there is no changing it. If one is gay, one is ill and it is something that they will gladly help you deal with—they will 'cure' you. One would never be allowed to rise up in the levels of Scientology unless one was cured of his homosexuality. You spend lots of time in counseling—called auditing—working out this kind of stuff and trying to 'cure' yourself."

Lindeman and Tom both felt guilty about having sex and eventually told their counselors. "I just had to bring it up," Lindeman says. "You had to be honest in the counseling and besides, I wasn't feeling good about this. The counseling is like a therapy session—one hour long—that you go to every day. Homosexuality is so abhorrent that every day they'll just keep trying to talk you out of it. It keeps you so busy that—between counseling, taking classes, and then working for the church—you don't actually have time to be *gay.*"

Lindeman and Tom came under much scrutiny; both were instructed that their relationship was to stop. They were told that it was unhealthy and wrong. "An ethics officer was called in," Lindeman says. "They had their own ethical system and if someone is in violation, they call you in for extra counseling, some ethics counseling, to examine whether your behavior is right or wrong. Tom and I were forced to go our separate ways."

Lindeman left Ohio and moved out to Lake Tahoe, Nevada. There he met a woman, a member of the church, and they married. Scientology encourages its members to meet members of the opposite sex, he says. "I'd have bathroom sex while I was married, in the late seventies and into the eighties," he says. "It was all homophobic homosexual sexual activity. I was really fighting with my sexuality. I wanted to just be straight. I kept going to classes and counseling, anything to completely block out homosexuality as an option, and suppress sexuality entirely."

He and his wife, Lana, moved to L.A. and had a child. "Soon, I was working in the design industry," he says, "and meeting fags like crazy. I began traveling for work, and I had a series of affairs with guys I'd meet. I had sexual desires. I knew I yearned for men and male companionship, a gay relationship. It was just torture."

Throughout that time, a twelve-year period, Lindeman still went to daily counseling and still put himself through the church's homophobic ethics sessions, in which they'd tell him how unacceptable these desires and actions were. But after all those years, his homosexuality was beginning to overpower even the church.

"What happened was," he recalls, "Lana met another man and fell in love, and I saw how happy she was. I then met a man who at first was a friend. It grew and we fell in love and I simply realized I had to get away from Scientology." The church tried valiantly to get him back, calling him up at home, telling him he had to come in for counseling and sending counselors out to him. But, as hard as it was for him, he resisted—overpowered, perhaps, by love, as his relationship with the man had grown.

Lindeman says he has been deeply scarred by the years of trying to repress his homosexuality. Even thinking about Scientology makes him shudder, and talking about it openly is frightening for him. This is the first time he has discussed it publicly.

Lindeman is bitter about all the lost years and all the pain he suffered during those years. He describes Scientology as the perfect vehicle for anyone who is forced to suppress his or her homosexuality. Lindeman is concerned that Scientology might use his files against him.

The *Time* magazine article that is the subject of Scientology's libel suit stated that "high-level defectors claim that Travolta has long feared that if he defected, details of his sexual life would be made public." William Franks, the church's former chairman of the board, was quoted in the magazine as saying that Travolta "felt pretty intimidated about this getting out and told me so. There were no outright threats made, but it was implicit," he said. "If you leave, they immediately start digging up everything." *Time* also noted that "the church's former head of security, Richard Aznaran, recalls a Scientology [leader] repeatedly joking to staffers about Travolta's allegedly promiscuous homosexual behavior." Lindeman says that not only is it common for church officials to encourage marriage between members, but in his case they apparently did so hoping it would help him go straight.

"As soon as I gave that interview to the *Enquirer*, I said, 'John is going to be married inside of a year,'" recalls Paul Barressi.

By January 1991, two weeks after the *Enquirer* story ran, the previously never married John Travolta was engaged to actress Kelly Preston, a fellow Scientologist. On September 5, 1991, they were married by a Scientologist minister in Paris. They now have a child, and Travolta's lawyer has dismissed questions about his client's sexuality as "bizarre."

In February 1993, *Redbook* published a cover story about Travolta's happy marriage and the joys of fatherhood, with a cover photo of Travolta and his wife and child and the headline FORGET THE RUMORS AND THE LIES . . . JOHN TRAVOLTA TELLS THE TRUTH. In the article Travolta said of the tabloid stories: "We get used to everything being said about us. You wish that stuff weren't there, but on the other hand, you accept yellow journalism as a way of life." The article also quoted him as saying, "I go to Scientology classes almost every night."

· · · · ·

The fact that individuals in Hollywood are forced to extremes, subjecting themselves to psychological terror and abuse, underscores Mary Buck's and Maxine Lapiduss's contention that actors are given no choice by the industry but to remain closeted. This view is shared by almost everyone in the industry. But the argument actually comes from two different perspectives with two distinct rationales. One of these is, perhaps, pragmatic, but the other is simply homophobic. The pragmatic one, articulated by Buck and Lapiduss, is concerned with the livelihood of the actors and their ability to work in a system that right now will not take a chance on employing anyone who is openly queer. This rationale leaves open the possibility that sometime in the future, when homosexuality is more accepted by society, the industry can allow people to be out. (Although it is naïve to think this kind of change will happen in society *without* gay public figures, such as those in Hollywood, coming out first.)

The second rationale, however, is based on the premise that a mass audience cannot tolerate knowing that an actor is queer; thus, lesbian and gay actors will *never* be able to be out of the closet because the audience will never be able to believe it when they play heterosexuals. Some have even applied this warped rationale to *closeted* actors, claiming that the audience can sometimes even tell that an actor is gay, and will then reject him or her. In his inimitable style, Howard Rosenman observed in *L.A. Weekly* that audiences unconsciously know who's gay: "It's not that they discriminate, but the audience knows when an actor is kissing a girl but would rather be sucking a dick."

Some of the most enlightened people, both inside and outside Hollywood, share this opinion, though it is steeped in fear and grossly underestimates an audience's ability and desire to fantasize. Hollywood is, after all, about fantasy, about the fantasy that is created in spite of the reality of actors' lives or the times that we live in. If filmgoers are able to believe that an actor is a gladiator or a disciple of Jesus or a general in World War II or an anthropologist or a pilot or a Zulu tribal leader, why can't they believe in a queer actor playing a heterosexual? The actor who plays a general, for instance, may in real life despise the military and announce that he is a pacifist. In such a case the entertainment media and the gossip columns would exploit the fact—and discuss why the actor took the role—before the film's release. It would be considered a good angle and one that shows an interesting, novel contradiction. The film would benefit from the publicity. If the actor was a good actor, the public would go and see the film and talk about how convincing he was.

There's no reason why the same couldn't be true of openly lesbian and gay actors playing heterosexual roles—or even playing homophobes. Some people argue that sex symbols who become bigger than life offscreen and are icons to millions of the opposite sex would suffer if they were known to be gay. But many heterosexual actors are still worshiped and desired though they are in reality married and unattainable. Stars are also sometimes shorter in person, or less attractive, or boring and stupid. The public fantasizes about the images and tries not to think about the realities.

The argument that sex and passion are too powerful and stereotypes about sexuality too strong to break down is ridiculous. For years lesbians and gay men have watched the few films about gays that both Hollywood and independent filmmakers have produced, most of which have starred heterosexual actors playing homosexuals. In the cases where the players were good actors, the homosexual audience had no problem believing in their performances. No one got up and walked out because heterosexuals playing gays somehow seemed unrealistic. Most lesbians enjoyed watching Susan Sarandon and Catherine Deneuve in *The Hunger*, while gay men were perfectly content to watch Harry Hamlin and Michael Ontkean in *Making Love*. The notion that heterosexuals are unable to fantasize in the same manner is insulting to the intelligence of straight people.

Rosenman's argument that some actors who are closeted and gay might even be recognized as homosexual by an audience is probably true in a way. Gay people have always claimed to have a "radar" that is able to pick out fellow queers. There's no reason to believe that straight people don't have it as well. Gay or straight, we all unconsciously pick up and send out signals. And if straight people pick up that someone is gay, that isn't necessarily detrimental to the gay person's attractiveness. Many would argue that Rock Hudson's homosexuality was evident, on a subconscious level, and that it was what gave him that extra something that both women and men connected with. Similarly, some would say that Jodie Foster's tomboy nature and Sapphic energy are part of what makes her immensely appealing.

In reality, a Hollywood star has *less* to lose in being openly gay than does a member of Congress. While sex scandals can and do ruin the careers of politicians—because the public associates their ability to perform their jobs with character issues that involve sexual behavior—Hollywood, on the other hand, thrives on—and expects—sex scandals. Rarely do they ruin Hollywood careers; some would argue that they enhance them.

Queer actors are forced into the closet not because the public can't tolerate them but because, as Mary Buck says, "they'll get nailed" by the powers that be if they come out. No one in power is willing to take a risk on how the public will react. It is the industry and the power brokers who are responsible for the hellish lives that queer actors live. (Of course, actors certainly make a conscious decision to hide their homosexuality, and thus perpetuate heterosexism and homophobia in return for getting work—and unparalleled financial benefits.) And it is the industry that refuses to portray the reality of queer life and continues to demonize us, thus helping to keep homophobia firmly entrenched—which keeps power brokers from coming out, which keeps everyone else in the business from coming out, which keeps the actors from coming out, which keeps America ignorant of the many lesbian and gay lives of their favorite actors, which keeps homophobia so entrenched in the larger society that Hollywood power brokers are afraid to make films about queers. By adamantly insisting that actors mustn't come out, by crying censorship when queers complain about negative depictions of them, and by refusing to produce positive gay-themed films because of financial considerations, Hollywood has been completely unreasonable, unwilling to bend in the slightest to help solve a dreadful problem that affects the lives of so many people who work in—and own and operate—the very industry that is propagating homophobia and gay invisibility in America.

Is Hollywood exaggerating, living in the past? Does being revealed as gay ruin careers? Thirty years ago Sheila Kuehl was fired from the *Dobie Gillis* show simply because of a rumor. Today, both Jodie Foster and Kristy McNichol have been outed on a grand scale, discussed fully in the gay press, splashed across the covers of supermarket tabloids, and mentioned as having been outed in story after story in the mainstream press, but nothing has happened to them—or to Richard Chamberlain, John Travolta, and others who've been outed. McNichol, outed by the tabloids in 1990, still had her hit TV show as of summer 1992. Foster, after her 1991 outing, went on to win a second Academy Award in 1992 and continued to be inundated with potential film deals. Chamberlain was living quietly in Hawaii, discussing future television projects, and Travolta was mulling over some scripts he'd been offered. Since their outings were so public, it would appear homophobic to suddenly fire or blacklist them. So they kept working, and the public was able to prove that it didn't care. Hollywood couldn't afford to appear publicly antigay—just as the Pentagon didn't want to appear that way by firing Pete Williams. Perhaps we have reached a point where outing actually ensures job security and being outed as a *homophobe* is something to avoid.

Of course, all those recently outed either had no comment or denied their homosexuality. It might be different if they came out on their own or spoke out on gay issues. Still, the outings' nonresults reflect a change in the industry. Even after such public discussion of their alleged homosexuality, these actors' work wasn't interfered with, while thirty years ago, mere unprinted rumors about Sheila Kuehl got her television show killed. Nowadays, it appears that outing doesn't ruin careers.

·····

In response to the activists' other demand, that gays in the business be held accountable to the lesbian and gay community and produce films about queer lives, Hollywood denies that there is big money to be made. "When gay sells," says Howard Rosenman, "when the zeitgeist allows for gay to sell, trust me, you'll see thousands of pictures with gay heroes." That argument doesn't explain why films that aren't necessarily about queers can't have a lesbian or gay character or two who, though tangential to the plot, are not evil or stereotypical—just as there are now blacks and Hispanics and members of other minorities sprinkled throughout films. It also doesn't explain why so many films that originally have benign lesbian or gay characters are altered before release. In most cases the characters are cut because the filmmakers, by testing audiences and giving them leading questions, decide that the audience simply won't like gay characters in the film. The mere fact that they're still asking audiences about gay characters and tailoring films to such whims betrays the industry's homophobia.

As to why Hollywood doesn't make gay-themed films, Rosenman's argument that the "zeitgeist" isn't ready is disputed throughout the industry. Many others in Hollywood see the situation differently, noting that Hollywood has never really explored the profitable gay market in the way that other industries, such as publishing, have. Every now and then Hollywood will gamble on a safe, mediocre film like *Making Love* or *Personal Best.* When they don't see big returns on such projects, power brokers decide that "gay" doesn't sell. Rather than try to tap the lesbian and gay audience—or even one consisting of gay and enlightened straight people—Hollywood seems hell-bent on proving that "gay" will not bring in the dollars.

In an article in *L.A. Weekly,* casting agent Mary Buck explained how a company will set itself up for defeat with regard to gay projects, seemingly to put the kibosh on such material:

> I had just finished casting on a CBS pilot called *Nights of the Living Table.* [There were] four characters: a brother, a sister and two neighborhood kids who grow up together. . . . The female in the show was going to be a lesbian. They opened it with her playing with two Barbie dolls. She gets caught by her brother who calls her a pervert. When you meet her again in the next scene, at 25, the brother's come home from the Marines and Marla has to come out to him.
>
> The night we taped it, all the people who were in the industry—agents, managers—came up and said it was one of the best things ever seen. Then CBS tests it, but instead of testing it with what I felt was a cross-section audience, they used a *Price Is Right* audience. And surprise: the *Price Is Right* audience isn't okay with the lesbian issue. At one point, CBS thought they'll change the little girl and not make her a lesbian. Ultimately, they decided not to buy the show at all.

In *Backlash,* Susan Faludi similarly showed how television executives, so utterly homophobic and threatened by images of independent women and of women who might appear to be lesbians, actually forced *Cagney and Lacey,* a successful show, to become unsuccessful, just so that they could cancel it:

> It was the CBS male programmers, not female viewers, who were uncomfortable with the two strong women of "Cagney and Lacey." [CBS vice president Arnold] Beck complained at the time that the show's women were "inordinately abrasive, loud, and lacking warmth." Another CBS executive told *TV Guide* that the heroines "were too harshly women's lib. . . . These women on 'Cagney and Lacey' seemed more intent on fighting the system than doing police work. We perceived them as dykes. . . ."
>
> In 1983, CBS canceled "Cagney and Lacey." After tens of thousands of letters poured in from loyal viewers (an avalanche outstripping the last leading fan-mail recall campaign, for "Lou Grant," by ten to one), after Tyne Daly (Lacey) won the Emmy for

best dramatic actress, and after the show scored number one in the ratings during summer *reruns,* the network backed off and put the show back on the air. The program went on to win five more Emmys, including best dramatic series. Nonetheless, in the fall of 1987, CBS pulled "Cagney and Lacey" from its regular time and reassigned it to a doomed time slot. By the following season, "Cagney and Lacey" was gone for good.

Richard Kramer is adamant when he says that if a film or television studio had the slightest desire, it could make money by aggressively marketing to the gay audience. A solution he and others have put forth is for a film studio to hire a vice president who is openly gay, who would be in charge of a few movies a year in which the themes are primarily queer. "Each film would be budgeted with a certain amount of money—but real money," he explains. "These films would then be aggressively marketed not only to the U.S. at large but to a specifically gay market. And then see what the returns are. It doesn't even have to have a gay director, but be a film about and for gays. You need a brilliant, revolutionary thinker to do this, somebody who's going to come along and understand the needs of an audience in an original and striking way."

Such solutions, activists contend, do not see the light of day simply because the charges of homophobia against Hollywood have consistently fallen on deaf ears. The only way to make Hollywood listen is to create a grand spectacle. The Christian right, using high-profile politicians like Joseph McCarthy and Dan Quayle, has known this for years. And in the early nineties, queer activists learned it too.

13

....

Outing, Part III

....

Seventy-two-year-old Morris Kight came out of the closet in 1958 and became a gay activist in Los Angeles.[16] "Right now, some of the historic revisionists have it that everyone was out back then," he says, regarding the homophile era of the fifties and early sixties. "It's just not true. The handful of people who worked in our movement were largely arch-conservative and they went under assumed names. They were all part of that homophile movement, and they were cautious in their approach to the public. Of course, I don't blame them; it was just the thing to do. The number of people who were out was small. Being out was a very hard thing to do."

By 1969, after New York's Stonewall riots and after the formation of the radical Gay Liberation Front, that caution began to evaporate. The quiet, discreet homophile movement of the previous decade, which emphasized behind-the-scenes, circumspect tactics as a way of creating change, began to come under pressure from the new out-of-the-closet activists. Almost immediately after the GLF was formed in July 1969, some gays began to publicly take on Hollywood. Their tactics included meetings, attacks through the media, and some protests. At that time, Kight was very active in the GLF in Los Angeles. Today, the white-haired elder statesman still lives in the heart of

Hollywood, where his home has become a virtual museum of gay history, referred to by local activists as "the Collection." Kight is still active in the gay community, but is a little more laid-back these days, spending much of his time in his yard entertaining guests, telling stories of yesteryear to young queers who come from all over to pay tribute to him. But back in the sixties and early seventies he was an energetic agitator pushing the conservative homophile establishment of the time to take a more vocal and visible stance. Kight and the GLF also advocated that everyone come out.

"The last gas bubble, I believe, was a conference of an outfit that had this insufferable name: The North American Conference of Homophile Organizations," he remembers. "It was in San Francisco in the summer of 1970. Despite my radical leanings, they invited me to come to be a speaker. I stood up and said to them, 'I'm here to tell you that you must change your ways. Lovingly, let me tell you that this act of yours is over. You've had it, guys! You can't do this anymore—you can't do those arch-conservative things, you can't do those closeted things, you can't call yourselves homophiles anymore. You simply have to pay attention to what's happening in the world and if you wish to be a party to it, well, I tell you, it's all terribly exciting. We welcome you. The door is open.' When I left, the radicals from the Gay Liberation Front from San Francisco came marching into the meeting and said, 'We're here to be a part of this conference.' Before the weekend was out, the homophiles had locked themselves in the offices of one of their closeted organizations, SIR [Society for Individual Rights], barricaded the office door with desks, and called the police to arrest the GLF folks. Happily, somebody talked them out of having the radical lesbians and gays arrested. The GLF had gotten its point across."

Kight says that he and his comrades had a more "universalist" approach and believed that taking on all aspects of society, including its art and culture, was as important as taking on government. He led one of the first protests against Hollywood, a demonstration at the premiere of *The Boys in the Band* in 1971 at the Westwood Theater in Los Angeles. The film had been controversial in the gay community: Some were happy to see any gay representation on screen, but many others were angered by the film's stereotyping of gay men as weak, "effeminate," troubled people.

"It was a hysterically, stunningly homophobic film in our minds," Kight says. "We marched on the theater that night [of the premiere]. These large men, big guys with three-piece suits and big diamond pinkie rings and who were smoking huge cigars, tried to stop us. They were used to having things 'handled.' And they were used to ordering servants around. They called the police and said, 'Handle it.' An Officer Sherman came, and he knew me. We were ancient enemies, as I was always having run-ins with him at demonstrations. He said to the large men, 'Oh, it's him. Look, forget it. These people have read the Constitution of the United States. They can quote the First Amendment back to you. Don't fight them. Just go with it.'

"So we marched in front of their theater. They had bands and choruses and valet parking. And the stars were arriving in their limousines. The crowd was inside this glass dome. The windows go up three floors and all of the people were all looking at us. The columnist Army Archerd [of *Daily Variety*] came out and interviewed me and said, 'What's the problem?' I said, 'We object to the film.' He told me that a lot of gay people love the film. I said, 'I'm sorry they do, but I think that they haven't analyzed it. Look, there is not a single character in the film I don't know. I know the drunk. I know the pill head. I know the pimply queen. I know every one of them. They're very real. But they're only a part of this community—and happily they're a dying breed. There are so many more of us now, proud gay types, who are out there living and achieving, not worried about pimply skin, not drinking, and not popping pills. We're not distraught.' "

Archerd's column portrayed the GLF and their complaints positively, and, Kight says, it helped him and others gain an audience with studio heads such as Lew Wasserman and Darryl Zanuck. "I think, at that time, a number of the heads had some decency," he says. "Now it's only about money, but then there was some desire to accommodate. They would at least listen to us." Kight says he met several times in the next few years with film and television executives and held other demonstrations. "We picketed the Academy Awards in 1974," he recalls, "and we issued a press release and everything. All kinds of homophobes showed up to counterdemonstrate. They called us dirty. We screamed back at them, 'You're the dirty ones! You filthy, homophobic pigs! Clean up your act!' "

The Gay Activist Alliance, which grew out of the GLF in late 1969, was determined to be less radical than its parent group, to work for change from the inside. Beginning in 1973, the Los Angeles chapter of the GAA met several times with the Association of Motion Picture and Television Producers, bringing with them a set of guidelines that they and the then New York–based National Gay Task Force (the word "Lesbian" had not yet appeared in the organization's name) had drawn up. These meetings were successful in forcing television to offer a slightly more balanced presentation of gays in the seventies. Activists of the time contended that it was a fear of advertiser boycotts that had the television industry paying attention: The NGTF launched successful letter-writing campaigns that discouraged advertisers from buying time on shows that were antigay.

The late *Village Voice* columnist Arthur Bell published two articles in *The New York Times*, printed one year apart in 1973 and 1974, attacking homophobia in films. Both articles received some attention. He railed against the industry throughout the seventies and spearheaded the protests sparked by *Cruising* in 1979 and 1980. However, as right-wing groups rose up in the eighties and flexed more muscle than the gay community had so far mustered, and as the AIDS crisis and the backlash against the feminist movement took hold, the new sensitivity in both television programming and film was relatively short-lived.

In 1985, the Gay and Lesbian Alliance Against Defamation formed in New York, in response to the rising tide of gay-bashing and AIDS-phobia in the media. GLAAD focused mostly on news organizations but also paid some attention to film and television. The now-defunct Association for Gay and Lesbian Artists in the Entertainment Industry was also founded in Los Angeles that year. That group mostly gave out awards to positive projects but occasionally reviewed scripts and lodged complaints. Rich Jennings, a lawyer at the time, was involved with the group. When it folded in 1988, he cofounded the Los Angeles chapter of GLAAD; that chapter became the first full-time gay group to put pressure on the film and television industry, although it also focuses on the major media organizations of southern California.

"When we first started, we kept trying to get meetings," Jennings recalls. "It wasn't until the Andy Rooney controversy [the *60 Minutes* commentator made antigay remarks in early 1990] that we began to get a foot in the door with news departments of local TV and radio stations. But with the studios, it was much harder."

Toward the end of 1990, Jennings says, GLAAD began to make a little bit of headway in getting meetings with the studios. The group took out full-page ads in the trade publications *Daily Variety* and *The Hollywood Reporter*, pointing out the industry's homophobia. But it wasn't until the angry protests and attacks on Hollywood from radical queers in 1991 and 1992 that GLAAD suddenly gained more access to the industry—and the industry suddenly began bending over backward to respond. "The protests, Queer Nation, all of the actions, it certainly all made a difference," Jennings says. "All of a sudden, the industry didn't know where it was going to get hit from next. I'd been brainstorming with people for a couple of years on how to do it. I never in my wildest dreams would have expected this much entrée so soon.

"There was the *Silence of the Lambs* controversy. Then there was the impact of the *Basic Instinct* protests—the fact that people would be willing to risk arrest to disrupt the filming of something. It was like the Nazis marching in Skokie, having a gay-bashing film shot in a place [San Francisco] where people go to escape oppression. It touched off a violent reaction in Hollywood, especially among closeted people.

"Outing certainly had an effect too. I'm sure it really hurts when you are gay or lesbian in the industry and suddenly all of these gay people are attacking you. It's got to make you stop and think about what you're doing, and how you can change it. It's a concept that we at [GLAAD] didn't really have, as we were trying to be mutually supportive of those gays in the industry. But the idea that you can label someone as an internal enemy is a new political idea. It suddenly became a lot easier for us to get hearings."

Indeed, outing had rocked Hollywood more forcefully than any earthquake the town had ever felt.

· · · · ·

Annette Wolf's breakfast one Monday in mid-April 1990 could not have been a pleasant one. That morning, the Hollywood publicist sat in her L.A. office and blankly stared out the window, overcome with trepidation. The phone was ringing off the hook, and reporters from around the country were lobbing questions at Wolf. She tried to keep calm as the realization of what had happened sunk in: Over the weekend the *Star*, the *National Enquirer*, and the *Globe*, which have the largest circulations in America (their combined readership tops five million), had all printed front-page stories saying that Richard Chamberlain was gay.

The supermarket tabloids, notorious for printing the most out-landish and shocking stories, were only just beginning to get their feet wet with outing. While homosexuality was still scandalous, it was now—thanks in no small part to the visibility produced by the burgeoning queer activism of the previous few years—moving from being unprintably scandalous to being acceptably scandalous. Times were changing and the tabloids were simply living up to their role in society: remaining at the cutting edge of what was wildly—but *acceptably*—scandalous. Noting the "expanding limits of the public's tastes and curiosity," the *Los Angeles Times* quoted the *Star*'s editor, Richard Kaplan, who explained that the tabloid was "now treating gay liaisons with about the same nonchalance as we do heterosexual ones. What wasn't permissible a number of years ago is now permissible."

Initiating its newfound freedom in reporting homosexuality, the *Star* had outed Chastity Bono, Cher's daughter, in January 1990, several months before the Chamberlain affair. This was the tabloid's first major outing. There was speculation among many in the entertainment business at the time that Chastity's was, at least in part, a vendetta outing: In a highly publicized altercation several months earlier, Cher's then-boyfriend, Rob Camilletti, had allegedly hit a *Star* photographer who got too close, and had also allegedly showered him with expletives. Whether or not it was meant as revenge, the outing of Chastity Bono by the *Star*, although as highly sensational as any other story the tabloid splashes across its pages, was handled with something as close to sensitivity as a tabloid can muster—even in a manner considered by many actually to be progay.

According to the *Star*, Chastity had come out to her mother, who had difficulty dealing with her daughter's orientation and tried to make Chastity change. But the story turned more on Cher's not accepting Chastity's sexuality than on Chastity's being a lesbian. The problem was couched not as Chastity's but as Cher's, and it alleged that Cher had entered therapy over the matter. A sidebar story, offering helpful information for parents who find out that their children are gay or lesbian, included several of the "most often asked questions," answered by Paulette Goodman, the then-president of Parents and Friends of Lesbians and Gays.

While queers were happy about the *Star* story, the outing seemed to send the increasingly commercial Cher—who by then was hawking all sort of products, from exercise videos to soft drinks—into a tizzy. The very symbol of sexual liberation and free living when she was married to Sonny Bono in the sixties and seventies, Cher didn't need this kind of controversy—and, for sure, neither did the various companies she was endorsing. Her publicist, the tough, shrewd Lois Smith of the internationally known entertainment PR firm PMK, began practicing spin control. The method is always to attack tangential inaccuracies and thus imply that the point of the story is inaccurate as well—even if it's not.

According to sources close to Cher, she was not personally upset about Chastity's lesbianism and had known about it for a long time, and she most certainly was not trying to change Chastity into a heterosexual. But Cher was apparently concerned about the effect the publicity might have on Chastity's rock music career.

Several weeks after the story in the *Star*, an item appeared in the *New York Post*'s widely read "Page Six" column: "Chastity Bono—perhaps reacting to stories in the *Star* that she prefers the company of women—has been seen around town with two guys lately." Those "guys," the *Post* later reported, were members of Chastity's band—called Vicious Rumor—who the *Post* said were asked to be seen in public with her. Soon after, almost every gossip columnist in New York had heard another piece of information, which may have been apocryphal: A young gay man who worked for PMK told people that he had been asked to take Chastity out on a date, and he blabbed about it to too many of his gay friends. Columnists at New York's dailies began calling PMK for verification, and plans for the "bearding" date were canceled. Lois Smith's assistant denied that there was any setup date whatsoever, and PMK vice president Alan Eichorn said that the information was "absolutely false," noting that PMK "is not a pimping agency. . . . This is not Hollywood of the 1940s," he said. "It's the 1990s. We don't do things that way."

But one week later came a brilliantly orchestrated piece of damage control: The *National Enquirer* printed a homophobic front-page story headlined BRANDED A GAY, CHER'S DAUGHTER CHASTITY FIGHTS BACK: THE TRUTH ABOUT CHER, MEN AND ME, EXCLUSIVE INTERVIEW. Of course, the first question one might ask is, Why would Cher and Chastity, burned by the tabloids in the past, now cooperate with them? Why would Chastity give the *National Enquirer* an interview?

Actually it has never been uncommon for stars to give these publications exclusive interviews when they want to control the story themselves. The tabloids are not in the business of reporting news or telling the truth; they exist solely to make money. An exclusive interview with Chastity at the height of this scandal would bring in big money. A good publicist like Lois Smith knows this only too well, and also knows that planting a refutation of the *Star*'s story in a rival publication that has a similar circulation (and probably the same readers) would be the best way to counteract the original unwanted publicity.

The point of the *Enquirer* interview was, of course, to convince readers that Chastity does not sleep with women and was the victim of a horrible smear. But she never once said in the interview that she was not a lesbian. She called the *Star*'s article "phony" and said it was all "lies." She said that she and her mother were never in therapy. She said that she and her mother have a great relationship. She said her mother was not pregnant (as had also been reported in the *Star*). And she even said that she "dates men." But nowhere in the article did she deny her homosexuality. The accommodating *Enquirer* editorialized that "Chastity is so furious over the gay reports that she refuses to even dignify them with a lengthy denial." Cher was quoted several times also making vague statements, and even Lois Smith stated for the article that "Cher is sick and tired of vicious rumors and outright lies contained in published reports about her and her daughter." But the damage control didn't end the story. Within weeks "Page Six" at the *New York Post* was once again reporting on Chastity's lesbian girlfriends.

The *Star*'s outing issue and the *Enquirer*'s "inning" issue both sold well. And the *Star*'s experiment in celebrity outing proved successful in terms of monetary gain. It also didn't cause the uproar that many people, including the *Star*'s editors, expected. In fact, rather than seeing the lesbian and gay community and others seethe with rage over the supposed invasion of privacy, the *Star* was actually *praised* by the established gay media watchdog group, GLAAD, for its positive presentation. Judging from sales and general interest, the tabloid's readers seemed to like the articles too. If all of this was a sign of how the public was going to react to outing of big-name celebrities, the message to the tabloids was clearly an encouraging one.[17]

Soon after the relatively well-received Chastity outing came *Out-Week*'s highly publicized outing of Malcolm Forbes. The editors of these publications felt that queers were now giving them carte blanche to expose the closeted rich and famous. They also realized that the public was fascinated with the topic—at least for the moment—and wanted more. Previously, common knowledge had it that the public did not want to know that its stars were gay. Now enquiring minds wanted to know. Richard Chamberlain is a big name in the world of the tabloid reader—bigger than Chastity Bono or Malcolm Forbes. His was an outing they could make a mint on.

But the Chamberlain outing was induced neither by the tabloids themselves nor by gay activists. It was, in retrospect, a fascinating media blunder that got out of control and unintentionally turned into the first major salvo in what would become the gay war against Hollywood. The whole affair was a mistaken coming-out story—which made it perhaps the most unique, subversive, and powerful kind of outing imaginable.

It began, at least in this country, with Rex Wockner, a gay reporter who has for several years run his own wire service, Outlines News Service, which sells stories to gay newspapers throughout America. Many of Outlines' stories are covered by Wockner himself, either from Chicago, where he is based, or from wherever he happens to be reporting from in his travels. Outlines is a clearinghouse for gay news from around the world. The service subscribes to over seventy gay publications from over fifty countries; Wockner and his staff scour them for news not previously reported in the States. In March 1990, Wockner noticed that many Western European gay publications were reporting that Richard Chamberlain had come out. The articles, which appeared in French, German, Swedish, Danish, and Norwegian gay publications, all quoted an interview with Chamberlain that had run in a French women's magazine, *Nous Deux*, in December 1989. According to the *Nous Deux* interview, Chamberlain said: "I've had enough pretending. I'm officially moving in with my friend, Martin Rabbett. We have been lovers for twelve years now and we have been building a house on the beach [in Hawaii] which will be our home. And too bad for people who are upset by it."

Wockner made sure to get a copy of *Nous Deux* himself. He then called Chamberlain's publicist, Annette Wolf, several times for confirmation, but she never returned his calls. He included a report of Chamberlain's supposed coming-out in *Nous Deux* in his international-news roundup, a five-thousand-word report he sends out on his wire. The roundup lists news country by country, and countries are listed alphabetically. The Chamberlain item ran no more than five sentences under the heading "France," buried in the middle of the roundup. Wockner included in the story the fact that Chamberlain's publicist did not return repeated inquiries on the subject.

One of Wockner's major subscribers, the *Bay Area Reporter*, a gay weekly in San Francisco, used the item from the middle of Wockner's roundup as a news story, which they threw on the front page of their March 22, 1990, issue with the headline RICHARD CHAMBERLAIN COMES OUT. By then, the story had already jumped from the European gay press to the mainstream media in Europe, with the London *Daily Mail* being one of the first major dailies to run with it.

After seeing the *Bay Area Reporter*'s treatment of the story, other U.S. subscribers to Wockner's service decided to give the story big play too. By the first week of April 1990, the story ran prominently in San Diego's *Update*, Philadelphia's *Au Courant*, Los Angeles's *Frontiers*, Minneapolis's *GLC Voice*, *The New York Native*, Florida's *Weekly News*, *The Baltimore Alternative*, Phoenix's *The Western Express*, Indianapolis's *Heartland*, Pittsburgh's *Out*, *The Seattle Gay News*, and several other lesbian and gay publications.

The American mainstream media began to take notice, seeing that their European counterparts were already going with the story and seeing the gay press in the U.S. making it big news. Reporters began calling Annette Wolf, who was taken completely by surprise. She denied all the reports immediately, said that Chamberlain had never made such statements to *Nous Deux,* and denounced the publications that had run with the story. While this kept the mainstream U.S. newspapers away from the issue for a little while, it was by no means enough to stop the supermarket tabloids, who now went ahead with their investigations. The hawks had spotted a snake in the grass and they weren't about to let it wriggle away.

The events caused Wolf to finally return Wockner's telephone calls. "There's absolutely no truth to the statements whatsoever," she told Wockner in an interview for a follow-up story he did, which ran with the headline CHAMBERLAIN SAYS HE'S NOT "OUT." Wolf stated flatly, "I have worked with Mr. Chamberlain for six years and there's nothing to this whatsoever. He is heterosexual."

Wolf told Wockner that neither Chamberlain nor the Annette Wolf Agency would sue for libel, "because you come up against these things all the time in regard to the client's personal life. I've gotten calls from England saying 'We have a death certificate,' when the client is sitting right here in my office."

Wolf also gave Wockner her opinion as to how the supposedly untrue rumors about Chamberlain started: "These are difficult times because of the added danger to people's sexual preferences. There's so much more information to spin off on this. There's a big issue in regard to leading men who are romantic heroes; people like to come up with the most horrifying stories. I'm very sorry about this. Richard Chamberlain is a very big star in Europe and people have always wanted to marry him off and whatever. That has something to do with stories getting fabricated. There is also a very big difference in culture between here and Europe. People are more lenient about things in Europe than we are here. I go through this all the time in regard to clients and they're happily married."

Two weeks later, knowing that the three front-page supermarket tabloid stories were about to send shock waves throughout Hollywood, Wolf changed her story. By then she'd been under siege by the press, including the tabloid press, and she knew that if the press wanted to prove something and reporters could get their hands on the facts, there was nothing she could do. Perhaps the media barrage had affected her, or perhaps she and Chamberlain had developed a different strategy regarding inquiries.

"I am in complete disagreement with the whole philosophy of

what you do," she told me when I called from *OutWeek*. There was desperation in her voice and, rather than refuting the reports as she'd done before, she argued against outing: "I saw you people on the *Today* show [*OutWeek* editor in chief Gabriel Rotello had been on that morning news program discussing Malcolm Forbes's homosexuality]. That was terrible. It is surely a person's own business. I am not going to have Richard Chamberlain talk to you and lower himself to have this conversation. You're doing yourself a major disservice and also doing the same to your community. You cannot invade people's privacy. You have absolutely no right to disclose anything about anyone. Richard Chamberlain is quite personal and will not discuss his personal life. What possesses you to do this? It is none of your business. It is wrong to go into people's personal lives. We disagree morally on this. Richard Chamberlain has never discussed his personal life—not getting married, having children, not having children. There are people who simply do not want to discuss their personal lives. This is about an incredible invasion of people's privacy. It is nobody's business who you go to bed with. This country stands for freedom of choice. Richard Chamberlain has made his decision not to talk. I think, with regard to what you're doing, it may be an issue with a politician, but I don't think it's an issue with regard to a performer."

Wolf said that there was "no man" in Chamberlain's life and that she did "not know any person named Martin Rabbett."

That was odd. Eight months earlier, on September 17, 1989, an interesting item had appeared in the "Personality Parade" feature in *Parade* magazine:

Q. It's no secret that Richard Chamberlain—the handsome star of *The Thornbirds, Shogun* and other TV miniseries—lives a quiet, peaceful, wifeless life in Honolulu when he's not before the cameras. Isn't it a secret, however, that he recently was involved in some environmental violation, the details of which the news media willfully killed or ignored?

—LANI SHAW, *Waikiki, Hawaii*

A. You are in error about the Chamberlain story. It was neither killed nor ignored. Earlier in the year, the *Honolulu Bulletin* reported that the

54-year-old actor had testified before the state board of land and natural resources that he and one Martin Rabbett were owners of a 42,527 square foot lot on Round Top Drive in the posh Tantalus area of Honolulu. They had removed some 60 trees from their property without the necessary prior permission, for which they were fined $31,000. An eloquent plea by Chamberlain got the fine reduced to $9,600. It was not much of an article and it received the space it deserved.

Presented with this item, Wolf said, "Richard has many business partners and people with whom he owns land. I don't know all of them." Certainly, as his publicist, she'd have heard of Martin Rabbett, even if she hadn't read the *Honolulu Bulletin* report. She would definitely have read the item in *Parade*. Inserted into millions of Sunday newspapers each week, it has one of the largest circulations of any publication in the country. "Personality Parade" is a major break that publicists kill for. In fact, publicists usually send the questions and answers in themselves, plugging their own clients.

At Mike Hall Associates, we regularly sent several pages of copy to "Personality Parade" and other Q-and-A-format features. Some questions and answers were about our clients, others were "free" items. The Chamberlain item was probably not sent by Wolf, since she wouldn't want to bring attention to Rabbett's existence; more than likely, the bit was a free sent by some other publicist. It was a well-written, juicy free in that it referred subtly to Chamberlain's alleged homosexuality. The question mentions his "wifeless" life (a strange description), while the answer notes that he's clearing land— something one usually does when building a home—that he owns with another man. Whether or not Wolf was pleased or angered by the *Parade* item, it's highly unlikely that she didn't know about it, and improbable that she never heard of Martin Rabbett.

In his follow-up story, Wockner noted that "sources for the original article in *Nous Deux* remained unknown at press time because the journalist who wrote the report is hospitalized for treatment of cancer, according to a spokeswoman for the magazine. The spokeswoman said the magazine's editors did not know where the reporter got the story."

Wockner says that, in retrospect, he believes that the *Nous Deux*

interview never actually occurred, that many of the European mainstream magazines bend the rules in the same way that the supermarket tabloids do here. It's his hunch that Chamberlain was at a party
or some other public affair, and that either the reporter overheard the
statements herself or someone she trusted heard them and reported
back to her. To print them was unethical by traditional journalistic
standards but par for the course in the gossip field. "I think he said
it," says Wockner. "I just don't think he said it for publication."

The Richard Chamberlain outing made Hollywood stand up and
take notice. Previously, gay street activists had targeted politicians.
With regard to Hollywood, gay journalists had focused on gossip
columnists, media power brokers, studio heads, and business mag-
nates—the behind-the-scenes people who were perpetuating homophobia and the closet. The tabloids had generally stayed clear of
naming celebrities they believed to be gay. The exception was Chastity Bono, and in that case there was strong speculation that it was
a vendetta outing.

But Richard Chamberlain was a television star in his prime who
hadn't discussed his personal life in years. Previously, he had been
linked to several actresses, but none of these liaisons ever became a
full-fledged romance. His outing sent unprecedented fear through all
of Hollywood, where image is money and where people make money
off many gay stars' perceived heterosexuality. This particular case, a
highly visible one, caused the mainstream media to begin analyzing
outing more thoroughly. If the Forbes outing sparked the straight
media's first true interest in the closet, the Chamberlain outing—and
the subsequent tabloid reports on John Travolta and Kristy McNichol—made outing a hotter story that encompassed not only the
Washington governmental bureaucracy and the New York media
hierarchy, but also the glamorous world of Hollywood. Soon many
mainstream papers were covering the outing phenomenon and using
names. And that caused even more alarm in Hollywood.

"What began as a gay political tactic has heated up the tabloids and
shifted into the mainstream press," the *Los Angeles Times* reported in
a four-thousand-word in-depth story in July 1990. "Now Hollywood
is grappling with the ethics, emotional impact and economic consequences of publicizing the alleged homosexuality of celebrities. . . .
Names have been named, photos published and details of sex lives

discussed. . . . Not surprisingly, it's causing anger, anxiety and fear in Hollywood, where a sexy, heterosexual image seems crucial to many lucrative careers."

According to the article, the terror pervading Hollywood was such that "many power brokers and image makers in the entertainment industry consider outing an issue unfit for print, and declined to discuss the subject."

The industry perceived the Chamberlain report as the first massive assault on it by queer activists, even though activists had nothing to do with it. Many in Hollywood—including Annette Wolf—were convinced that the entire controversy had been orchestrated by militant gays. The tabloids, in fact, so characterized the episode in their accounts, saying that Chamberlain was the "victim" of "radical" gay publications. If those in the industry didn't believe that queers and their publications had actually calculated the entire scenario, they believed that the outing phenomenon itself was responsible for the tabloids' willingness to run with the Chamberlain outing. In Hollywood's eyes, gay militants had, with the Malcolm Forbes story, test-fired a new weapon.

For the lesbian and gay community, this particular event, perpetrated not by gay activists but rather by the media themselves, was a watershed of sorts, not because it did anything in and of itself for queers, but rather because it stripped away Hollywood's tough outer shell and revealed a vulnerable, frightened industry. Queer activists saw that they could make Hollywood quake—even when they didn't carry out the action themselves. They learned from the Chamberlain incident that the way to attack Hollywood was to rip down its façade and expose its duplicity. Hollywood is all about making money, protecting that money, and making more money. Unlike Washington's, Hollywood's power brokers are not elected officials with responsibilities, even though what they produce has a tremendous bearing on people's lives. Hollywood, like all private enterprise, is a power structure that responds only to those who threaten its ability to make money. Anything that embarrasses it in the eyes of the public and thus affects its ability to make money is a potential tool against it. While outing wouldn't necessarily be the only or even the most efficient tool, it had revealed to queer activists fault lines and soft spots in a previously impenetrable industry.

.....

Soon after the Malcolm Forbes outing in March 1990, while the Chamberlain story was appearing in the tabloids, I blasted David Geffen and other prominent people, penning a broadside in *OutWeek*. Though there were specific reasons to attack Geffen—his defense of his antigay band Guns N' Roses and his promotion of Andrew Dice Clay—I was at this particular time attacking them because I felt they weren't using their influence enough to end the AIDs crisis:

THESE SELFISH BASTARDS SIT QUIETLY AND WAIT TO SIGN THAT NEXT MILLION DOLLAR CONTRACT. They're running companies and selling real estate and voting in Congress. Though they're invisible as gays and lesbians, their faces flash out at us all day long on the television, in the newspapers, on the streets. They're doctors, artists, actors, lawyers, directors, models, producers, editors, politicians, writers, athletes, designers, gossip columnists. AND THEIR SILENCE IS KILLING US.

I met a man the other night in a club. He was a typical Upper East Side sort who, like many, had disagreed with me a year ago, but now was saying that he understood, shared and supported many of my motives and tactics. He brought up a sad thought: If Rock Hudson, Perry Ellis, Barry Diller, Liz Smith, David Geffen and Malcolm Forbes had held a joint press conference back in 1982 at the beginning of the AIDS crisis, think of the effect it would have had. Think of the power it would have unleashed. Think of the visibility it would have created. THINK OF THE LIVES IT MAY HAVE SAVED.

The column caused a stir in New York and Hollywood. Most alarming to some was that I had declared a "revolution" and issued to closeted queers in the New York/Hollywood status quo the following ultimatum:

EITHER YOU JOIN US OR WE WILL BEGIN IMMEDIATELY TEARING DOWN EVERY WALL, EXPOSING YOUR HYPOCRISIES. We are on the move, joining forces, arming ourselves for battle—and we're about to make an assault on the ALMIGHTY CLOSET. We'll end its tyranny and bury this archaic relic. And it's your decision which way you want to go. But don't think too long. Time is running out.

The mainstream media were churning out their first round of outing stories in the wake of the Forbes affair and the tabloids were outing more Hollywood celebrities. Activists, in turn, seeing Hollywood come to a standstill for the first time, reveled in the tabloids' exposures. Some activists even helped the tabloids. Everyone in the glamour circles of New York and Hollywood was up in arms—and my column seemed to them to be ground zero. I came under enormous attack—in the media, on the telephone, at the supermarket, on the streets. But there was something that felt right about what I was doing. I continued launching salvo after salvo at media and entertainment figures, and always in capital letters.

Two months later, *OutWeek* hit the stands with an entire issue devoted to a discussion of outing. The community was yearning for in-depth discussion of the controversy. The cover featured the headline SMASHING THE CLOSET: THE PROS AND CONS OF OUTING and the issue included seven essays, some in favor of outing, others opposed. On the same day, *USA Today* ran a big outing story, giving that week's magazine a great plug: "Today's issue of 'Outweek,' which gave birth to outing in its 'Gossip Watch' column last year, looks back on what it has wrought." *USA Today* chronicled the fear and paranoia, of course, quoting Hollywood publicists calling it a "witch hunt" and reporting that "the industry is buzzing about outing."

My attacks became more personal after David Geffen publicly criticized the AIDS service group Gay Men's Health Crisis as "a bunch of assholes" because they refused to have Guns N' Roses—whose lyrics had railed against "faggots" spreading a disease—perform at a benefit. "I don't care what Guns N' Roses' record is," Geffen said. "When you need a blood donor and the only person who can give you a transfusion is Hitler, you take the blood." I printed Geffen's office telephone number in large type in the middle of the column and urged readers to call him in a "Gossip Zap!" I was steaming mad:

GEFFEN, YOU PIG, WE DEMAND THAT YOU IMMEDIATELY STAND UP FOR YOURSELF AND THIS COMMU-

NITY AND DENOUNCE AND DROP GUNS N' ROSES. We demand an apology for their gross, violence-inciting statements—both from you for not saying anything as they spewed such venom and from them for their ignorance.

I don't care how much blood money you've given to fight AIDS. You slit our throats with one hand and help deaden the pain with the other. You, David Geffen, are the most horrifying kind of nightmare I've come to study in the grotesque mosaic of the media swirl. The more I hear about you, the bigger my file grows and the more ammunition we have to fire.

Geffen, still closeted at the time, became quite defensive, telling the *Los Angeles Times* a week later: "It's a bogus issue. Homosexuals see homophobia everywhere. They have such a 'victim' mentality. I see so little homophobia in Hollywood." Privately, people were saying that he was developing a "victim" mentality himself. Perhaps that was justified.

Two weeks later, Geffen's good friend, then–*Vanity Fair* editor Kevin Sessums, wrote me a letter, which he intended for publication. I printed it in my column. "By rallying your readers to your own luridly reactionary lockstep, they have in turn called Geffen's office with threats of bombings and even death," he said. "This is a form of terrorism; this is 'blood' journalism." Sessums branded me a "self-appointed leader of this new strain of activism that can best be labeled 'tantrum politics.' "

He had a point—though I refused to acknowledge it. I responded that I thought it was valiant of him to stick up for the "poor, little, picked-on billionaire" but said that "I won't be polite about how I achieve ends and I will use the tools and tactics of my oppressors against them—and against the vile lesbian and gay traitors who've sold out for a few crumbs." I can't say I felt great about all of this. It wasn't the outing I had a problem with, but the fact that I was using it as a bludgeoning and blackmailing tool. That wasn't what I originally had in mind.

But as has been true in every revolution, there is always a person or group who kicks things off by doing something brutal. Most movements, including the gay movement, have been invigorated by riots. We were under siege at the time, and I was operating with a siege mentality. Friends were dying every week. The AIDS crisis was escalating and the right wing was turning its screws on Washington. Meanwhile, Hollywood—our supposed "liberal" friend—was demonizing queers. Worse yet, the system was all but impenetrable. My tirades were the only way to get a message out about homophobia in pop culture and start to see it dismantled.

In the past, when we attacked Hollywood, the industry's PR would churn out press releases about First Amendment rights and that would be the end of it. But now we had all of Hollywood quaking. Publicists, petrified about the "witch-hunt," were for the first time returning activists' calls. Producers and agents were predicting financial ruin and pleading with queers to stop this madness. And power brokers were asking their friends to write letters to *OutWeek* to defend them.

Week after week throughout 1990, I continued my capital-letter attacks on the Hollywood establishment. In June, I went after Diller, Geffen, and others who were behind the controversial comedian Andrew Dice Clay, whose act was viciously antigay. Diller had given Clay a three-picture deal at 20th Century Fox, and Geffen Records was the distributor for his live album. His agent was Sandy Gallin, an openly gay man who'd done some work for high-visibility gay and AIDS benefits in Hollywood. The immediate impetus for my attack was the fact that Clay had been interviewed for *Vanity Fair* by another openly gay man, Bob Colacello, who sang the comedian's praises. In the article, Colacello quoted only one individual criticizing Clay, the comedian Bob Goldthwaite, but ten people, including Clay's handlers and fans, speaking glowingly of him. There were no quotes from gay leaders, feminists, or others who found Clay objectionable. David Geffen, already having experienced the wrath of activists, refused comment for the article. Colacello quoted Barry Diller as saying that he didn't find Clay's comedy offensive.

When I called Geffen's office for comment, letting them know I was writing a column about the *Vanity Fair* article, his PR person, Bryn Bridenthal, was very accommodating. Only weeks earlier, before my assault on him regarding Guns N' Roses that had elicited phone calls and attacks from the public, she had been quite nasty and had released a statement about the First Amendment. Now she assured me that Geffen was trying to distance himself from Clay, which was why he refused comment for Colacello's article. She also said that he was "contractually bound to distribute all Def American records" but that, for the first time, Geffen had taken his company's name off a record. The Geffen logo would not appear on Clay's live album, just being released. Bridenthal said that was their "protest," their way of "expressing" their opinion of the record.

Diller's PR person, Dennis Potrosky, said that Diller had been misquoted in *Vanity Fair*, that he never really said he didn't find Clay offensive, but that he had nothing more to say on the matter. Sandy Gallin's office referred me to Clay's publicity agency, Solters, Roskin and Friedman. The famed Lee Solters himself, a friend of Gallin's, got on the phone. An influential Hollywood figure, Solters had been in the business for fifty years and was among the most powerful of the publicists. He said that he took my call because this was an "important" matter.

"Sandy is a very active gay person," he said. "He's been very, very prominently involved in gay rights; he gives donations, sponsors concerts and events. Mr. Gallin has asked Dice Clay—which he has done—to delete all offensive remarks—right now—to the gay community. And he did do that. I know for a fact that Sandy asked him to delete any remarks which were offensive to the gays. Sandy is an active gay person, very, very prominently involved in gay activities and raising funds. Nobody can challenge that."

People were beginning to squirm. The tactics were working.

By July, Andrew Dice Clay billboards all over Los Angeles were spray-painted with various insults to Barry Diller. Meanwhile, the mainstream media, spurred by such activism, were pummeling Clay, interviewing feminists and queers about his bigoted brand of comedy. This only bolstered the use of in-your-face tactics: The mainstream media, so afraid of offending those in power in Hollywood, wouldn't do stories on their own, but would do stories when activists launched attacks.

By mid-July, Diller had killed the second picture of Clay's three-picture deal which was of one of Clay's live concerts; he was offended by Clay's act and afraid of the brouhaha that might ensue, sources said, after the live concert film was released. The film had a lot of antigay material.

By September, Geffen had dumped a band whose album he was about to distribute, the Geto Boys, because some of their lyrics attacked people with AIDS and advocated shooting them and chopping them up with chain saws. In a press release, Geffen articulated the difference between his actions and censorship, saying that as a private company and not a government entity he had the right to distribute or not distribute what he deemed insensitive. It was a proper decision, although many anticensorship types weren't happy.

The censorship issue is the one that gets many purists, especially on the left, riled up about queers' and others' attacks on pop culture. The critics fail to see that this is less about censorship and more about promoting homophobia for the sake of making money.

Perhaps, as some liberals and civil libertarians would say, more speech is the best speech, and we have all become much too "sensitive." Perhaps it is better to hear the extremes of all sides on a debate than no sides at all. This rationale, however, is utopian. It assumes that "more speech" also means that all sides are represented in the debate. Unfortunately, in this society—a capitalist one—that is not the case. "More speech" all too often means more hate speech, which, it seems, can always be mass-marketed and exploited. While the Andrew Dice Clays and Sam Kinisons were becoming superstars in the eighties, no major record company had signed and vigorously promoted an openly lesbian or gay comedian who attacked homophobes (though there certainly are many talented and hilarious gay comics). Similarly, while gays were turning up as villains in film after film, no films showed gays as heroes.

That is the essence of queers' attacks on pop culture: Contrary to what many have perceived as our goals, it is not censorship of the ugliness that is sought, but rather a serving up of something else—the full reality of gay lives would be a nice start—that offers balance. However, as gay-bashing and AIDS hysteria escalated in the late eighties, the entertainment industry and the mass media refused to offer that balance. Geffen's actions were a good start, but activists were not satisfied.

Later that month, Geffen's name, along with Diller's and Gallin's, appeared on the benefit committee for AIDS Project Los Angeles's annual Commitment to Life benefit, on a list that included some straight Hollywood liberals as well as several prominent closeted stars and some individuals whose sympathy to gays was questionable.

The L.A. group Artists Confronting AIDS sent a letter of protest to APLA: "In looking over the ill-conceived list of notables chosen to promote the benefit, we noticed a startling number of closet-case celebs listed alongside some of Hollywood's most notorious homophobes. Is this an AIDS fund-raiser or a monument to show-biz self-hatred? . . . Commitment to Life?! Honey, next year call it what it really is: Commitment to the Closet."

On the night of the benefit, the Los Angeles chapter of Queer Nation showed up outside. The signs the activists held, as well as fliers the group distributed, depicted photos of Geffen, Gallin, and Diller, captioned MISS GEFFEN, THE RECORD PRODUCER; MARY GALLIN, THE AGENT; and LA DILLER, THE MOVIE MOGUL.

Within two weeks, Geffen Records dumped Andrew Dice Clay, severing its relationship with Def American Records entirely. Bridenthal was quick to say that this was because of a difference in "creative philosophy," not because of pressure from lesbians and gays. But Rick Rubin, Def American's founder, told *OutWeek:* "David Geffen is a good friend of mine. I believe strongly in my artists and am willing to personally defend them. I am upset that David was put in a position where he was forced to defend them, especially from fringe organizations." In my column, I wrote that "David Geffen should be commended—at least a little." Diller, who friends say was mortified by the protest, was also moved to action. He shelved the third movie in Clay's three-picture deal, and that was pretty much the end of Andrew Dice Clay. These actions were highly publicized; the clear message was that Geffen and Diller, perhaps the most powerful men in Hollywood at the time, were saying no to homophobia and—perhaps most significantly—were responding to pressure from activists.

Diller and Geffen set an example in Hollywood. While Diller rarely gave interviews, Geffen was very visible, commenting frequently on his highly publicized selling of MCA to Japanese businessmen. In those profiles and interviews, intimate details of his life were brought forth—but there was no mention of homosexuality.

In December 1990, in reaction to several of these interviews, I urged readers to "ZAP GEFFEN AGAIN!" I was angered by a *Newsweek* interview that talked about Geffen's alleged affair with Cher years ago, but said nothing about his queer life. I was also angry about a *Forbes* article in which he was portrayed as being "well on his way to being Hollywood's first billionaire" and "a bachelor to boot." What incensed me most was that these reporters perpetuated the lie, because, like everyone in the business, they knew that Geffen was gay. Their own heterosexism, I charged, had claimed Geffen as an available, eligible "bachelor," one that any straight yuppie woman could have:

> My heart goes out to any of those hetero girls who might be reading this.... It's terrible that *Forbes* is once again misleading you poor dears . . .
> And it is up to David Geffen himself to tell that to the media. HERE IS THIS ALL-POWERFUL QUEER GETTING HIM-SELF ON THE COVERS OF MAGAZINES—AND HE CAN'T EVEN STAND UP, BE PROUD AND GIVE VISIBILITY TO THIS COMMUNITY.

Two months later, in February 1991, Geffen came out as "bisexual" in an interview in *Vanity Fair,* saying that he went from being "in love with Cher to being in love with Marlo Thomas to being in love with a guy from Studio 54." The writer, Paul Rosenfield, seemed intent on making this appear to be no big deal—even though he spent a lot of time talking about it. Both he and Geffen also were intent on giving activists no credit, and even tried to float the idea that Geffen had been out all along:

> Geffen is not like some married producers in Hollywood who lead double lives, pretending to be straight; he shows up at dinner parties with whomever he's seeing at the time, whether a man or a woman. "I have not kept any secrets," Geffen says. "There's not a person who does not know my story." Referring to threats from certain quarters of the gay press that they would "out" Geffen, he says, "No one can threaten me with exposure of something I'm not hiding." The fact is, sex is a non-issue, and non-problem. And nobody's business.

Over the next couple of years, Geffen, in public appearances and interviews, became more astute about gay issues, and he publicly donated millions to AIDS Project Los Angeles and other gay and AIDS organizations. More important, he sent a message throughout the industry that not only was it okay to come out, but that antigay projects should not be encouraged or tolerated. Then, at the end of 1992, receiving an award from APLA for his contributions, he came out fully—as "a gay man"—remarking that he'd "come a long way."

· · · · ·

At around the same time that Geffen gave his interview to *Vanity Fair* the debate over *The Silence of the Lambs* began to rage. Larry Kramer made an impassioned speech at the memorial service for Vito Russo in December 1990, as usual turning a eulogy into a rallying cry. He spoke of the upcoming film, mentioning that the serial killer in the film was gay. "Thanks a lot for starring in it, Jodie Foster," he said.

Many people assumed that Kramer was exaggerating, as he was always prone to hyperbole. But the film did indeed turn out to contain a cross-dressing killer who has a poodle named Precious and who we're told in the film, had a "lover," a male, who became one of his victims. I wrote a column railing against the film, its supposedly hip and sensitive director, Jonathan Demme, and Jodie Foster, for playing the heroine who kills the deranged transvestite faggot. I also attacked all the gay writers and critics who had praised Demme's work and were now blinded to his bias.

GLAAD also condemned the film, and debate exploded throughout the mainstream press. I reviled *Lambs* for weeks, once again incurring the wrath of *The Village Voice,* several of whose writers fired back at me. Some were angry about my attacking their take on the film, but others just didn't like anyone attacking Jodie Foster.

Again, I must admit, I was hard on Foster. I knew several women who'd gone to Yale with her; they said they knew her as a lesbian and that she had a girlfriend, and had even attended meetings of one of the lesbian organizations there. I thought it would be disingenuous to discuss the film's homophobia without talking about what responsibilities, if any, its star had to the lesbian and gay community. If a black actor starred in a film that had been charged with perpetuating racism, certainly that actor's presence would be discussed and a debate would ensue as to what responsibility, if any, he or she had to the African-American community.

The controversy went on for weeks. Queers all over the country, in Queer Nation chapters and other groups, targeted Demme, Foster, and Orion Pictures (which had produced the film) with fax and phone zaps. The *Star* outed Jodie Foster at that point, saying that she had drawn gay activists' anger because she, a lesbian, had made a film that they felt was antigay. Jodie Foster stayed silent throughout the debate.

Jonathan Demme was very defensive, spitting out explanation after explanation of how the film was not homophobic. His defenders in the press did the same. Some of those who had always championed him, like the *Voice*'s Gary Indiana, refused to explain how the film was not homophobic, instead attacking me and my tactics. Some feminist writers, like the *Voice*'s B. Ruby Rich, seemed to hold the opinion that, even if there were problems with the film's portrayal of gay men, it should be deemed unassailable because it was a feminist film with a strong female lead. Others, like C. Carr, refused to see the film's homophobia at all, rationalizing that the killer wasn't gay and that we had misinterpreted (even though Demme eventually admitted to *The Advocate* that the character had killed his male lover). To these writers, the film couldn't be good in one respect and bad in another; it had to be all good or all bad. They were not, in their criticisms, treating *Lambs* the way they treated films by minority directors, like Spike Lee's *Do the Right Thing*, a powerful film for the black community that was blatantly sexist, or *Longtime Companion*, a film about gay men dealing with AIDS, which was an important film for queers but had racist elements. While those films had their flaws exposed amid the praise of them, Demme was being let off the hook.

Other writers and cultural critics, male and female and gay and straight, also looked at *The Silence of the Lambs* and did not find it homophobic. They refused to see how such images affect people who grow up in a homophobic society that doesn't tell them anything positive about gays and only perpetuates myths. The film—vigorously marketed to the mass audience—only validates people's worst fears and beliefs about gays. It was reported, soon after the film opened, that people had screamed, "Kill the faggot!" during it: chilling and compelling proof of the activists' arguments.

While the debate over the film grew heated and sometimes ugly, overall it was enormously healthy for both the community and Hollywood. The new queer activists were deconstructing films as Vito Russo had taught them to, and they were now teaching the media and public how to do it too.

Not surprisingly then, only a month or so later, a new controversy began. As *Basic Instinct*, starring Michael Douglas and Sharon Stone, was filming in San Francisco, Queer Nation protestors shut down the set, angered by the film's portrayal of lesbians and bisexual women as ice-pick murderers. The mêlée went on for weeks, with a San Francisco Queer Nation subgroup, Lesbian and Bi Women in Action (LABIA), focusing solely on *Basic Instinct*.

Activists from Queer Nation, GLAAD, and other groups met with the film's producer, Alan Marshall, its director, Paul Verhoeven, and its screenwriter, Joe Eszterhas. These meetings produced small changes to the script, but in general the plot of *Basic Instinct* remained the same. Eszterhas expressed his desire to change the film further, but Verhoeven refused. The activists continued their protests. On one occasion arrests were made.

The national media were mesmerized by the entire *Basic Instinct* flap. At the time of the film's shooting, I called for a march on Hollywood, and activists began discussing the idea.

In the meantime, the Los Angeles chapters of Queer Nation and ACT UP took on the 1991 Academy Awards several weeks after the first *Basic Instinct* protests. ACT UP sent letters to a thousand Academy members, asking them to discuss AIDS issues at the awards (the letter included detailed information about AIDS). A SILENCE = DEATH button was included in each envelope. No one spoke about AIDS that year, and only two celebrities (*Longtime Companion* star Bruce Davison, and Susan Sarandon) wore their buttons.

But the message got through. Fifty ACT UP members protested outside the awards. Activists Judy Sisneros, Terry Ford and Dale Griner pulled up to the entrance in a limousine, pretending to be invited guests, and upon exiting the car tossed around a bunch of fliers and chanted, "Lights, cameras, AIDS action now!" Inside, one protestor, David Lacaillaide, got as far as the orchestra in his attempts to take the stage. He'd gained entrance by using tickets donated by a well-known gay Academy member. He chanted, "A hundred thousand dead from AIDS! What are you doing?" All heads turned as he was hauled out by security and arrested. The disturbance wasn't heard or seen on camera.

Later that night, about a hundred people, members of ACT UP and Queer Nation, took on Spago, the swanky restaurant where agent Irving "Swifty" Lazar throws his star-studded annual post-Oscar bash. Facing the stars' limousines at various corners and at the front door, the activists held up huge banners that read COME OUT QUEER HOLLYWOOD; COME OUT OF THE CLOSET; "THE TRUTH SHALL SET YOU FREE"—VITO RUSSO; and GAY STARS SHINE BRIGHTEST WHEN THEY ARE OUT. They did not go unnoticed by the horrified celebrities who arrived at Spago that night; many of the partiers were realizing that this crowd couldn't be kept at bay much longer and that something had to be done.

Throughout the year, activists refused to let up, staging demonstrations and fax-zapping and phone-zapping the studios about everything from *Basic Instinct* to the dearth of films about AIDS. When actor Brad Davis died of AIDS, leaving an angry letter condemning the industry for its horrendous treatment of actors with AIDS, a personal blow was dealt to an already beat-up industry. In October 1991, Barry Diller and Universal Pictures CEO Sid Sheinberg announced the formation of Hollywood Supports, an organization that was to deal with AIDS discrimination and homophobia in the industry. Both Diller and Sheinberg gave lengthy interviews to *The Advocate*, discussing Hollywood's homophobia for the first time. The activists' message had by then become focused, and the media were beginning to pick it up. The power brokers had no choice at that point but to address the activists' concerns; there could be no other damage control.

"I think it would be irresponsible for a senior executive in this community not to speak to the issue [of homophobia]," Diller told *The Advocate*, speaking out about the issue for the first time. "As attention has focused on the responsibilities of the media, the people in the media should not remain silent. I think the obligation we have is to stop saying things automatically. This pointless acceptance about what an audience will or will not accept has got to stop. We've got to start busting the myth that audiences won't accept gay material. We have no evidence of people running screaming from the theater."

None of this could stop what was about to come down the pike that fall. Like an avalanche, a series of stereotyped, antigay, or "de-homosexualized" films gushed out of Hollywood, films that had been in the works during the previous few years. And nothing could stop queer activists' response. GLAAD was gaining more access to Holly-wood and the gay community was now educated on the issues. On the heels of *The Silence of Lambs* and in the midst of the highly charged *Basic Instinct* controversy, several films brought events to critical mass.

The makers of *Welcome Home, Roxy Carmichael* removed the original lesbian theme from its screenplay. In *L.A. Story*, the dyke character was made more ambiguous. A lesbian love scene was completely cut from *Switch* when test audiences were uncomfortable with it. The lesbian lovers in the book *Fried Green Tomatoes at the Whistle Stop Cafe* became straight pals in the film version. And then came *JFK*, Oliver Stone's highly controversial version of history, which portrayed Kennedy's assassination as a rubout at the hands of a cabal of sleazy gay operators while District Attorney Jim Garrison was portrayed as an honest, straight family man (when, in actuality, he was a pedophile who'd had a scrape with the law himself). The film sent queers into a fury. *The Advocate*'s film critic David Ehrenstein called it "the most homophobic movie ever made."

GLAAD, Queer Nation, and a newly formed group of gays in the industry, Out in Film, sprang into action, condemning *JFK*. Scott Robbe of Out in Film went so far as to demand that Oliver Stone not direct *The Mayor of Castro Street*, a movie based on Randy Shilts's book about Harvey Milk, the slain openly gay San Francisco supervisor. Stone had bought the rights and was set to produce and direct. The *JFK* debate went on for months—for as long as the rest of the controversy swirling about the film lasted.

As one queer attack on Hollywood dissipated, it seemed that another began. When the announcements for the 1992 Academy Award nominations were made public, Jennie Livingston's independently produced *Paris Is Burning* was not nominated. Livingston, a lesbian, had been lauded by critics and given several major awards for her documentary about black and Latino gay men and their lives in the voguing subculture of New York. The media, which had rightly given her and her film much publicity when it was released, inquired as to the oversight, eliciting a homophobic response from the Academy of Motion Picture Arts and Sciences. Comparing *Paris Is Burning* to the documentaries that were nominated, Sy Gomberg, chairman of the Academy's nominating committee, said that a film about "drag queens" didn't come "anywhere near" the other films "in terms of importance." Livingston replied with a condemnation of the Academy. Out in Film expressed outrage. And once again the industry was on the defensive, continuing to rationalize its homophobia.

In March, *Basic Instinct* opened; renewed protests at theaters around the country garnered enormous publicity. A lesbian group in San Francisco called itself "Catherine Did It!" in an attempt to ruin the film's ending by revealing the murderer. Once again, the critics, especially at *The Village Voice*, split hairs about the film's lesbophobia. So did some women in the lesbian and gay community, who said that they personally found the killer "empowering." In that spirit, the *Voice*'s C. Carr predictably articulated her displeasure with activists' attacks, but again she didn't address how a film like *Basic Instinct* affects a culture devoid of images of queers. The vast majority of Americans, taught very little about lesbians, were getting the message not only that lesbians and bisexual women kill but also that men who have sex with a lesbian—which is what they're told lesbians really need and want—may lose their lives. On the heels of the protests, the National Gay and Lesbian Task Force Policy Institute released a report showing that violent crimes against gay men and lesbians had risen 31 percent in six cities that year. The organization laid the blame partly on Hollywood, pointing to *The Silence of the Lambs* and *Basic Instinct* as perpetuating negative stereotypes while the industry offered no positive ones.

At that time, some activists had decided to take up my call for a march on Hollywood. It was announced in the media that queers would be storming the 1992 Academy Awards. Hollywood's homophobia finally became a major story.

"I had read *The Celluloid Closet* a long time ago," says Judy Sisneros, a lesbian who moved to Los Angeles in the early eighties after living in San Francisco's punk-rock underground throughout the seventies. "A lot of the stuff that Vito was talking about, I had always seen for myself in films and on TV. But he put it all together."

Sisneros, whose long jet-black hair is the only trace left of her former punker self, joined the Los Angeles chapter of Queer Nation, formed in the summer of 1990. Later, propelled by her increasing interest in how queers were being portrayed in the popular media, she became a major figure on its Hollywood Homophobia Committee. At thirty-eight, Sisneros was older than most members of the group and had a bit more experience in activism. "I was in the pro-choice movement, doing clinic defense for a while," she says. "Then I found out that a friend, a woman, was HIV-positive, and it really affected me. I joined ACT UP/LA in 1989, before going on to Queer Nation."

By spring of 1992, Sisneros found herself at the epicenter of queer activists' assault on Hollywood. She had worked at the same job for five years, as an administrative assistant in an advertising agency. "It keeps a roof over my head so I can do my activist work," she says. But in the weeks leading up to the Academy Awards, Sisneros suddenly had a second full-time job as a spokeswoman for angry queers, giving interview after interview about the community's protests against the industry—protests that brought international attention to the issue of Hollywood homophobia and jolted the industry as it had never been jolted before. The Academy Awards protests—and, more important, the media buildup to them—were a culmination of two years of brash, in-your-face, and sometimes questionable tactics that antagonized and pushed Hollywood much faster than twenty years of sporadic protest and insider politicking ever had.

A full three weeks before the Oscars, *Advocate* columnist Lance Loud reported that a Queer Nation protest would interrupt the awards. Before Loud's column hit the newsstands, Ryan Murphy, a reporter for *The Miami Herald*, reported the content of Loud's column in the Florida paper. Within hours the story was on the wires. The New York *Daily News* put it on the front page, reporting that other sources said there would be a "powerful disruption."

In Hollywood, this news was not taken lightly—nor was it treated that way by the entertainment press that covers the industry. The

Academy Awards is to Hollywood what high mass at St. Patrick's Cathedral is to Catholics; disrupting the awards is a sacrilege equivalent to ACT UP's 1989 invasion of St. Patrick's.

The media switched into high gear, as members of the Academy and the industry attempted to defuse the situation. For weeks, stories appeared almost every day in newspapers and on television about the impending action and the issues behind it. The hype snowballed beyond anyone's wildest imagination, and Judy Sisneros and two other queer activists, Michael DuPlesis and Kathleen Chapman, fielded calls day and night for two weeks straight.

Across the country, stories landed on the front pages of scores of gay publications. Radio talk shows chatted incessantly about *JFK*'s cabal of killer queers and *Fried Green Tomatoes*'s invisible dykes. Television served up a banquet of pieces on gay-bashing in films. Most critics and commentators sided with the activists, and Gene Siskel on *CBS This Morning* summed up the basic consensus: "Hollywood is getting what is coming to it." *The New York Times* even weighed in days before the awards with a huge piece in the Sunday Arts and Leisure section by gay author John Weir, headlined "Gay Bashing, Villainy and the Oscars." Suddenly, Hollywood's decades of homophobia and neglect were a huge story—ten years after Vito Russo first threw the book at Tinseltown.

Meanwhile, activists were ingeniously harnessing the immense power of the supermarket tabloids. Spinning themselves into their usual hysterical frenzy, these publications startled the industry in the week prior to the awards. GAYS PLOT TO "OUT" 60 STARS AT OSCARS, blared the headline of the *Star*, next to a photograph of Jodie Foster. The tabloids sensationalized the activists' hints that they were going to pass out maps to closeted gay stars' homes; what activists actually did pass out were maps to the homes of homophobes. The *National Enquirer* warned America that "gay terrorists" had plotted to "ruin Oscar night." The hype was welcome to the activists, and the *Los Angeles Times* and *The Hollywood Reporter* tracked the industry's frightened response daily. ACADEMY ASKS GAY ORGS FOR RESTRAINT, read the headline on the front page of *Daily Variety*.

Fittingly, the night of the awards played out just like a movie, eerily reminiscent of *The Day of the Locust*. Several hundred queer activists took to the streets outside the pavilion, armed with a vast array of slickly produced, colorful signs. STOP CENSORING OUR TRUE QUEER LIVES, read some. PARIS WAS BURNED and WORST PICTURE: SILENCE OF THE LAMBS, read others. Nearby, a smaller group of antigay demonstrators had shown up, carrying crudely lettered signs that read NO GAY FILMS. Limousines carrying the stars, directors, screenwriters, and producers had to meander through this maze of queer and antigay protestors who vied for their attention on either side of a huge, fifty-foot replica of the Oscar.

An audience of about a hundred was seated in bleachers not too far away, just at the entrance to the pavilion, so that as the stars arrived and exited their cars, there was an audience of adoring fans waving and cheering for the purposes of television. The protestors were far louder than the audience, belting out chants, blowing whistles, and sounding foghorns. But the audience was miked. On the street, all one could possibly hear when Jonathan Demme or Oliver Stone appeared were boos and whistles as angry demonstrators let their message be heard; on television, the only thing to be heard was the cheers and applause of the tiny audience; all that was to be seen were the smiling and waving stars.

Several people, Judy Sisneros among them, were arrested for performing civil disobedience in the streets, providing footage for television news teams from around the world. The story had gone international, and Hollywood, behind all the glitter and the makeup, was scrambling for damage control. Virtually every star in attendance wore the red AIDS ribbon. Several stars gave quotes to the media sympathizing with the protestors. "We're in the business of telling about people's real lives," said Whoopi Goldberg. "And that's what we should be doing." During the ceremonies, thick with tension over the possible "powerful disruption," host Billy Crystal explained what the red ribbons meant and presenter Richard Gere called on the government to put more money into the fight against AIDS.

·····

The disruption of the 1992 Oscars never happened. It didn't need to, and anyway it was partly a figment of the media's hype. If the purpose of the protest was to focus attention on gay-bashing in films and get the powers that be to respond, then that purpose had already been achieved by the night of the awards. As one member of Queer

Nation put it: "This is a postmodern demonstration: We announce the action, the media create it, and then whatever happens happens."

A lot, it seems, did happen. "It was only last spring that gay activists . . . organized street protests and threatened to make a mess of the Oscar ceremony," reported the *Chicago Tribune* in September 1992. "Now a bumbled, nervous Hollywood may be responding quicker than you can yell, 'Homophobia!' " The paper was referring to an article about Hollywood's new attitude, written for *Out* magazine by *Daily Variety* reporter Richard Natale. Indeed, suddenly power brokers were making the right deals. Filmmakers were pitching the right projects. Studio spokespeople were giving the right sound bites. The entertainment press was zeroing in on homophobia. And queers in Hollywood were edging forward.

By late 1992, GLAAD was having more meetings with insiders than ever before. Hollywood Supports was making headway in getting companies to offer domestic-partnership benefits, with MCA Pictures and Viacom (Showtime and MTV) already having announced their plans to do so and 20th Century Fox and Columbia expected to follow.

Joe Eszterhas, the screenwriter of *Basic Instinct,* let it be known that he was writing a script in which the hero was a gay cop. *Silence of the Lambs* director Jonathan Demme announced his plans to shoot *Philadelphia,* a film about an HIV-positive lawyer who suffers discrimination. Several other films in development in 1992 were to deal with the AIDS crisis, including *Good Days,* written by David Leavitt for *Midnight Cowboy* director John Schlesinger, and *Family Values,* which openly gay producer Barry Krost sold to Columbia. Still other AIDS films were suddenly in the early stages of production—a development so astounding that publications from *Daily Variety* to *The New York Times* remarked on it, noting that in ten years of a ravaging epidemic not one major studio had tackled a work focusing on the disease.

On television, where shows like *Roseanne, L.A. Law,* and *thirtysomething* had only been able to go so far as having gay characters make guest appearances, there was a new move to establish regular gay characters. On *Roseanne,* the year after Martin Mull first played a gay man, a character played by Sandra Bernhard announced that she was a lesbian and fell in love with a character played by Morgan Fairchild. The Fox show *Melrose Place* featured a regular gay character who dealt with gay-bashing, police insensitivity, and discrimination—all in one episode. And the daytime soap opera *One Life to Live* made history, becoming the first of its genre to offer a regular gay character. On still other series that had never had a lesbian or gay male character in even one episode, gay characters began making guest appearances.

The industry, having previously shied away from specifically queer events, was also suddenly more supportive in lending itself and its money to the cause of gay rights. On a hot August night in 1991, three hundred of Hollywood's glitterati gathered in a home in Los Angeles's Westside for a sold-out benefit for the National Gay and Lesbian Task Force. The benefit was organized by openly gay Hollywood attorney Alan Hergott, who had set an example for years as one of the few Hollywood gay men who takes his lover to events. His lover is Curtis Shephard, cochair of the NGLTF. The benefit was the first event of its kind to finally put queers up there with Hollywood's other causes, such as women's rights and Israel. The *L.A. Times* was quick to note that the benefit was coming "after at least a year of contentious relations between the entertainment Establishment and some members of the gay community." The paper noted that "some gay activists have inflamed relations with a spate of 'outings' earlier this year" and that "the industry has also been rocked by a series of articles discussing gays within the show business power structure, including a cover article in the national gay publication *The Advocate* on 'Homophobia in Hollywood,' and another in the *L.A. Weekly* entitled 'The Hollywood Closet.' "

Among the members of the host committee at the benefit were Warner Brothers chairman Bob Daly, ABC Entertainment president Robert Igor, International Creative Management chairman Jeff Berg, MCA, Inc., president Sid Sheinberg, Walt Disney Studios chairman Jeffrey Katzenberg, and the man regarded as perhaps the most powerful in Hollywood, the superagent who was chairman of Creative Artists Agency, Michael Ovitz. A year later, several months after the Academy Awards protests, the event was repeated. This time five hundred people attended. The benefit was underwritten by the Sony

Corporation, the David Geffen Foundation, the Diller Foundation, Fox, Warner Brothers, and, amazingly, the Walt Disney Company. pany.

Oliver Stone, who had been all set to produce and direct *The Mayor of Castro Street,* had initially become enraged by activists' attacks on *JFK,* and at the height of the protests he just about abandoned the Harvey Milk biography. But after negotiations, both among queers and between them and Stone, the director seemed to realize that *Castro Street* was a historic project of great importance to the gay community, and one that should be in the hands of gays. Still the producer of the film, Stone announced in the summer of 1992 that Gus Van Sant would make the film—something that Out in Film's Scott Robbe had suggested when *JFK* was rigorously criticized almost a year earlier. (However, in April 1993, Van Sant pulled out of the project, citing creative differences, and the film seemed up in the air once again.)

Suddenly, it wasn't so risky for stars themselves to spearhead gay causes. In late 1992, Barbra Streisand called for a boycott of Colorado, where voters had rescinded existing gay-rights laws. While much of the media and the community focused on those who spoke out against the boycott (like Barry Diller) or remained silent (like Jodie Foster), it almost went unnoticed that much of Hollywood, from Liza Minnelli to Jonathan Demme, immediately joined the boycott—something few would have expected only five years earlier.

Indeed, the entire two-year period beginning in 1990 seemed like an Academy Awards production in and of itself; a fantasy epic in which an industry begins to deal with an oppressed minority it has continually mistreated. Though they are just a start, the changes are amazing in comparison to the conditions prevailing only two years before. These events proved what could be done when the system was taken on full force and an assault was made on the closet. Outing was only the beginning of the queer activists' steadfast work in dismantling the closet in America.

14

##########

The Resurrection

##########

# of Sheila Kuehl

##########

When Zelda Gilroy was written off *The Many Loves of Dobie Gillis*, Sheila James Kuehl felt as if her life had been destroyed. Certainly her career had been. In the next few years she played some bit parts, but they were few and far between. After a while, she couldn't land any work at all. "I couldn't even get a commercial," she says. She entered a serious depression; a drinking problem, which she says began when she was worried about being closeted and acting, got worse. But Kuehl pulled herself together, sought help, and went on with her life. Like Zelda Gilroy, Sheila Kuehl had always been strong, strong enough to withstand what many others couldn't.

She moved in with her girlfriend, Kathy, and began working at UCLA in the student activities office. She went on to help students organize around the many political movements that were exploding during the sixties.

Kuehl has since had several lovers and has been active in the women's movement for twenty years. She eventually attended Harvard Law school and received her law degree in 1978. She came out as a lesbian slowly, over many years, to all of her friends and family. Today, she is an attorney for the California Women's Law Center in Los Angeles.[18] While what happened to her was a devastating blow,

Kuehl is happy today. She says that it's more important to be out of the closet and out of the business than to be acting but forced to remain closeted in Hollywood. "My life is much better not acting and being a radical feminist activist attorney," she says, laughing. "It is joyful to be who you are and say who you are and fight the good fight."

After three decades, in October 1990, Kuehl decided it was time to tell the public, including many of her fans who remember her, that she is a lesbian. At the time, her lover was Torie Osborn. Osborn is now the executive director of the National Gay and Lesbian Task Force in Washington, but at that time she was the executive director of the Los Angeles Lesbian and Gay Community Services Center.[19] Governor Pete Wilson of California had just vetoed AB101, a bill that would have ended legal discrimination in the state against lesbians and gays in housing and employment. Queers erupted with rage when Wilson withdrew his support and refused to sign the bill. Riots and massive demonstrations took place in San Francisco, Sacramento, and Los Angeles. The events, which some dubbed "Stonewall West," galvanized the community, especially in L.A., injecting new political energy. Like those in Washington, gays in L.A. have never been as overtly political as their counterparts in New York and San Francisco. "Hollywood is a very important place for them to keep us invisible," Kuehl notes, echoing the sentiments of many inside and outside the business. "If a famous actor was allowed to come out and he was allowed to be working it would appear to be saying this 'lifestyle' is acceptable, which is the last thing in the world that the homophobes want to allow. So it's important for them to keep them locked in the closet." The veto brought new people to action, bringing some out of the closet as well.

"After AB101, Dick Sargent called Torie and said, 'I'm mad! What can I do?'" Kuehl recounts, regarding the actor who is most remembered for playing Darrin Stephens, husband of the witch Samantha, played by Elizabeth Montgomery, on the very popular sixties sitcom *Bewitched*. "He's a moral man, not the bravest man you'll ever meet, but there's a time for everything."

Unlike Kuehl, whose career was destroyed when she was rumored to be a lesbian, Sargent worked in the business for forty years, keeping his homosexuality a secret. He had spent his entire career closeted, something he describes as "a terrible way to live."

Sargent lived for twenty years with a lover, a screenwriter who died in 1980. Especially in the early years, in the fifties, they were very guarded. "It totally felt dirty and second-class and had all of those negative emotions," he says of living in secrecy. "Nobody should have to do it."

Like Kuehl, Sargent never discussed his homosexuality with anyone else, not even with other gays in the business—not even those he worked with closely. "My first agent was gay, and I didn't even talk to him about it," he says. In the early years, while he was working in films, he put a fictitious ex-wife in his bio, at his lover's suggestion. "Nobody ever checked it," he says, laughing.

When Sargent starred in *Bewitched*, from 1969 to 1972, things had loosened up. By the late sixties, a rumor that someone was gay would not necessarily ruin his or her career. But if push came to shove, that person would be expected to deny it. Sargent was sure that many in the cast and crew of *Bewitched* thought he was gay, but it was never acknowledged, or even hinted at. This silence was perpetuated even though veteran actress Agnes Moorehead, who played Samantha Stephens's mother, Endora, also a witch, and comedian Paul Lynde, who played the role of Uncle Arthur, a warlock, both now deceased, were also closeted queers, as were several other members of the cast. Still, homosexuality was simply not up for discussion, even among themselves.

"Of course Liz Montgomery knew, but we never talked about it at all back then," Sargent recalls. "We never discussed it even though she and her husband and my lover and I socialized. We'd play tennis together, have Christmas parties, that kind of stuff, but [Liz and I] never discussed my being gay until years later. As long as you didn't say anything, nobody ever gave a damn in that [*Bewitched*] crowd. Paul Lynde was always around, always coming to parties and he was flamboyant and obvious and always trying to shock people. Everyone had to know, but it was never talked about."

Sargent was sometimes even more afraid of fellow gay colleagues, such as Paul Lynde, than he was of straight ones. "Paul was just a basket case," he recounts. "As soon as he smelled the cork of a bottle, he was a different person. When he was drunk he was vicious and mean. I'm sure that was how he was dealing with the situation of being gay. I'm sure he probably knew [about me], but I didn't talk to him about it because I didn't want any part of his life and I didn't want him having any part of mine. He was a sad character, always with some tired hustler, or some new 'lover' who'd be gone in a few weeks. He was so flamboyant in that way. I stayed away from him because if it had come out publicly about me, my career would be down the toilet."

When Sargent's lover died of a cerebral hemorrhage in 1980, it was the beginning of a change for Sargent. "I've never really gotten over it," he says. He began to get out a bit more and notice what was happening in the gay community and in society. "I've always been the type of person who always told the truth," he comments. "I just wasn't liking living a lie." He began to socialize more with gays who were out, not ever acknowledging his homosexuality publicly but being less secretive than formerly.

In April 1991, Sargent was outed by the *Star*. "It was terrible, that way," he says. "But it probably pushed me. It made me realize that I needed to live my life honestly."

Pete Wilson's refusal to sign AB101 was the catalyst that finally made Sargent speak out, as it had moved so many other gay Californians to go public. Torie Osborn had the publicist at the community center book Sargent on *Entertainment Tonight* with Sheila James Kuehl, in a segment produced by *ET*'s openly gay Hollywood correspondent, Garrett Glazer.

Dick Sargent was most excited about coming out on the show, he says, because he felt that gay children needed someone like him, someone who could be an adult role model.

"For the first time I feel cleansed," Sargent says. He's also become a zealous activist. "I can't stop myself now from telling everyone to come out," he says with a laugh. "I've approached other actors and told them, 'You're going along with everyone else who says you don't deserve rights if you stay in the closet.' They haven't come out—not yet, anyway. They look at me like they don't know what to do. They know I'm right but they just don't want to talk about it."

For Kuehl there was an uncomfortable reality to coming out. "It bothers me that, being a celebrity, there are a million people watching, who know me, but who now hate me," she says sadly. "Actors really want to be loved. They thrive on it." Still, the reactions she's gotten in person have been positive. "People stop me on the streets to tell me that they're proud of what I did," she says.

Kuehl and Sargent made history in 1992, becoming among the very first television actors to come out. They were joined by Sandra Bernhard, who finally declared her queerness and even played an out dyke on *Roseanne*.

It was a long time since Zelda Gilroy was crucified for being "just a little too butch."

Epilogue

Epilogue

The future of lesbians and gay men in America is intertwined with that of the religious right. As the religious right continues to gain power at the state and local levels, one of its greatest weapons against homosexuals is the closet. Forcing their antigay agenda on local governments, the armies of the religious right often

QUEER

IN AMERICA

go unchallenged by the most powerful gay people in their communities because those people are closeted. By maintaining a hateful climate, the religious right keeps the closet even more tightly closed.

The future of the gay community is also intertwined with that of high technology. For various reasons, homosexuals are among the people who dominate the young, tolerant computer industry centered in northern California. More often than not, Silicon Valley's many gay people are out of the closet and highly organized.

In recent years lesbian and gay activists have successfully employed high technology. Gay men and lesbians within the computer industry continue to develop innovative technologies that activists will use in the future to do battle with their enemies.

High technology will also be utilized in the future to bring people out of the closet. It will make the coming-out process less painful. Technology will put the armies of the closeted to work. They will be the anonymous frontline soldiers of the Queer Revolution of the 1990s, as they ready themselves to take those first giant steps out.

15

....

The Oregon

....

Nightmare

....

Just outside the town of Newport, on the pristine Oregon coast, three lesbians live together in a big old house. They spent almost every day in October 1992 putting signs on their front lawn before going to work. The signs, which read VOTE NO ON 9, had become as natural to the Oregon landscape that year as the spotted owl.

So had signs that read VOTE YES ON 9.

In the rural area where these women lived, however, unlike in Newport or in the big city of Portland, there were far more YES ON 9 than NO ON 9 signs. Each day, when the women came home, their NO ON 9 signs were gone, torn off of their lawn. After a few weeks, the women finally decided to put the signs out of reach. One morning before work, they climbed several tall trees in their front yard and placed the signs in the uppermost branches.

When the women came home that day, all of their trees had been chopped down.

.....

Ballot Measure 9 was an infamous proposal put on the Oregon ballot in the fall of 1992 by the Oregon Citizens Alliance, a right-wing religious fundamentalist group backed financially by Pat Robertson's Christian Coalition. If passed, Measure 9 would have had the Oregon constitution deem homosexuality "abnormal, wrong, unnatural and perverse." No state funds could have been used to "promote, encourage or facilitate" homosexuality.

Ballot Measure 9 wasn't the first antigay referendum Oregon voters saw: In 1988, a measure put on the ballot by the OCA rescinded the governor's executive order barring discrimination against lesbians and gays in state jobs. In May 1992, voters in the town of Springfield voted to stop the town from "promoting" homosexuality, yet another OCA victory.

If Measure 9 had passed, all gay civil-rights laws already in effect, such as an antidiscrimination law in the city of Portland, would have been voided. Libraries, some legal experts said, could have been cleared of all books about gay life. Teachers would not have been able to instruct students that they should be tolerant of gays but would instead have been forced to tell them that homosexuality is "wrong." Guidance counselors would not have been allowed to help gay teens deal with their homosexuality but would have had to tell them that they are "perverse." Any out-of-the-closet teachers or other state workers would have been fired. Gay parents could have had their children taken from them, since the parents would have been deemed "abnormal."

Forty-two percent of the Oregon voters cast their ballot in favor of the measure. Oregon is considered a liberal, progressive state, and many were amazed that such a repressive proposal could get as much support as it did. Equally jarring was the fact that voters in Colorado, another progressive state, narrowly passed an antigay measure with softer language that November, voiding existing gay-rights laws in Denver, Aspen, and Boulder.

Lon Mabon, the leader of the Oregon crusade against homosexuals and the man who put Measure 9 on the ballot, vowed to come back with a "Colorado-style" measure the following year. By the end of the nineties, in the absence of a federal gay-rights bill, activists expect that such a measure could be put on the ballot in a majority of states.

In Oregon, Measure 9 depleted and drained the lesbian and gay community, which poured whatever resources it had into fighting the fundamentalists. The battle created a statewide atmosphere of hate against homosexuals that resulted in far worse than a few trees being chopped down. During the whole campaign, and in the months following, homes and businesses that bore signs opposing the measure were vandalized. Churches that condemned the measure were torched. Crosses and swastikas were set ablaze on the lawns of homes owned by gays. Three gay men who lived in a trailer were shot at on several occasions by antigay attackers. All over the state, people were taunted and threatened, and many queers suffered savage physical attacks. A lesbian and a gay man who lived in Salem were murdered by neo-Nazis who threw a firebomb into their living room. The town of Springfield had passed an antigay measure months before the Measure 9 vote; local gay leaders had the windows of their cars and homes shattered in the middle of the night.

It didn't matter that Ballot Measure 9 didn't pass: Simply by gaining a large chunk of the vote and injecting hate into the Oregon political landscape, Lon Mabon had won the "first battle"—as he said on election night—of a long and bloody cultural jihad that the far right had declared for the coming decade. In the 1992 political season, Oregon was the gay community's Selma, Alabama.

Lon Mabon's greatest asset in the war against homosexuals in Oregon—far more powerful than neo-Nazis, skinheads, or Bible-thumping volunteers—is and will continue to be the almighty closet.

·····

Historically, Oregon has been a pioneer state. It was, in fact, the first state in the union to introduce ballot measures as a way of attaining purer democracy. Like much of the West and the Northwest, Oregon in recent years has been an attractive place for many looking for a fresh start in a less developed but hip environment.

Oregon's major city, Portland, is a storybook town of the future, a modern, clean urban center nestled in a valley below white-capped Mount Hood, on the Willamette River. With a progressive city government, it has always been a mecca for individualists and liberals—and queers. It is a city especially known for its large, vocal lesbian community, many of whose members settled there in the seventies and eighties to start families and raise children in a tolerant environment. A large number of these lesbians live in the middle-class and working-class northeast section of the city. But both gay men and lesbians live all over the city, which tends to be a fairly open, relaxed community.

High up the hills, however, to the north of the city, sit Portland's closets of power. All male, the people in these closets are mostly from "old money." Their names are the names of Portland's shopping centers and stadiums and public squares and streets. They are among the most powerful people in Oregon politics, media, and business. Some of them give money to gay causes, and they gave to the No on 9 Campaign, but often they claim that gay groups are too "radical" and that they feel as if they were throwing their money away. They get angry when gay groups endorse only Democratic candidates or align themselves with more liberal and leftist segments of the community.

"We've never really supported the fund-raisers," says Ron, a handsome twenty-nine-year-old blond who lives with his lover, Ted, a wealthy sixty-one-year-old businessman. They live in a posh condominium. "I don't really want to be represented by a drag queen or Queer Nation or these people who are obviously into S and M," Ted explains. "My clients wouldn't give a hoot [if they knew I was gay], but they would be upset and offended if they saw me associating with any of those people. They'd paint us all with one brush."

Ted and Ron define themselves as "out." "We're not really, you know, *closeted*—although I don't want my name used in this," remarks Ted. "We always ask for a queen-size bed when we travel. But then all of these people say that we have to scream and yell, that people are getting thrown out of their jobs or their houses. Where? I mean, I just don't see it."

"Actually," Ron says, correcting him, "we do know one person who lost his job at a bank because he got up and said, 'I'm gay. I'm queer.' And the board of directors were upset and said, 'You're out!' " Ron defines "out" in a particular way: "If you're quiet and discreet and mind your own business, nobody cares, but if you yell and scream, people don't like it."

"There'll come a time," says Ted, "not in my time, but it will come, when two men can get up and dance and not worry about what people think."

What if two people decided that now is that time and simply got up and danced?

"No, no, no," Ted answers. "You must do things slowly. You can't shove things down people's throats."

"The whole gay movement," says Ron, "is in a disastrous mess. They're all fighting each other and all the ideas are just washed up. First there was the regular gay movement. Then came Queer Nation and now the outing people have come along. They're all opposing each other."

"Who *are* the outing people?" Ted asks him. "Aren't they the same as the Queer Nation crowd?"

"Well, no, are they?"

"I haven't got a clue what goes on with any of these people," answers Ted, "but I tell you, if I ever met one of these outing fellows I'd certainly give him a talking-to. Who in God's name do they think they are?"

The Hill Crowd, as Portland queers call them, are not only out of touch with the mainstream of gay politics, they're racist and anti-Semitic. They regularly throw cocktail parties in their beautiful homes overlooking the city, and they invited this visiting New York journalist with a northern Italian name, although they knew little or nothing about me. But Jews who grew up in Portland, even those from the wealthiest families in town, are kept out of the clique and not allowed at these parties.

Fifty-four-year-old Sandford Director is from one of the five prominent Jewish families in Portland. For several decades his family has owned and run Director Furniture, known throughout Oregon. In the early 1960s, in a scandal that rocked Portland, young Sandford was arrested for running a male prostitution ring. Director now says that his arrest was a relief of sorts because it got him out of the closet. He became a well-known drag queen in town and has raised a lot of money over the years for AIDS and other charities in the community by holding fund-raisers.

"The Hill Crowd is all old Portland people," says Director. "This is all blue blazers and button-down types. You have to be in couples—they don't take to singles and they don't take to 'divorces': When you're in that crowd, you're with your companion for life usually, even though they're all fooling around on the side, going up to pick people up at the path up at Washington Park.

"All they do is sit around and talk about their privileges. They'd only very rarely go to a gay event. And never a gay bar or a disco or something—that would be mixing with the multitudes. They don't take to newcomers, even with a lot of money. Right now there are some couples coming up from San Francisco who are loaded and who are trying to break into this crowd, throwing parties, but they're getting a hard time. The only way to really break into that crowd is to 'marry' in. But if you're Jewish, you can't even do that. They still won't accept you."

"I realize he's done a lot of work [in the community]," says a prominent physician, one of the Hill crowd, talking about Director. "But what an embarrassment he was—to his family, to everyone. Oh, no, it's not because he's Jewish, although there are no Jews in our crowd, I'll admit. The drag queens and all that bit, we were never into that—and we're still not. It's outlandish. We didn't ever advertise our sexuality. We frowned on that. We have always had lots of dinners and we used to dress up, you know, in coats and neckties. Now, it's the same crowd but we wear sweaters."

Not all of the Hill Crowd is closeted. Even some of the oldest members are publicly known as gay and do give their time and money to the cause. But they are the exception, as are the few who "married in" and are more out of the closet. Frank came from New York. He "married in," to John, a WASP who is more closeted. Both in their fifties, they live on the Hill in a beautiful home, go to many parties, and gossip incessantly about everyone. John is from a very prominent Portland family.

"I really don't understand this circle," Frank says. "They're completely out of touch. I mean, I've told John for years, 'Do something about AIDS—give money or speak or something.' But he'd always just say to me, 'But I don't know anyone with *that*.' And he really believed it. Their world is so rarefied, and they're afraid of anyone finding out anything. Now a friend of ours has gotten sick, a young guy we know, and John has suddenly started donating some of his time, driving around people with AIDS."

"Most of the Hill crowd will say they're not closeted, but they all are," says Sandford Director. "Most of them don't donate to causes, although some give money anonymously, but only to the most conservative kinds of gay causes. It maddens us. They have all the money in town—the money we need."

While the OCA campaigned to put a measure on the ballot in 1988 to rescind the governor's executive order barring antigay discrimination in state jobs, the Hill Crowd threw their cocktail parties.

While the OCA spent much of 1991 and 1992 feverishly collecting names on petitions in shopping malls to put its next measure on the ballot, the Hill Crowd threw their cocktail parties.

And while the OCA waged its campaign to change the Oregon constitution, winning 42 percent of the vote, the Hill Crowd threw their cocktail parties.

At one such party, in the home of a prominent architect, people chattered and laughed and looked out the bay windows at the extraordinary view. "Oh, now really," said one guest, "why ask about the OCA here? This is a party. We don't discuss those things."

"They are all so prominent," says Director. "If they stood up and came forward, it would carry a lot of weight against the OCA, but they stay silent because they have to guard their closets."

· · · · ·

Many people believe that the closet contributed considerably to the OCA's 42 percent. Much of the gay community's response was carried out with a closeted mentality. The No on 9 Campaign, some charged, refused to take a forthright approach. It cut out the Lesbian Community Project, headed by tireless activist Donna Red Wing. She and other activists, like Scott Seibert—a dissenting voice on the No on 9 steering committee—were pushing for a campaign that would emphasize and enhance lesbian and gay visibility. "This was not a grass-roots campaign and not a gay/lesbian–positive campaign," Seibert later commented.

Most of the No on 9 people were worried. Many were closeted themselves. Others were concerned about the fact that they were getting money from closeted people—the Hill Crowd—who wanted things done in a very low-key manner. Kathleen Saadat, a lesbian who, like Seibert, was a dissenting voice on the No On 9 steering committee, described her feelings to *The Advocate*: "No on 9 staff members did not really want to talk about homosexuality or things that people were concerned about, like pedophilia. While you don't make those the big pieces of your media campaign, you have to make them significant pieces of your educational campaign."

The way that the OCA operates is to lie and distort. For months before the election the group mailed out propaganda saying that "homosexual men on average ingest the fecal material of 23 different men per year" and "homosexuals are 15 times more likely to commit murder than heterosexuals." But their greatest rallying cry—one that worked especially well in a depressed economy—was that homosexuals are seeking "special rights." By saying that the equal rights that gays seek as an oppressed minority are really special rights that they're trying to get for their "behavior," the OCA was able to manipulate much of the public into voting for its agenda. Outside of big cities, the gross distortions and trick rationales worked because people had never known any homosexuals—or at least, they thought they hadn't.

Instead of showing the populace that gays are a people with a culture, and that we are normal everyday folks, the No on 9 Campaign's strategy was to appeal to people on a "human rights" level, attempting to convince them that this was the beginning of an attempt to eventually take away their rights too. Not only did this seem farfetched to most people, it didn't do anything to change their feelings about queers.

That same year, gay people in Portland, Maine, fought a more vigorous, high-visibility campaign against a ballot measure to repeal the city's ban on antigay discrimination. Not only did voters reject the measure, but the school board later voted to enact its own ban on antigay bias, and the Christian group that had pushed the measure backed off, dropping plans to seek signatures to put an antigay measure on the statewide ballot. "While organizers in Maine focused on the discrimination that gays and lesbians would suffer if the referendum were passed," reported John Gallagher in *The Advocate*, "activists in Oregon focused on the OCA itself, alleging that the initiative was part of a broad right-wing strategy that threatened all Oregonians." Portland, Maine, city council member Peter O'Donnell explained their approach: "We got the local gay people involved in the campaign as role models and put them up front. Once the voters saw that these people were incredibly productive and give a lot to our city, it was hard for them to discriminate."

Fighting a similar statewide antigay ballot measure in Colorado, activists used a low-visibility strategy like the Oregonians'. There, the antigay measure, less severely worded than the Oregon one but nonetheless repressive, passed.

"While the OCA kept pounding away these lies that gays are pedophiles and perverts," says documentary maker David Meiran, "the No on 9 Campaign's television PSAs didn't even mention the words 'lesbian' or 'gay.' They would have straight people on these PSAs. And even in the public debates, they'd never have gays, but straight people defending this as a human-rights issue, not as a lesbian and gay issue. The biggest problem was invisibility. There was no visibility campaign."

The OCA made a videotape that was distributed to church groups around the state and played on cable television. The tape, called *The Gay Agenda,* depicted gays as sex maniacs intent on recruiting and molesting children. Meiran, a videomaker with the Testing the Limits collective in New York, was in Portland covering Ballot Measure 9. He did much undercover work, even going to OCA meetings.

"One meeting was called the OCA 'Get Out the Vote' meeting," he says. "It was like looking into a warped mirror image. It was like an ACT UP meeting except the politics were completely opposite. They had a table with literature. They made a call for volunteers to do the busywork. They had a parade of speakers get up and tell their stories—always about how the 'militant homosexuals' were taking over. Everyone would yell 'Amen.' They announced that the OCA needed money for media ads and passed around a big Kentucky Fried Chicken basket. These were all lower-middle-income people throwing in fifty- and hundred-dollar bills. There were maybe only two hundred and fifty people there, but they collected several thousand dollars. Then they gave out the videotapes—thousands of them. People were taking handfuls of them, five or ten each, so that they could give them out to their neighbors."

With such an aggressive campaign and an army of volunteers—the opposite of the No on 9 Campaign's strategy—the OCA was able to convince great numbers of people to vote in its favor. The OCA controlled the debate: The voters were not getting the truth from the other side. They really weren't getting *anything* from the other side. The other side was engaging in the closet strategy: Pray and duck for cover.

"In our exit polls," Meiran recalls, "people who appeared to be straight liberals, people who voted for Bill Clinton, would say, 'Oh, well, I voted in favor of Measure 9 because I was thinking of the children,' and then they'd hug their child who came with them."

The No on 9 Campaign never stated the reality that gays are less likely to molest children than are straights. It never did anything to show that gays are not monsters but real people. "I think," says Meiran, "people in the end voted on whether or not they knew a lesbian or gay man. If they knew gay people, they knew this propaganda couldn't be true. But if they didn't, then they suspected that there could be some morsel of truth to the propaganda, and they voted in favor of it just to be safe."

Many believe that things would have turned out worse had it not been for Donna Red Wing and others who managed to create visibility in spite of the efforts to squelch them. And many felt that the work of queers outside of the state, who'd managed to garner much support and turn the vote into a national media story, had helped. In the last few weeks of the campaign, some even more radical queer tactics came into play too. The ever enterprising Michael Petrelis knew that Senator Mark Hatfield of Oregon had remained silent about the OCA, while Oregon's other senator, Bob Packwood, as well as the majority of state and local politicians, had condemned it. When asked, Hatfield had given some flimsy excuse about not getting involved in local issues; in reality, he'd actually backed the OCA in the past and, as someone who had positioned himself as a religious man, did not want to jar that constituency. But Michael Petrelis also knew that Hatfield had been outed two years before—and had strenuously denied he was gay—and might not want a repeat. He called Hatfield's office and said that he was planning to out Hatfield all over again. Two days later, the *Oregonian* ran with the headline MARK HATFIELD OPPOSES MEASURE 9, followed by the subhead "The senator did not say why he changed his position on the anti–gay rights initiative."

For some voters, that was the only thing that got them to vote no.

If Oregon's powerful closeted men had been out, not only would the populace have known more gay people but also the mentality that trickled down from the closets of power to the No on 9 Campaign would not have existed. The desire to be "discreet" and unaggressive is a product of the closet. As a tactic, it simply doesn't work, because homophobes aren't closeted about their homophobia.

·····

On election night, there were two victory parties in Portland and one makeshift memorial service. One was the No on 9 Campaign's victory party, where the closeted and their coconspirators danced and drank as balloons flew about—living, as they do, in denial, thinking that they'd really won something. The other victory party was at OCA headquarters, where Lon Mabon was grinning at having gotten the numbers he did. He called his 42 percent a victory and vowed to be back. "We'll get them next time," he said.

The memorial service was at the Metropolitan Community Church, where Donna Red Wing and the other queer activists who saw the future met to console each other. "The tragedy of this campaign is that it didn't change how Oregonians feel about lesbian and gay people," Donna Red Wing said. She and her compatriots knew the truth: All that had happened was that they'd bought a little time.

They knew that somewhere Pat Robertson was saying, "If we got forty-two percent in a so-called progressive, liberal state like Oregon—and with such a drastic measure—imagine how we'll do in Texas and Florida."

They knew that, if we all are to win the war, the closet, as a weapon, must be stolen from the right forever.

16

....

The Silicon

....

Solution

....

Your video display terminal is a battleground.

Your weapon is a modem. Your ammunition, electronic mail. On computer bulletin-board services, you rally the troops. You drop in on several "electronic cafés," where dozens of queers exchange news, information, and instructions. Within minutes you've let scores of people in on your plan; in turn, each of them has passed it on to scores more. Then, with the push of a button, you and thousands of others launch fax zaps, mail zaps, and phone zaps, bombing your enemy with a continuous stream of raw data, printed messages, and recorded voices. Instantly, you're taking to task a newspaper that printed a homophobic article, a member of Congress who refused to sign on to a progay bill, a religious zealot who preaches hate from his pulpit, and a corporation that hasn't expanded its bereavement-leave policy to include gays.

Press another button and you receive your customized electronic newspaper: all the news about gay issues and your other favorite topics from mainstream newspapers around the country and the world is downloaded onto your screen. A similar service brings you the gay press as well: You read the *Bay Area Reporter* online, then *The*

Washington Blade, then *The Philadelphia Gay News.* You punch in a code and get your own personalized AIDS update, complete with current information on drug research and drug trials.

While you are reading, a red button flashes on the terminal, indicating an emergency. You press the button and receive a news flash from a just-formed group called the No on 26 Campaign, headquartered in the Montana capital of Helena. Montana fundamentalists have just put Measure 26 on the state ballot; the measure would outlaw gay teachers, who quickly organized a counteroffensive. They need to do a media blitz, which will cost them a lot of money. You are offered several options and press the button for the first one: $3.00 will be taken directly from your bank account and sent to the campaign; for $1.75 more, a scorching letter will be sent to all of Montana's newspapers and the governor's office, threatening a boycott of the state's products and services should the measure pass. Hundreds of thousands, perhaps millions, of queers across the country receive this urgent appeal at the same time that you do. Within minutes, dollars and letters pour into Montana. Later on, trying to assess the situation and come up with a grander strategy, you'll communicate online with lesbians and gays from around the country on the Nationwide Queer Town Hall.

"We already have an edge over the religious right in terms of utilizing this kind of technology," says Tom Rielly, director of strategic relations at SuperMac Technology, a maker of computer hardware.[20] Rielly is speaking about the above scenarios, which he sees as taking place in the not-too-distant future. "When it comes to setting trends, queers are always at the vanguard, and the computer revolution is no different. From my experience, there are higher numbers of out lesbians and gays in the personal-computer field than in other industries. I think a higher percentage of queers than the general population probably own computers."

Over the past few years, gay and lesbian activists, perhaps more than other activists, have been developing advanced techniques to take on the system. "It all started with ACT UP," observes Susan Schuman, a lesbian who is manager of communications products for Apple Computer's Personal Interactive Electronics Division. Apple, like Supermac, is located on the peninsula in northern California between San

Jose and San Francisco known as Silicon Valley, the center of the personal-computer industry in America. Schuman is a telecommunications expert who has been in the field for over fifteen years.

"People have different thoughts on ACT UP, but ACT UP was very smart," she says. "They used technology—satellite transmission, fax, computers. They organized around manipulating and managing the media and excelled at the transfer of information back and forth. It was grass-roots organizers taking advantage of high technology instead of being afraid of it." Rielly adds that when desktop publishing was developed, "it was immediately adopted by both ACT UP and Queer Nation to communicate in-your-face messages with slick graphic designs—all realized within minutes on personal computers and then run off on high-speed photocopiers."

"Now, a whole new younger generation of more out gays and lesbians is coming up," notes Schuman, "and they're going to be even more [technologically] literate. I think there was a period of time when the religious right was ahead of us in this regard—*they* had control of the media, control of the newspapers. Then came a time just recently where we were sort of equal—we started to get some access to the media and they held on to the access they had. Now, all of a sudden, we're surpassing them in terms of the way we take on the media and the way we use the technology."

Of course the religious right, as well as the rest of society, will also be able to get any new technology that comes into the marketplace. And certainly the right can train people to use it. But many lesbians and gays in the computer field feel that, in this area, the right will be a few steps behind queers for quite some time—and may never be as fluent or as advanced in computer technology. "We'll have an edge because the more we can communicate the more we'll win," says David Stewart, who left the computer industry to become operations manager for the National Gay and Lesbian Task Force. "We have never really had as much access to the means of communication as the religious right, but when we do get some access our message is convincing because we are right. And people eventually realize our enemies are wrong. An example was the Republican Convention [of 1992]. They were able to get the platform to communicate, but what they had to say scared the daylights out of people."

Others say the reason queers will have an advantage and always be one step ahead of the religious right with regard to high technology is simply because large numbers of lesbians and gay men are among the people who dominate the world of computers and work at the cutting edge of new technology. According to Overlooked Opinions, a Chicago-based market-research firm, ten times more queers work in the computer industry than in the fashion industry. And unlike their brothers and sisters in the older industries of Hollywood and the New York media world—and certainly unlike those within Washington's political system—queers in Silicon Valley are much less likely to be locked in the closet. They are visible, organized, and highly productive.

· · · · ·

Perhaps it was not a coincidence that one of the earliest developers of computing, Alan Turing—who in World War II aided the Allies by cracking the Nazi's Enigma code—was gay. Or that the modern gay movement and the computer industry were both born at roughly the same time in the late sixties by people who were breaking with convention. Or that both thrived and grew within the liberal political climate of northern California.

Ironically, it is often the closet that brings queers and computers together. "I believe that when you're in the closet as a child you tend to sublimate all your sexual energy into some kind of pursuit," observes Rielly. "I know I did. Personal computers and telecommunication services are private and fascinating. They're unconditionally supportive activities that require a single pursuit. The computer is a place where you can escape from predominantly heterosexual role models."

"I think there is a tendency for alienated people, straight or gay, to go into industries where you only have to focus on what you are doing and you are not interacting with other people," says Ben Templin, a former writer and editor for the computer magazine *MacUser*. A thirty-four-year-old gay man, he now develops software and creates databases for ZiffNet, the online service of the computer publishing giant Ziff-Davis. "Programming itself is like writing. There's a certain amount of escapism involved, where you create your own world that is probably very attractive to people who want to escape society. It's welcoming to people who have been abused."

In high school, Jonathan Rotenberg was very interested in computers. That was in 1976, when few people knew much about them. "I had heard about these new microcomputers that were coming onto the market," he remembers. "So I inquired about them." A few months later, at the age of thirteen, Rotenberg founded the Boston Computer Society, a group dedicated to helping people learn about the personal computer at a time when this technology was completely alien. Within a year, the society experienced a 300 percent growth in membership, from ten people to several dozen.

But that was just the beginning. The computer industry began to explode as the eighties began. Heading the society—whose membership would eventually top 31,000 worldwide—Rotenberg became a teenage CEO and was soon internationally famous. By the time he was nineteen, he had been on the front page of *The Wall Street Journal* and was named one of the ten most eligible bachelors in Boston by *The Boston Herald*.

Thoughout all of that time, Rotenberg was completely in denial about his homosexuality—or any sexuality; he poured all of his energy and time into computers. He didn't have sex and didn't really fantasize about it either. "Every once in a while, I'd get concerned about it," he says. "I thought I was awkward and not polished with women and thought that it would just happen someday."

He attended Brown University, and came to know gay people, but, after briefly entertaining the notion that he might be gay, he recoiled from it because it was something he didn't want to be. "There was a tremendous amount of grief at that time," he remembers. "I would pour myself into work and try to ignore it. I kept giving myself warning signs that there was a dilemma, but I ignored them too, and just kept punching away. A lot of problems developed, all of these irrational things: A fear of flying—just a total meltdown. I just was fighting this so hard." His only recourse, he says, was to bury himself deeper and deeper into computers.

It wasn't until years later, in 1990, at the age of twenty-seven, that Rotenberg came to terms with the fact that he was gay. That was after a lot of soul-searching and years of therapy while he went to Harvard Business School.

"I looked around the class one day," he says. "I realized that people my age were starting to look older. I realized that I wasn't going to have my youth and vitality forever. So at that point I decided to call the president of the Gay and Lesbian Students Association." Rotenberg's plan was just to "explore." He was an "uncommitted."

"Their meeting was the first gay anything I ever went to," he says. "Within thirty minutes there were all of these people who were saying, 'He's the president of the computer society.' There were actually three members there. I felt comfortable."

Today, Rotenberg is a corporate-strategy consultant in Cambridge, Massachusetts. Looking back, he observes that he was forcing himself to suppress his sexuality by escaping. "I wasn't allowing myself to feel these things," he says, "and was putting all of my energy in the society and computers.

"I think in general you find much greater diversity of people at all levels of the computer industry, especially in personal computers, than in other industries," he observes of Silicon Valley. "It's a new industry and doesn't have any of the baggage and the old-boy networks that are very integral to other industries. As a result you find a lot of interesting situations in the personal-computer industry. People who could never be mainstream businesspeople in other industries rise to the top. You have a lot of young people who drop out of college and become the wealthiest people in America. In any other business the idea of a twenty-year-old doing that is unthinkable. But in this industry, having a track record, a long career, playing golf with the right people, and all of those things that are important in other jobs just aren't important. It all boils down to one thing: If you see the future better than other people, you can be very successful."

At twenty-four, Ben Waldman, a software engineer and manager of Macintosh technology at Microsoft, is a millionaire, as the shares of stock that he received when he began working at the company several years ago have soared. Waldman also is openly gay and very active in organizing around gay issues in the company. "It's absolutely one of the most tolerant industries," he says. "In this business, you need bright and talented people. Companies just look for the best people with the best qualifications. Other things don't matter." Waldman believes that he's more politically aware and active because of his company's gay-friendly atmosphere. "In college, I wasn't political at all," he remembers. "At the time I was wondering what the outside world would be like and I was worried, so I didn't get involved in anything. I didn't know what to expect in this business, but I'm very happy and I'm also more political now."

Some people in the personal-computer field are even encouraged by their bosses to use their jobs to advance gay rights. Jeff Pittelkau is laboratory director at *MacUser* magazine. "I was basically outed in front of a former boss years ago by a colleague," he says. "My boss was very accepting and asked, 'Why didn't you tell me?' A couple of years later I had another boss who I spoke to about whether or not I should move into another position, my current one, because it's very public in terms of interfacing with vendors who make many of the products we evaluate. He advised me to take the job, saying: 'This is a rare opportunity for you to use your position in the industry to stand on a soapbox for gay rights.' I was astonished."

Unlike the rest of the business world, where discretion is thought of as the better part of valor, the computer industry fills some of its highest positions with gay people who are out of the closet and politically active. Tim Gill is the founder, senior vice president of research and development, and chairman of Denver-based Quark, Inc., makers of QuarkXPress desktop-publishing software.[21] In November 1992, he was an outspoken leader in the fight against the antigay measure put on the ballot in Colorado. Gill was the single-largest contributor to the antihate campaign. In the fight to overturn the antigay Amendment 2, Quark pledged $1 million toward education efforts. He also led a boycott of the state, telling his own customers that he understood if they had to participate in the boycott. By threatening to pull $20 million in accounts, Gill forced one of Quark's banks, Norwest, to immediately institute a gay-inclusive nondiscrimination policy in the wake of the vote.

"I was an introverted kid—even before I knew I was gay," Gill recalls. "Being gay tends to make you introverted. I think that, for me, the computer was a little world all its own—all of a sudden this world and everything in it could be mine. I could control it and certainly there's a tremendous feeling of power that gives you, especially if you feel powerless." As chairman of Quark, Gill now heads a $50 million, world-renowned company that in eleven years has become the leader in desktop publishing, including most of the largest media and publishing companies in America among its clients.

"Because the industry is northern California–based, near San Francisco, a lot of gay people work in it, and the political climate of the entire area is liberal," he says. "It's a younger industry and more tolerant. But also, there's a desire for talent, for the best people. The problem with discrimination in hiring is that you lose people. The computer industry has fewer talented people than it needs. Nondiscrimination is a way that you keep a higher number."

"It's a real renegade industry that has prided itself on breaking the rules," observes Karen Wickre, a multimedia developer at 3DO in San Mateo and a member of Digital Queers, a group of industry professionals founded in 1992 by Tom Rielly. "The business itself broke the rules in the way it grew and developed. It's this sense of progressiveness, of not doing business as usual, that has affected a lot of personnel policies and human-resources departments of the companies here."

Over fifty Silicon Valley companies, including Apple, DEC, Tandem, IBM, Oracle, and Intel, have policies banning discrimination on the basis of sexual orientation. Almost all of them make *The San Jose Mercury News's* annual list of the top hundred companies in the area. As of 1992, domestic-partnership benefits were being instituted among companies in the computer industry faster than in any other industry. That is true not just among Silicon Valley companies, but throughout the industry nationwide. Boston-based Lotus Development Corporation became the first to offer domestic-partnership benefits. It was followed quickly by Borland, ASK Ingres, Silicon Graphics, Sybase, and several others throughout the United States. Some believe the reason is that most of the major companies are located in areas where gays are concentrated and have gained political clout, and thus forces both inside and outside the companies have brought pressure to bear. "There's the high-tech industry in Silicon Valley, which is very close to San Francisco and the Bay Area, which has a huge gay population," observers Susan Schuman. "And then there are technology focal points in the Boston area, the New York area, and the Washington and Chicago areas—all large metropolitan areas for gay people." Each of those cities has computer companies that have instituted or are negotiating domestic-partnership benefits for gay employees.

"It's now about competition," notes Jeff Bowles, a manager at ASK

Ingres, a maker of database software. "Nobody wants to be beaten out by the other companies, especially since they're afraid that all of their talented lesbian and gay employees will leave a company to get better benefits elsewhere."

The competition over domestic-partnership benefits in particular began in 1991, when Lotus granted its employees such benefits.

"When I came to Lotus I assumed that they were so liberal that I simply applied for benefits for my partner and was very politely told that she wasn't covered," recalls Margie Bleichman, a principal software engineer. Soon after being turned down, Bleichman, together with senior administrative assistant Polly Laurelchild-Hertig and a third woman who has since left the company, began researching domestic-partnership benefits. "We ran into lots of surprises," says Laurelchild-Hertig. "We found that only Levi Strauss had what were considered great benefits for lesbians and gays, and they were only for bereavement leave. We realized that no one really had great benefits."

That was in the spring of 1989. Working with a small group of people from within the company and with the National Center for Lesbian Rights, the trio came up with a proposal. "They were very receptive and positive," Bleichman says of the Lotus management. "But it took a long time to put it through the bureaucratic process. At another company, the first barrier would have been homophobia, but that was not the case with us." After three years of research, proposals, and monthly meetings, the policy was instituted. To the surprise of the company and the lesbians who'd pushed the benefits through, there was a media frenzy. *The Wall Street Journal* and *The New York Times* put the story on their front pages. Indeed, it was a major matter: Lotus, a publicly traded company, had charted territory that most of corporate America and all the high-tech companies were steering clear of.

To the delight of Lotus executives, their pioneering turned into phenomenal PR for the company. "There were some negative letters, but most were positive," says Laurelchild-Hertig. "What we didn't expect was that there were people who wrote in and said they were going to buy the product because of this. I got a letter from one guy who said he saw the story in *The Wall Street Journal* about Lotus offering such benefits and he decided not to buy from our competitor because of the stand that we took."

In the first few weeks there were inquiries from eighty companies about Lotus's domestic-partnership benefits and how they were instituted; within the first year and a half there were over four hundred inquiries. Many calls also came from lesbians and gays in other high-tech companies who began organizing for similar benefits.

In that respect, many lesbians and gay men in the industry say they are comfortable being open and organizing within their companies, often with the approval and encouragement of management.

Apple Lambda formed in 1986. "We serve as a social group, a support group, and a place for lesbian and gay employees to network," says the group's president, Bennet Marks. "We work with the company. When we started, Apple didn't have a nondiscrimination policy. We pushed them on that. We also got them to write a letter condemning the governor's veto of AB101. We celebrate National Coming Out Day at the company and we march in San Francisco's parade with the company's banner." At Microsoft, there is GLEAM—Gay, Lesbian and Bisexual Employees at Microsoft—whose members worldwide communicate, like most gay groups in the industry, through the company's electronic-mail system. GLEAM has its own mailing list—called an "alias"—of lesbian, gay, and gay-friendly employees who belong to the group. Printed rules and regulations govern use of the alias, among them: "Assume that everyone (even knuckleheads) acts/speaks from caring (or at worst ignorance) rather than malice. (Or at least write/speak as though you assume it!)"; "Respect the confidentiality of the alias. Not everybody is out everywhere. Not everybody on the alias is queer"; and "Don't flame (especially to the entire alias, or personally without care. Try a constructive approach)." ("Flaming," in computer lingo, means ranting and carrying on, usually in capital letters.)

There are industry-wide groups as well. High-Tech Gays, which meets monthly at the San Jose Gay Community Center, boasts over five hundred members. The group regularly hosts speakers' forums as well as social functions for queers throughout the industry. High-Tech Gays was founded in the eighties by several employees at Lockheed, the aerospace company whose largest client is the Penta-

gon. Companies with military contracts tend to be much more homophobic than others in Silicon Valley, and that was one reason why
High-Tech Gays focused initially on getting security clearances for
gays working in such companies. Later, the group broke ground in
getting companies in the San Jose and Santa Clara valleys to institute
sexual-orientation nondiscrimination policies.

Digital Queers was founded in 1992, when Tom Rielly and several
of his friends began having informal social gatherings. Soon, the
group was organizing in the political arena as well; it focuses primarily on the personal-computer industry and its emerging links with
telecommunications. "The world of personal computers is merging
with the world of telephones and the world of television," Rielly
observes. "Pretty soon you won't be able to see the difference between a computer, a phone, and a TV. The technological revolution
is inevitable and queers have to harness it to our aims."

Rielly is a dynamo among dynamos—confident, poised, and determined to enlist advanced high technology in the pursuit of gay civil
rights. He wasn't always so self-assured.

"In high school, I used to stand in front of the mirror with a razor
blade and chant, 'If you are one of them, you have to kill yourself,' "
he recalls, describing his personal motivation for activist work today.
"I finally did try to kill myself three times, overdosing on drugs. I just
don't want any more kids to kill themselves. I want to make sure that
accurate information gets to kids in the fastest ways possible."

For Rielly, it's imperative that the entire movement become computer literate, speeding up communication. In January 1993, he and
Digital Queers organized an unprecedented benefit for the National
Gay and Lesbian Task Force aimed at bringing the Washington
group to the forefront of the digital age.

"Their computers were ten years old," says Rielly of the NGLTF.
"Their system was primitive. They needed help."

The benefit was held during the MacWorld Expo in San Francisco.
At MacWorld, one of the largest computer trade shows, 60,000 people in the industry gather twice annually. Before the benefit, Rielly
and fellow Digital Queer Jeff Pittelkau went from booth to booth
soliciting software to present to NGLTF at the benefit. "It was
astonishing," says Pittelkau. "People were just handing software over

to us. We explained what Digital Queers was and what the NGLTF was. The fact that they were gay organizations didn't faze anyone. They were more interested and excited about the fact that we were switching NGLTF over to the Macintosh system."

Four hundred people showed up for the benefit, which took in $50,000 in cash. Over $75,000 in computer software and $75,000 in consulting services had also been donated to the NGLTF. Several senior management consultants from top firms have developed a strategic technology plan for the organization, also as a donation. "I can't describe to you what it was like for me to go to San Francisco and just walk around and ask for stuff and have everyone say yes," says NGLTF operations manager David Stewart. "It was exhilarating."

Digital Queers has "adopted" NGLTF, in the words of Rielly. Their goal is to aid NGLTF in acquiring more computers and software, installing the systems, and teaching the NGLTF staff how to use them. "We're going to create NGLTF Online—a national computer network on which anyone can access important queer info at a moment's notice and which NGLTF can use to send out E-mail to scores of people," Rielly says. "They'll also be able to do an enormous amount of desktop publishing, getting information out to the public at amazing speeds. And we can put all of the volumes of information on homosexuality and a history of the gay movement on CD–ROM. We'll also be able to connect all of the gay groups around the country—hundreds of them—online. The idea is to get gay individuals connected to gay groups, which are all connected to each other, all part of one big online queer universe. It keeps the groups more in touch with their constituents. It also fosters electronic democracy and participation in political discussion."

In 1993, NGLTF and Digital Queers began a pilot program to connect many other lesbian and gay grass-roots organizations, using personal computers and electronic mail. Aware that technology often only goes to those who can afford it, Digital Queers and NGLTF committed themselves to making sure the capabilities were made available first to the groups with most need and least money. Among the groups to receive priority for software and hardware were the National Black Gay and Lesbian Leadership Forum, the Little

Rock–based Arkansas Women's Project, the National Center for Lesbian Rights, and the Latino(a) Lesbian and Gay Organization.

"That benefit in San Francisco was the start of something big," says Elizabeth Birch, senior litigation counsel for Apple Computer (worldwide), referring to the benefit at which Digital Queers made its commitment to NGLTF.[22] "It was seeing people like Tom Rielly speaking—a true technoqueer, someone who loves technology and loves his people. And it was seeing all of these gay high-technology people in a room together for the first time." Birch, like Rielly, combines her unique skills as a legal and high-technology professional with political activism. The highest-ranking gay person in the corporate area, she became cochair of NGLTF's board in late 1992.

In February 1993, Birch helped organize a historic meeting between lesbians and gays at Apple and the company's president, the influential John Sculley. The night before the meeting, both she and Tom Rielly briefed Sculley about queer issues, sending him a load of information via electronic mail. At the meeting, which attendees describe as exhilarating, Sculley announced that Apple would extend benefits to domestic partners. But more important, say some who attended, Sculley, who has Bill Clinton's ear, was visibly moved, and he genuinely committed himself to furthering gay rights. "As Apple goes, so goes Silicon Valley," comments Rielly, referring to Apple's power and influence in the industry.

"This is a sort of progressive telecommunications movement now forming," Birch says. "When you have people with this tool, there's no telling how far you can go. We gays and lesbians in the high-technology business are a group of people whose skills and influence are the envy of the world. We are very well paid and very well taken care of. Now we can offer our services to the community. Until now the company gay groups have been inwardly focused—on things like domestic partnership—but now we're moving en masse to the outside, to the world, putting our skills toward the gay movement."

Birch sees the growing power structure of Silicon Valley eventually influencing and changing the Hollywood power structure, which will perhaps in turn have an effect on the Trinity of the Closet, breaking down homophobia. "You see this technology now seeping into the entertainment industry and you see this cross-fertilization," she observes. "This is because in the future, beginning in a very significant way in the 1990s and completing in the twenty-first century, entertainment and high technology will commingle. Entertainment will be computer-based and the software will come from Hollywood. Everything will be interactive media: Your television will be like a computer, where you order up what you want to see and experience. What you will have is a situation where Hollywood will also adopt the values of this industry, in terms of the way they treat the work force—instituting enlightened policies, because they will be the only policies under which the high-technology people will work."

. . . . .

While the way that Silicon Valley's queers organize themselves politically and deal with management is completely out of synch with the way that queers elsewhere—on Wall Street, say—operate and are treated by their employers, gays in the industry are quick to point out that Silicon Valley is by no means a utopia. It is, like the rest of corporate America, and certainly like Wall Street, a predominantly straight, white, male industry with a glass ceiling when it comes to women and minorities.

"There's more of an effort in this industry to exhibit some consciousness," says Bryan Simmons, a black gay man who is manager of corporate public relations at Lotus. "It is a younger industry, but it's still mostly white and mostly male. There's the same amount of racism here as throughout society. I think it is still difficult for someone who is openly gay, or black, or a woman, to become a senior executive in these companies."

"I would say there are pockets in the industry that are much more tolerant," says Schuman, "but there is still a closet." She also feels that the industry is far from treating women equally with men—and that includes lesbians and gay men. "This industry might not have an old-boys' network, but it has a young-boys' network," she notes. "There's also a male network as opposed to a female network, especially among gays." Schuman says that gay men, often comfortable in the industry, still treat lesbians the way straight men often treat women. "I've seen instances where people, because they're male and gay, moved up," she says. "There's sort of this split of the sexes that goes on with gays. And there is a glass ceiling for all women." Schuman feels somewhat isolated as a lesbian in a key position. "As a woman, you're fighting all the sexism, and it is a male-dominated industry," she says. "There is not that network for lesbians. It seems to take quite some time for lesbians to get together, and gay men in the industry have made lesbians invisible by not including women in things as much."

Karen Wickre agrees: "It seems like there are a lot of gay people, but it's a very extensive gay male network—not as many lesbians. The lesbians just aren't as networked and organized. They also seem to be left out by the men." Yet Wickre notes that women, in general, probably do better in this industry than in others. "There are a lot more women in power," she says. "I think it's probably easier to attain that power here."

Homophobia is also far from nonexistent in Silicon Valley. While many of the personal-computer companies are gay-positive, others, especially aerospace companies and those that supply technology to the U.S. military, can be hostile toward gays. "There is a night-and-day difference between Lockheed and Apple or Tandem," observes Don Nelson, who works at Lockheed. Gays and lesbians are not made to feel included there, Nelson says, and negotiating domestic partnership or other policies is years away. There is a gay group, GLOBAL, but the company forced it to change the word that the second "L" originally stood for: " 'GLOBAL' now stands for 'Gays, Lesbians and Bisexuals Achieving Leadership,' " Nelson says, "but it used to be 'Gays, Lesbians and Bisexuals at Lockheed.' The company asked us not to use their name and they made an implicit threat in the request. They gave the excuse that it was a proprietary name and could not be used in any way, even though other minority groups in the company use the name."

Even at the more enlightened companies, bigotry consistently rears its head. Apple's Bennet Marks notes that, while he encounters neither directly antigay company policy, nor homophobic actions by staff members, he does experience homophobia on the company computer bulletin board, on which all of Apple's 12,000 employees nationwide have regular discussions and share their opinions. "People can contribute to it anonymously," he says. "There have been complaints about Apple Lambda on the board. Every time we plan some event, or participate in a public event like a parade, using the company's name, there are complaints on the board and a discussion about whether or not we should be doing that. The nastiest things have been said about me on there. What really shows progress is that many of the gay people and the progay straight people vigorously attack the homophobes—using their own names."

Of course a Silicon Valley company like Apple is way ahead of most companies in America merely in having an online bulletin board where all employees can discuss and debate gay issues. Though problems exist, queers of both sexes, especially those who've worked outside the computer industry, agree that theirs is a more comfortable place to work than others. Some of those who do gay organizing in the industry also feel that if it weren't for the tolerance of the industry—and, more important, the easy access to technology—they might not be involved in political issues at all.

"Sometimes I wonder just how involved I would have gotten in political activism if it weren't for desktop publishing," says Bennet Marks. His job alone takes up most of his time. Organizing the employees would normally take a lot of extra time somewhere else. But he can utilize electronic mail and bulletin boards, and can make fliers and printed materials in a fraction of the time it would take to communicate by more conventional means.

Via electronic mail, Jeff Bowles was able to organize the employees at his company, Boston-based ASK Ingres, to push for and win domestic-partnership benefits. "With E-mail somebody can just send mail throughout the entire company," he says. "It's useful for information-sharing, organizing, getting opinions on issues. It doesn't require a control queen in the middle. Certainly it's leadership by the many instead of leadership by the few."

More support can be garnered through E-mail because closeted people can be involved in decision-making and can add their opinion and their vote by communicating anonymously through the computer. "The future of every company in America—indeed, eventually every household—is E-mail," says Tom Rielly, noting that E-mail is fast replacing traditional interoffice mail services in American corporations far beyond the computer industry itself.

Both E-mail and bulletin boards are having an effect on the gay community at large. There are now over three hundred lesbian and gay bulletin boards through which individuals may send private E-mail to other members, or on which people may speak publicly to the entire board. Some are local bulletin boards on which people from the same state or region speak regularly. Four national networks, CompuServe, Genie, America Online, and Internet, have queer bulletin boards. Every day, across the country, tens of thousands of queers organize, debate, and just plain chat. There are also several boards just for sex; people fill out questionnaires describing what they like in hopes of meeting someone with similar tastes.

"What happened in the early eighties," says Tom Rielly, "was that all of these closeted queers who were putting their sexual energy into the computer were suddenly presented with new technology—the modem—which would allow them all to communicate with each other via the telephone lines."

Every day now, many of the closeted are speaking to each other, using anonymous names. They're also speaking to those who are out of the closet and who offer them encouragement. For perhaps the first time, the closeted individuals can be themselves within a community—the online community—without putting up fronts. Slowly, they may decide to actually meet some of the people they're talking to, and eventually they're on the road to coming out.

"So many people grew up in a repressive environment," says Ben Templin, who himself came out through the bulletin boards eight years ago, when he was in his mid-twenties. "It was a way for me to get away from that environment, to escape. I could create my own personality—or rather, show my real personality—online. By not having to face another person you can develop your personality naturally. You're taking away face-to-face communication, but you're still in communication with other people. In that sense, while I was coming out, I didn't run the risk of embarrassing myself or being found out—I could hang up immediately if I got scared. I was able to ask the questions I wanted to ask and get so many answers right away. I was more honest on the bulletin board."

Twenty-nine-year-old Martin Chavez, who founded his own company, Quorum Software, in 1989, is active in Digital Queers. But until two years ago, he was locked in the closet. He'd never had sex, and he forced himself not to think about sex either.

"I'd known for a long time emphatically that I was gay," he says, "but I also believed that I was going to spend eternity in hell if I acted on it, so I sublimated all my love and libidinous impulses into creating software." During his teens and into early adulthood, while he attended high school, college (at Harvard), and medical school (at Stanford), Chavez did, however, experience the gay life—on the computer bulletin boards. Eventually, via the gay BBS, he would meet his first love and come out.

"I'd known about this one gay bulletin board since I was sixteen years old," he recalls. "I read it all the time. On one level I would read it and say, 'This is revolting,' but on the other level it was one of my many steps and it would educate me. I was reading about people's coming-out stories, parties at The Saint [a nightclub in New York City], sexual practices, you name it. I was getting this vast derivative knowledge about being gay. When I finally came out ten years later, I had all of this gay culture even though I'd never read a gay book, magazine, or knew anyone who was gay."

After many years of reading the board, Chavez decided to communicate with the people on it. "I sent what they call a message in a bottle," he says. "I told my story—but anonymously. I got back a flood of replies. Hundreds from all over the world." One man from Colorado particularly interested Chavez, and the two began communicating regularly, falling in love—online. "We wound up exchanging a huge volume of mail—poems and short stories, confessions and sexual fantasies," he says. "It went on for four months." Eventually they met and had a long relationship. And Chavez has been stridently out ever since.

Tom Rielly says that, while in college, he found the queer bulletin boards by accident. People who subscribe to an online service automatically get lists of all available boards. Thus anyone—including closeted teens in need of people to talk to—who subscribes to an online service will be presented with the option of logging on to the gay boards. "People usually go on to CompuServe, which offers a variety of information services, and then they find out that there are these bulletin boards," Rielly says. "They get on one of the gay boards, and watch on the screen as people have conversations about gay issues. There have been huge debates on the boards, for instance, about outing and the word 'queer.'"

The bulletin boards, Rielly and many others say, provide a network for the closeted. As the price of an average personal computer and modem continues to plunge, and as computers become more available in public facilites like schools and libraries, queer activists in the computer industry see computers becoming a major organizing tool, and a device to help the closeted come out on a massive scale. By the late nineties, says Rielly, nearly every household will have a computer and a modem.

New technology is also enabling some gays in the industry to come up with still more innovative ways of educating both gay and straight people as well as ways to systematize the coming-out process and make it easier. Jonathan Rotenberg has developed an audiotext system to do just that.

"I realized how similar homophobia was to computerphobia," he says, only half joking. "I saw so many parallels. People who grow up with computers and are fluent in them have no fear of them at all. Similarly, people who grow up with gay people don't see what the problem is. I began thinking about how in business school we were being trained to take on complicated problems. We have a whole set of techniques to do so. I came up with a strategy for the gay community, a twenty-page strategy for coming out, for lesbian and gay groups to utilize. I figured if coming out could be broken down into a series of little steps—rather than one big [one]—it would be easier for people. So I put together an audiotext system, a telephone system that could give people information. I put together a group of fifteen who began to do research on it. We've now got 150 topics on the system, with information from why people are straight or gay to what meetings take place each week at the community center." The system, utilizing push-button technology and automated messaging, currently services the Boston area. There are now also privately owned systems providing information to lesbians and gays in other cities as well. Rotenberg soon hopes to create a national system, providing 800 and 900 numbers that would be vigorously advertised on radio and television.

With audiotext, E-mail, and bulletin boards, activists in the computer industry are joining those who use more traditional strategies in making a major assault on the closet.

Not only will people in closets be provided with safer, easier ways to emerge from the dark caverns they were forced into as children, but they will also be put to work while still closeted. Without having to identify themselves, they will launch attacks on bigots, voice their opinions to politicians, tell their companies what problems they're experiencing, and network with other closeted people—all with the speed and efficiency that computer technology offers—as they take those first steps out.

In these and many other ways, the fascinating connection that has always existed between two contemporary revolutions—the high-technology movement and the queer movement—will become more profound. Ironically, the closet has been the unifying force that has brought these two movements together; now they are conspiring to blow the closet doors off.

Not only, as Elizabeth Birch points out, will the high-technology industry merge with the entertainment power structure, bringing the values and policies of Silicon Valley to Hollywood, but high tech will become firmly rooted in the political system and in the media as well.

Early on in his 1992 presidential campaign, Bill Clinton saw the potency of Silicon Valley. Not only was the most sophisticated technology used in running the campaign, but Clinton also vigorously courted the high-tech vote and even brought Apple Computer president John Sculley into his trusted circle of advisors. Clinton has been called the "high-tech president" who "talks technospeak," while Vice President Gore—a computer nerd from way back—has been dubbed the "technology czar." The burgeoning companies of Silicon Valley, important to an administration intent on revitalizing the American economy, will become more involved in Washington in the nineties. Meanwhile, activists will use high technology to take on government as much as government will use high tech to get its own work done. Washington's ambitious plan for a network of information highways will have queer activists and other lobbyists tapped into the White House, which, when Bill Clinton arrived, created its own bulletin board. In the not-too-distant future, Washington will run on electronic mail.

The New York media world, where immediacy is vital, will also continue to be affected by Silicon Valley in significant ways. Almost all of New York's top publications—from *The New York Times* and *Newsweek* to *Entertainment Weekly* and *Vogue*—are produced using

Quark Xpress, the desktop publishing software produced by Tim Gill's Quark. Every reporter now uses Nexus, the computerized database that catalogs past and present articles from major American publications. Television news is being revolutionized by computer graphics, and editors at publications like *Time* and *People* couldn't operate under the gun today without sophisticated word-processing software and electronic mail.

As the three older power structures that form the Trinity of the Closet collide and merge with the rising power structure of Silicon Valley, the high-technology companies and their younger, more enlightened, and very openly queer executives and work force will greatly influence and change Washington, Hollywood, and New York. Those changes will ultimately affect all of politics and corporate America. They will alter even the most conservative institutions, transform mass culture on a grand scale, and aid in dismantling the closet in American society forever.

17

A Queer Manifesto

TO ALL QUEERS

There is no "right" to the closet.

If you are in it, it is not by your choice. You were forced into it as a child, and you are being held captive by a hypocritical, homophobic society.

Now is the time to plan your escape. The power to do so is inside of you, and only you can unleash it.

Stop sitting around blaming your parents, your school, the government, the media.

Stop whining about your existence and wallowing in self-pity.

Stop wishing yourself dead.

If you are already out of the closet, it is your obligation to help all those who are still being held prisoner.

If you are not yet out of the closet—if you are a teenager dependent on your parents, if you are trapped in a homophobic town or a rough city neighborhood where they beat up queers, if you are in any way in danger—hold on and plan for the day when you are older, when you have saved some money, when you can leave that place, when you can stand up on your own two feet and take charge of your life. No one can keep you where you are—except yourself. But you must come out wisely.

Everyone must come out of the closet, no matter how difficult, no matter how painful.

We must all tell our parents.

We must all tell our families.

We must all tell our friends.

We must all tell our coworkers.

These people vote. If they don't know that we're queer—if they think only the most horrible people are queer—they will vote against us.

What was done to us when we were children was nothing less than child abuse: Our psyches were tampered with, our personalities stunted.

Now we have a responsibility to speak out when we witness such crimes. If a child being viciously beaten by his parents confided in another child, would we expect the second child to respect the "privacy" of the other child's pain? Or would we praise him or her for speaking out?

Liberate yourself and all others who are locked in the closet. Don't be codependent with those whose dysfunction enables the bigots who bash us.

Badger everyone you know who is closeted—your friends, your family members, your coworkers—to come out. Put pressure on those in power whom you know to be queer. Send them letters. Call them on the phone. Fax them. Confront them in the streets.

Tell them they have a responsibility: to themselves, to you, to humanity.

Tell them they have to face the truth. And tell the truth yourself.

Tell them that you will not stop until they are out—until their closets no longer affect your life.

Remember that all those in the closet, blinded by their own trauma, hurt themselves and all other queers. The invisibility they perpetuate harms us more than any of their good deeds might benefit us.

As the demagogues of the religious right push ahead with their campaign of hatred against homosexuals, the moment of truth is upon us.

Now is the time for all queers to come out and be counted.

TO THE CLOSETED IN POWER

Get yourself some professional help.

The walls are caving in around you, and there's nothing you can do. Your future is going to be painful and difficult, and you would be wise to seek counseling rather than continue to live in denial. While it is hard for you to think rationally about coming out, try just for a moment:

An army of lovers is marching forth: women and women, men and men, arm in arm, hand in hand. Our numbers keep growing every day as we become more and more impatient with the likes of you. All of the hell you've lived through—the hiding, the sweating, the crying, the lying—is only going to become more unbearable. Unless you come out, you'll eventually be revealed as just another cowering, sad, self-loathing homosexual. You'll be remembered as just another Roy Cohn, just another Terry Dolan, just another J. Edgar Hoover.

Deep down, you know you have no "right" to be where you are, that you were shoved in your closet a long time ago. Deep down, you know why you must now come out and why it is wrong for you not to. It's better if you do it yourself. It's liberating and invigorating and empowering.

And it's time.

Just think: You'll be one of the people who have decided to be honest and make the world a better place for all queers. You'll be another Barney Frank, another Martina Navratilova, another k. d. lang, another David Geffen. You'll be a hero.

Now is the time for those who occupy the closets of power to come out and be counted.

TO THE SYMPATHETIC STRAIGHTS

From now on, discount the opinions of the closeted gays around you. Everything they have to say is colored by the closet, tinged by the repressed and fearful existence they lead.

Talk to the out-of-the-closet people you know, talk to several who represent a spectrum of opinions and experiences.

Admit it: All of you have some discomfort with homosexuality.

Your minds have been as polluted as ours by the homophobic society in which we live. You must now be part of changing that society, beginning in your own home. Your children must be brought up without the hatred, without the slurs, without the closet. They must be taught not only that they should have respect for lesbians and gay men but also that it's okay if they are gay themselves. And this honest, compassionate teaching must come not only from you but from their schools and from their churches.

Your queer children must not be forced into the closet.

If your children are being closeted—by you, by their teachers, or by their churches—you are engaging in child abuse, brutal psychological terror, the kind that may lead them to consider or even commit suicide. Stop the terror. Stop other parents from engaging in such abuse. Start thinking about the future, about constructing legislation that will punish people who abuse their children in this way.

Teach your straight children that it's okay if their brothers, their sisters, their cousins, their friends, their uncles, their aunts—even their moms or dads—are gay. Understand this: If your children are straight they cannot be made gay, but they *can* be made into gay bashers.

Those of you in positions of power, stop rewarding the closeted around you for being "discreet." Be there for your closeted friends and colleagues, help them and comfort them. Let them know how much you care. But do not aid in their self-destructive behavior. If a heroin addict were looking for a fix, wouldn't you help him through the withdrawal, no matter how painful it was?

If you really and truly love your closeted friends—as well as all humanity—you will not be party to maintaining their closets.

Now is the time for sympathetic straights to help their queer friends come out and be counted.

TO THE RELIGIOUS RIGHT

You say we're coming for your children, and you're right.

We're coming for your *queer* children. We *are* your queer children.

God—your God, our God—made us that way. And there's nothing you can do about it.

So now we have to be saved—from you—because you do nothing but warp innocent minds.

We will not allow you to force future generations into the closet.

We will not allow you to abuse them in that way.

We will not allow you to poison all of American life.

We will not allow you to breed hatred in our schools.

We will not allow you to create queer bashers and murderers.

We will not allow you to push us all back into the closet—in the military, on Capitol Hill, in Hollywood, or on Main Street.

We are never going back into the closet.

Your most articulate and ardent spokespeople and politicians still claim that homosexuality is a "choice."

This we find curious.

Sexuality is not a choice—it is a natural, immutable orientation. It's those who speak of "choice" who made a choice—a choice to fight their own queer urges. Many of them are repressed bisexuals and homosexuals, obsessed with routing out of society what is coming from deep inside them. Quite a few of them—we know for a fact—are even active but deeply closeted homosexuals who preach the gospel of homophobia.

But the army of lovers will no longer be silent; the greatest casualty in this war you've declared will be the closet.

TO ALL QUEER ACTIVISTS

We have come to an exciting, critical juncture, one for which we have all worked hard.

But we are fractured, split into a million opposing factions. It is essential that we put our differences aside, at least for this crucial moment in history.

We must focus not on that which divides us—our genders, races, classes, ages, political ideologies—but on the one powerful enemy that we all have in common: the closet.

Our diversity is in fact our greatest weapon.

Now is the time for the gay Republicans and the black lesbian mothers and the computer nerds and the congressional staffers and the queer radicals and the gossip columnists and the AIDS activists and the television executives and the gay lobbyists and the record moguls and the outing proponents and the businesspeople and the drag queens to come together.

Our brainpower, resources, talent, and experiences will break down the closets of power forever.

And future generations will be able to be out, proud, and queer in America.

ACKNOWLEDGMENTS

This book represents a mosaic of thoughts and ideas of people who, over the past several years, took time out to engage me in lively discussion. Some of these individuals have been at odds with each other; several have been at odds with themselves. But all of them are queer American heros to whom I am greatly indebted: Maxine Wolfe, Larry Kramer, Gregg Bordowitz, Peter Staley, Ann Northrop, Karl Soehnlein, Heidi Dorow, David Corkery, Michael Nesline, Mark Harrington, Liz Tracey, Alan Klein, Michael Petrelis, Maria Maggenti, Sydney Pokorny, Scott Robbe, Jim Provenzano, Sarah Schulman, Avram Finkelstein, Charlie Franchino, Andrew Beaver, John Weir, Jean Carlomusto, Ken Woodard, Brian Zabcik, David Barr, Bradley Ball, Catherine Saalfield, Douglas Crimp, Walter Armstrong, James Conrad, Scott Tucker, Spencer Cox, Andy Velez, Tom Kean, David Robinson, Betty Berzon, Morris Kight, Jamie Green, Bill Dobbs, Scott Gorenstein, Garance Franke-Ruta, David Feinberg, Joe Ferrari, Lee Schy, Robert Bray, Stephen Gendin, Tom Blewitt, Robert Hilferty, Robert Warnock, Urvashi Vaid, Vic Basile, Jamie Leo, Dale Peck, Ron Goldberg, Phillip Hopbell, Michael Musto, Greg Scott, Tom Rielly, Ggreg Taylor, Adam Block, Steve Beery, Marc Geller, Kevin Lyons, Judy Sisneros, David Burns, Barry Krost, Kevin Lindsay, Rosemary Caggiano, Elias Farajeje-Jones, Wayne Harris, the late Bob Rafsky, the late David Wojnarowicz and the late Vito Russo.

I am grateful to the AIDS Coalition to Unleash Power (ACT UP), a learning institution that offered me the kind of instruction no university could, and to the now-defunct *OutWeek* magazine for allowing me to apply that education to its fullest. My talented colleagues there—Gabriel Rotello, Sarah Pettit, Andrew Miller, Nina

Reyes and Victoria Starr—deserve much credit, as the opinions that flowed from our myriad polemical debates are in these pages. The works of authors Martin Duberman and Eve Kosofsky Sedgwick provided necessary background for this book. I am also thankful to former *Advocate* editor Richard Rouilard, current *Advocate* editor Jeff Yarbrough, *Village Voice* executive editor Richard Goldstein, *Out* magazine editor Michael Goff, *Los Angeles Times* reporter Victor Zonana, Dr. Lawrence Mass, Virginia Uribe of Los Angeles's Project 10, and Larry Gross, professor of communications at the Annenberg School of Communications at the University of Pennsylvania, all of whom have supported me in my previous work and encouraged me in this endeavor.

Throughout this project, many people were generous enough to open their homes to me. In Washington, I lived for several months on Capitol Hill with Greg Scott, a tireless activist who I'm convinced is the proudest queer in America. Tom Rielly, David Carney and Andy Gombiner, put me up for several months in their home in Beverly Hills, an experience I will truly never forget. Wayne Harris and Tom Scholder, a happy queer couple, were my hosts in Portland, Oregon. And in San Francisco, Kevin Lyons gave me a room in his apartment.

In New York, my downstairs neighbor and close friend, Jay Blotcher, was invaluable to me. A gifted writer, publicist, and activist, he not only supported me during the frustrating low points, but read and edited copy, transcribed tapes, offered his professional public-relations services and cared for my cat while I was traveling.

I am lucky to have an out and proud agent, Jed Mattes, who wholeheartedly believed in this project. Similarly, this book wouldn't have been realized had it not been for my dynamic, openly queer editor, Mitchell Ivers. He shared my vision, pushed me hard, and propelled this book forward. I was also privileged to have had as a copy editor Jolanta Benal, an out lesbian who had a comprehensive knowledge of the material.

Lastly, a special thanks to Frank Gollmann of Munich, Germany, whom I met toward the end of this project and who made me very happy.

Afterword

As I wrote in the last section of "A Queer Manifesto," 1993 proved to be a critical time in gay history, and many lesbians and gay men rose to the occasion. Soon after *Queer in America* appeared in stores, I began to receive hundreds of letters from people all over the country, people who said they understood my impassioned call and were now going about the gradual task of coming out of their closets. Many said they were looking at the world differently, with a fresh, unobstructed perspective, rather than the prism of the closet. They said that, though they were inspired by the visibility that gays were suddenly receiving in the media, they realized that for as much as the media wrote about queers there was perhaps ten times more that was kept hidden. Many wrote specifically to tell me about well-known public figures, some dead for many years and others who are alive, who they knew to be closeted gays and who, in some cases, had truly sad and painful stories. Others wrote to tell me about closeted public figures who died in 1993, and how they had taken note, perhaps for the first time, of the media's willful cover-up of these people's homosexuality in stories about their lives that had appeared after their deaths.

On September 13, 1993, veteran film and television actor Raymond Burr, a man most famous for playing the attorney Perry Mason and later the wheelchair-bound lawyer Ironside on television, died. On October 31, 1993, young, talented actor River

Phoenix, known for his acclaimed performance as a gay hustler in Gus Van Sant's *My Own Private Idaho*, died. Contrary to how the media portrayed these stars to the public, Burr was gay and Phoenix, it appears, was bisexual.

Unless there is a belated media feeding frenzy regarding these actors' sexuality between the time I write this afterword (January 1994) and the time it appears, or unless one or more future biographies of these actors reveal the truth, this is most likely one of the few places you will read these accounts.

Raymond Burr had for many years been living a gay life; he had a longtime lover and was out to most or all of his friends. Known as a gay man to many people in Hollywood, he rarely "bearded" himself with someone of the opposite sex and often brought his lover to parties and other affairs. A few years before his death, I had spoken to several gay men who were friendly with Burr and knew him as gay, and one had had an affair with him many years ago. I know the supermarket tabloids had also been privy to this information in the eighties, since several reporters from these publications had contacted me several times, alerting me that they were "investigating" Burr, although, for reasons I don't know, their stories never appeared.

Raymond Burr was also known to be gay by many if not all of the mainstream journalists who cover the entertainment industry. Since he did not want this fact about him made public (falling back on the excuse that it would hurt his career) reporters and their news organizations complied with his wishes and always kept his sexuality a secret while he was alive. But even after Raymond Burr's death—after the "invasion of privacy" issue was moot and there was no longer a career that could be ruined—these reporters and editors still kept him in the closet. In the hundreds of stories that appeared about the actor shortly after he died of natural causes, all of the most personal and intimate details of his life, including alleged heterosexual affairs from the past, were fleshed out. On one network television tribute, a former female lover from many years back talked about Burr and about their relationship. No care seemed to be given as to what Burr might have thought of such an interview. Since he was dead, Burr's opinion didn't matter anymore; how he would be remembered would now be left to journalists and historians to decide, based on what they thought were the most important facts about his life—and his homosexuality, in their eyes, clearly was not among those facts.

Similarly, River Phoenix, who was known to have dated actress Martha Plimpton, was also known in some gay male circles to have been sexually involved with men. He had in fact been involved with several different men at various times; moreover, he had openly gay friends and always supported gay rights. Some people said he was "confused" or that he was young and experimenting; others said he was most certainly bisexual. Whatever the case, many people in the entertainment industry and in the media knew of his sexual ambiguity, and of those who hadn't previously known, many found out about it in the course of researching his life after his death.

When Phoenix died, the cause of death was not officially known, with strong speculation that it was a drug overdose. Before an autopsy confirmed this theory over a week after his death, many stories appeared in which journalists speculated about Phoenix's underground life as a drug user and how this contradicted the public image he had cultivated as a health-conscious, clean living youth. The media were fascinated by the fact that the actor was leading what they saw as a double life—promoting himself to the media in a way that was culturally acceptable, while secretly leading a life-style that was the opposite—and certainly thought it was important to uncover the truth.

Just before the autopsy revealed that Phoenix's death was due to a lethal mixture of several different drugs, *People* magazine, next to a photograph of the actor, ran a headline on its cover, THE SECRET LIFE OF RIVER PHOENIX. Inferring from the headline, I most certainly expected to read about the actor's bisexuality or at least about speculation in that regard, but the story made no mention of it. The profile was mostly about his drug use and reinforced his image as a heterosexual by referring only to his relationship with Martha Plimpton. While many publications felt it was important to delve into the actor's drug use—a "secret life"—they didn't think there was any reason to discuss his sexuality—another "secret life"—nor did they see any merit to such a discussion, though they knew much about his sexuality. While the editors of *Entertainment*

Weekly would argue that "Drugs and Young Hollywood" (the special issue they published about Phoenix and the drug scene in Hollywood shortly after his death) was an immensely important story to do because it brought attention to a problem plaguing many young people across the country, they clearly did not feel the same toward Phoenix's sexuality, even though it would have highlighted and validated the problems of many young *gay, lesbian, and bisexual* people in America. (Five months after his death in March, 1994, only one major publication, *Esquire*, had seen fit to discuss Phoenix's bisexuality in a story about his life.)

In both cases, of Raymond Burr and River Phoenix, the ingrained homophobia of members of the media prevented them from reporting the truth. As in the past, the silence implied that homosexuality is the most invasive, horrible circumstance that could be revealed about someone after death—far worse than digging up past *heterosexual* liaisons or, in the case of Phoenix specifically, telling us every minute detail of his substance abuse.

Some reporters and editors might argue that we don't really need to know the facts of these stars' sexuality, that they are not pertinent to the stories of their deaths. But when public figures die almost every fact about their lives from birth on—facts we have no need to know—are brought forth, and they often include details that had not been reported previously. The information reported about a public figure after his or her death helps to better our understanding of the person, to look more honestly at the individual now that he or she—and others—are not guarding certain facts. Reporting these facts is viewed as important in insuring that the historical record is correct, whether or not we like what those facts represent and whether or not the public figure wanted those facts to be known. It is also understood that because the person is dead, such reporting will not hurt his or her career or interpersonal relationships. And how the public figure's surviving family or loved ones feel about any posthumous revelation is never taken into account. Clearly, there is no valid reason to keep a public figure's homosexuality secret after his or her death—unless those doing the reporting feel that it is not the way *they* want the person remembered.

• • • • •

Looking at the instances of Burr and Phoenix it would appear that the media have not changed since the debate over outing began several years ago—or even since *Queer in America* was first published in May 1993. But that is not true. In fairness, these and several other cases were the exceptions rather than the rule. On the broad issue of homosexuality the media are and will continue to be in a state of great flux, in a period where coverage is uneven. Much of the media, especially in 1993, actually did change dramatically with regard to outing. They changed in subtle ways, pushed by the enlightened straights among them, as well as by the gay men and lesbians among them who came out and stood up to homophobia. Though reporters would never say they were "outing," many actually were, bringing up public figures' homosexuality—or asking public figures about their sexuality—when it was pertinent to the story, which is what I and others had asked them to do since the beginning of the debate. Often these occurred at the very news organizations that had previously condemned the idea.

In September of 1993 a major controversy erupted in New York City regarding the conservative incoming schools chancellor, Ramon Cortines. The seven-member New York City Board of Education, controlled by four ideological conservatives who had been dubbed by media pundits as the "Gang of Four," had previously ousted liberal chancellor Joseph Fernandez, with whom they had butted heads often. Specifically, Fernandez had clashed with the four on his distribution of condoms in city high schools (without an "opt out" provision allowing parents to keep their children from getting condoms without parental consent) and his "Children of the Rainbow" curriculum, which included as suggested reading for first-graders books titled *Heather Has Two Mommies*, *Gloria Goes to Gay Pride*, and *Daddy's Roommate*.

Far different from Fernandez, Cortines is a conservative who, as schools chancellor in San Francisco, had fought gay activists regarding these same issues. He first refused to allow condom distribution, then later allowed such a program, but only with the inclusion of a parental opt-out provision. He had fought activists over providing a vital counseling service for gay and lesbian youth in city schools—the kind of service that even Governor William Weld of Massachusetts, a Republican, introduced as an important tool in preventing suicides among gay teens. Cortines, however, resisted, saying that he worried about "enticing young people as it relates to their sexual orientation."

An unmarried sixty-one-year-old man, Cortines was, at the height of these controversies in San Francisco in 1990, also accused of being a hypocritical closeted gay man in an article that appeared in a local gay publication, *The Sentinel*. But, while the *San Francisco Examiner*, in a story on outing the week Cortines was attacked in the gay press, referred to a "city official" who'd been outed, the San Francisco papers did not name Cortines nor discuss the controversy surrounding him.

But now he was headed for New York, and it was three years later—three years in which the debate over outing had continued. In a testament to how far the media had come on the issue, almost immediately upon his arrival, Cortines was bombarded with questions from the press about his sexuality. At a hastily convened press conference, however, he refused to answer the questions, becoming quite annoyed—and stunned—when reporters wouldn't let up. "When I have not recommended things that community wanted they have gone after me personally," Cortines said. "I understand that and that's their point of view. But I'm not going to be intimidated. I'm not going to be blackmailed. As it relates to me personally, I've said previously that I'm not going to discuss that. And I won't discuss it now." The answer did not satisfy reporters, however, who asked the question several more times, as Cortines became increasingly angered and each time refused to answer.

Five years earlier reporters would have thought it the most terribly invasive and unnecessary question to ask, but now they saw that the issue was pertinent to the story of Cortines's appointment: He was coming to a city and a school system where sexuality—particularly homosexuality—was the issue of the day and his sexuality—particularly, if it were true, his homosexuality—was relevant. Their reasoning echoed that of gay activists. "Cortines's sexuality is an extremely important issue," said Denny Lee of ACT UP to *New York Newsday* at the time. "We can't have a chancellor who is closeted head the largest educational system in this country. The media has no qualms about discussing other parts of his personal history—everything from his childhood to his ulcer, but when the issue is homosexuality the media fall silent."

Reporters and columnists at *The New York Times*, *New York Daily News*, *New York Newsday*, and *New York Post* discussed the issue for several days. "He's a closet gay who is a homophobe, kind of like an Uncle Tom," an unnamed liberal member of the Board of Education told *New York Newsday*'s Liz Willen in describing Cortines. Referring to the board's Gang of Four, Willen quoted the board member as saying, "He was their kind of gay: against condom distribution, against gay rights, very, very conservative. He was their kind of gay."

Though they dealt with the issue directly rather than avoiding it, the New York papers' had in fact held off on disclosing this part of the controversy at first, debating in their newsrooms for days as to what they should do. At *Newsday* Gabriel Rotello had written a column about the issue early on, only to have it killed by editors, who said that the paper had a policy against outing. Ironically, a day later *Newsday* became the first paper to bring up the issue in print, obviously seeing it as pertinent. "Ramon Cortines was approved as New York City's schools chancellor at an emotionally charged meeting in which . . . gay activists raised questions about whether Cortines may be a closeted homosexual who is being hypocritical," read the lead of *Newsday*'s September 1, 1993, story. *Newsday* was soon followed by the other three daily papers as well as by television and radio news organizations. On September 2, *The New York Times*—which several years earlier would refer to the dead Malcolm Forbes in a story on outing only as "a recently deceased businessman" and which stayed as far away from the Pete Williams story as possible—reported on the press conference held by Cortines:

> [Cortines] took questions and one of the first came from a television reporter. "Some have raised the question as to whether you are gay and haven't disclosed it." Even before his arrival in the city members of gay advocacy groups were calling news organizations with claims that Mr. Cortines was a closet homosexual. In San Francisco, Mr. Cortines faced criticism from some gay advocates because he modified their proposals for school counseling and other programs for gay and lesbian students.

The *Times* had come a long way on this issue, but it would soon go even further. On September 26 sports columnist Robert Lipsyte, who has a keen understanding of gay issues and has offered some of the *Times*'s best coverage about gays and sports, interviewed one-time diving champion Greg Louganis. The profile was an example of the kind of journalism that no *Times* reporter would have done only five years before—and an example of the kind of journalism that no *Times* editor would have previously allowed.

On September 7, 1993, Greg Louganis began starring in Paul Rudnick's award-winning off-Broadway play *Jeffrey*, about gay life in the age of AIDS. Louganis was playing Darius, a gay Broadway chorus boy with AIDS. Lipsyte's column focused on his transition from sports to acting and on why Louganis had not, like so many other Olympic stars, endorsed dozens of products, been the subject of a made-for-TV movie, or even written a book.

"Outside the subculture of competitive diving, where he was simply the best of all time, Greg Louganis has never received the attention his four Olympic gold medals, his discipline, his performing beauty seemed to deserve," began Lipsyte's first paragraph, which ends with the jarring question, "Was it because of the whispers that he was gay?" Lipsyte held off for several more paragraphs before offering up an even more startling question, the first question he asked Louganis in their interview: "So, does this mean you're out?" Louganis, who Lipsyte described as becoming "briefly zoned," responded by asking the question back: "Out?" He then reminded Lipsyte that this subject had come up in a previous interview that the journalist had conducted with him five years before. They had decided to drop the issue in that previous discussion. But not this time, and Lipsyte explained to Louganis, and to his readers, why:

> It's different now. I asked the question then because there were so many rumors, and I didn't include the answer in my report because it ultimately had nothing to do with the story of you preparing for the 1988 Olympics in Seoul.
> "But now," I gestured to the empty stage, "you are in a gay role in a gay play."

Louganis, offering some further insight into his life and the tough decisions he has had to face, finally answered the question by saying, "I'm working on things," and Lipsyte concluded, "We'll just leave it that you're working on things."

Elsewhere in the media, the homosexuality of figures once considered untouchable was also revealed, and the relevance made apparent. *New York* magazine—a publication whose media critic, Edwin Diamond, once referred to me as a practitioner of the "fascistic art of outing"—outed Barry Diller in a November 1, 1993, cover story about the highly publicized hostile takeover bid for Paramount Pictures by Diller's QVC Network. "Few details of Barry Diller's private life have ever reached print," *New York*'s Christopher Byron wrote up-front in the article. "*Spy* magazine has referred to Diller and [David] Geffen as part of Hollywood's powerful gay tong."

Later in the article, Byron gave the reason why this reference was pertinent to his story: Paramount Communications includes Paramount Publishing, formerly Simon and Schuster, over which Diller would have direct influence if QVC purchased Paramount. "More and more book publishers in America are now owned either directly or indirectly by a media conglomerate with investments in Hollywood," Byron noted. "But a pattern has developed lately in which publishers sign-up—then eventually end up spiking—books on the industry that threaten to embarrass their corporate parents and affiliates. . . . Dutton [owned by Viking/Penguin] yielded to pressure from a lawyer representing Geffen and Diller, and spiked an exposé on the Beverly Hills gay scene by a homosexual poet, Gavin Geoffrey Dillard. . . . It does look like more than a coincidence when the subject matter [of books that are canceled] turns out time and again to be media personalities seeking to control what the press says about them or their companies."

These were only a few among several instances in which the media delved into public figures' sexuality with or without their cooperation because it was relevant to a larger news story; there were many more examples where members of the media, during direct interviews, asked celebrities if they were gay—even when it wasn't necessarily pertinent. This was amazing, considering that such a question had been an utter taboo prior to 1990. In November 1993, *TV Guide* popped the question to Dolly Parton, and it became news, running on the Associated Press wire: "You've had the support of your best friend Judy Ogle. Are you disturbed by the published rumors about your relationship with her?" The fact that rumors had been published in the supermarket tabloids a long time before and dismissed then would suggest, according to the media's previous logic, that there was no reason to bring them up now. "Judy and I have been best friends since we were seven," Parton responded. "We have done everything together—but not *that*. I've often said I am closer to Judy than I am to [my husband] Carl, and it's true. But what would be the big deal if the rumors were true? There are a lot of gay people in the world! I'm just not one of 'em."

Perhaps the most telling indicators that the national media had changed the way it handled discussion of public figures' sexuality were the reviews of *Queer in America* in newspapers and magazines across the country. The majority of the reviews, in both the mainstream media and the gay press, were thoughtful. In many cases reviewers admitted to having had a distorted view of what outing was about, and many said they had changed their minds on the issue. Even in those cases where writers remained ambivalent about outing—or opposed to it—many expressed a realization that outing was not about "McCarthyism," that the motive was to equalize the discussion of homosexuality and heterosexuality in the media. In almost all cases, whether or not they opposed outing, the writers talked about the closet and why it was necessary to break it down.

There were, however, those who just didn't get it—or who perhaps did get it but, for various reasons, refused to break out of their rigid mentality. While *Newsweek* opined that *Queer in America* "argues persuasively that outing hypocritical, closeted gays is just good reporting," *Time*, which one would assume has similar if not identical standards of journalism, called the book "rancid gossip repackaged for national distribution" and advised that "readers looking for consistency should open a jar of peanut butter rather than read this screed." *Time* reviewer C. H. Sheppard did not recount what *Queer in America* was about—the closet and its de-structive influence—and instead wrote that I was an "egotist" who "touts himself as the pioneer of 'outing,' the distasteful practice of publicizing the private lives of homosexuals who do not feel the need to advertise what goes on in their bedrooms."

Similarly, Tom Goldstein, dean of the graduate school of journalism at the University of California, Berkeley, writing a review for *The New York Times*, neglected to discuss the closets of power and what they do to gay people. Instead, he confined himself to lambasting outing, which he described—perhaps in a moment of wishful thinking—as "a fleeting phenomenon."

Rather than explain accurately and take seriously the issues put forth in *Queer in America* and then disagree with them—as some others had—these and a few other writers chose to dismiss the book, distort radically what it was about, and simplify its arguments. Perhaps the book's issues incensed or scared them so much that they were intent on destroying it without a fair hearing. This disinformation seemed to reveal a subtle form of homophobia: the usual fear and revulsion of homosexuality on the part of some heterosexuals disguised as a disdain for the tactics of the "gay radical," as opposed to the behavior of the "good" gay.

The demonizing of gay writers and activists as "radicals" and "extremists"—and thus providing a way to bash all queers—is a fairly common occurrence. In 1993, however, as gays became more visible and prominent, this trend picked up steam dramatically.

Increasingly, many of those doing the demonizing are openly gay themselves, as a new dynamic has come into play. As had been true in the past with blacks and later with women, lesbians and gay men had reached the point in 1993 where they simply could not be ignored and kept at a distance. And as had been the case with African-Americans and women, some of America's bigots would handle the situation by reiterating their bigotry loudly and publicly while others would play a shrewder game, bringing the conservatives among us into the fold and using them to attack the activists.

•••••

It would be too easy and quite unfair to lump together all gay conservatives or to make them all out to be self-loathing, evil people, as some gay activists have done; there are many gay men and lesbians who are conservative in their thinking, their values, and even their politics but who do not attack gay activists continually and who certainly understand the complexities and diversity of the gay movement. Even many gay Republicans who want to carve out a place for gays in the Republican party work with, have a mutual respect for, and fully appreciate gay activists from across the political spectrum. We should use our diversity to its advantage; instead of attacking gay Republicans, we should welcome their organizing so that we are not always captive to Democratic politicians, and also because much of the legislation that we need passed will require bipartisan support and bipartisan organizing.

The gay and lesbian community faces too many important issues across the political spectrum for us to refrain from dialogue. The message about the destructiveness of the closet, for instance, is one that must transcend political parties and ideological beliefs. For that reason, in the face of criticism from some on the left, I spoke in 1993 at the national convention of the Log Cabin Federation, the national gay Republican group. I met many interesting and intelligent people—people who understand that the closet must be abolished—and many were very supportive of the work that gay activists on the left do.

However, there is a strain of gay conservatives who could accurately be called the Gay Right, not only because they use the same tactics as the Religious Right—demonizing and marginalizing all gay activists—but because on many issues they have a rigid ideology that does not permit dissent, an ideology in which everything is black and white, with no shades of gray. Ironically, this ideology is as rigid as that of the so-called "politically correct" of the left, whom the Gay Right continually attack. Often, in fact, these people behave exactly like the people they criticize. As African-American scholar Cornel West, in his 1993 bestseller, *Race Matters*, observed of black conservatives and their relationship to black liberals, those on the right denounce what they describe as the liberals and leftists' recoiling to victimology, even as they complain about their own victimization by the left.

Conservative and openly gay Andrew Sullivan of *The New Republic* has often told reporters that he is hounded by crazed gay radicals who supposedly throw drinks at him in bars and call him all sorts of terrible names. In an April 1993 *New Republic* cover article, "Straight America, Gay America," he collapsed together many different people from across the gay political spectrum and who often have very different opinions. Sullivan painted them all as immoral people with no self-control who hold bizarre beliefs. In his eyes, all queer activists are mad extremists who believe, for instance, that homosexuality is a "choice." There is, of course, a broad spectrum of beliefs on this subject even in the small sliver that Sullivan would like to dub the Gay Left. And of this group only a small minority in fact believe their sexuality to be of their own choosing.

Yet according to Sullivan—and others in the Gay Right—the queer radicals' deranged beliefs and behavior work unwittingly with the Religious Right to bring down the gay movement. According to Sullivan, both the queer radicals and the Religious Right favor outing, which he describes as a "punitive" tactic. This is of course an oversimplified analysis. Most antigay zealots on the right are in fact very wary of outing, perhaps because they realize that it helps gay visibility. Outing has been attacked by conservatives from Patrick Buchanan and right-wing former California congressman William Dannemeyer to Phyllis Schlafly and the viciously antigay Reverend Lou Sheldon. More important, there are many so-called queer radicals and straight leftists who have opposed outing. Most of the editorial staff of the *Village Voice*, which Sullivan would say is a queer radical primer, have opposed outing. And some gay conservatives, such as Marvin Leibman, a founder of the conservative movement, have favored outing. Like most issues the Gay Right tries to make black and white in order to further their simplistic and orthodox viewpoints, outing is more complex than they allow.

Sullivan has often spoken out against people who hamper debate, censor discussion, and encourage group think, but he has refused to allow any discussion of outing in the *New Republic* that does not describe it as "punitive," "authoritarian," or include other negative knee-jerk characterizations. I have never read anyone straight or gay putting forth a pro-outing position in his magazine, nor have I read any interviews in the *New Republic* with people who hold such positions. When attacking outing, Sullivan hasn't even first presented the arguments favoring it as a way of normalizing the media's treatment of homosexuality: He simply has dubbed it "punitive" and "blackmail," as if he were afraid to truly flesh out our positions.

So it was predictable that in a lengthy December 1993 *New*

Republic essay headlined THE GAY AWAKENING, a review of nine recent and not so recent gay books, writer Paul Berman, echoing Sullivan's previous articles, demonized queer activists, refused to discuss outing in its complexity, distorted what *Queer in America* was about, and dismissed me as a "conspiracy theorist":

> The "outing" of fellow homosexuals serves, in effect, to blackmail influential persons into helping the gay cause, as interpreted by the blackmailing "outer." Yes, there might be a personal or professional cost to the poor soul who has been "outed." . . . But what is that to Robespierre? Show me a guillotine and I will show you a career ladder. Among the several books on gay themes that have recently been published is one called *Queer in America* by a public relations flack named Michelangelo Signorile, who went from the service industries of the Broadway gossip columns to a giddy career of Yippie agit-prop for Queer Nation, where his proudest achievement, recounted in cheerful detail in his book, is to have become famous for harassing one of George Bush's assistant secretaries of defense. Signorile telephoned his chosen victim at home in the middle of the night and then, not liking the assistant secretary's way of talking, took it on himself to reveal this man's homosexuality to the world.

This was cynical and disappointing coming from a magazine at which the editor is gay and well versed in these issues. Even one of Sullivan's fellow gay conservatives, Jonathan Rausch, an editor at *The National Journal* and a contributor to *The New Republic*, has praised *Queer in America* for its analysis of the closet while he has respectfully disagreed with me over outing.

Sullivan would rather marginalize gay activists by distorting their opinions than present them responsibly. Only a "punitive" Gay Left gives him the martyr status he presents to his straight and often homophobic colleagues. It also gives those colleagues a scapegoat—"gay radicals"—to direct their homophobia toward rather than at him.

An article such as Berman's thus helps Sullivan maintain his view of the horrible activists, the bad apples who spoil the whole bunch. The conclusion of Berman's piece in fact is that the gay movement, in spite of "embarrassments and misfortunes" such as our "invention of a kitschy cultural identity on the basis of sex," our "ensuing campaigns to eroticize art and culture," "the snarly air of intolerance radiating from the radicals," our display on Gay Pride Day of "parading fetishists," and "the maneuverings of the flacks and the conspiracy theorists," in spite of all this, *somehow* we had survived as a movement, albeit a "muddled" one. But alas, implies Berman, the Gay Right—with all of their superior intellect and moral righteousness, of course—have finally arrived to deliver us all from evil. He then goes on glowingly to review books by members of the Gay Right whose points of view predictably mimic all of Sullivan's black and white contentions about the demonic radicals who sully the name of the great church-going, suit-and-tie masses of the gay community.

"If anyone was going to work up some genuinely new thoughts and give those thoughts a sharp enough edge to command attention, it would be intellectuals of the sort who don't mind a little unpopularity," wrote Berman. "And if any such people existed they would probably have to be a new generation entirely—just the way that, among black intellectuals, only an unpopular and sometimes conservative new wave of writers in the course of the 1980s was able to challenge the old Black Power orthodoxies from those same radical 60s."

That statement is interesting, considering Cornel West's analysis in *Race Matters* of the impact of black conservatives. The bid for "conservative hegemony in black political and intellectual leadership in the post–Civil Rights era," West notes, "has been highly unsuccessful, though it has generated much attention from the American media. . . . The new black conservatives have been unable to convince black Americans that conservative ideology [is] morally acceptable and politically advantageous. . . . Black Americans have rejected the arguments of the new black conservatives."

Similarly, the new Gay Right received much attention in 1993. The media use these people to bash what they perceive to be the more threatening elements of the community.

Just as black Americans have rejected the arguments of the black conservatives, gay Americans will by and large reject the arguments of the new Gay Right, for most gay Americans are too smart, and their lives too complex, to follow black and white rules. They seek liberation from moralists, not yet another lockstep mentality that passes judgment on people. The writers in the Gay Right continually assert that they represent the "silent majority" of gay people, those people whom the Gay Right claim to be average, everyday folks who are not activists. But that is a bald assumption; there is no empirical evidence to support their claim. In my own experience I have received hundreds of letters from readers, and met thousands while on tour—doctors, lawyers, students, sales clerks, engineers, priests, military people, mothers, fathers, grandparents, and other "everyday" folks. I have met the "silent majority," and the Gay Right is in for a surprise. The "silent majority" have a great respect for and support gay activists and some, once a year, even march in Gay Pride parades, proud of who they are and proud of their community. Perhaps because they don't represent the extremes of the community—and also because many are closeted—they are not the people one might see on the news on the night of the parade. But these people rightfully put the responsibility for that on the media—not gay activists, gay "fetishists," or gay "conspiracy theorists" and others whom the Gay Right vilify.

The Gay Right's logic regarding the responsibilities of the closeted and the out is in fact backward: They put the burden of gay representation not on those who remain closeted—including closeted public figures—and thus deny themselves and the community its visibility and diversity, but on those people who have already come out but whose physical appearances and political viewpoints are not to the Gay Right's liking. Thus they believe that an outspoken and very public gay man who likes to do drag or who celebrates his sexuality by dressing in an overtly sexual manner or whose political ideologies and tactics are far to the left is giving the community a bad name, making Americans believe that all gay people are just like him. According to the Gay Right, that person has a responsibility to restrain himself from such expressions. Of course, this line of reasoning fails to account for the basic individual freedom of that public gay man, someone who took great risks to come out of the closet and who is now expressing himself as he sees fit, in a manner that he does not view as wrong. In this way, the

Gay Right has no tolerance for openly gay people whose views of right and wrong differ in the slightest from theirs.

One of the Gay Right's newest spokespersons, for instance, is Bruce Bawer, a self-described gay neoconservative who wrote a book published in the fall of 1993 called *A Place at the Table*, a bilious attack on every conceivable aspect of gay culture. Few gay people are spared by Bawer, who admonishes even the most mainstream and politically moderate of gay writers—from Paul Monette to Edmund White—practically all gay activists, cross dressers, people who go nightclubbing, people who view sex in any way other than Victorian, and just about anyone who marches in a Gay Pride parade. In Bawer's view, drag queens and gay people who are into the leather scene are exhibiting a great deal of "self-disgust," "self-hatred," and a "lack of self-respect," and activists in groups like ACT UP are driven to direct-action activism because of their "self-loathing" and "self-destructiveness."

In his book as well as in interviews, Bawer engages in much name-calling directed at well-known openly gay people working within the lesbian and gay community. In a December 1993 interview in *The Advocate*, in a throwback to McCarthy-era hysteria, he even went so far as to label Urvashi Vaid, the hard-working lesbian activist and former director of the very mainstream National Gay and Lesbian Task Force and a woman who is of Indian descent, "anti-American."

Ironically, the premise of Bawer's book is that the gay movement needs to put forth a squeaky clean, nonthreatening, friendly image so that America will embrace it. The Gay Left, he opines, must stop being what he views as "intolerant" of those in the community whose opinions are different from theirs, and gay activists as well as all those gay people who march in Gay Pride parades must alter their behavior so that they will not feed the public's various negative stereotypes about gays. And yet, Bawer seems unaware of how ugly his own intolerance is, how unattractive his own name-calling and demonizing is, how negatively stereotypical of gay men his own petty, bitter, Miss Manners–like behavior is.

This ignorance of the consequences of their own actions and behavior is typical among those in the increasingly intemperate, doctrinaire Gay Right. They complain about what they perceive to be the extremism and the rigid orthodoxy of most of the organized gay community, and yet seem oblivious to the fact that they have become their own worst nightmare.

If the individuals in the Gay Right truly desire to advance the gay cause, as several of them have claimed, rather than demonizing their opponents as a way to distinguish themselves, they would make an effort to find common ground with people within the gay movement with whom they disagree, so that we can all move forward.

· · · · ·

While *The New Republic*'s rejection of even a healthy discussion of outing suggests an editorial contempt for gay activists, it also reveals how much the Washington political elite are under the influence of "the Beltway mentality," far removed from what is happening in the real world. They seem almost blind to the fact that on the issue of outing, the mainstream media outside the Beltway are moving at a dramatic pace. It is in fact a measure of the national media's movement on the issue of outing that *TV Guide*, perhaps the most mundane, "middle American" publication there is—and the publication with the highest circulation in the country—would practice the kind of journalism that only three years earlier was labeled by media people as "fascistic," "McCarthyistic," and an "invasion of privacy" by asking Dolly Parton if she was having a lesbian affair. Or that *The New York Times* would go so far as to ask Greg Louganis if he were "out." Or that Katie Couric, interviewing me on *Today*, would treat the issue of outing as a small aside to the much larger problem of the closet.

On April 3, 1993, *The Boston Globe* published a front-page article headlined: 'OUTING' SEEN AS POLITICAL TOOL, DISPUTED STRATEGY OF NAMING PROMINENT GAYS GAINING FAVOR. In addition to noting the change in the media, the article said that even some "moderate activists" were no longer condemning outing. "I am unwilling to criticize people who engage in telling the truth about public figures who are members of the community," Kevin Cathcart, director of the largest gay legal advocacy group, Lambda Legal Defense and Education Fund, told *The Globe*. "I think it's important that people have privacy, but public figures in this country give up a lot of their privacy rights."

The *Globe* story was picked up by several other papers at the time. Throughout 1993 still other papers and some television news shows carried their own stories on the issue, with most noting a change in the rules about when and how to report on a public figure's homosexuality.

This shift was in part due to the fact that by 1993 queer issues had taken center stage, forcing members of the media to think out topics fully that they previously had tried to marginalize and put out of their minds.

In late April of 1993, on the eve of the march on Washington, at the time the first copies of *Queer in America* appeared in bookstores, gay issues dominated the media, captivating the country. The amount of attention devoted to the march before it actually occurred was staggering. At any other time there would have been no media buildup to a gay march and little coverage afterward, as was the case with the 1987 march on Washington. But in 1993 the media had finally "discovered" homosexuals and were uncovering every aspect of our lives. Three significant circumstances, all of which give credence to the argument that breaking down the closet is the only way that the gay movement will move forward, led to this sudden visibility in the media:

- Beginning in 1987 AIDS and queer activists seized the media, utilizing attention-grabbing tactics, charging out of the closet and forcing America's news organizations to cover an explosion of activity in the gay community.

The debate over outing, and later the debate about the military's ban on gays, focused attention, perhaps for the first time, on the closet and, more important, on what a destructive—rather than protective—place the closet can be. Many previously closeted gay people, inspired both by the proud street activists and by the patriotic military gays, rose to the occasion and came out themselves. Among these people were lesbians and gay men in newsrooms across America. In 1991, the National Lesbian and Gay Journalists Association formed. At its first conference, in June 1992 only three hundred people attended. In September

1993, five hundred lesbian and gay journalists from mainstream media organizations around the country came to the group's second conference, held in New York City, where Tom Brokaw, Dan Rather, Judy Woodruff, and Robert MacNeil, all presumably heterosexuals who now felt it was important to support their gay colleagues, sat on the opening night panel. Queers in the media realized that they had a responsibility—not simply as people who were part of a community that was fighting back but as journalists—to push editors in newsrooms to cover the gay community in depth and accurately, to go beyond the activists, to show the full spectrum of the gay community.

• From 1990 to 1992 *The New York Times*, the newspaper of record that sets an example for all others, transformed itself into a leader among the media by both covering the gay community in depth on its news pages and advancing the cause of gay rights on its editorial pages. The changes had come after decades of entrenched homophobia, when former publisher Arthur Ochs Sulzberger passed the torch to his young and enlightened son Arthur Sulzberger, Jr., and after twenty-year veteran *Times*man Jeffrey Schmalz came out of the closet—both as a gay man and as a person with AIDS. It was AIDS, in fact, that outed him; he suffered a seizure in the newsroom and could no longer keep his medical condition and his sexuality private.

I was privileged to facilitate Schmalz's public coming out in an interview for a lengthy *Advocate* article (May 1992) I wrote about the dramatic changes at the *Times*. Schmalz, who had by then been out to his colleagues in the newsroom for several months, told me at that time that he'd wished he'd come out years before, that he realized how beneficial it would have been.

Soon after coming out publicly in *The Advocate* Schmalz devoted himself to writing articles dealing with gay and AIDS issues, crowning his work with a lengthy November 29, 1993, *New York Times Magazine* cover story, "What Ever Happened to AIDS?" It was an unfinished article which rebuked the media for slacking off in its coverage of AIDS. Schmalz died shortly before the article appeared, on November 6. Schmalz's work, and more significant, his editors' support of that work, had a major

effect on all of the media's coverage of gay issues, as *The New York Times* is watched and followed by many other news organizations.
• Bill Clinton, the first presidential candidate to campaign and win with an overtly progay platform, had ushered in what some had called the Queer Nineties. It was openly gay political organizers, however, many of whom had been organizing within the Democratic party for years and some of whom were friends of Clinton and his wife, Hillary, who pushed the Democrats and Clinton to support gay rights. Clinton's initial promise to end the ban on gays in the military, and the enormous controversy in early 1993 that erupted over that promise, had the media riveted. Gay issues were for the first time on the front pages for days.

Soon after Bill Clinton was elected president it appeared to many lesbians and gay men as if we were going to win our full civil rights at the end of the next soundbite. Privately, I was cautioning friends against this exuberance, and in public I had written columns for *The Advocate* months earlier, during the presidential campaign, which warned readers that Bill Clinton was not a savior of the gay community and would probably not keep his promises.

I had no inside knowledge of this but simply a gut feeling that all of the organizing, protesting, and closet-busting by gay activists, as well as the explosion of visibility in the media, would soon be met by a fierce backlash. The signs of the backlash were already apparent; they had been apparent throughout the eighties, as the Religious Right organized at the grassroots level in cities and towns across the country and had just won a ballot measure in Colorado. But the media, in its excitement, had glossed over that backlash, and perhaps unwittingly lulled many people into thinking that homosexuality and gay rights were more understood and sanctioned in society than had been the case. When the press did focus on where antigay measures were passed, such places were treated as isolated cases, as exceptions to the norm rather than as part of a large and powerful concerted national effort on the part of antigay bigots.

The barrage of positive stories about gay life, it appeared, had a very seductive effect; they had convinced liberal straights, and many lesbians and gay men as well, that Americans had somehow actually *accepted* queers more than they had previously. Many people believed that the kind of hatred that Patrick Buchanan had displayed at the Republican convention had somehow been toppled with Bill Clinton's election. They believed that Buchanan and the ugly propaganda he floats had been discredited and that Americans were beginning to welcome lesbians and gays into the fold.

In truth, most Americans had never seen or known homosexuals previously but were now being bombarded for the first time with people who had been kept hidden from them for many years and who forced them to deal with issues they'd always been taught were shameful and taboo. While visibility is the first step toward winning our rights, it will be a long time before Americans are desensitized to gays, before age-old prejudices will be dissolved. In 1993, the mask was off, but the fear was still there, and that fear could—and would—easily be manipulated.

For those reasons I wasn't surprised by our loss of the battle of the ban or by the forces that antigay bigots had been able to muster against us. But, while the main culprits in our loss had been the right-wing and the Religious Right, we have to admit that we were equally disorganized and that our leaders showed an enormous amount of naïveté. Intoxicated by Bill Clinton's win, expecting that they were going to get everything that was promised and that the right-wing was out of commission for the time being, gay leaders were caught with their guard down.

All of the visible signs of that demise were there; as early as the day after the election the controversy over lifting the ban had begun. There was a news vacuum, as there usually is directly after a presidential election, and the media went for the most contentious issue they could find, putting President-elect Clinton on the spot about lifting the ban. It was then that the national gay organizations in Washington should have begun organizing vigorously. Instead, leaders of the Human Rights Campaign Fund (HRCF), executive director Tim McFeeley and communications director Gregory King specifically, told the press over and over again that they had complete faith in the President and continually dismissed—to the media as well as to the gay community—any suggestion that there would be impediments in the way of lifting the ban.

Meanwhile, as the controversy over the ban mushroomed and as our enemies gained ground, the National Gay and Lesbian Task Force (NGLTF) was replacing an executive director who knew the ways of Washington with someone who came from as far away from the Beltway as one could get—California. It was a case of bad timing, at perhaps the most crucial point in the gay and lesbian civil rights movement, NGLTF's tireless Urvashi Vaid was stepping down at the end of 1992—something that had been planned long before the election—with the position passed on to Torie Osborn, former head of the Los Angeles Lesbian and Gay Community Center. In January 1993, after Vaid had already left but before Osborn assumed her position, Bill Clinton was under attack and backtracking on his promise. This left NGLTF virtually leaderless while the media was looking for some direction from the gay community. Osborn took the helm just as the huge controversy was exploding, precisely as she attempted to adjust to a demanding new job. (Eventually, six months after taking the post, Osborn resigned.)

At the same time, a new group, backed by newly visible and well-heeled queers, emerged in the power vacuum: the Campaign for Military Service (CMS). Founded in January 1993 by David Mixner and Tom Stoddard as a vehicle to wage a media campaign to lift the ban, CMS was in reality not putting its resources toward that goal but instead began to duplicate the work of the other groups. "CMS hired lobbyists, policy analysts, and researchers and tried to mobilize grassroots support, even though NGLTF, HRCF, and the Victory Fund already had these in place," reported Andrew Beaver in *Out* magazine in November 1993. As has been reported in several gay publications, CMS tried to take over the entire fight. A turf war ensued that pitted NGLTF, HRCF, and CMS against each other. Theoretically, the group that would come out on top in this battle would, once we won the lifting of the ban, be the new gay power brokers of Washington. And so, with our leaders caught in a power struggle, the enemy organized with the precision of a fighter battalion and eventually blew us out of the water.

The President is not free from blame; he proved to be as

disingenuous as the few gay skeptics—Michael Petrelis most prominent among them—predicted during the election. He was, after all, just another heterosexual trying to save his own skin throughout the ban fiasco and looking for a way out of this mess. Openly gay congressman Barney Frank provided him with that out, caving in to Sam Nunn's "Don't Ask. Don't Tell" compromise without consulting with any of the four embattled gay groups—thus making the ultimate power play over all of them.

It seemed we'd been let down across the boards. Even David Geffen, who had taken a leadership role for gays as the Clinton administration took power, rather than send a clear message to the President and the Democrats for wimping out, continued to give money to the Democratic National Committee before, during, and after the ban debate, and even hosted a grand Hollywood fundraiser in the fall of 1993 that honored the President and Hillary Rodham Clinton.

• • • • •

Many have said that the gay community was so out organized by the right that it wouldn't have mattered if we had been better equipped. Perhaps, but that stance seems to be yet another excuse on the part of people who don't want to accept where our weaknesses lie. Such a statement is still an admission that we were ill-prepared, and if we don't fix what's broken we will continue to lose ground on all levels of political action.

If the lesbian and gay movement, a relatively young one, is to grow and mature as other communities have, then we must hold our leadership—whether they are Washington gay advocates or Hollywood power brokers—accountable; it is after all *our* rights they are supposed to be fighting for; *we* have allowed them to speak for us.

Some gay leaders, perhaps in an attempt to further take blame off of themselves, particularly in the wake of the loss over lifting the ban, have said that criticizing them is "cannibalism," that in doing so we are "eating our own."

These rationalizations must be resisted; such reasoning is an insult to the intelligence of all those queers out there who have valid opinions about how things should be done. Yes, there are some people in the gay activist community—as in every community—who *are* cannibalistic, who are vicious, mean, and unfair to other activists, and they should be and are criticized for their tactics. But it is cowardly and cynical when gay organizations and their leaders exploit the attacks as a way to end all criticism against them.

It is important that we watchdog our leadership, and our gay press needs to be vigilant in exposing incompetence within gay organizations. If gay leaders cannot take being under hot lamps, and cannot accept culpability for their actions, then they were never cut out for the job to begin with. In 1993 the entire lesbian and gay community underwent a traumatic and difficult experience in which the highs were high and the lows were low. In the end, for many, the sense of loss was great. The greatest leaders of all would be the ones who, rather than deflecting criticism and screaming "cannibalism," would wear the badge of responsibility for mistakes made, be open to suggestions from a range of queer activists—men and women, young and old, Republican and Democrat—and draw upon the enormous talents in the gay community rather than shut people out in an effort to retain personal and political power.

• • • • •

Though we lost the battle of the ban, and though our march on Washington wasn't the magic bullet we hoped for, in the big picture we weren't really losers.

That is because in 1993 we *had* won something: The right to have our grievances aired. We'd also won the right to have the fight we've been picking for over twenty years, regardless of how we eventually handle that fight. Previously our enemies had ignored us, but beginning in 1993 we were taken seriously, and that in and of itself is a victory. Our march on Washington galvanized lesbians and gay men throughout America, brought many out of the closet, and sent a powerful image to homophobes. Nineteen ninety-three was a year that marked the very beginning of a long war. It will be a ten-year battle at least, and one that may perhaps be violent and bloody. Before things get better they will probably have to get far worse. Looking at other conflicts between the far right and the rest of

America confirms this belief. In two separate incidents in 1993, doctors who perform abortions were shot by religious fundamentalists; one of these shootings was fatal. These and dozens of other attacks on prochoice doctors and clinics are an indication of the extremes to which the Religious Right will go and of the desperation, however realistic or unrealistic, they are experiencing.

For queers, that violence has already begun. In Colorado gay-bashing rose 300 percent in the wake of the passage of antigay Amendment 2, with homophobes feeling they now had carte blanche to attack queers. In Oregon, the Measure 9 campaign unleashed hatred that the state had never seen before, with people being shot at and one gay man and a lesbian murdered when their home was firebombed by neo-Nazis. By the end of 1993 several states and dozens of localities had passed measures banning gay rights laws—or were about to. The long and arduous process of winning our civil rights through the courts has begun. We've already had some court victories with regard to the military ban and Colorado's highest court has overturned Amendment 2. But the Religious Right will not give up easily. The lesbian and gay community, and our allies, would be foolish to think that this opposition, this hatred, with be rooted out without a nasty fight.

Compounding this state of affairs is the AIDS crisis, which had been allowed to get so out of control in the eighties that seemingly nothing done now—short of an outright cure—can change its magnitude. The epidemic will continue to weaken our spirits, deplete our energy, and kill our people. We will be fighting continually on both fronts, torn between the fight for a cure and the larger battle to end the homophobia that exacerbated the AIDS crisis from the beginning.

As AIDS activists have realized, so too queer activists must understand that it is time for new strategies and that some of the old strategies might be doing more harm than good. Our brash, attention-grabbing tactics were previously appropriate and highly effective. Now, not only are they old hat, but they increasingly turn people off. Screaming and yelling was more than cathartic; it drew attention to our cause and galvanized our people to action. Now that we have the spotlight, our message must be more focused, direct, and logical. It was easy to galvanize the like-minded, but changing the thinking of the not-so-like-minded is a harder task that requires clear, rational argument.

That is something I learned myself—the hard way. After having been dismissed by many people, I learned that the only way to have a chance to change the minds of people who don't agree with you—after you get their attention, that is—is by presenting the arguments rationally and respectfully. That was part of my motivation for writing *Queer in America*—to present the logic behind the passion, the reasoning behind the rage, and thus reach a wider audience and participate in a dialogue rather than merely have a temper tantrum.

I bring this up here because, in traveling around the country speaking at colleges and universities, I met so many intelligent people, committed queer and AIDS activists who have challenged the established activists and the powers-that-be in their communities with a very compelling, and what I believe to be an absolutely on-target, message. But because their tactics were so abrasive they were sloughed off easily, easily couched as lunatics. They and all of us must keep our ideas from being discarded by reevaluating our methods and strategies for getting our messages across.

There is another reason to change our tactics. Our enemies have caught up with us and have figured out how to turn our tactics back against us. The Religious Right is making propaganda videos that present homosexuals as powerful, evil monsters who are set on destroying the fabric of American life. They have turned themselves into the victims and turned us into the victimizers. By breaking down their church doors, by spitting and hurling four-letter words at them, by threatening them and behaving in a violent manner (as much as all of this feels good and is perhaps not morally inappropriate considering what they have done to us), we only give them further ammunition.

I am in no way seeking to champion the opinions of those in the Gay Right who say that Gay Pride parades, drag queens, leather men, and angry protesters are the real problem and that, if we are to get anywhere, we must somehow stop these people or at best *hide* them. Not only is this unrealistic, it's dishonest; we have to present our community with all of its diversity and desensitize people to those elements of the community that they might fear.

Communication based on visibility is the only way we will really win.

But now that we have the spotlight, now that the media will show when we schedule a demonstration (or any event, for that matter), our protests must incorporate tactics that can't be used *against* us but will rather work *for* us. One of the most effective demonstrations I read about in 1993 occurred in a church in Brooklyn. Roman Catholic bishop Thomas Daley had come out against gay rights laws in a strong political statement. Protesters went to his service the following Sunday and wore T-shirts with messages on them—messages that drove the point home that Daley was a bigot who was putting their lives in danger, but were not vulgar or disrespectful. The protesters stood up and turned their backs on him during the service in a silent protest. The demonstration garnered much television and print media coverage—positive coverage that portrayed the activists as good people fighting for their rights. Daley tried to present himself to the media as the victim, but it didn't work because he *wasn't* a victim; the protesters were too dignified and respectable to be seen as aggressors. Daley, in his attempt to play the victim, came off as cynical.

To this end, queer activists should look to the real experts on civil disobedience and protest, people like Mahatma Gandhi, who championed the kind of civil disobedience that never cost him his self-respect and dignity and never turned his oppressors to victims.

That is not to say that bold and strident protest is uncalled for; used when appropriate, powerful disruptions can be very effective. On December 1, 1993, World AIDS Day, a member of ACT UP named Luke Sissyfag (his legal name) took Bill Clinton to task as the President gave a speech to students and researchers at Georgetown Medical Center. As Clinton, with panels from the AIDS Memorial Quilt as his backdrop, took note that AIDS had receded from public consciousness and urged people to get "revved up" about the disease, Sissyfag rose up, marched to within twenty feet of the President, and delivered his compelling missive:

> If you're so concerned about AIDS, where's the Manhattan Project on AIDS that you promised during your campaign? One year, lots of talk, no action! Thirty recommendations of

the National Commission on AIDS go sitting on a shelf gathering dust in your White House, Bill, while me and my community are dying in ever-increasing numbers, and all you do is talk! Talk is cheap, and we need action! You're hiding behind the quilts! You are doing nothing! Look at your record, Bill! One year, no results. The Manhattan Project on AIDS that you promised during the campaign, where is it? Thirty recommendations of George Bush's Commission on AIDS. . . . Where are they? One year! Slick Willy! The Republicans were right! We never should have trusted you.

Sissyfag's message was focused, rational, and direct. While he was abrupt and strident, his protest was just short of crossing the line where it would have made the President a victim. Sissyfag garnered much attention and got his point across while keeping his own dignity and self-respect and without turning his target into someone for whom the media—and America—should instantly have sympathy. In fact, Clinton's response to Sissyfag—defending his administration's efforts on AIDS while admitting that more could be done and saying, "part of my job is to be a lightning rod"—only validated the protester's charges.

Beyond protest, the most dignified, self-respecting—and yet direct and focused—action that the average gay person can take in the nineties, the person who is not an activist and is simply living his or her life quietly somewhere, is to come out of the closet, something I cannot say enough times. If you take one action for your community and for yourself the one that is far more important than all of the dollars you can give and all of the time you can volunteer is to gradually tell all those people around you—your friends, your family, your co-workers—that you are gay.

The one thing we learned from the turn of events in the pivotal year of 1993 was this: Abolishing the closet will do more to disarm our enemies and win us our rights than any heterosexual progay politician—or even an army of them—will ever do.

When it comes to our liberation, the only people who will save us are ourselves.

Queer in America 2003

In October 1999, over one hundred openly lesbian and gay elected officials gathered in Providence, Rhode Island, to discuss a topic that had grown dramatically in the 1990s. It is a topic that the Internet has had, and continues to have, a major role in shaping. It is the topic that obviously is the focus of this book: When and how a public figure's undisclosed homosexuality should be made public.

Ten years after outing first came to the forefront of the media and eight years after *Queer in America* was published, that topic was still the focus of attention at events like the one in Providence. The elected officials had come from all corners of North America: The mayors of Winnipeg, Manitoba, and West Hollywood, California, and Tempe, Arizona; a member of Congress from Wisconsin and one from Massachusetts; state assembly and senate members from California, Texas, Florida, Oklahoma, Hawaii, Minnesota, New Jersey, New York, Rhode Island, Maryland, Connecticut, Colorado, and Oregon; and council members from dozens of urban centers, small towns, and rural areas.

It wasn't the first time that a group of gay leaders had gathered to discuss the topic of the "closets of power," but this meeting was very different from any that had taken place in earlier years. One reason was simply that there were so many openly gay elected officials, all sitting in one room. In 1989 one could have counted the number of openly gay officials nationwide on both hands.

The difference that stood out even larger, however, was the fact that the people in the room were almost unanimous in their opinions on the topic of discussion: The homosexuality of public officials should be reported on when relevant to a larger story, and the media have a responsibility to report on public figures' homosexuality in the same way they report on public figures' heterosexuality—rather than treating homosexuality as a dirty secret.

At the meeting in Providence I led a plenary session for the elected officials titled "Our Closeted Colleagues: What Should We do About Them?" Over the previous ten years the closet had more uniformly come to be seen as a destructive force that kept people personally imprisoned and as something that kept the gay movement back by maintaining gay invisibility. That I—once considered a radical on the topic of journalism's role in reporting the homosexuality of public figures who had not declared themselves gay—would be invited to speak about the issue and lead a plenary session at such a mainstream gathering was in itself an indication of how far the gay movement, and the larger culture, had come in the years since *Queer in America* was first published.

And yet, even as American culture has changed markedly regarding homosexuality and the gay closet, the closet survives as an institution in 2003, proving itself quite resilient, responding to challenges by remaking and redefining itself.

Looking back at the afterword to the paperback edition published in 1994—as well as chapter 16, about the rise of the high-technology industry—it's clear changes that took place in those first few years of the '90s, and in 1993 in particular, continued throughout the decade. Still, I was overly optimistic about some of these changes and at other times perhaps not optimistic enough. Having the distance of ten years now we can reflect on some important events, looking at what ways there have been dramatic change and what ways there have not.

DE-CLOSETING AMERICA: THE 1990S

So many events that occurred over the past ten years—the most pivotal decade in the gay rights movement so far—were enormously important, each of which could fill several books (and some of these events have filled books) and each of which highlights how our ideas about the closet have changed. Just because an issue isn't covered here doesn't mean it wasn't significant, or that it didn't warrant more discussion. This chapter confines itself to covering a few controversies that became symbolic or indicative of others.

Before looking at a few specific controversies regarding outing and the closet, however, it's important to outline, briefly, some of the changes and larger discussions relevant to gay and lesbian rights that occurred in America in the 1990s.

- In the early to mid-'90s the country was torn by an often heated but sometimes quite productive debate over whether gay men and lesbians should serve in the military openly, out of the closet; that debate has only intensified as injustice in the military continues to be revealed, and as the "don't ask, don't tell policy" has only resulted in more discharges of gay men and lesbians than ever before.

- Throughout the '90s and into the first years of the new century, mainstream celebrities such as Ellen DeGeneres and Rosie O'Donnell and pop stars such as Melissa Etheridge and k. d. lang have come out, impacting the culture and influencing new generations of gay people to come out and to have much less tolerance for the closet in their own lives.

- In public schools across the country the issue of homosexuality, and why gays from a very young age feel shamed into hiding, is for the first time being discussed openly; the hot button issue of homosexuality moved to local school boards by the late '90s, causing heated debates, and it seems that it will continue to do so well into the twenty-first century.

- More open gays and lesbians were elected to local and state offices across the country in the five-year period from 1998 to 2003 than in the entirety of the previous thirty years since the Stonewall riots ushered in the modern gay rights movement.

- In the '90s, President Bill Clinton brought in a new era for gays and lesbians working in the White House and the federal government— a far cry from the 1950s, when gays were purged from the federal government. Clinton signed executive orders barring antigay discrimination in the civil service and hired many openly gay men and women for staff positions. This has had a lasting impact on the Republican Party as well, which has had a more recent history of being hostile toward gays: Republican President George W. Bush, even with the religious right protesting loudly, has been forced to hire openly gay individuals to posts within his own administration and had no choice but to meet with gay Republicans during the election campaign.

• Issues such as same-sex marriage (highlighted by Vermont's passage in 2000 of a civil unions law for gays, and other states' rush to outlaw same-sex marriage), antigay hate crimes (highlighted by the slaying of the Wyoming student, Mathew Shepard in 1998), and discrimination against gays in housing and employment (highlighted by the push by gay advocates to pass the Employment Non-Discrimination Act in Congress beginning in the latter part of the '90s and by the actions of influential states such as New York, which in 2002 joined those states that outlaw discrimination against gays and lesbians) came to the forefront of the national political debates in the 1990s and are continuing well into the first decade of this century.

All of these events and issues intersect with, recast, reorganize, and break down the closet. They demand that both private individuals as well as public figures rethink the whole idea of being out and put pressure on the media to report more on how public figures identify themselves.

For example, several closeted members of Congress who voted in favor of the Defense of Marriage Act in 1996—a federal statute promoted by right-wing conservatives that outlawed same-sex marriage—eventually saw their homosexuality, to varying degrees, discussed in the press.

OUTING THE INTERNET

Rather than diminishing, the issues of the closet and outing have thus become more broadly debated and discussed over the ten years since *Queer in America* was first published. Fascinatingly, in some sectors outing has become so commonplace that it doesn't create a whimper, while in other areas of life it continues to whip up controversy and create dialogue. That discussion, however, is smarter than it used to be and is less sensational. The mainstream media now seem more compelled, and perhaps more emboldened, to honestly report on the lives of prominent gay people, even if the public figures have been circumspect about their sexuality. Once taboo, such reporting is now more accepted (within certain parameters), even if it is uneven, and even if the media are sometimes confused about which direction to go with such coverage.

Perhaps the single greatest influence on the entire issue of outing over this past decade has been the Internet, which was not in widespread use in the late '80s and early '90s. As the Internet revolutionizes communication and media, as average folks are more able to affect public debates through e-mail, Web sites, "blogs," and chat rooms, the discussion of public figures' homosexuality is no longer solely in the hands of the media elite. It is more so being moved by gay citizens across America.

Thus, in recent years specific events that shine a spotlight on homosexuality have brought the issue of outing to the forefront. The final chapter of the original *Queer in America*, "The Silicon Solution," looks to high technology as a tool that would be used to break down the closet in America. The Internet was still very new when I wrote that chapter in 1991; many gays and lesbians in the high-technology industries were interviewed for that epilogue, and they discussed the role they saw the Internet having in the future. In many ways, the chapter was utopian and didn't live up to expectations. The religious right and the larger conservative movement, contrary to what many activists believed, have in fact organized online on a grand scale. And the online world itself, economically at least, became a bubble that eventually burst by the end of the decade. It was not the panacea—economically, culturally, politically— for which many had hoped.

But in other astonishing ways, a great many of the activists' predictions in that chapter about how the Internet would be used for activist purposes have come true and continue to come true. The year 1996, for example, was the year of the antigay Defense of Marriage Act (DOMA) and endless media debates about when and whether to recognize gay and lesbian unions. But perhaps more interesting was how the issue of outing flared up. The anger unleashed by the legislation, which banned federal recognition of same-sex marriage and allowed states to do the same, radicalized and reenergized many lesbian and gay Americans and had them again looking at the "closets of power."

Many were shocked that legislators whom they knew or thought to be closeted gay men and lesbians could vote for this particularly nasty, antigay bill.

In the midst of the debate over DOMA that summer, the Internet became ablaze with outings, as many of the staid and often-conservative gay marriage advocates teamed up with more seasoned queer activists. For perhaps the first time, information about American legislators' sexuality raced around the globe, popping up on home pages, in e-mail messages, on bulletin boards, in newsgroups, on Web sites, in chat rooms. The mainstream and more traditional media became almost beside the point. Not all of the tales were well documented, of course, and some were mere speculation based on apocryphal anecdotes.

Regardless, in light of the passage of DOMA, many gay men and lesbians felt it was well within their rights to speculate about which Senate and House members might be gay or lesbian. Certainly, wondering whether someone might be gay or lesbian was not in and of itself a bad thing, they reasoned. Eventually, many of the online outings spilled over onto gay radio broadcasts and gay cable TV shows, into the gay and alternative print media, and then often, when there was enough to go on, into the mainstream media. Several members of the House and Senate, even if they denied assertions that they were lesbian or gay, or if they refused to answer the question at all, were that year asked point-blank by reporters about their sexual orientation. And one, Congressman Jim Kolbe, simply came out, perhaps realizing it was exhausting to stay closeted.

Such questioning would have been unthinkable in years past. What was perhaps most remarkable about all of this, however, was how *unremarkable* it all was. Several of the Internet-driven outings made it into the mainstream with little of the moral outrage we'd come to expect from the national media on the issue. Though Representative Mark Foley of Florida, a pro-DOMA Republican, would neither confirm nor deny reports in the gay press about his sexual orientation, for example, those reports eventually surfaced in the *St. Petersburg Times* (the hometown paper of the district he represents) and other newspapers, with barely a whimper from the privacy purists in the national press. (Later, in 2003, Foley's homosexuality was discussed even more openly in the media as he made a run for the U.S. Senate, even as Foley himself refused to discuss it.)

CHANGING TIMES

Perhaps the most definitive example of the sea change that had taken place by 1996 was the *New York Times*'s own coverage of the man who, for better or worse, will always be remembered in any discussion of the history of outing: the late multimillionaire publisher Malcolm Forbes, whose homosexuality I'd revealed in an article in *OutWeek* back in 1989, shortly after his death, kicking off the outing debate (all of which is discussed at length in *Queer in America*). The *New York Times* and much of the media refused to report on Forbes's homosexuality at the time when I wrote my story; the *Times*, in a story about the cultural implications of outing, reported that "a recently deceased businessman" had been outed. But in February 1996, in a lengthy front-page, above-the-fold story about Republican presidential primary candidate Steve Forbes headlined, "In Political Quest, Forbes Runs in Shadow of Father," the *New York Times* not only finally told its readers about "the first published reports in the gay press of his father's homosexuality," but went on to question Steve Forbes about the issue and to enlighten us about the fact that "in the last five years of his life, Malcolm Forbes became increasingly indiscreet, and he was seen regularly roaring up on his motorcycle in tight black leather to Manhattan nightclubs and, according to current and former workers at *Forbes* [magazine], pursuing some of his young male employees."

As the *Times*'s Forbes turnaround underscores, journalistic outing never really went away and has only progressed as time has gone on. Its perimeters are still hazy and unstable, changing as often as the public's feelings about homosexuality itself change, and there are no hard-and-fast rules. The simple fact is that more and more journalists are coming to realize that there are times when a public figure's undisclosed homosexuality is relevant and proper to report on or to speculate about, regardless of whether that person is directly engaging in antigay behavior or not.

The highly publicized revelations of Assistant Secretary of Defense Pete Williams in 1991, a story I wrote for the *Advocate* and documented further in this book, perhaps gave much of the media the first clear-cut example of the so-called hypocrisy argument for outing: Williams was a spokesperson for the Pentagon, an institution that had a particularly vicious policy against allowing gay men and lesbians to serve in the armed forces, regularly conducting witch-hunts to purge gay service members. But, as discussed in several chapters of *Queer in America,* while most of the press picked up the story, they were baffled as to how to treat it: Some news organizations ran the story prominently and named Williams; others buried it, saying only that "a Pentagon official" had been outed. Fast-forward four years: By the time *Rolling Stone* publisher Jann Wenner left his wife in 1994 for former Calvin Klein employee Matt Nye, the idea of relevancy as distinct from hypocrisy had become established. The *Wall Street Journal* published a front-page piece on Wenner's divorce and the effect it would have on his business empire (his wife was his business partner), clearly seeing the relevance of reporting the fact that Wenner left his wife for a man. Had Wenner left his wife for a woman, the paper's editor reasoned when asked about the revelation by other reporters, it would have reported that and other facts about her. The rest of the media quickly picked up the Wenner story. In its report the *Washington Post,* as if the editors there had come up with the idea on their own, decided all of this needed a new name: the "equalization" of homosexuality and heterosexuality.

By the end of the '90s even the gay conservative Andrew Sullivan, who had excoriated me and others relentlessly in the early '90s, calling us "authoritarians" because we pushed for the media to treat gay public figures equal to their heterosexual counterparts, had a change of heart (though he was loathe to admit that). In the *New York Times Magazine,* chastising such individuals as Rosie O'Donnell (then closeted), Ricky Martin, then Health and Human Services secretary Donna Shalala, then Attorney General Janet Reno, Gore campaign manager Donna Brazile, former New York City mayor Ed Koch, and fitness guru Richard Simmons because they refused to declare their sexual orientation, Sullivan expressed his impatience: "There comes a point, surely, at which the diminishing public stigmatization of homosexuality makes this kind of coyness not so much understandably defensive as simply feeble: insulting to homosexuals, who know better, and condescending to heterosexuals, who deserve better. It's as if the closet has had every foundation and bearing wall removed but still stands, supported by mere expediency, etiquette and the lingering shards of shame. Does no one have the gumption just to blow it down?" And when Koch fumed to the *New York Post* the following week that Sullivan is like "the Jew-catcher of Nazi Germany," it certainly brought back memories for me; the difference this time around, however, was that few other prominent voices came to Koch's defense.

Perhaps there's no better indicator of the mainstream media's values and shifts than the work of Barbara Walters, the reigning queen of television news. By 2000, she was knocking down closet doors too. Walters wouldn't relent when interviewing Ricky Martin on her ABC-TV Oscar night special in March 2000. After Martin evaded her first inquiry about "rumors that question and talk about [his] sexual orientation," Walters pushed on: "You could say, as many artists have, 'Yes, I am gay,' or you could say, 'No, I'm not.'" And when Martin continued to dodge the question, Walters pressed on further: "It's in your power to do it." Martin was forced to feebly utter, "I understand. . . . [but] I just don't feel like it."

That same year, MSNBC.com columnist Jeanette Walls published her book, *Dish: The Inside Story on the World of Gossip,* in which she discusses the sexual orientation of the cyber-gossip Matt Drudge, who'd been at the center of efforts to expose President Clinton's sex life. Seeing it as relevant to the story of Drudge's own reporting on private lives, Walls interviewed several men who say they dated him, and spoke to former friends who knew him as gay, such as Dan Mathews, campaign director of People for the Ethical Treatment of Animals.

All of these instances—speculating, asking, and outright reporting—would have been dubbed "outing" ten years ago, attacked by pundits of media outlets such as the *New York Times* and ABC-TV as the worst breach of privacy. Today, however, these practices have simply been folded into journalism. What we did in the gay press has clearly pointed the way for many at today's mainstream outlets. "Equalizing" has, in many cases, become reality.

THE LIMITS OF EQUALIZING

Though we may be getting there, "equalization" is not quite as equal as many of us would like it to be. While outing is now within the realm of popular journalism, much of the media all too often still duck for cover when it comes to the lives of public figures who are gay or lesbian, not quite knowing how to proceed, often fearful of coming under attack if they move too quickly, if at all. Still holding most of the cards—the Internet notwithstanding—the mainstream media often make arbitrary decisions about who to out and who not to out.

For example, when Republican political strategist Arthur Finkelstein—a man who worked for such illustrious homophobes as Republican Senators Jesse Helms, Launch Faircloth, and Don Nickles—was revealed by *Boston* magazine in 1997 to be gay and living with another man and their two adopted children in a posh corner of Massachusetts, much of the media seemed to walk on eggshells. The story swirled around a bit, surfacing in the *Village Voice,* getting a mention in *Newsweek,* a blurb in the *New York Post,* and a relatively short segment on *CNN Headline News.* Finkelstein clearly didn't want this information about his life plastered across the media (as it could, and probably did, cost him clients like Mr. Helms); he refused to speak on the record with the *Boston* magazine reporter about the topic and later issued a statement saying he was "disappointed" with the story: "I keep my private life separate from my business life."

The story died for a while, going nowhere. But claiming that it was because Finkelstein, in the statement of his disapproval of the revelations, noted that his "family" knew he was gay, the *New York Times* eventually saw it fit to print. The eagle-eyed columnist Frank Rich wrote a stinging column about Finkelstein, strangely making sure to excuse himself from participating in outing by noting that Finkelstein was out to his family. But mentioning this fact seemed to be splitting hairs: For all practical purposes, the *Times* was of course outing Finkelstein, a private man who, by his own refusal to speak on the record about his sexuality with the *Boston* magazine reporter (or with the *Times* itself), did not want this information made public. The *Times* could say that it wasn't an outing, but there are many other public figures whose homosexuality is just as relevant as Finkelstein's and who have for years been just as out to their families, and even to their local communities (Congressman Kolbe and many other still-closeted members of Congress come to mind). And yet, the *Times* and many other media organizations do not report on these people's sexual orientation unless these individuals come out themselves.

Similarly, until 2002, when she came out of the closet with great fanfare (discussed later in this chapter) talk show host and actress Rosie O'-Donnell stayed mum for much of the '90s about her sexual orientation. And much of the media went along for the ride, allowing O'Donnell to live in a glass closet: Most people assumed the unmarried O'Donnell was a lesbian—and if they glanced at the supermarket tabloids throughout the '90s, they knew that she held the record for a star being photographed with a lesbian lover—but the word was never spoken in the mainstream press, nor was O'Donnell ever asked the question. The glass closet is a phenomenon that has always been around (Liberace was among its most famous occupants) but by 2000 it had become something much larger in popular culture, and it was often allowed to exist by a complacent gay movement—as indirectly pointed out by none other than neo-outer Andrew Sullivan himself.

While stars who sell their sex appeal, such as Tom Cruise, saw their sexual orientation questioned over and over again in the '90s—including, in Cruise's case, in published rumors that moved him to launch a highly publicized lawsuit disputing the claims, a lawsuit he won—stars like O'Donnell, who had virtually desexualized themselves (i.e., playing the role of the clown, of the overweight woman, or of the mom), often weren't asked the gay question in the way that Barbara Walters put the question to Ricky Martin.

THE FADING OF ACTIVISM

Influencing much of this unevenness is the lack of a sustained, grass roots gay activist movement putting pressure on both the media and on public figures who remained closeted. While events like the signing of DOMA in 1996, or the brutal, nationally publicized murder of Mathew Shepard in 1997, did galvanize activists—and in the case of DOMA renewed the issue of outing among activists—the pressure has not been as constant and relentless as it was in the late '80s and early '90s, when the urgency of the AIDS epidemic was at its peak.

ACT UP and later Queer Nation were a driving force in pushing the issues of gay visibility, coming out, and outing in the late '80s and early '90s. In the afterword of *Queer in America* I discussed the need for tactics to change, as the media had gotten used to the loud, attention-grabbing protests. But that doesn't mean that vigorous protest should fade entirely and activism become completely muted and compromised.

But through the 1990s, ACT UP, Queer Nation, and other grass roots activists that came off the streets in the early '90s shrank and often collapsed entirely. Much of that, at least with regard to AIDS and ACT UP, was due to the arrival in the mid-'90s of protease inhibitors, the so-called triple-combination drug therapy, that dramatically and wonderfully brought so many gay men back from the brink of death. Suddenly, AIDS was not a death sentence—though these drugs are far from a cure and have brutal side effects—and for many, it became all about going back to their lives.

Unfortunately, but perhaps not unexpectedly, complacency set it in with regard to AIDS—not just politically, but when it came to safer sex among gay men as well, even as the epidemic was far from over and AIDS was far from cured. Unsafe sex among gay men, particularly among younger generations and African American and Latino gay men, rose dramatically in the '90s, as did infection rates. And some men, young and old, even gave up condoms consciously, seeking "bareback" sex online, believing that AIDS was no longer a problem. The horrific side effects of the drugs—and the fact that they didn't work for many—was obscured by the reports of people going on with their lives, miraculously having battled AIDS.

Many men with HIV, using testosterone as therapy, began looking better and more muscled than a lot of HIV negative men. AIDS went back into a closet of its own. (That was perhaps no more evident than when the famed fashion photographer Herb Ritts died of AIDS complications at the end of 2002 and major news organizations, in a throw back to the '80s, reported his death as due to "pneumonia." Few asked if it was AIDS, and the family was not initially forthcoming.)

Thus, in the mid- and late '90s, some of the most heated debates in the gay world—certainly among gay writers and journalists like myself—were about this seemingly willful ignorance and the political, cultural, and epidemiological consequences of the bareback phenomenon rather than the government neglect or homophobia. That only added to the diminished state of gay activism: Some of the most outspoken activists and writers were too busy talking about internal issues to be focused on the outside world.

The decline in grass roots activism was followed by a rise of more mainstream, tepid, and accommodating gay advocates, as well as the even further rise in the media of the gay conservatives such as Andrew Sullivan, who left the *New Republic* and became a writer for the *New York Times Magazine* for several years.

Sullivan himself, however, lost some of his luster by the decade's end, as his own hypocrisy was revealed: In a widely circulated article in the gay paper *LGNY* in early 2001, I wrote how Sullivan, who has moralized about the gay community, was himself soliciting "bareback" sex on the Internet. Having come out as HIV positive in the mid-nineties, claiming he got infected through oral sex, which he described as "innocent" behavior, Sullivan now had to fend off charges that he was acting recklessly. While many on the right defended him, it did appear that his star had faded among many heterosexual liberals who'd previously found themselves gravitating toward him.

But the gay right, as a phenomenon, having come to the surface in the early '90s, only grew bigger as the decade wore on, more endeared to a mainstream media that found the gay right less threatening. (In 2002, *Village Voice* editor Richard Goldstein wrote a book about the gay right, *The Attack Queers*).

The gay right provided a buffer between gay activists, who were waning on their own, and the straight liberal and conservative establishments. Once the pressure from activists was removed, it became easier for the closet to remain or to reconstitute, even if it had been dealt a severe blow years earlier. One outcome of that is that now, as before, there are many in Hollywood and Washington who remain deeply closeted even as some, and particularly those behind the scenes in Hollywood (producers, directors, agents), have come out.

THE GLASS CLOSET

Another outcome of the decline in activism has been the toleration of the glass closet—a closet in which the individual's sexual orientation is known but where the individual feels no pressure to simply go the extra step and come out. And for complicated reasons, the media feel less of an obligation to push the issue with these individuals than with others. When these people do decide to come out, curiously, they often don't want attention focused on it—they want to have been perceived as being out all along. (For example, Rosie O'Donnell has said that the media made a big deal of her coming, but that she'd never hidden anything, thus implying that she'd always been out.)

The public figure in the glass closet and the media play an odd dance. Perhaps one positive development regarding the glass closet dance is that, while celebrities or politicians might not want to be out for fear of how it might affect their careers, they are embarrassed about being perceived as closeted as well—and when they do come out, they want us to believe they've always been open.

The media, meanwhile, don't want to be perceived as having pushed them. And that gets at part of the reason for some of the media's unevenness, strange rationalizations, excuses, and splitting of hairs about reportage on various individuals. The word *outing* itself is something no one wants to be associated with (and despite even the *Washington Post*'s best efforts, *equalizing,* as a term, is still not catching on), much less accused of promulgating. Just like the words *feminist* and *liberal,* the word outing has been demonized even more in the past ten years than in the years prior to *Queer in America*'s first publication, even though most people probably believe in its basic tenets or support it to some extent. In a statement that betrayed this fear—not to mention defensiveness—the *New York Times* denied it was outing, even when Andrew Sullivan had named so many names in his *Times* magazine piece, claiming that Sullivan was simply "questioning" these people's coyness.

Similarly, when the producers of the late '90s sitcom *Ellen* finally decided to make the lead character come out as a lesbian, *Time* magazine let us know that *Ellen* star Ellen DeGeneres's own sexual orientation "is a topic of much speculation," and that was almost a year before DeGeneres herself came out, ironically on the cover of *Time.* It was relevant for *Time* to discuss the "speculation" of the real-life Ellen's sexual orientation now that the fictional character of the same name was coming out—in any other instance, reviewers and critics would certainly discuss what an actor brings from his or her own personal life to a role he or she is playing—but *Time*'s editors would be loath to admit that by mentioning the "speculation," they were participating in "outing," the egregious activity whose name they'd coined six years earlier. But they most certainly were.

GOING BACK

The '90s clearly were a time in which the entire culture was embarking on a new path with regard to gay issues, and without a road map. But without a force of activism pushing through that uncharted path it's understandable that there sometimes was an impulse to just turn around and go back. Perhaps that kind of "three steps forward, two steps back" phenomenon is present in every social change movement. And as I discussed in the afterword, there certainly was a fierce, religious-right-fueled backlash against gay rights in the early '90s. Even among liberals and the mainstream, however, the guard was let down throughout the '90s.

One example that so potently underscores how quickly the media and others can at any time revert to their base impulses on homosexuality and, in effect, demonize gays is the massive media coverage of the serial murderer Andrew Cunanan soon after he'd killed the fashion designer Gianni Versace in 1997. Not only was Cunanan dubbed the "gay serial killer"—before gay media groups could even send out directives on how to cover this huge and sensational story responsibly—but speculation commenced immediately about how Cunanan's homosexual passions might have fed into his pathological behavior and the murder of five men.

On *NBC Nightly News,* Tom Brokaw described Cunanan as a "homicidal homosexual," conjuring up the stereotyped image of the desperate, sex-crazed gay who will stop at nothing to get what he wants. *Vanity Fair* writer Maureen Orth claimed on *Dateline* that Cunanan had become increasingly involved in gay S & M sex and that this dark obsession was somehow tied to his killing spree. Reports were widely disseminated that Cunanan might have AIDS—though there was no proof of this and an autopsy of Cunanan's body later disproved it—further sexualizing Cunanan, and playing upon one of the most ugly media myths of the 1980s: The vengeful, sexually ravenous and dangerous gay AIDS victim on a rampage.

Throughout the manhunt television news reports referred ad nauseam to a "gay sexual underworld." Announcers would glibly refer to this "underworld," as a sinister, kinky place where people like Cunanan lurk—and where in fact he could be hiding out. One news magazine editor called to ask me to write a piece showing how a particular segment of the gay male community that I studied in my third book, *Life Outside*— the gay party circuit, with its sexy muscle men and often drug-fueled dance events—was tied to the murder. I explained that neither Cunanan nor Versace were part of that scene, that in fact the gay world was as complex as the straight world, encompassing many different kinds of people. But the editor simply moved on; someone else was lined up to write about what he several times described to me as a "shadowy, dangerous gay underground" that was the "backdrop" for the murder of Versace.

It was *Vanity Fair*'s Orth who floated the idea that that there was a prior meeting (read: sexual interaction) between Cunanan and Versace, and many in the media took this story and ran with it. The media in fact seemed split on how to treat Versace: Some emphasized Orth's theory of a prior meeting, making the murder seem like perhaps another seedy gay crime in which the victim might have brought on his own destruction by becoming sexually involved with the wrong person. Others downplayed any prior meeting with Cunanan and desexualized Versace by rendering almost invisible his longtime companion Antonio D'Amico. In this scenario, almost all of the media played up Versace's family ties, pressing family members for interviews, but tended to ignore D'Amico, his partner of eleven years. Whatever way they portrayed Versace the depictions relied upon age-old stereotypes of gays as shameful, closeting aspects of his life.

Had Versace been a married heterosexual man, his wife would have been bombarded with reporters and photographed continuously—as were the wives of the two heterosexual-identified victims of Cunanan. In the case of D'Amico, much of the media seemed to have suddenly decided they needed to respect the privacy of the murder victim's closest survivor.

These actions are often couched as exercises in liberal tolerance and respect, and as concerns for privacy and decency. But their uneven application betrays a double standard when it comes to straights and gays, and it is one that often still exists. Through the gay movement's sheer fortitude in the '90s, much of popular culture may now allow for people, even public figures, to state that they are homosexual. But visibly acting on that homosexuality—in the way that heterosexuals act on their sexuality—appears to be something that the larger heterosexual culture is still quite uneasy about, demonizing gay sexuality or trying to brush it away, out of sight and out of mind.

QUEER IN AMERICA TODAY

The events of the new century, including the arrival of a conservative Republican presidential administration in Washington as well as the events that faced us all in the aftermath of the September 11 terrorist attacks, raise new issues for the gay, lesbian, bisexual, and transgendered movements. As in the Andrew Cunanan scenario, these events allow for biases against gays to surface within the media and political cultures, showing that there still is a long way to go.

Soon after the September 11 attacks, for example, Pat Robertson and Jerry Falwell blamed "gays and lesbians and feminists" for bringing on the attacks—God's retribution for our evil ways. It was encouraging that the two were condemned by many—even by many conservatives—for their horrendous attempt to demonize gays in the midst of the worst terrorist attack in American history.

Still, the two religious zealots' comments showed that the impulse to demonize gays is alive and well, particularly in times of high anxiety. Gays, lesbians, bisexuals, and transgendered people—who became more visible in the '90s as transgendered rights came to the forefront—will for some time remain in a precarious place and must always be on guard against such demonization, a fact that makes the further push to break down the closet even more important.

Gays and lesbians may be more accepted in society, and may be more visible in films and on television, and transgendered people may be increasingly discussed in the media, but there is still no national legislation protecting gays, lesbians, bisexuals, and transgendered people. Only a handful of states (fifteen) outlaw discrimination against gays and lesbians, and none protect transgendered individuals. While several states are exploring giving partnership rights or marriage rights to gays, only one, Vermont, has legalized gay relationships, in the form of civil unions, while many states have outlawed gay marriage.

QUEER IN WASHINGTON 2003

The importance of guarding against demonization is particularly true in a conservative time and under a conservative presidency. George W. Bush has been hostile toward the gay movement, has supported sodomy laws in the past, and has come out against gay-inclusive antidiscrimination laws, marriage rights for gays, and adoption rights for gays. Eager to appease the religious right, whom he courted throughout his campaign, Bush has several times in his presidency played into the religious right's demonization of homosexuals.

In July 2001, for example, it was revealed in the *Washington Post* that White House mastermind Karl Rove had cut a deal with the Salvation Army, promising that Bush's new faith-based initiative programs would make the not-so-gay-friendly group exempt from antidiscrimination laws that protect gays. (Though the White House initially dropped the plan once it was exposed, little over a year later Bush signed executive orders that in effect did exactly as the Salvation Army had wanted, allowing the group to exclude hiring those who do not follow their faith in the way they determine—such as gays, lesbians, bisexuals, and transgendered people.)

And in January 2003 an appointee to the presidential AIDS panel, Pennsylvania marketing consultant Jerry Thacker, withdrew his name—under pressure from the White House—after the *Washington Post* reported that he had in the past called AIDS the "gay plague," had attacked the gay "death style," and had promoted the idea of "rescuing" homosexuals from their sin. Had reporters not seized upon Thacker's past words—which Thacker had purged from his own Web site—he'd have remained on the AIDS panel.

The closet in Washington—and in the Bush administration—is not only alive and well, it's far bigger under the Bush administration than under the Clinton administration, representing a few steps back. While there were over one hundred openly gay appointees in the Clinton administration (several of whom were high level), there are only six or so openly gay appointees under Bush.

But there are many closeted individuals working in the administration, even in high positions, known to gays in Washington and aware that they must remain low-key for fear of embarrassing the president. While we might have reached a point where the religious right can tolerate a few openly gay appointees, certainly a mass coming out—particularly of people in key positions—would be unacceptable.

In early 2003 I received information that one Washington individual supported by the president for a position in the government was in fact a deeply closeted individual who was vocally antigay—not only to colleagues at work but even, apparently, toward the men with whom he has sex. One man told me about how this individual told him, after they had sex, he was going to burn in hell because of the actions he'd just committed. Other men came forward telling me of come-ons and unwanted sexual advances this man made in the locker rooms and steam rooms of Washington gyms. One man explained how this individual grabbed his penis in the steam room and was shocked when the advance was rebuffed.

All of these men who made the charges are professionals and highly credible. None of these men, however, would go on the record, fearful that their reputations and livelihoods would be destroyed, in the way Anita Hill's reputation and integrity were attacked by Republicans when she spoke out against Supreme Court nominee Clarence Thomas.

The anguished, deeply conflicted closeted individual, meanwhile, is speaking out against gays in his job, almost as a way of fighting his own impulses.

Indeed, by all indications the Washington closet, particularly in conservative Republican circles, is as prevalent as ever. One story that went national in 2002 was David Brock's, whose book *Blinded by the Right* became a *New York Times* bestseller. Though his story is about how he operated as a closeted gay man during the '90s in conservative circles, it opens a window into how so many others—including, he notes, the cyber-gossip Matt Drudge—still travel in those circles while living in fear of details being made public about their sexual orientation. It also sheds much more light on the events surrounding Anita Hill's charges of sexual harassment against Thomas back in the late '80s, during his confirmation hearings, charges that are discussed in earlier chapters of *Queer in America*.

As a closeted gay right-wing journalist in the late '80s and early '90s, Brock worked with such illustrious gay-bashers as religious zealots James Dobson and Pat Robertson, *Weekly Standard* editor Bill Kristol, then *Washington Times* editor John Podhoretz and *American Spectator* editor R. Emmett Tyrrell. He conspired with them and many others against what they saw as the evils of liberalism. In the guise of journalism Brock cooked up, as he describes it, a "witches' brew of fact, allegation, hearsay, speculation, opinion, and invective" about Anita Hill and, later, an equally toxic potion of often unsubstantiated allegations about President Clinton. All the while Brock secretly harbored a libido that was precisely of the kind that many of his coconspirators were railing against.

Looking back, I'd wondered why I'd not outed Brock myself in those years, long before he had written his infamous "Troopergate" Clinton hit piece in the *Spectator* (which launched the Paula Jones lawsuit) and before he'd become so valuable to the right that they'd just accept him as another house homosexual rather than dump him because of an embarrassing exposure.

When I told him, during an interview I conducted with him in 2002, that I should have outed him, he half-jokingly replied, "I'd have been outraged at the time—but I certainly deserved to be outed."

It's a response that goes a long way toward showing the sincerity of Brock's apology for his past recklessness, as well as the validity of the political conversion from right to left that he lucidly details in his book.

Truth be told, Brock hardly dated and kept his secret tightly hidden in the early years as he moved through conservative circles; he wasn't as sloppy as the closeted Pentagon officials and Republican staffers on Capitol Hill—and even some closeted members of Congress—who often socialized in gay circles and even in gay establishments. Brock wanted fame and fortune so badly, and was so "self-loathing" and in search of validation, he says, that he'd do whatever it took. And as his secret became more well-known in the early '90s, Brock then just came out himself—prodded by some right-wing colleagues' impressions of a critical Frank Rich column in 1994 that they claimed was sexually suggestive (though that was hardly the case).

As Brock describes it, at that point, after the runaway success of his first book, *The Real Anita Hill,* and other attention-getting articles in the *Spectator,* he was worth too much as a hired character assassin for his homosexuality to matter to his benefactors. It was only when Brock, in his second book, 1996's *The Seduction of Hillary Rodham,* offered a more balanced look at the First Lady—rather than a hit job connecting her to criminal activity, which many expected—that his patrons on the right began to abandon him. That book, he says, was the very beginning of his long journey away from the right.

The cast of hypocrites, vipers, and freaks doesn't get any more perverse than those in *Blinded by the Right.* There's the story about the often self-righteous media pundit and hate radio talk show host Laura Ingraham—one of Brock's gaggle of "fag hags"—who, "in a drunken stupor, crawled . . . on her hands and knees," looking for Brock at a dance club. There's the truly demented pundit Ann Coulter, who, Brock writes, "seemed to live on nothing but Chardonnay and cigarettes." (Brock told me in an interview that Coulter, another of his "fag hags," used to give him "ex-gay" literature, trying to "convert" him to hetero-

sexuality.) Former Clarence Thomas aide and radio talk show host Armstrong Williams—who was sued by a male bodyguard a few years ago
who claimed he was sexually harassed by Williams, a case that was settled out of court—appeared to have come on to him at Williams's apartment, writes Brock, while asking him whether he was "dominant or
submissive in bed." (This is the same Armstrong Williams who wrote a
column in March 2003 lambasting Rosie O'Donnell supporters for using children "to push alternative lifestyles into the mainstream.")

There's also Brock's reporting about Web gossip Matt Drudge, who
has reveled in exposing Clinton's sexual affair with Monica Lewinsky, in
addition to spinning out sexual innuendo, half-truths, and lies about others. Brock says he went on a date with Drudge (though Brock wasn't really interested in him) shortly after Brock and Ingraham cohosted a dinner party for Drudge in June 1997 to draw Drudge closer into the
right-wing cabal. While at the gay dance club Rage in L. A., Brock
writes, the jealous Drudge purposely stepped on the foot of a man dancing nearby who was flirting with Brock. A few weeks later the heartsick
Drudge sent Brock an e-mail saying that Ingraham was spreading the rumor that Brock and Drudge were "fuck buddies," opining that he should
only be "so lucky."

Some in the media understandably raised the question of Brock's
credibility upon the publication of *Blinded by the Right*, asking how anything he says can now be trusted, and a few have summarily dismissed
him for that reason. But some of the media dismissals may have been
about something else: self-preservation. Certainly many reporters and
editors would rather forget about those ugly times than reexamine their
own roles in having furthered Brock's vicious tales. Many in the mainstream media are implicated in *Blinded*, including *Newsweek* reporter
Michael Isikoff who, Brock writes, "had passed on to me a handful of
Clinton sex stories that he was not able to get past his editors in the hope
that I would follow them up," presumably so that Isikoff could then write
about them after Brock did. And who can forget the glowing reviews of
The Real Anita Hill, including one from the *New York Times*'s Christopher Lehmann-Haupt? By now admitting that the book was a pile of
trash, Brock reveals what biased fools such respected reviewers were—
particularly since many others saw the book for what it was at the time.

Some of the media's impulse to dismiss *Blinded* was even on display in
March 2002 when the *Washington Post* had the gay conservative author

Bruce Bawer review Brock's book. Predictably, Bawer slammed the book and mocked its author. After a number of complaints the *Post*'s editors admitted that Bawer shouldn't have reviewed the book because he had been a writer at the *American Spectator* as well. The decision to use Bawer seemed to betray an attempt, conscious or not, to marginalize *Blinded* by serving up a review that was a less-than-serious side-show—two queens, now political opposites, having a cat fight—rather than examining some of the disturbing issues and events that Brock's confessions raise.

Some might say I believe Brock because I want to believe him. But, actually, I'd been quite skeptical of Brock and his several-year-long conversion for some time, both to colleagues and in print; in 1998, I was strongly critical of him in a piece I wrote for the *New York Observer*. I still have some lingering doubts about his motivations, as I'm sure Brock hopes his confessions are as financially successful as his lies were (then again, who wouldn't?). But I'm glad that, unlike the notorious McCarthy sidekick Roy Cohn and many others, Brock isn't going to his death working for those who work against his own kind, taking all of the secrets with him.

Instead, Brock offered, for the new century, a powerful and important blueprint for how the Washington closet operates, one that can be used by journalists and activists for a long time to come.

HOLLYWOOD'S FINAL FRONTIER

Like the Washington closet, the Hollywood closet went through some transformations. Controversies surrounding it in the past few years became indicative of just how the Hollywood closet operates.

There's no question that gays have come out a great deal among Hollywood's elite and that gay and lesbians are much more visible in popular culture. From *Will & Grace* to *Queer as Folk* to *Six Feet Under*, television—on the networks and on cable—has embraced gay and lesbian storylines. In films too, gays and lesbians have arrived. The year 2003 alone saw *The Hours*, a film with lesbian themes, and *Far from Heaven*, about a closeted, tormented married gay man in the 1950s, garner prominent Oscar nominations.

People like Alan Ball, director of *American Beauty* and the creator of the HBO hit *Six Feet Under*, and *Will & Grace* co-creator Max Mutchnik are among the new openly gay power brokers in Hollywood, along with so many others who are out. Showtime was even set to launch a gay-themed cable network by 2003.

Yet, there is still no leading movie star who is openly gay or lesbian in Hollywood after all these years of change and after the Hollywood community has done so much to rally around gay rights. While there have been some actors, such as Nathan Lane and Rupert Everett, who have commendably come out, there has not been a leading actor, let alone a romantic lead, who has come out. There have been many attempts to negate gay rumors about certain stars at all costs.

Hollywood's power brokers, still fearful about the box office, will go to whatever lengths they have to in order to keep stars from coming out—or even being thought of as gay—fearing how the public would respond to a star believed to be homosexual.

In the late nineties and early part of the new century actor Kevin Spacey several times denied and deflected rumors that he was gay. When *Esquire* magazine ran a front page profile of Spacey in 1997, titled "Kevin Spacey Has a Secret," that speculated on his sexual orientation, the denunciations came fast and furiously from Hollywood's titans. Spacey himself released a statement calling the article "McCarthyism," though he did not deny he was gay at the time. The William Morris Agency, which handles Spacey, released a statement saying it would "strongly advise all of the agents to dissuade their clients from doing interviews with *Esquire*."

Little more than a year later Spacey told *Playboy:* "It's not true. It's a lie. . . . It wasn't that I cared if they [*Esquire* magazine in 1997] inferred I was gay, because I believe people in this country are more advanced than certain members of the media who try to use their medium as a weapon. But I felt betrayed."

But then, just a week before the 2000 Academy Awards—for which Spacey had been nominated (and won) for best actor for *American Beauty*—the *Star* tabloid claimed Spacey had a hot and heavy daytime romp in a park with a hot young Hollywood male model. And the magazine printed thirteen photos to back up the assertion, all of which show the men touching, hugging, and fondling.

"For two hours," the tabloid claimed, "the pair chatted, held hands, cuddled, stroked and massaged each other hidden behind a rock in Oakland Memorial Park near Topanga, close to where Spacey grew up."

There was no response from Spacey. But he did show up at the Oscars the following week with a girlfriend no one had previously known about or heard about, and to whom he made a loving tribute in his acceptance speech. But it wasn't enough to stop the gossip mill. When a study showing a correlation between homosexuality and finger length became publicized a couple of years ago, Nathan Lane cracked in an interview, "It's hard to believe that's true—although the very same day, Kevin Spacey was spotted shopping for mittens."

Spacey himself continues to have overheated reactions to questions about his sexuality. In early 2003 he snapped at a reporter in London when asked whether he preferred the "lifestyle of London rather than that of Los Angeles." "What do you mean by 'lifestyle'?" Spacey shot back. And when another reporter asked specifically about the gay rumors, Spacey thundered, "Don't ask me about that crap!"

The Spacey case shows how far the media, much more than in the past, is pushing when it comes to the issue of homosexuality and asking the question. But the Hollywood power brokers and the celebrities themselves are pushing back fiercely, still finding the mere question appalling and scary.

CRUISE CONTROL

No series of events, however, shows Hollywood power brokers' outright fears of an actor even being thought of as gay as those that played out when Tom Cruise sued a man in 2001 for $100 million for claiming he was gay. As *Queer in America* shows in detail in the chapters on Hollywood, high-powered lawyers and publicists have always been at the core of Hollywood's power, making sure the big bucks keep rolling in. That is as true now as it was in 1993.

Since Hollywood is all about images that are packaged and sold, sometimes it's the lawyers' and publicists' job to promote a specific image—and other times it's their job to squash it.

Fearsome publicists such as Pat Kingsley make sure that certain discussions about stars—Hollywood's glittering cash cows—do not get in print. As MSNBC columnist Jeannette Walls described in an entire chapter in her 2000 book *Dish*, one of Kingsley's tasks for years has been to make sure that magazine writers and other journalists do not ask Tom

Cruise about the gay rumors surrounding him—often by threatening the magazines' editors from having access to other stars. For Hollywood's titans, having a discussion of the Cruise gay rumors—even if they are not true—would raise the issue of why Hollywood is so afraid of having openly gay leading men, and that's a discussion they do not want to broach.

Thus, the story of Cruise filing a defamation suit in March 2001 because of a report that he had a gay affair at least had the potential of underscoring Hollywood's queasiness about known gays in its midst and the lengths to which the industry will go to protect its stars. Not to mention that, as an extra-added bonus, it brought the rumors about Cruise to international attention and thrust them into the mainstream media once and for all. Some people even thought that there was a chance it would end with the rumors about Cruise confirmed.

But the Hollywood machine is too well oiled for that. Cruise and company would not have proceeded with such a suit, elevating an obscure, foreign report, unless they knew exactly where this would go. With the Cruise lawsuit, they indeed seem to have made sparkling California lemonade out of some pretty bad lemons. The whole affair, by the end, began looking like a remake of *The Talented Mr. Ripley*—yes, with perhaps yet another very confused homosexual at the core.

Cruise, a member of the highly litigious Church of Scientology, sued gay male porn star Kyle Bradford for $100 million for allegedly giving an interview to a French gossip magazine saying he'd had a sexual tryst with the actor. Cruise's lawyers denied that Cruise is gay and called such a characterization "vicious." The suit claimed that rumors of Cruise being gay could "cost Cruise very substantial sums" because of the macho roles he plays and the public's perceptions of him, implying of course that all homosexuals are mincing pansies, or at least that most people think that. Bradford denied that he gave the interview, in a brief statement on his Web site: "I have never been to France, I have never spoken with *Actustar* magazine, and have never said any of the statements allegedly said by me."

It was not exactly a denial of knowing Cruise, however, and certainly kept the gossip columnists jumping for the next several days. Not to mention that Nicole Kidman, perhaps playing hardball in the divorce proceedings and trying to get as much as she could, refused to offer any comment to columnists looking for confirmation of Cruise's heterosexuality. Some reports pointed to Bradford's past conversations with friends about knowing Cruise and the possibility that he'd given an interview to a different magazine, the information from which somehow made its way to *Actustar*. (*Actustar* has since printed a retraction and an apology.)

But soon enough *Village Voice* columnist Michael Musto interviewed Bradford's ex, Randall Kohl, who implied that Bradford (a.k.a Chad Slater, a.k.a. Phil Navarone), if he did indeed tell people that he knew Cruise, was perhaps being a bit creative.

"I was with him almost a year, but I didn't really know him until after about six months," Kohl told Musto. "I noticed his lying when he said he was going to appear on [the British music show] *Top of the Pops* and he didn't—he actually went to Europe to wrestle. He said he did a Kentucky Fried Chicken commercial that I found out was not true."

Said Kohl: "He wants to be like Tom Cruise. Deep down, Chad thought he was Tom in his mind. He thought he looked a lot like him—he told me he did." According to Kohl, before all of this, Bradford did give an interview about a supposed relationship with Cruise to the *London Daily Mail*, but it never ran, as the paper reportedly had doubts about it.

Bradford, obviously feeling the heat from lawyers, eventually changed the statement on his Web site. It soon referred to "the false and vicious stories that I had a gay sexual affair." Bradford said that he "doesn't know Tom Cruise and never said" that he did know him. "I haven't the slightest evidence of Tom Cruise being gay," Bradford stated unequivocally. "I understand Mr. Cruise's anger over this article. It is disgusting. I am equally angry. If I can assist him in discovering the person or persons who started this completely false story, I will."

Soon the story had gone from one that might have unsheathed Hollywood's homophobia, or at least provided us with some juicy gay dirt, to one that perhaps was created in the mind of an overzealous young man, to one in which that same young man, no doubt with a gun held to his head by shrewd Hollywood lawyers, is forced to describe a revelation of homosexuality as "vicious" and "disgusting." In early 2003, Cruise won his lawsuit and was awarded $10 million.

Score another one for the Hollywood machine.

ROSIE'S ENDLESS OUTING

One event in 2002 that revealed just how the media, centered in New York and a major subject of *Queer in America*, had changed both on the issue of outing and on it's approach to the closet in the new century was Rosie O'Donnell's coming out. It was an event I wrote about and reported on in columns in *New York Press,* incurring the wrath of Rosie herself.

In retrospect I was a bit hard on Rosie, putting the entire onus on her for the way her coming out was engineered, packaged, and perceived. Rosie's coming out was also a product of a media that was titillated by the idea of gay celebrities, more willing than ever before to push open that closet door just a little bit more—and more willing to be used to maximum advantage.

If the journalistic definition of outing is reporting on an individual's undisclosed homosexuality, then in a six week period in early 2002 Rosie had been outed at the very least 10,800 times (that's the number that came up when one did a Google search of "Rosie O'Donnell and gay" at the time). That's not including the supermarket tabloids, where Rosie perhaps held the record for celebrity outings during the '90s. Rosie had yet to say the words "I'm gay" herself on camera or in print but nonetheless we were assured for weeks and weeks by CNN, the *New York Times,* the Associated Press, Barbara Walters, and everyone else participating in the hype machine that it is absolutely true, and that Rosie would soon say so to the world—promise!

Yes, she would do it in her now defunct magazine *Rosie,* she would do it in her then best-selling book *Find Me,* she would do it in a highly publicized *Primetime Thursday* interview, and she would even do it on the still-running *Rosie O'Donnell Show.* It's true that Ellen DeGeneres was the first big TV star to jump into the self-outing media whirl, but she just didn't have such a lucrative product line—all she had was a bad sitcom—not to mention that Rosie had a serious cause to champion (which, in p.r. terms, will blunt charges of crassness and opportunism), as she took up the issue of lesbian and gay adoption, a personal issue for her as a mother. The love that dare not speak its name, in that great American way, had been transformed into high-concept, cross-promotional marketing brilliance.

But that too is progress. And it's certainly true that with a prominent spokesperson, activists trying to change laws that ban adoptions by gay people got a boost. From the standpoint of some lesbians and gays—and certainly from that of fearful entertainment industry executives—it was smart for Rosie to first establish her career, define herself as a devoted mother and as one of America's favorite talk show hosts, then announce that she is a lesbian later.

Still, it was hard not to be a bit cynical when discussing a woman who waited until she was almost forty years old and until after she grew tired of doing her TV show—which she packed in by mid-year—to come out. Rosie's people were trying to spin the media, putting out the idea that this is all not really a big deal, that Rosie's never really hidden her sexuality or tried to appear heterosexual. But if her being a lesbian had never been a big deal—and if she wasn't hiding anything—why not just say it, instead of offering the vagaries Rosie had offered in the past?

Still, it was a great thing that someone as visible as Rosie finally came out and began speaking up about gay rights issues. And since she's come out, Rosie's moved further along. Not only did Rosie contact me by e-mail about criticisms I made of her in response to her claiming she'd never been closeted (and further criticisms I made in response to other statements she'd initially put forth about the gay movement) but we eventually met and had a passionate, off-the-record discussion about the issues affecting gay people. I realized that there was a lot we didn't know about her that affected her thinking and how she viewed gay issues. She perhaps realized she could say things better when speaking on the important issues facing gay people. And she soon did, in an interview with Larry King. One thing about being out is that it opens up a whole new world and once they are out, people continue to change and grow. And they should be commended for it.

Barbara Walters, meanwhile, emerged in the Rosie coming out story as today's outing warrior extraordinaire—she knows a ratings-grabber when she sees it. She and ABC's Diane Sawyer fought over the Rosie story and though they've both denied any animosity between them, Walters reportedly was miffed that Sawyer got the Rosie coming-out interview. So Walters apparently picked up the phone, called up Rosie to get the scoop and then, on *The View* weeks before Sawyer's *Primetime Thursday* interview, confirmed the rumors and announced Rosie's plans to take up the adoption issue, stealing Sawyer's thunder.

There was a time not long ago when you couldn't get journalists to report on gay public figures who were already out, let alone get them to push the closeted ones to fess up. Now they're undermining one another to be first with the coming out scoop. That actually shows progress too.

THE VATICAN'S CLOSET

As sexual abuse scandals rocked the Catholic Church in the first months of 2002, the skeletons in the Vatican's vaults began popping out like there's no tomorrow. And since the Catholic Church has an enormous influence on American culture, the scandal had an impact on the discussion of homosexuality in America, particularly when the Vatican began stoking the gay issue.

Some people were shocked and horrified by what they'd heard from the Vatican during that time, talk that sounds like a new Inquisition, this time focused on gay priests, whom the Vatican has blamed for the sex abuse cases. But really, before hatred can be purged it needs to be drawn out, like puss from a boil. That is the process we're going through right now. It'll probably get uglier before it gets better—and, at the rate the Catholic Church moves, it may take a century or so—but it needs to happen.

The issues the crisis underscored brought me back to a column I wrote for *New York Press,* syndicated to other papers around the country, in November 2001, just before the scandals exploded. The column was about Pope John Paul's acceptance of the helmet of Mychal Judge—the gay New York Fire Department chaplain who was killed in the September 11 attacks at the World Trade Center—in a ceremony in St. Peter's Square. I contended that it was a supremely hypocritical action on the Pope's part because of the Vatican's position that homosexuality is "evil" and "objectively disordered," terminology that in my view amounts to gay-bashing. Here was the Pope honoring a man who embodied the very "evil" and "disorder" he rails against, accepting a hero's helmet that he surely didn't deserve.

I was lambasted in some circles for that column. James Taranto and the other conservative moral arbiters at the *Wall Street Journal*'s Opinion Journal Web site put me on their "Stupidity Watch." The Catholic League sent around a breathless alert, quoting the organization's pit bull president William Donohue actually making a tasteless sexual reference—opining how "surprising" my comments were coming from someone who has so much "practice" at "turning the other cheek."

The angry letters came pouring in. I was a sinner, a monster, and the devil incarnate, not to mention, according to several of the Catholic letter writers, "a faggot." In corresponding with some of these individuals, it became clear to me that it didn't matter to them that I was speaking as someone who was raised Catholic, who attended ten years of Catholic school, who was an altar boy, and who, for a brief period as a teen, even entertained the notion that I might become a priest. As far as they were concerned, any strong criticism of any kind of the church, and more so of the Pope, made me a Catholic-basher, end of story.

The more intelligent of the negative letters, the ones that went into a bit more detail, all seemed to make the same point: "The church doesn't condemn homosexuals—it condemns homosexuality." In other words, the church doesn't engage in gay-bashing, it engages in homosexuality-bashing. There is of course no difference between the two. Apologists have a way of splitting hairs to the point of ridiculousness. They cling to this explanation—the "love the sinner, hate the sin" policy—because it comforts them as they blindly go along lock, stock, and barrel with a church that promotes hatred against an entire group of people, the kind of hatred that results in violence.

Five months after I'd written that column and incurred the angry reactions, the church was embroiled in a sexual controversy that finally had some prominent, long-time Vatican defenders for the first time offering blistering criticisms. And lo and behold, the two issues they seem to be focused on are hypocrisy and gay-bashing.

In op-ed pieces across the country, religious Catholics and theologians were speaking out. Many clearly saw that the same church that ostracizes divorced and gay Catholics, and tells us all that sex outside of heterosexual marriage for the purpose of procreation is "evil," protects pedophile priests, allowing them to continue in their duties even after knowing they've abused the very young people who put their trust in them. And after remaining silent for weeks, the Vatican began its inquisition talk, something few could ignore: It announced that the entire pedophile scandal was the fault of those homosexual priests—no matter, it seems, even if they've remained celibate—who must be banned outright from the priesthood.

"People with these inclinations just cannot be ordained," the Pope's spokesman, Dr. Joaquin Navarro-Valls, said.

As Web columnist John Aravosis observed in "The List," his widely e-mailed column, "it now seems the Pope may be returning that helmet." Desperate, the church was looking for a scapegoat, and that old standby—equating pedophilia with homosexuality—was its new strategy. (Never mind that most pedophiles are straight men who molest little girls, and that banning gays will have little impact on that). This is not exactly the supposedly nurturing and understanding "love the sinner, hate the sin" policy toward homosexuals. It sounds more like a "blame all of our centuries-in-the-making, self-inflicted problems on the poor sinner, and then throw the sinner out" policy.

Of course, banning gays from the priesthood—which, according to some estimates in the media, may be as much as 50 percent gay—would not only be an end to the already dwindling priesthood; it would go far toward dismantling the homosexual closet in America and I suspect other countries, as the priesthood has been a refuge for a lot of confused and struggling gay men who turn to it, with its vow of celibacy, rather than come to terms with their sexual orientation. But how on earth the Vatican would go about instituting such an inquisition is mind-boggling. And in a way it doesn't matter. Novarro-Valls's words brought the war between the church and gays to a new level. Whether or not the Vatican actually tries to ban gays, its gay-bashing is now completely out of the closet.

The Vatican has finally articulated that it believes homosexuals—not just homosexuality—are bad, and that they must be ostracized from the church clergy. The church apologists can no longer realistically split hairs about the loving church having compassion for the homosexual who doesn't act on his desires. And bringing the gay-bashing out of the Vatican closet is the first step toward exorcising it forever.

In the process, the gay closets of many in the church, from gay priests to those in the highest reaches of the Vatican, may also be cracked open as the war will no doubt heat up in coming years. (As of this writing, the Vatican is reportedly set to formally ban gays from the priesthood.)

CARDINAL SPELLMAN'S DARK LEGACY

If the Vatican's closets come under the spotlight as we move into the future, more attention will perhaps be paid as well to the closets of past figures in the church, which can only shed a light on the problem of homophobia in the church.

In mid-April 2002, at the height of the church's sex abuse scandal, the rector of St. Patrick's Cathedral in New York, Monsignor Eugene Clark, gave a homily that inspired the kind of PRIEST BLASTS GAYS headlines that New York's tabloids thrive on. Standing in for the embattled Cardinal Egan (who, like Cardinal Law in Boston, had been accused of looking the other way of pedophile priests,) blamed the sex abuse scandal on gays, railed against homosexuality as a "disorder," and said it was a "grave mistake" to allow gays into the priesthood.

It may have been another trial balloon as the Vatican desperately attempted to change the subject and scapegoat gays. Or it may simply have been further ineptitude on increasingly feeble Cardinal Egan's part, putting the wrong person at the pulpit while he scampered away to the Bronx amid the crisis. The New York archdiocese later distanced itself from—though didn't refute—Clark's comments, and a discombobulated Egan offered a bizarre nonresponse when asked in Rome about homosexuals in the priesthood: "I would just say this. The most important thing is to clean up the truth. And the truth is I have never said anything." (Egan seemed just a bit too desperate not to be on the record saying "anything" about homosexuality, perhaps fearful that his position might be pointed to, for whatever reason, in the future.)

Whatever Clark's rant was meant to convey, it represented a dangerous path for the Catholic Church to embark upon, one that will only embolden media-savvy gay activists in the future—and a press corps much less loyal to the church than in years past—to begin exposing the many twisted, personal sexual hypocrisies that envelop the increasingly tainted, lying bishops and cardinals who are running the church.

Clark's deceptions included equating homosexuality with pedophilia, the ugly lie we've been hearing from the Vatican and the American cardinals, both before and during the sex abuse summit. But seventy-six-year-old Clark also engaged in a larger, less-defined but more powerful deception. In putting forth the idea that homosexuality is a "disorder," and that it is a "grave mistake" to ordain gay priests, he implied that only the lowly priests—the alleged child abusers among them—are afflicted with the so-called "disorder." He wouldn't, after all, accuse any bishops or cardinals themselves of having the "disorder," nor would he say that it was a "grave mistake" to have ordained them, would he?

Yet, among the several skeletons in gay-basher Clark's closet is that he in fact dutifully worked as secretary for one of the most notorious, powerful, and sexually voracious homosexuals in the American Catholic Church's history: the politically connected Francis Cardinal Spellman, known as "Franny" to assorted Broadway chorus boys and others, who was New York's cardinal from 1939 until his death in 1967.

The archconservative Spellman was the epitome of the self-loathing, closeted, evil queen, working with his good friend, the closeted gay McCarthy henchman Roy Cohn, to undermine liberalism in America during the 1950s communist and homosexual witch hunts. The church has squelched discussion of Spellman's gay life quite successfully, most notably by pressuring the *New York Times* to don the drag of the censor back in the 1980s. The *Times* today may be out front exposing every little nasty detail in the Catholic Church's abuse scandal—a testament to both the more open discussion of such issues today and the church's waning power in New York—but not even twenty years ago the *Times* was covering up Spellman's sexual secrets many years after his death, clearly fearful of the church's revenge if the paper didn't fall in line. (During Spellman's reign and long afterward, all of New York's newspapers in fact cowered before the Catholic Church. On Spellman's orders many of New York's Catholic-owned department stores pulled ads from the then liberal *New York Post* in the 1950s after publisher Dorothy Schiff wrote commentary critical of his right-wing positions; Schiff was forced to back down on her positions.)

In the original bound galleys of former *Wall Street Journal* reporter John Cooney's Spellman biography, *The American Pope*—published in 1984 by Times Books, which was then owned by the New York Times Co.—Spellman's gay life was recounted in four pages that included interviews with several notable individuals who knew Spellman as a closeted homosexual. Among Cooney's interview subjects was C. A. Tripp, the noted researcher affiliated with Dr. Alfred C. Kinsey of the Institute for Sex Research, who shared information that he had on Spellman regarding the prelate's homosexuality. In a telephone interview with Tripp in early 2003, he told me that his information came from a Broadway dancer in the show *One Touch of Venus* who had a relationship with Spellman back in the 1940s; the prelate would have his limousine pick up the dancer several nights a week and bring him back to his place. When the dancer once asked Spellman how he could get away with this, Tripp says Spellman answered, "Who would believe that?" The anecdote is also recounted in John Loughery's history of gay life in the twentieth century, *The Other Side of Silence*.

"In New York's clerical circles, Spellman's sex life was a source of profound embarrassment and shame to many priests," Cooney had written in the original manuscript of his book. When Mitchell Levitas, who was then the editor of the *New York Times Book Review*, received the manuscript for review, he realized it was a book that would make big news; he sent the book over to Arthur Gelb, who was then the managing editor of the *New York Times*. Gelb assigned reporter Ed McDowell to the story. McDowell interviewed Cooney and went about interviewing others who were relevant to the story, including church officials.

The archdiocese, however, went ballistic when presented with the information and became determined to keep it from being published. Chief among those orchestrating the cleansing of Spellman's past sex life was none other than the current gay-basher Monsignor Clark, who, in an interview with the *Times*, called the assertions "preposterous," commenting that "if you had any idea of [Spellman's] New England background" you'd realize these were "foolish" charges. The church sent John Moore, the retired U.S. ambassador to Ireland and a close friend and confidant of several church officials, to appeal to Sidney Gruson, then vice chairman of the New York Times Co. "The *Times* was going to report that Cardinal Spellman was a homosexual," Moore later told journalist Eric Nadler, who wrote a piece for *Forum* about the ugly little cover-up, "and I was determined to stop it." Moore told Nadler that this was the "third or fourth" time he had appealed to the *Times* regarding a sensitive church matter. "They've always done the right thing," he said.

As Cooney describes it, he was soon told by his editors at Times Books that his sourcing wasn't good enough, and that the four pages would have to be cut. He could keep a paragraph that alluded to the "rumors," but he would have to state that the rumors had been strongly contested by many people—even though, in his research, that had not truly been the case. The discussion of Spellman's homosexuality in the book was reduced to mere speculation, which was branded as irrelevant:

For years rumors abounded about Cardinal Spellman being a homosexual. As a result, many felt—and continue to feel—that Spellman the public moralist may well have been a contradiction of the man of the flesh. Others within the church and outside have steadfastly dismissed such claims. Finally, to make an absolute statement about Spellman's sexual activities is to invite an irresolvable debate and to deflect attention from his words and deeds.

The dutiful *Times* then had another former U.S. ambassador to Ireland and friend of the church, William V. Shannon, review *The American Pope* for the *Book Review*. Shannon's review was scathing, attacking Cooney for even bringing the subject up at all: "Prurient interest in the sex lives of public figures serves no useful purpose."

A Jesuit priest wrote a letter to the *Book Review*, published a few weeks later: "Cardinal Spellman's sex life does not matter, but [his] homosexuality does. . . . It matters to thousands of people whose jobs, relationships and whose very lives are threatened because of their sexuality, all the while being forced to view and eat the hypocrisy of their church. And it enrages people that church men and women can retain their jobs, hiding behind their clerical and religious statutes while their own people suffer persecution, disease and discrimination."

Sadly, the Jesuit's words still ring true today, almost twenty years later. While Spellman has been long dead, his legacy of hypocrisy lives on: There are closeted homosexuals—often condemning "sexual immorality" publicly while having gay sex privately—throughout the uppermost echelons of the church today. The gay movement in the past fifteen years has taken on the Hollywood closet and the Washington political closet, both with much success, beginning a process that only continues—and both those institutions have public relations operations far more sophisticated than the Vatican's antiquated machine, which can't even seem to get the aging cardinals to attend a press conference.

The media these days also has a much greater appetite for exposing sexual hypocrisy, and is no longer cowed by the Catholic Church. Going down this treacherous road of increased gay-bashing and scapegoating, the Vatican perhaps doesn't realize what it may be unleashing upon itself.

THE TWENTY-FIRST CENTURY CLOSET

As the events of the early part of the twenty-first century have shown, though we've come a long way there are further battles and coming wars for the gay movement, many still focused on the closet and its enduring strength even as so much has changed.

When I first began researching and writing this chapter, I wasn't so sure that there was much more left to do in breaking down the closet and pushing for gay and lesbian rights. Of course there were many legislative battles—from hate crimes legislation and antidiscrimination laws to marriage rights and adoption issues—but those were different from culture, visibility, and the closet. Looking around, seeing so many who'd come out, including within popular culture, and seeing the enormous coverage of gay issues today, you can often have a warped impression. And sometimes, if you don't feel the oppression personally and in a heavy way, you can convince yourself it doesn't exist—for others and for the community as whole.

Many of us who remember how bad things were in the past, particularly when AIDS hit full force during the antigay Reagan administration, can easily be quite seduced by the idea that we've "arrived." A similar phenomenon was experienced by the generation prior, who remembered how horrific things were in the 1950s and the McCarthy days and believed that by the 1970s everything was great for gays simply because gay ghettos and discos had become so public, visible, and seemingly accepted. Then AIDS came and woke people up.

So, it's easy to see how older generations can believe that our work is almost finished. And younger people often take things for granted, not moved to action unless something dramatic occurs (as what happened to the '80s generation with regard to AIDS), suddenly instilling in them the sense that homophobia is rampant even though it was thought be beaten down.

It's only when you look carefully at the landscape that you realize that we still have our work cut out for us. My hope for this book is that it can serve as a marker of how far we've come, a reminder of how far we have to go, and an example of how much we truly can change attitudes and perceptions in America.

NOTES

1. After seventy-six years in business, the Russian Tea Room closed its doors in July 2002, citing financial pressures due in part to the depressed post–September 11 economy in New York.

2. Liz Smith is now at the *New York Post*.

3. Richard Johnson is today back at the *New York Post*, writing and editing "Page Six."

4. A pioneer in lesbian and gay journalism, Sarah Pettit went on to co-found *Out* magazine with one-time *Outweek* columnist Michael Goff in 1992, and she became arts editor at *Newsweek* in 1999. We worked together at *Out*, where I was a columnist in the mid-nineties, and we remained close friends until her stunning death from complications of lymphoma, at the age of thirty-six, in early 2003.

5. Steven Gunderson eventually became more open about being gay, and became a voice for gay Republicans. He left politics in 1996 after sixteen years in the House, and is currently on the board of the Human Rights Campaign, the Washington gay lobby.

6. Marvin Liebman died in April of 1997, at the age of seventy-three.

7. The Human Rights Campaign Fund changed its name to the Human Rights Campaign, and both Tim McFeeley and Gregory King left the group in the early '90s.

8. Gerry Studds left the House and political life at the end of 1996, after rep-

resenting his southern Massachusetts district for almost twenty-five years. He has worked since then as a consultant and as the executive director of the New Bedford Aquarium.

9. Richard Rouilard died of complications from AIDS in 1996.

10. Frank Bruni is now a reporter at the *New York Times.*

11. Andrew Sullivan's editorship at the *New Republic* ended in 1996, at which time he revealed that he was HIV positive.

12. Pulitzer Prize–winning reporter and theater critic William Henry III died of cardiac arrest in 1994 at the age of forty-four, taking to his grave the secret that had so colored his coverage of outing and which should have disqualified him from reporting on the topic: Though married, he had many clandestine boyfriends and male sex partners over the years and was known as gay and closeted to many gay men in the theater.

13. Tom Stoddard died of complications from AIDS in 1997.

14. Tim Donohoe died in 1999 at the age of fifty-four, having apparently suffered a heart attack.

15. Rich Tafel left Log Cabin in late 2002.

16. Gay rights pioneer Morris Kight died of natural causes in early 2003, at the age of eighty-three.

17. In the '90s, Chastity Bono became a gay rights leader, authoring books, writing columns for the *Advocate,* and working for the Gay and Lesbian Alliance against Defamation. She discussed her own experience in detail and talked about the detrimental effects of the closet.

18. In 1994 Sheila Kuehl was elected to the California State Assembly, becoming the first gay or lesbian person elected to the California Legislature. She served in the assembly for six years and in 2000 was elected to the California State Senate.

19. Torie Osborn left the National Gay and Lesbian Task Force in the mid-'90s.

20. Tom Rielly went on to found Planet Out, which by the mid-'90s became the most highly visible Web site serving the gay community. It eventually merged with Gay.com, taking the name Planet Out Partners, which serves millions of gays, lesbians, bisexuals, and transgendered people worldwide.

21. In 1994 Tim Gill established the Gill Foundation, an organization committed to funding lesbian, gay, bisexual, and transgendered nonprofit projects as well as those focused on HIV and AIDS. The Gill Foundation has granted over $27 million to groups and organizations across the nation since its inception.

22. Elizabeth Birch became executive director of the Human Rights Campaign, the nation's largest gay lobby, in 1995. She stepped down in 2003.

Index